—— *Welcome to* ——

I M M E R S E
The Bible Reading Experience

The Bible is a great gift. The Creator of all things entered into our human story and spoke to us. He inspired people over many centuries to shape words into books that reveal his mind, bringing wisdom into our lives and light to our paths. But God's biggest intention for the Bible is to invite us into its Story. What God wants for us, more than anything else, is that we make the Bible's great drama of restoration and new life the story of our lives, too.

The appropriate way to receive a gift like this is to come to know the Bible deeply, to lose ourselves in it precisely so that we can find ourselves in it. In other words, we need to immerse ourselves in it—to read God's words at length and without distraction, to read with deeper historical and literary perspective, and to read through the Bible with friends in a regular three-year rhythm. *Immerse: The Bible Reading Experience* has been specially designed for this purpose.

Immerse: The Reading Bible presents each book of the Bible without the distractions of chapter and verse markers, subject headers, or footnotes—all later historical additions to the text. The *Holy Bible*, New Living Translation, is presented in a single-column format with easy-to-read type. To provide meaningful perspective, book introductions give historical and literary context, and the books are often reordered chronologically or grouped with books that share similar ancient audiences. Every feature in this unique Bible enhances the opportunity for readers to engage with God's words in simple clarity.

A more complete explanation of this unique Bible presentation can be found in the articles that begin on page 329 at the back of this volume.

—— *Introduction to* ——

BEGINNINGS

THE BIBLE TELLS THE STORY of how our world that's gone wrong is being made right again. God's creation was intended to be beautiful and harmonious, but due to the deception of evil powers and human disobedience, the creation became broken and disordered—cursed. Yet ever since the Fall, God has been working patiently and carefully to restore humanity to his presence and the whole creation to its lost beauty and harmony.

The biblical narrative of restoration and renewal takes a significant step forward every time God establishes a covenant. These covenants are God-initiated sets of promises and obligations that establish a binding relationship between God and his people. In our day, we are more familiar with contracts: agreements enforceable by human law. But in the ancient world, people made covenants, which carried the expectation that God would bless them for keeping the covenant's terms or curse them for breaking them. And as a full participant in the covenants he makes, God actually puts himself under his own curse should he break the terms.

The goal of these God-initiated covenants is to gather people into communities that will live the life he intends for everyone. Through communities deeply connected to their Creator, this life will spread outward to other people as well. Starting with chosen individuals, then a family, and then a nation, God moves in the interest of winning back all things in heaven and on earth. The first five books of the Bible tell the story of the first three covenants God makes with Noah, Abraham, and Moses—who act as humanity's representatives.

The first nine books of the Bible, Genesis through Samuel–Kings, are actually one continuous narrative. Sometimes referred to as Israel's primary history, this saga covers the story from the birth of the world to the painful account of God's people being exiled from the Land of

Promise. The first five books have a special status of their own and in Christian tradition are known as the *Pentateuch* (meaning "five books" in Greek). But its ancient Hebrew name, *Torah*, reveals the purpose of these books more clearly.

Torah is probably best translated as "instruction." As God's covenant community follows these instructions, they not only receive God's blessings but also are uniquely positioned to bring renewal and healing to the world, as implied in God's promises to Abraham. God's instructions to his people are the catalyst for their movement to show all peoples the true character and nature of God. The community of God's people is being sent on a mission to renew the world, and these instructions are its marching orders.

This *Torah* is conveyed through a variety of literary genres, or kinds of writing. About two-thirds of these first five books consist of laws that instruct people on how to live the life that God intends. These laws appear both in general terms ("love your neighbor as yourself") and in specific cases ("If you come upon your enemy's ox or donkey that has strayed away, take it back to its owner"). These laws were given to govern the covenant relationship between God and his people. It is important to understand that these laws are for God's people in a particular historical and cultural setting and in an early stage of God's story with respect to the world. Many of the particular laws are not God's final, timeless answers about how we should live. The entire Bible tells this ongoing story, and more light is shed as the story moves forward.

In addition to stories and laws, we find songs and poems that celebrate special events or anticipate the future. There are family trees (genealogies) listing people in relation to their ancestors and descendants, locating their historical place in the community that experienced God's faithfulness generation after generation. Other kinds of lists appear as well, detailing kings, spies, stopping points along a journey, job assignments, and so forth. These books also contain elaborate blueprints for a place of worship and its furnishings, and even census reports for the population of Israel.

All of these different kinds of writing are woven together into a single work, whose overall purpose is to describe the formation of the covenant community. This community—the ancient nation of Israel—will constitute God's people on earth for the first three-quarters of the Bible. Over the course of these first five books—*Beginnings*—we follow the community from its earliest ancestors to the moment it is poised to enter the land God promised them. There, the community can begin living a life that will lead the surrounding nations to exclaim, "How wise and prudent are the people of this great nation!"

IMMERSED IN GENESIS

THE FIRST BOOK OF THE BIBLE lays the foundation for the rest of the Bible's story. It reveals God as the world's sovereign Creator. It shows his intention to bring blessing to people—his image-bearers—and for all life to thrive by living in his presence. Genesis tells us about the entrance of evil into the world and the commencement of God's struggle against it, a theme that flows through the whole Bible. God created the world as his own temple, intending to live here among humanity for their well-being. But how will God achieve his goal in the face of rebellion and disobedience?

Genesis tells the story of God's dealings with humanity from the world's creation to the time when Abraham's descendants were beginning to grow into the nation of Israel. It does this by giving the "accounts" (the word that marks the major divisions of the book) of notable people. The most important figures are part of the covenant lineage and therefore advance the ongoing story. Others, described much more briefly, represent offshoots that will be drawn back in later as the reach of the covenant community spreads to all of humanity.

In the first four accounts, human disobedience leads to evil and violence that corrupt the created world. Seeing that everything people think or imagine is "consistently and totally evil," God is sorry he made them. He destroys wicked humanity in a great, cleansing flood but spares Noah and his family—the only righteous people left. After the Flood, Noah worships God, and God makes his first covenant. With Noah serving as their representative, humanity and all animals on earth receive God's promise: "Never again will floodwaters kill all living creatures."

God then makes a second covenant, one that will ultimately transform humanity, starting with only a small group. God promises a man named Abram (later renamed Abraham) that "all the nations of the earth" will be blessed through him and his descendants. God tells him to leave his home and move to a new place: the land of Canaan. Abraham essentially becomes a wanderer in that land and eventually has a son named Isaac, who becomes the heir to all that God has promised. God renews his covenant with Isaac and then again with Isaac's son Jacob, who then has twelve sons of his own. These twelve sons will become the ancestors of the tribes of Israel.

The book concludes by describing the life of Joseph, one of Jacob's sons. Joseph is betrayed and cast off by his jealous brothers, but he ultimately has a surprising role in preserving the family so that it can expand into a nation. Throughout Genesis, we see God relentlessly pursuing his plans to renew humanity and the rest of creation, blessing the covenant community in their obedience and overcoming their disobedience.

Genesis consists mostly of stories. But family trees, which connect the stories of people in different generations, also play a big role. Ancient Hebrew writers loved to tell stories using the literary form of *chiasm*, in which the first and last episodes/elements are paired, then the second and next-to-last episodes/elements are paired, and so forth. This literary structure lays out a series of situations that are resolved in the reverse order of their initial appearance. (The formatting of this edition of Genesis will single out the separate elements of the chiasms as they appear.) Here's a brief example from the account of the Flood:

> A Noah builds an ark.
>   B God tells Noah to enter the ark.
>   C The waters rise.
>   D The waters flood the earth.
>   C' The waters recede.
>   B' God tells Noah to leave the ark.
> A' Noah builds an altar.

The overall story in Genesis has an artistic shape. Its eleven accounts, together with its prologue about creation, give it twelve parts, mirroring the twelve tribes Abraham's descendants would grow into.

The storytelling in Genesis is marvelous, and it's best to read continuously through the whole book. The stories are set in an ancient world very different from our own, so don't be surprised at the strangeness of some of what we encounter. But the characters in these stories are human and very much like us in crucial ways. God is wrestling with them to slowly bring his redemptive purposes into our world. The name Genesis means "beginnings." It is the perfect introduction to the entire Bible, giving us the framework for understanding everything that follows.

GENESIS

✢

In the beginning God created the heavens and the earth. The earth was formless and empty, and darkness covered the deep waters. And the Spirit of God was hovering over the surface of the waters.

Then God said, "Let there be light," and there was light. And God saw that the light was good. Then he separated the light from the darkness. God called the light "day" and the darkness "night."

And evening passed and morning came, marking the first day.

Then God said, "Let there be a space between the waters, to separate the waters of the heavens from the waters of the earth." And that is what happened. God made this space to separate the waters of the earth from the waters of the heavens. God called the space "sky."

And evening passed and morning came, marking the second day.

Then God said, "Let the waters beneath the sky flow together into one place, so dry ground may appear." And that is what happened. God called the dry ground "land" and the waters "seas." And God saw that it was good. Then God said, "Let the land sprout with vegetation—every sort of seed-bearing plant, and trees that grow seed-bearing fruit. These seeds will then produce the kinds of plants and trees from which they came." And that is what happened. The land produced vegetation—all sorts of seed-bearing plants, and trees with seed-bearing fruit. Their seeds produced plants and trees of the same kind. And God saw that it was good.

And evening passed and morning came, marking the third day.

Then God said, "Let lights appear in the sky to separate the day from the night. Let them be signs to mark the seasons, days, and years. Let these lights in the sky shine down on the earth." And that is what happened. God made two great lights—the larger one to govern the day, and the smaller one to govern the night. He also made the stars. God set these lights in the sky to light the earth, to govern the day and night, and to separate the light from the darkness. And God saw that it was good.

And evening passed and morning came, marking the fourth day.

Then God said, "Let the waters swarm with fish and other life. Let the skies be filled with birds of every kind." So God created great sea creatures and every living thing that scurries and swarms in the water, and every sort of bird—each producing offspring of the same kind. And God saw that it was good. Then God blessed them, saying, "Be fruitful and multiply. Let the fish fill the seas, and let the birds multiply on the earth."

And evening passed and morning came, marking the fifth day.

Then God said, "Let the earth produce every sort of animal, each producing offspring of the same kind—livestock, small animals that scurry along the ground, and wild animals." And that is what happened. God made all sorts of wild animals, livestock, and small animals, each able to produce offspring of the same kind. And God saw that it was good.

Then God said, "Let us make human beings in our image, to be like us. They will reign over the fish in the sea, the birds in the sky, the livestock, all the wild animals on the earth, and the small animals that scurry along the ground."

So God created human beings in his own image.
   In the image of God he created them;
   male and female he created them.

Then God blessed them and said, "Be fruitful and multiply. Fill the earth and govern it. Reign over the fish in the sea, the birds in the sky, and all the animals that scurry along the ground."

Then God said, "Look! I have given you every seed-bearing plant throughout the earth and all the fruit trees for your food. And I have given every green plant as food for all the wild animals, the birds in the sky, and the small animals that scurry along the ground—everything that has life." And that is what happened.

Then God looked over all he had made, and he saw that it was very good!

And evening passed and morning came, marking the sixth day.

So the creation of the heavens and the earth and everything in them was completed. On the seventh day God had finished his work of creation, so he rested from all his work. And God blessed the seventh day and declared it holy, because it was the day when he rested from all his work of creation.

+ + +

This is the account of the creation of the heavens and the earth.

When the LORD God made the earth and the heavens, neither wild plants nor grains were growing on the earth. For the LORD God had not yet sent rain to water the earth, and there were no people to cultivate the soil. Instead, springs came up from the ground and watered all the land. Then the LORD God formed the man from the dust of the ground. He breathed the breath of life into the man's nostrils, and the man became a living person.

Then the LORD God planted a garden in Eden in the east, and there he placed the man he had made. The LORD God made all sorts of trees grow up from the ground—trees that were beautiful and that produced delicious fruit. In the middle of the garden he placed the tree of life and the tree of the knowledge of good and evil.

A river flowed from the land of Eden, watering the garden and then dividing into four branches. The first branch, called the Pishon, flowed around the entire land of Havilah, where gold is found. The gold of that land is exceptionally pure; aromatic resin and onyx stone are also found there. The second branch, called the Gihon, flowed around the entire land of Cush. The third branch, called the Tigris, flowed east of the land of Asshur. The fourth branch is called the Euphrates.

The LORD God placed the man in the Garden of Eden to tend and watch over it. But the LORD God warned him, "You may freely eat the fruit of every tree in the garden—except the tree of the knowledge of good and evil. If you eat its fruit, you are sure to die."

Then the LORD God said, "It is not good for the man to be alone. I will make a helper who is just right for him." So the LORD God formed from the ground all the wild animals and all the birds of the sky. He brought them to the man to see what he would call them, and the man chose a name for each one. He gave names to all the livestock, all the birds of the sky, and all the wild animals. But still there was no helper just right for him.

So the LORD God caused the man to fall into a deep sleep. While the man slept, the LORD God took out one of the man's ribs and closed up the opening. Then the LORD God made a woman from the rib, and he brought her to the man.

"At last!" the man exclaimed.

"This one is bone from my bone,
    and flesh from my flesh!
She will be called 'woman,'
    because she was taken from 'man.'"

This explains why a man leaves his father and mother and is joined to his wife, and the two are united into one.

Now the man and his wife were both naked, but they felt no shame.

The serpent was the shrewdest of all the wild animals the LORD God had made. One day he asked the woman, "Did God really say you must not eat the fruit from any of the trees in the garden?"

"Of course we may eat fruit from the trees in the garden," the woman replied. "It's only the fruit from the tree in the middle of the garden that we are not allowed to eat. God said, 'You must not eat it or even touch it; if you do, you will die.'"

"You won't die!" the serpent replied to the woman. "God knows that your eyes will be opened as soon as you eat it, and you will be like God, knowing both good and evil."

The woman was convinced. She saw that the tree was beautiful and its fruit looked delicious, and she wanted the wisdom it would give her. So she took some of the fruit and ate it. Then she gave some to her husband, who was with her, and he ate it, too. At that moment their eyes were opened, and they suddenly felt shame at their nakedness. So they sewed fig leaves together to cover themselves.

When the cool evening breezes were blowing, the man and his wife heard the LORD God walking about in the garden. So they hid from the LORD God among the trees. Then the LORD God called to the man, "Where are you?"

He replied, "I heard you walking in the garden, so I hid. I was afraid because I was naked."

"Who told you that you were naked?" the LORD God asked. "Have you eaten from the tree whose fruit I commanded you not to eat?"

The man replied, "It was the woman you gave me who gave me the fruit, and I ate it."

Then the LORD God asked the woman, "What have you done?"

"The serpent deceived me," she replied. "That's why I ate it."

Then the LORD God said to the serpent,

"Because you have done this, you are cursed
    more than all animals, domestic and wild.
You will crawl on your belly,
    groveling in the dust as long as you live.
And I will cause hostility between you and the woman,
    and between your offspring and her offspring.
He will strike your head,
    and you will strike his heel."

Then he said to the woman,

> "I will sharpen the pain of your pregnancy,
>   and in pain you will give birth.
> And you will desire to control your husband,
>   but he will rule over you."

And to the man he said,

> "Since you listened to your wife and ate from the tree
>   whose fruit I commanded you not to eat,
> the ground is cursed because of you.
>   All your life you will struggle to scratch a living from it.
> It will grow thorns and thistles for you,
>   though you will eat of its grains.
> By the sweat of your brow
>   will you have food to eat
> until you return to the ground
>   from which you were made.
> For you were made from dust,
>   and to dust you will return."

Then the man—Adam—named his wife Eve, because she would be the mother of all who live. And the Lord God made clothing from animal skins for Adam and his wife.

Then the Lord God said, "Look, the human beings have become like us, knowing both good and evil. What if they reach out, take fruit from the tree of life, and eat it? Then they will live forever!" So the Lord God banished them from the Garden of Eden, and he sent Adam out to cultivate the ground from which he had been made. After sending them out, the Lord God stationed mighty cherubim to the east of the Garden of Eden. And he placed a flaming sword that flashed back and forth to guard the way to the tree of life.

Now Adam had sexual relations with his wife, Eve, and she became pregnant. When she gave birth to Cain, she said, "With the Lord's help, I have produced a man!" Later she gave birth to his brother and named him Abel.

When they grew up, Abel became a shepherd, while Cain cultivated the ground. When it was time for the harvest, Cain presented some of his crops as a gift to the Lord. Abel also brought a gift—the best portions of the firstborn lambs from his flock. The Lord accepted Abel and his gift, but he did not accept Cain and his gift. This made Cain very angry, and he looked dejected.

"Why are you so angry?" the Lord asked Cain. "Why do you look so dejected? You will be accepted if you do what is right. But if you refuse to do what is right, then watch out! Sin is crouching at the door, eager to control you. But you must subdue it and be its master."

One day Cain suggested to his brother, "Let's go out into the fields." And while they were in the field, Cain attacked his brother, Abel, and killed him.

Afterward the Lord asked Cain, "Where is your brother? Where is Abel?"

"I don't know," Cain responded. "Am I my brother's guardian?"

But the Lord said, "What have you done? Listen! Your brother's blood cries out to me from the ground! Now you are cursed and banished from the ground, which has swallowed your brother's blood. No longer will the ground yield good crops for you, no matter how hard you work! From now on you will be a homeless wanderer on the earth."

Cain replied to the Lord, "My punishment is too great for me to bear! You have banished me from the land and from your presence; you have made me a homeless wanderer. Anyone who finds me will kill me!"

The Lord replied, "No, for I will give a sevenfold punishment to anyone who kills you." Then the Lord put a mark on Cain to warn anyone who might try to kill him. So Cain left the Lord's presence and settled in the land of Nod, east of Eden.

Cain had sexual relations with his wife, and she became pregnant and gave birth to Enoch. Then Cain founded a city, which he named Enoch, after his son. Enoch had a son named Irad. Irad became the father of Mehujael. Mehujael became the father of Methushael. Methushael became the father of Lamech.

Lamech married two women. The first was named Adah, and the second was Zillah. Adah gave birth to Jabal, who was the first of those who raise livestock and live in tents. His brother's name was Jubal, the first of all who play the harp and flute. Lamech's other wife, Zillah, gave birth to a son named Tubal-cain. He became an expert in forging tools of bronze and iron. Tubal-cain had a sister named Naamah. One day Lamech said to his wives,

"Adah and Zillah, hear my voice;
   listen to me, you wives of Lamech.
I have killed a man who attacked me,
   a young man who wounded me.
If someone who kills Cain is punished seven times,
   then the one who kills me will be punished seventy-seven times!"

MESSIAH

8-WEEK READING PLAN

4 Questions to get your conversations started:

1. What stood out to you this week?

2. Was there anything confusing or troubling?

3. Did anything make you think differently about God?

4. How might this change the way we live?

IMMERSE
The **Bible** Reading Experience™

QUICK START GUIDE

3 ways to get the most out of your experience

1 Use *Immerse: Messiah* instead of your regular chapter-and-verse Bible. This special reader's edition restores the Bible to its natural simplicity and beauty by removing chapter and verse numbers and other historical additions. Letters look like letters, songs look like songs, and the original literary structures are visible in each book.

2 Commit to making this a community experience. Immerse is designed for groups to encounter large portions of the Bible together for 8 weeks—more like a book club, less like a Bible study. By meeting every week in small groups and discussing what you read in open, honest conversations, you and your community can come together to be transformed through an authentic experience with the Scriptures.

3 Aim to understand the big story. Read through "A Sacred Saga" (p. A8) to see how the books of the Bible work together to tell God's story of his creation's restoration. As you read through *Immerse: Messiah*, rather than ask, "How do I fit God into my busy life?" begin asking, "How can I join in God's great plan by living out my part in his story?"

IMMERSE Resources:

- Custom Immerse audio Bible
- Weekly preview videos
- Digital eBook version
- Pastor's Guide
- Group Host Guide
- Family Guide

Tyndale

INSTITUTE FOR BIBLE READING

Available at **ImmerseBible.com/Messiah**

Adam had sexual relations with his wife again, and she gave birth to another son. She named him Seth, for she said, "God has granted me another son in place of Abel, whom Cain killed." When Seth grew up, he had a son and named him Enosh. At that time people first began to worship the LORD by name.

+ + +

This is the written account of the descendants of Adam. When God created human beings, he made them to be like himself. He created them male and female, and he blessed them and called them "human."

When Adam was 130 years old, he became the father of a son who was just like him—in his very image. He named his son Seth. After the birth of Seth, Adam lived another 800 years, and he had other sons and daughters. Adam lived 930 years, and then he died.

When Seth was 105 years old, he became the father of Enosh. After the birth of Enosh, Seth lived another 807 years, and he had other sons and daughters. Seth lived 912 years, and then he died.

When Enosh was 90 years old, he became the father of Kenan. After the birth of Kenan, Enosh lived another 815 years, and he had other sons and daughters. Enosh lived 905 years, and then he died.

When Kenan was 70 years old, he became the father of Mahalalel. After the birth of Mahalalel, Kenan lived another 840 years, and he had other sons and daughters. Kenan lived 910 years, and then he died.

When Mahalalel was 65 years old, he became the father of Jared. After the birth of Jared, Mahalalel lived another 830 years, and he had other sons and daughters. Mahalalel lived 895 years, and then he died.

When Jared was 162 years old, he became the father of Enoch. After the birth of Enoch, Jared lived another 800 years, and he had other sons and daughters. Jared lived 962 years, and then he died.

When Enoch was 65 years old, he became the father of Methuselah. After the birth of Methuselah, Enoch lived in close fellowship with God for another 300 years, and he had other sons and daughters. Enoch lived 365 years, walking in close fellowship with God. Then one day he disappeared, because God took him.

When Methuselah was 187 years old, he became the father of Lamech. After the birth of Lamech, Methuselah lived another 782 years, and he had other sons and daughters. Methuselah lived 969 years, and then he died.

When Lamech was 182 years old, he became the father of a son. Lamech named his son Noah, for he said, "May he bring us relief from our work and the painful labor of farming this ground that the LORD has cursed." After the birth of Noah, Lamech lived another 595 years, and he had other sons and daughters. Lamech lived 777 years, and then he died.

After Noah was 500 years old, he became the father of Shem, Ham, and Japheth.

Then the people began to multiply on the earth, and daughters were born to them. The sons of God saw the beautiful women and took any they wanted as their wives. Then the LORD said, "My Spirit will not put up with humans for such a long time, for they are only mortal flesh. In the future, their normal lifespan will be no more than 120 years."

In those days, and for some time after, giant Nephilites lived on the earth, for whenever the sons of God had intercourse with women, they gave birth to children who became the heroes and famous warriors of ancient times.

The LORD observed the extent of human wickedness on the earth, and he saw that everything they thought or imagined was consistently and totally evil. So the LORD was sorry he had ever made them and put them on the earth. It broke his heart. And the LORD said, "I will wipe this human race I have created from the face of the earth. Yes, and I will destroy every living thing—all the people, the large animals, the small animals that scurry along the ground, and even the birds of the sky. I am sorry I ever made them." But Noah found favor with the LORD.

+ + +

This is the account of Noah and his family.

Noah was a righteous man, the only blameless person living on earth at the time, and he walked in close fellowship with God. Noah was the father of three sons: Shem, Ham, and Japheth.

Now God saw that the earth had become corrupt and was filled with violence. God observed all this corruption in the world, for everyone on earth was corrupt. So God said to Noah, "I have decided to destroy all living creatures, for they have filled the earth with violence. Yes, I will wipe them all out along with the earth!

"Build a large boat from cypress wood and waterproof it with tar, inside and out. Then construct decks and stalls throughout its interior. Make the boat 450 feet long, 75 feet wide, and 45 feet high. Leave an 18-inch opening below the roof all the way around the boat. Put the door on the side, and build three decks inside the boat—lower, middle, and upper.

"Look! I am about to cover the earth with a flood that will destroy every living thing that breathes. Everything on earth will die. But I will confirm my covenant with you. So enter the boat—you and your wife and your sons and their wives. Bring a pair of every kind of animal—a male and a female—into the boat with you to keep them alive during the flood. Pairs of every kind of bird, and every kind of animal, and every kind of small animal that scurries along the ground, will come to you to be kept alive. And be sure to take on board enough food for your family and for all the animals."

So Noah did everything exactly as God had commanded him.

When everything was ready, the LORD said to Noah, "Go into the boat with all your family, for among all the people of the earth, I can see that you alone are righteous. Take with you seven pairs—male and female—of each animal I have approved for eating and for sacrifice, and take one pair of each of the others. Also take seven pairs of every kind of bird. There must be a male and a female in each pair to ensure that all life will survive on the earth after the flood. Seven days from now I will make the rains pour down on the earth. And it will rain for forty days and forty nights, until I have wiped from the earth all the living things I have created."

So Noah did everything as the LORD commanded him.

Noah was 600 years old when the flood covered the earth. He went on board the boat to escape the flood—he and his wife and his sons and their wives. With them were all the various kinds of animals—those approved for eating and for sacrifice and those that were not—along with all the birds and the small animals that scurry along the ground. They entered the boat in pairs, male and female, just as God had commanded Noah. After seven days, the waters of the flood came and covered the earth.

When Noah was 600 years old, on the seventeenth day of the second month, all the underground waters erupted from the earth, and the rain fell in mighty torrents from the sky. The rain continued to fall for forty days and forty nights.

That very day Noah had gone into the boat with his wife and his sons— Shem, Ham, and Japheth—and their wives. With them in the boat were pairs of every kind of animal—domestic and wild, large and small—along with birds of every kind. Two by two they came into the boat, representing every living thing that breathes. A male and female of each kind entered, just as God had commanded Noah. Then the LORD closed the door behind them.

For forty days the floodwaters grew deeper, covering the ground and lifting the boat high above the earth. As the waters rose higher and higher above the ground, the boat floated safely on the surface. Finally, the water covered even the highest mountains on the earth, rising more than twenty-two feet above the highest peaks. All the living things on earth died—birds, domestic animals, wild animals, small animals that scurry along the ground, and all the people. Everything that breathed and lived on dry land died. God wiped out every living thing on the earth—people, livestock, small animals that scurry along the ground, and the birds of the sky. All were destroyed. The only people who survived were Noah and those with him in the boat. And the floodwaters covered the earth for 150 days.

But God remembered Noah and all the wild animals and livestock with him in the boat. He sent a wind to blow across the earth, and the flood-waters began to recede. The underground waters stopped flowing, and the torrential rains from the sky were stopped. So the floodwaters gradually receded from the earth. After 150 days, exactly five months from the time the flood began, the boat came to rest on the mountains of Ararat. Two and a half months later, as the waters continued to go down, other mountain peaks became visible.

After another forty days, Noah opened the window he had made in the boat and released a raven. The bird flew back and forth until the flood-waters on the earth had dried up. He also released a dove to see if the water had receded and it could find dry ground. But the dove could find no place to land because the water still covered the ground. So it returned to the boat, and Noah held out his hand and drew the dove back inside. After waiting another seven days, Noah released the dove again. This time the dove returned to him in the evening with a fresh olive leaf in its beak. Then Noah knew that the floodwaters were almost gone. He waited another seven days and then released the dove again. This time it did not come back.

Noah was now 601 years old. On the first day of the new year, ten and a half months after the flood began, the floodwaters had almost dried up from the earth. Noah lifted back the covering of the boat and saw that the surface of the ground was drying. Two more months went by, and at last the earth was dry!

Then God said to Noah, "Leave the boat, all of you—you and your wife, and your sons and their wives. Release all the animals—the birds, the live-stock, and the small animals that scurry along the ground—so they can be fruitful and multiply throughout the earth."

So Noah, his wife, and his sons and their wives left the boat. And all of the large and small animals and birds came out of the boat, pair by pair.

Then Noah built an altar to the LORD, and there he sacrificed as burnt offerings the animals and birds that had been approved for that purpose. And the LORD was pleased with the aroma of the sacrifice and said to himself, "I will never again curse the ground because of the human race, even though everything they think or imagine is bent toward evil from childhood. I will never again destroy all living things. As long as the earth remains, there will be planting and harvest, cold and heat, summer and winter, day and night."

Then God blessed Noah and his sons and told them, "Be fruitful and multiply. Fill the earth. All the animals of the earth, all the birds of the sky, all the small animals that scurry along the ground, and all the fish in the sea will look on you with fear and terror. I have placed them in your power. I have given them to you for food, just as I have given you grain and vegetables. But you must never eat any meat that still has the lifeblood in it.

"And I will require the blood of anyone who takes another person's life. If a wild animal kills a person, it must die. And anyone who murders a fellow human must die. If anyone takes a human life, that person's life will also be taken by human hands. For God made human beings in his own image. Now be fruitful and multiply, and repopulate the earth."

Then God told Noah and his sons, "I hereby confirm my covenant with you and your descendants, and with all the animals that were on the boat with you—the birds, the livestock, and all the wild animals—every living creature on earth. Yes, I am confirming my covenant with you. Never again will floodwaters kill all living creatures; never again will a flood destroy the earth."

Then God said, "I am giving you a sign of my covenant with you and with all living creatures, for all generations to come. I have placed my rainbow in the clouds. It is the sign of my covenant with you and with all the earth. When I send clouds over the earth, the rainbow will appear in the clouds, and I will remember my covenant with you and with all living creatures. Never again will the floodwaters destroy all life. When I see the rainbow in the clouds, I will remember the eternal covenant between God and every living creature on earth." Then God said to Noah, "Yes, this rainbow is the sign of the covenant I am confirming with all the creatures on earth."

The sons of Noah who came out of the boat with their father were Shem, Ham, and Japheth. (Ham is the father of Canaan.) From these three sons of Noah came all the people who now populate the earth.

After the flood, Noah began to cultivate the ground, and he planted a vineyard. One day he drank some wine he had made, and he became drunk and lay naked inside his tent. Ham, the father of Canaan, saw that his father was naked and went outside and told his brothers. Then Shem and Japheth took a robe, held it over their shoulders, and backed into the tent to cover their father. As they did this, they looked the other way so they would not see him naked.

When Noah woke up from his stupor, he learned what Ham, his youngest son, had done. Then he cursed Canaan, the son of Ham:

"May Canaan be cursed!
    May he be the lowest of servants to his relatives."

Then Noah said,

"May the LORD, the God of Shem, be blessed,
    and may Canaan be his servant!
May God expand the territory of Japheth!
May Japheth share the prosperity of Shem,
    and may Canaan be his servant."

Noah lived another 350 years after the great flood. He lived 950 years, and then he died.

+ + +

This is the account of the families of Shem, Ham, and Japheth, the three sons of Noah. Many children were born to them after the great flood.

The descendants of Japheth were Gomer, Magog, Madai, Javan, Tubal, Meshech, and Tiras.
The descendants of Gomer were Ashkenaz, Riphath, and Togarmah.
The descendants of Javan were Elishah, Tarshish, Kittim, and Rodanim. Their descendants became the seafaring peoples that spread out to various lands, each identified by its own language, clan, and national identity.

The descendants of Ham were Cush, Mizraim, Put, and Canaan.
The descendants of Cush were Seba, Havilah, Sabtah, Raamah, and Sabteca. The descendants of Raamah were Sheba and Dedan.

Cush was also the ancestor of Nimrod, who was the first heroic warrior on earth. Since he was the greatest hunter in the world, his name became proverbial. People would say, "This man is like Nimrod, the greatest hunter in the world." He built his kingdom in the land of Babylonia, with the cities of Babylon, Erech, Akkad, and Calneh. From there he expanded his territory to Assyria, building the cities of Nineveh, Rehoboth-ir, Calah, and Resen (the great city located between Nineveh and Calah).

Mizraim was the ancestor of the Ludites, Anamites, Lehabites, Naphtuhites, Pathrusites, Casluhites, and the Caphtorites, from whom the Philistines came.

Canaan's oldest son was Sidon, the ancestor of the Sidonians. Canaan was also the ancestor of the Hittites, Jebusites, Amorites, Girgashites, Hivites, Arkites, Sinites, Arvadites, Zemarites, and Hamathites. The Canaanite clans eventually spread out, and the territory of Canaan extended from Sidon in the north to Gerar and Gaza in the south, and east as far as Sodom, Gomorrah, Admah, and Zeboiim, near Lasha.

These were the descendants of Ham, identified by clan, language, territory, and national identity.

Sons were also born to Shem, the older brother of Japheth. Shem was the ancestor of all the descendants of Eber.

The descendants of Shem were Elam, Asshur, Arphaxad, Lud, and Aram.

The descendants of Aram were Uz, Hul, Gether, and Mash.

Arphaxad was the father of Shelah, and Shelah was the father of Eber.

Eber had two sons. The first was named Peleg (which means "division"), for during his lifetime the people of the world were divided into different language groups. His brother's name was Joktan.

Joktan was the ancestor of Almodad, Sheleph, Hazarmaveth, Jerah, Hadoram, Uzal, Diklah, Obal, Abimael, Sheba, Ophir, Havilah, and Jobab. All these were descendants of Joktan. The territory they occupied extended from Mesha all the way to Sephar in the eastern mountains.

These were the descendants of Shem, identified by clan, language, territory, and national identity.

These are the clans that descended from Noah's sons, arranged by nation according to their lines of descent. All the nations of the earth descended from these clans after the great flood.

At one time all the people of the world spoke the same language and used the same words. As the people migrated to the east, they found a plain in the land of Babylonia and settled there.

They began saying to each other, "Let's make bricks and harden them with fire." (In this region bricks were used instead of stone, and tar was used for mortar.) Then they said, "Come, let's build a great city for ourselves with a tower that reaches into the sky. This will make us famous and keep us from being scattered all over the world."

But the LORD came down to look at the city and the tower the people were building. "Look!" he said. "The people are united, and they all speak the same language. After this, nothing they set out to do will be impossible for them! Come, let's go down and confuse the people with different languages. Then they won't be able to understand each other."

In that way, the LORD scattered them all over the world, and they stopped building the city. That is why the city was called Babel, because that is where the LORD confused the people with different languages. In this way he scattered them all over the world.

+ + +

This is the account of Shem's family.

Two years after the great flood, when Shem was 100 years old, he became the father of Arphaxad. After the birth of Arphaxad, Shem lived another 500 years and had other sons and daughters.

When Arphaxad was 35 years old, he became the father of Shelah. After the birth of Shelah, Arphaxad lived another 403 years and had other sons and daughters.

When Shelah was 30 years old, he became the father of Eber. After the birth of Eber, Shelah lived another 403 years and had other sons and daughters.

When Eber was 34 years old, he became the father of Peleg. After the birth of Peleg, Eber lived another 430 years and had other sons and daughters.

When Peleg was 30 years old, he became the father of Reu. After the birth of Reu, Peleg lived another 209 years and had other sons and daughters.

When Reu was 32 years old, he became the father of Serug. After the birth of Serug, Reu lived another 207 years and had other sons and daughters.

When Serug was 30 years old, he became the father of Nahor. After the birth of Nahor, Serug lived another 200 years and had other sons and daughters.

When Nahor was 29 years old, he became the father of Terah. After the birth of Terah, Nahor lived another 119 years and had other sons and daughters.

After Terah was 70 years old, he became the father of Abram, Nahor, and Haran.

+ + +

This is the account of Terah's family.

Terah was the father of Abram, Nahor, and Haran; and Haran was the father of Lot. But Haran died in Ur of the Chaldeans, the land of his birth, while his father, Terah, was still living. Meanwhile, Abram and Nahor both married. The name of Abram's wife was Sarai, and the name of Nahor's wife was Milcah. (Milcah and her sister Iscah were daughters of Nahor's brother Haran.) But Sarai was unable to become pregnant and had no children.

One day Terah took his son Abram, his daughter-in-law Sarai (his son Abram's wife), and his grandson Lot (his son Haran's child) and moved away from Ur of the Chaldeans. He was headed for the land of Canaan, but they stopped at Haran and settled there. Terah lived for 205 years and died while still in Haran.

+

The LORD had said to Abram, "Leave your native country, your relatives, and your father's family, and go to the land that I will show you. I will make you into a great nation. I will bless you and make you famous, and you will be a blessing to others. I will bless those who bless you and curse those who treat you with contempt. All the families on earth will be blessed through you."

So Abram departed as the LORD had instructed, and Lot went with him. Abram was seventy-five years old when he left Haran. He took his wife, Sarai, his nephew Lot, and all his wealth—his livestock and all the people he had taken into his household at Haran—and headed for the land of Canaan. When they arrived in Canaan, Abram traveled through the land as far as Shechem. There he set up camp beside the oak of Moreh. At that time, the area was inhabited by Canaanites.

Then the LORD appeared to Abram and said, "I will give this land to your descendants." And Abram built an altar there and dedicated it to the LORD, who had appeared to him. After that, Abram traveled south and set up camp in the hill country, with Bethel to the west and Ai to the east. There he built another altar and dedicated it to the LORD, and he worshiped the LORD. Then Abram continued traveling south by stages toward the Negev.

+

At that time a severe famine struck the land of Canaan, forcing Abram to go down to Egypt, where he lived as a foreigner. As he was approaching the border of Egypt, Abram said to his wife, Sarai, "Look, you are a very beautiful woman. When the Egyptians see you, they will say, 'This is his wife. Let's kill him; then we can have her!' So please tell them you are my sister. Then they will spare my life and treat me well because of their interest in you."

And sure enough, when Abram arrived in Egypt, everyone noticed Sarai's beauty. When the palace officials saw her, they sang her praises to Pharaoh, their king, and Sarai was taken into his palace. Then Pharaoh gave Abram many gifts because of her—sheep, goats, cattle, male and female donkeys, male and female servants, and camels.

But the LORD sent terrible plagues upon Pharaoh and his household because of Sarai, Abram's wife. So Pharaoh summoned Abram and accused him sharply. "What have you done to me?" he demanded. "Why didn't you tell me she was your wife? Why did you say, 'She is my sister,' and allow me to take her as my wife? Now then, here is your wife. Take her and get out of here!" Pharaoh ordered some of his men to escort them, and he sent Abram out of the country, along with his wife and all his possessions.

✝

So Abram left Egypt and traveled north into the Negev, along with his wife and Lot and all that they owned. (Abram was very rich in livestock, silver, and gold.) From the Negev, they continued traveling by stages toward Bethel, and they pitched their tents between Bethel and Ai, where they had camped before. This was the same place where Abram had built the altar, and there he worshiped the LORD again.

Lot, who was traveling with Abram, had also become very wealthy with flocks of sheep and goats, herds of cattle, and many tents. But the land could not support both Abram and Lot with all their flocks and herds living so close together. So disputes broke out between the herdsmen of Abram and Lot. (At that time Canaanites and Perizzites were also living in the land.)

Finally Abram said to Lot, "Let's not allow this conflict to come between us or our herdsmen. After all, we are close relatives! The whole countryside is open to you. Take your choice of any section of the land you want, and we will separate. If you want the land to the left, then I'll take the land on the right. If you prefer the land on the right, then I'll go to the left."

Lot took a long look at the fertile plains of the Jordan Valley in the direction of Zoar. The whole area was well watered everywhere, like the garden of the LORD or the beautiful land of Egypt. (This was before the LORD destroyed Sodom and Gomorrah.) Lot chose for himself the whole Jordan Valley to the east of them. He went there with his flocks and servants and parted company with his uncle Abram. So Abram settled in the land of Canaan, and Lot moved his tents to a place near Sodom and settled among the cities of the plain. But the people of this area were extremely wicked and constantly sinned against the LORD.

After Lot had gone, the LORD said to Abram, "Look as far as you can see in every direction—north and south, east and west. I am giving all this land, as far as you can see, to you and your descendants as a permanent possession. And I will give you so many descendants that, like the dust of the earth, they cannot be counted! Go and walk through the land in every direction, for I am giving it to you."

So Abram moved his camp to Hebron and settled near the oak grove belonging to Mamre. There he built another altar to the LORD.

About this time war broke out in the region. King Amraphel of Babylonia, King Arioch of Ellasar, King Kedorlaomer of Elam, and King Tidal of Goiim fought against King Bera of Sodom, King Birsha of Gomorrah, King Shinab of Admah, King Shemeber of Zeboiim, and the king of Bela (also called Zoar).

This second group of kings joined forces in Siddim Valley (that is, the valley of the Dead Sea). For twelve years they had been subject to King Kedorlaomer, but in the thirteenth year they rebelled against him.

One year later Kedorlaomer and his allies arrived and defeated the Rephaites at Ashteroth-karnaim, the Zuzites at Ham, the Emites at Shaveh-kiriathaim, and the Horites at Mount Seir, as far as El-paran at the edge of the wilderness. Then they turned back and came to En-mishpat (now called Kadesh) and conquered all the territory of the Amalekites, and also the Amorites living in Hazazon-tamar.

Then the rebel kings of Sodom, Gomorrah, Admah, Zeboiim, and Bela (also called Zoar) prepared for battle in the valley of the Dead Sea. They fought against King Kedorlaomer of Elam, King Tidal of Goiim, King Amraphel of Babylonia, and King Arioch of Ellasar—four kings against five. As it happened, the valley of the Dead Sea was filled with tar pits. And as the army of the kings of Sodom and Gomorrah fled, some fell into the tar pits, while the rest escaped into the mountains. The victorious invaders then plundered Sodom and Gomorrah and headed for home, taking with them all the spoils of war and the food supplies. They also captured Lot—Abram's nephew who lived in Sodom—and carried off everything he owned.

But one of Lot's men escaped and reported everything to Abram the Hebrew, who was living near the oak grove belonging to Mamre the Amorite. Mamre and his relatives, Eshcol and Aner, were Abram's allies.

When Abram heard that his nephew Lot had been captured, he mobilized the 318 trained men who had been born into his household. Then he pursued Kedorlaomer's army until he caught up with them at Dan. There he divided his men and attacked during the night. Kedorlaomer's army fled, but Abram chased them as far as Hobah, north of Damascus.

Abram recovered all the goods that had been taken, and he brought back his nephew Lot with his possessions and all the women and other captives.

After Abram returned from his victory over Kedorlaomer and all his allies, the king of Sodom went out to meet him in the valley of Shaveh (that is, the King's Valley).

And Melchizedek, the king of Salem and a priest of God Most High, brought Abram some bread and wine. Melchizedek blessed Abram with this blessing:

"Blessed be Abram by God Most High,
    Creator of heaven and earth.
And blessed be God Most High,
    who has defeated your enemies for you."

Then Abram gave Melchizedek a tenth of all the goods he had recovered.

The king of Sodom said to Abram, "Give back my people who were captured. But you may keep for yourself all the goods you have recovered."

Abram replied to the king of Sodom, "I solemnly swear to the LORD, God Most High, Creator of heaven and earth, that I will not take so much as a single thread or sandal thong from what belongs to you. Otherwise you might say, 'I am the one who made Abram rich.' I will accept only what my young warriors have already eaten, and I request that you give a fair share of the goods to my allies—Aner, Eshcol, and Mamre."

+

Some time later, the LORD spoke to Abram in a vision and said to him, "Do not be afraid, Abram, for I will protect you, and your reward will be great."

But Abram replied, "O Sovereign LORD, what good are all your blessings when I don't even have a son? Since you've given me no children, Eliezer of Damascus, a servant in my household, will inherit all my wealth. You have given me no descendants of my own, so one of my servants will be my heir."

Then the LORD said to him, "No, your servant will not be your heir, for you will have a son of your own who will be your heir." Then the LORD took Abram outside and said to him, "Look up into the sky and count the stars if you can. That's how many descendants you will have!"

And Abram believed the LORD, and the LORD counted him as righteous because of his faith.

Then the LORD told him, "I am the LORD who brought you out of Ur of the Chaldeans to give you this land as your possession."

But Abram replied, "O Sovereign LORD, how can I be sure that I will actually possess it?"

The LORD told him, "Bring me a three-year-old heifer, a three-year-old female goat, a three-year-old ram, a turtledove, and a young pigeon." So Abram presented all these to him and killed them. Then he cut each animal down the middle and laid the halves side by side; he did not, however, cut the birds in half. Some vultures swooped down to eat the carcasses, but Abram chased them away.

As the sun was going down, Abram fell into a deep sleep, and a terrifying darkness came down over him. Then the LORD said to Abram, "You can be sure that your descendants will be strangers in a foreign land, where they will be oppressed as slaves for 400 years. But I will punish the nation that enslaves them, and in the end they will come away with great wealth. (As for you, you will die in peace and be buried at a ripe old age.) After four generations your descendants will return here to this land, for the sins of the Amorites do not yet warrant their destruction."

After the sun went down and darkness fell, Abram saw a smoking firepot and a flaming torch pass between the halves of the carcasses. So the LORD made a covenant with Abram that day and said, "I have given this land to your descendants, all the way from the border of Egypt to the great Euphrates River—the land now occupied by the Kenites, Kenizzites, Kadmonites, Hittites, Perizzites, Rephaites, Amorites, Canaanites, Girgashites, and Jebusites."

+

Now Sarai, Abram's wife, had not been able to bear children for him. But she had an Egyptian servant named Hagar. So Sarai said to Abram, "The LORD has prevented me from having children. Go and sleep with my servant. Perhaps I can have children through her." And Abram agreed with Sarai's proposal. So Sarai, Abram's wife, took Hagar the Egyptian servant and gave her to Abram as a wife. (This happened ten years after Abram had settled in the land of Canaan.)

So Abram had sexual relations with Hagar, and she became pregnant. But when Hagar knew she was pregnant, she began to treat her mistress, Sarai, with contempt. Then Sarai said to Abram, "This is all your fault! I put my servant into your arms, but now that she's pregnant she treats me with contempt. The LORD will show who's wrong—you or me!"

Abram replied, "Look, she is your servant, so deal with her as you see fit." Then Sarai treated Hagar so harshly that she finally ran away.

The angel of the LORD found Hagar beside a spring of water in the wilderness, along the road to Shur. The angel said to her, "Hagar, Sarai's servant, where have you come from, and where are you going?"

"I'm running away from my mistress, Sarai," she replied.

The angel of the LORD said to her, "Return to your mistress, and submit to her authority." Then he added, "I will give you more descendants than you can count."

And the angel also said, "You are now pregnant and will give birth to a son. You are to name him Ishmael (which means 'God hears'), for the LORD has heard your cry of distress. This son of yours will be a wild man, as untamed as a wild donkey! He will raise his fist against everyone, and everyone will be against him. Yes, he will live in open hostility against all his relatives."

Thereafter, Hagar used another name to refer to the LORD, who had spoken to her. She said, "You are the God who sees me." She also said, "Have I truly seen the One who sees me?" So that well was named Beer-lahai-roi (which means "well of the Living One who sees me"). It can still be found between Kadesh and Bered.

So Hagar gave Abram a son, and Abram named him Ishmael. Abram was eighty-six years old when Ishmael was born.

+

When Abram was ninety-nine years old, the LORD appeared to him and said, "I am El-Shaddai—'God Almighty.' Serve me faithfully and live a blameless life. I will make a covenant with you, by which I will guarantee to give you countless descendants."

At this, Abram fell face down on the ground. Then God said to him, "This is my covenant with you: I will make you the father of a multitude of nations! What's more, I am changing your name. It will no longer be Abram. Instead, you will be called Abraham, for you will be the father of many nations. I will make you extremely fruitful. Your descendants will become many nations, and kings will be among them!

"I will confirm my covenant with you and your descendants after you, from generation to generation. This is the everlasting covenant: I will always be your God and the God of your descendants after you. And I will give the entire land of Canaan, where you now live as a foreigner, to you and your descendants. It will be their possession forever, and I will be their God."

Then God said to Abraham, "Your responsibility is to obey the terms of the covenant. You and all your descendants have this continual responsibility. This is the covenant that you and your descendants must keep: Each male among you must be circumcised. You must cut off the flesh of your foreskin as a sign of the covenant between me and you. From generation to generation, every male child must be circumcised on the eighth day after his birth. This applies not only to members of your family but also to the servants born in your household and the foreign-born servants whom you have purchased. All must be circumcised. Your bodies will bear the mark of my everlasting covenant. Any male who fails to be circumcised will be cut off from the covenant family for breaking the covenant."

Then God said to Abraham, "Regarding Sarai, your wife—her name will no longer be Sarai. From now on her name will be Sarah. And I will bless her and give you a son from her! Yes, I will bless her richly, and she will become the mother of many nations. Kings of nations will be among her descendants."

Then Abraham bowed down to the ground, but he laughed to himself in disbelief. "How could I become a father at the age of 100?" he thought. "And how can Sarah have a baby when she is ninety years old?" So Abraham said to God, "May Ishmael live under your special blessing!"

But God replied, "No—Sarah, your wife, will give birth to a son for you. You will name him Isaac, and I will confirm my covenant with him and his descendants as an everlasting covenant. As for Ishmael, I will bless him also, just as you have asked. I will make him extremely fruitful and multiply his descendants. He will become the father of twelve princes, and I will make him a great nation. But my covenant will be confirmed with Isaac, who will be born to you and Sarah about this time next year." When God had finished speaking, he left Abraham.

On that very day Abraham took his son, Ishmael, and every male in his household, including those born there and those he had bought. Then he circumcised them, cutting off their foreskins, just as God had told him. Abraham was ninety-nine years old when he was circumcised, and Ishmael, his son, was thirteen. Both Abraham and his son, Ishmael, were circumcised on that same day, along with all the other men and boys of the household, whether they were born there or bought as servants. All were circumcised with him.

The LORD appeared again to Abraham near the oak grove belonging to Mamre. One day Abraham was sitting at the entrance to his tent during the hottest part of the day. He looked up and noticed three men standing nearby. When he saw them, he ran to meet them and welcomed them, bowing low to the ground.

"My lord," he said, "if it pleases you, stop here for a while. Rest in the shade of this tree while water is brought to wash your feet. And since you've honored your servant with this visit, let me prepare some food to refresh you before you continue on your journey."

"All right," they said. "Do as you have said."

So Abraham ran back to the tent and said to Sarah, "Hurry! Get three large measures of your best flour, knead it into dough, and bake some bread." Then Abraham ran out to the herd and chose a tender calf and gave it to his servant, who quickly prepared it. When the food was ready, Abraham took some yogurt and milk and the roasted meat, and he served it to the men. As they ate, Abraham waited on them in the shade of the trees.

"Where is Sarah, your wife?" the visitors asked.

"She's inside the tent," Abraham replied.

Then one of them said, "I will return to you about this time next year, and your wife, Sarah, will have a son!"

Sarah was listening to this conversation from the tent. Abraham and Sarah were both very old by this time, and Sarah was long past the age of having children. So she laughed silently to herself and said, "How could a worn-out woman like me enjoy such pleasure, especially when my master—my husband—is also so old?"

Then the LORD said to Abraham, "Why did Sarah laugh? Why did she say, 'Can an old woman like me have a baby?' Is anything too hard for the LORD? I will return about this time next year, and Sarah will have a son."

Sarah was afraid, so she denied it, saying, "I didn't laugh."

But the LORD said, "No, you did laugh."

+

Then the men got up from their meal and looked out toward Sodom. As they left, Abraham went with them to send them on their way.

"Should I hide my plan from Abraham?" the LORD asked. "For Abraham will certainly become a great and mighty nation, and all the nations of the earth will be blessed through him. I have singled him out so that he will direct his sons and their families to keep the way of the LORD by doing what is right and just. Then I will do for Abraham all that I have promised."

So the LORD told Abraham, "I have heard a great outcry from Sodom and Gomorrah, because their sin is so flagrant. I am going down to see if their actions are as wicked as I have heard. If not, I want to know."

The other men turned and headed toward Sodom, but the LORD remained with Abraham. Abraham approached him and said, "Will you sweep away both the righteous and the wicked? Suppose you find fifty righteous people living there in the city—will you still sweep it away and not spare it for their sakes? Surely you wouldn't do such a thing, destroying the righteous along with the wicked. Why, you would be treating the righteous and the wicked exactly the same! Surely you wouldn't do that! Should not the Judge of all the earth do what is right?"

And the LORD replied, "If I find fifty righteous people in Sodom, I will spare the entire city for their sake."

Then Abraham spoke again. "Since I have begun, let me speak further to my Lord, even though I am but dust and ashes. Suppose there are only forty-five righteous people rather than fifty? Will you destroy the whole city for lack of five?"

And the LORD said, "I will not destroy it if I find forty-five righteous people there."

Then Abraham pressed his request further. "Suppose there are only forty?"

And the LORD replied, "I will not destroy it for the sake of the forty."

"Please don't be angry, my Lord," Abraham pleaded. "Let me speak— suppose only thirty righteous people are found?"

And the LORD replied, "I will not destroy it if I find thirty."

Then Abraham said, "Since I have dared to speak to the Lord, let me continue—suppose there are only twenty?"

And the LORD replied, "Then I will not destroy it for the sake of the twenty."

Finally, Abraham said, "Lord, please don't be angry with me if I speak one more time. Suppose only ten are found there?"

And the LORD replied, "Then I will not destroy it for the sake of the ten."

When the LORD had finished his conversation with Abraham, he went on his way, and Abraham returned to his tent.

That evening the two angels came to the entrance of the city of Sodom. Lot was sitting there, and when he saw them, he stood up to meet them. Then he welcomed them and bowed with his face to the ground. "My lords," he said, "come to my home to wash your feet, and be my guests for the night. You may then get up early in the morning and be on your way again."

"Oh no," they replied. "We'll just spend the night out here in the city square."

But Lot insisted, so at last they went home with him. Lot prepared a feast for them, complete with fresh bread made without yeast, and they ate. But before they retired for the night, all the men of Sodom, young and old, came from all over the city and surrounded the house. They shouted to Lot, "Where are the men who came to spend the night with you? Bring them out to us so we can have sex with them!"

So Lot stepped outside to talk to them, shutting the door behind him. "Please, my brothers," he begged, "don't do such a wicked thing. Look, I have two virgin daughters. Let me bring them out to you, and you can do with them as you wish. But please, leave these men alone, for they are my guests and are under my protection."

"Stand back!" they shouted. "This fellow came to town as an outsider, and now he's acting like our judge! We'll treat you far worse than those other men!" And they lunged toward Lot to break down the door.

But the two angels reached out, pulled Lot into the house, and bolted the door. Then they blinded all the men, young and old, who were at the door of the house, so they gave up trying to get inside.

Meanwhile, the angels questioned Lot. "Do you have any other relatives here in the city?" they asked. "Get them out of this place—your sons-in-law, sons, daughters, or anyone else. For we are about to destroy this city completely. The outcry against this place is so great it has reached the LORD, and he has sent us to destroy it."

So Lot rushed out to tell his daughters' fiancés, "Quick, get out of the city! The LORD is about to destroy it." But the young men thought he was only joking.

At dawn the next morning the angels became insistent. "Hurry," they said to Lot. "Take your wife and your two daughters who are here. Get out right now, or you will be swept away in the destruction of the city!"

When Lot still hesitated, the angels seized his hand and the hands of his wife and two daughters and rushed them to safety outside the city, for the LORD was merciful. When they were safely out of the city, one of the angels ordered, "Run for your lives! And don't look back or stop anywhere in the valley! Escape to the mountains, or you will be swept away!"

"Oh no, my lord!" Lot begged. "You have been so gracious to me and saved my life, and you have shown such great kindness. But I cannot go to the mountains. Disaster would catch up to me there, and I would soon die. See, there is a small village nearby. Please let me go there instead; don't you see how small it is? Then my life will be saved."

"All right," the angel said, "I will grant your request. I will not destroy the little village. But hurry! Escape to it, for I can do nothing until you arrive there." (This explains why that village was known as Zoar, which means "little place.")

Lot reached the village just as the sun was rising over the horizon. Then the LORD rained down fire and burning sulfur from the sky on Sodom and Gomorrah. He utterly destroyed them, along with the other cities and villages of the plain, wiping out all the people and every bit of vegetation. But Lot's wife looked back as she was following behind him, and she turned into a pillar of salt.

Abraham got up early that morning and hurried out to the place where he had stood in the LORD's presence. He looked out across the plain toward Sodom and Gomorrah and watched as columns of smoke rose from the cities like smoke from a furnace.

But God had listened to Abraham's request and kept Lot safe, removing him from the disaster that engulfed the cities on the plain.

Afterward Lot left Zoar because he was afraid of the people there, and he went to live in a cave in the mountains with his two daughters. One day the older daughter said to her sister, "There are no men left anywhere in this entire area, so we can't get married like everyone else. And our father will soon be too old to have children. Come, let's get him drunk with wine, and then we will have sex with him. That way we will preserve our family line through our father."

So that night they got him drunk with wine, and the older daughter went in and had intercourse with her father. He was unaware of her lying down or getting up again.

The next morning the older daughter said to her younger sister, "I had sex with our father last night. Let's get him drunk with wine again tonight, and you go in and have sex with him. That way we will preserve our family line through our father." So that night they got him drunk with wine again, and the younger daughter went in and had intercourse with him. As before, he was unaware of her lying down or getting up again.

As a result, both of Lot's daughters became pregnant by their own father. When the older daughter gave birth to a son, she named him Moab. He became the ancestor of the nation now known as the Moabites. When the younger daughter gave birth to a son, she named him Ben-ammi. He became the ancestor of the nation now known as the Ammonites.

+

Abraham moved south to the Negev and lived for a while between Kadesh and Shur, and then he moved on to Gerar. While living there as a foreigner, Abraham introduced his wife, Sarah, by saying, "She is my sister." So King Abimelech of Gerar sent for Sarah and had her brought to him at his palace.

But that night God came to Abimelech in a dream and told him, "You are a dead man, for that woman you have taken is already married!"

But Abimelech had not slept with her yet, so he said, "Lord, will you destroy an innocent nation? Didn't Abraham tell me, 'She is my sister'? And she herself said, 'Yes, he is my brother.' I acted in complete innocence! My hands are clean."

In the dream God responded, "Yes, I know you are innocent. That's why I kept you from sinning against me, and why I did not let you touch her. Now return the woman to her husband, and he will pray for you, for he is a prophet. Then you will live. But if you don't return her to him, you can be sure that you and all your people will die."

Abimelech got up early the next morning and quickly called all his servants together. When he told them what had happened, his men were terrified. Then Abimelech called for Abraham. "What have you done to us?" he demanded. "What crime have I committed that deserves treatment like this, making me and my kingdom guilty of this great sin? No one should ever do what you have done! Whatever possessed you to do such a thing?"

Abraham replied, "I thought, 'This is a godless place. They will want my wife and will kill me to get her.' And she really is my sister, for we both have the same father, but different mothers. And I married her. When God called me to leave my father's home and to travel from place to place, I told her, 'Do me a favor. Wherever we go, tell the people that I am your brother.'"

Then Abimelech took some of his sheep and goats, cattle, and male and female servants, and he presented them to Abraham. He also returned his wife, Sarah, to him. Then Abimelech said, "Look over my land and choose any place where you would like to live." And he said to Sarah, "Look, I am giving your 'brother' 1,000 pieces of silver in the presence of all these witnesses. This is to compensate you for any wrong I may have done to you. This will settle any claim against me, and your reputation is cleared."

Then Abraham prayed to God, and God healed Abimelech, his wife, and his female servants, so they could have children. For the LORD had caused all the women to be infertile because of what happened with Abraham's wife, Sarah.

+

The LORD kept his word and did for Sarah exactly what he had promised. She became pregnant, and she gave birth to a son for Abraham in his old age. This happened at just the time God had said it would. And Abraham named their son Isaac. Eight days after Isaac was born, Abraham circumcised him as God had commanded. Abraham was 100 years old when Isaac was born.

And Sarah declared, "God has brought me laughter. All who hear about this will laugh with me. Who would have said to Abraham that Sarah would nurse a baby? Yet I have given Abraham a son in his old age!"

When Isaac grew up and was about to be weaned, Abraham prepared a huge feast to celebrate the occasion. But Sarah saw Ishmael—the son of Abraham and her Egyptian servant Hagar—making fun of her son, Isaac. So she turned to Abraham and demanded, "Get rid of that slave woman and her son. He is not going to share the inheritance with my son, Isaac. I won't have it!"

This upset Abraham very much because Ishmael was his son. But God told Abraham, "Do not be upset over the boy and your servant. Do whatever Sarah tells you, for Isaac is the son through whom your descendants will be counted. But I will also make a nation of the descendants of Hagar's son because he is your son, too."

So Abraham got up early the next morning, prepared food and a container of water, and strapped them on Hagar's shoulders. Then he sent her away with their son, and she wandered aimlessly in the wilderness of Beersheba.

When the water was gone, she put the boy in the shade of a bush. Then she went and sat down by herself about a hundred yards away. "I don't want to watch the boy die," she said, as she burst into tears.

But God heard the boy crying, and the angel of God called to Hagar from heaven, "Hagar, what's wrong? Do not be afraid! God has heard the boy crying as he lies there. Go to him and comfort him, for I will make a great nation from his descendants."

Then God opened Hagar's eyes, and she saw a well full of water. She quickly filled her water container and gave the boy a drink.

And God was with the boy as he grew up in the wilderness. He became a skillful archer, and he settled in the wilderness of Paran. His mother arranged for him to marry a woman from the land of Egypt.

About this time, Abimelech came with Phicol, his army commander, to visit Abraham. "God is obviously with you, helping you in everything you do," Abimelech said. "Swear to me in God's name that you will never deceive me, my children, or any of my descendants. I have been loyal to you, so now swear that you will be loyal to me and to this country where you are living as a foreigner."

Abraham replied, "Yes, I swear to it!" Then Abraham complained to Abimelech about a well that Abimelech's servants had taken by force from Abraham's servants.

"This is the first I've heard of it," Abimelech answered. "I have no idea who is responsible. You have never complained about this before."

Abraham then gave some of his sheep, goats, and cattle to Abimelech, and they made a treaty. But Abraham also took seven additional female lambs and set them off by themselves. Abimelech asked, "Why have you set these seven apart from the others?"

Abraham replied, "Please accept these seven lambs to show your agreement that I dug this well." Then he named the place Beersheba (which means "well of the oath"), because that was where they had sworn the oath.

After making their covenant at Beersheba, Abimelech left with Phicol, the commander of his army, and they returned home to the land of the Philistines. Then Abraham planted a tamarisk tree at Beersheba, and there he worshiped the LORD, the Eternal God. And Abraham lived as a foreigner in Philistine country for a long time.

+

Some time later, God tested Abraham's faith. "Abraham!" God called.

"Yes," he replied. "Here I am."

"Take your son, your only son—yes, Isaac, whom you love so much—and go to the land of Moriah. Go and sacrifice him as a burnt offering on one of the mountains, which I will show you."

The next morning Abraham got up early. He saddled his donkey and took two of his servants with him, along with his son, Isaac. Then he chopped wood for a fire for a burnt offering and set out for the place God had told him about. On the third day of their journey, Abraham looked up and saw the place in the distance. "Stay here with the donkey," Abraham told the servants. "The boy and I will travel a little farther. We will worship there, and then we will come right back."

So Abraham placed the wood for the burnt offering on Isaac's shoulders, while he himself carried the fire and the knife. As the two of them walked on together, Isaac turned to Abraham and said, "Father?"

"Yes, my son?" Abraham replied.

"We have the fire and the wood," the boy said, "but where is the sheep for the burnt offering?"

"God will provide a sheep for the burnt offering, my son," Abraham answered. And they both walked on together.

When they arrived at the place where God had told him to go, Abraham built an altar and arranged the wood on it. Then he tied his son, Isaac, and laid him on the altar on top of the wood. And Abraham picked up the knife to kill his son as a sacrifice. At that moment the angel of the LORD called to him from heaven, "Abraham! Abraham!"

"Yes," Abraham replied. "Here I am!"

"Don't lay a hand on the boy!" the angel said. "Do not hurt him in any way, for now I know that you truly fear God. You have not withheld from me even your son, your only son."

Then Abraham looked up and saw a ram caught by its horns in a thicket. So he took the ram and sacrificed it as a burnt offering in place of his son. Abraham named the place Yahweh-Yireh (which means "the LORD will provide"). To this day, people still use that name as a proverb: "On the mountain of the LORD it will be provided."

Then the angel of the LORD called again to Abraham from heaven. "This is what the LORD says: Because you have obeyed me and have not withheld even your son, your only son, I swear by my own name that I will certainly bless you. I will multiply your descendants beyond number, like the stars in the sky and the sand on the seashore. Your descendants will conquer the cities of their enemies. And through your descendants all the nations of the earth will be blessed—all because you have obeyed me."

Then they returned to the servants and traveled back to Beersheba, where Abraham continued to live.

Soon after this, Abraham heard that Milcah, his brother Nahor's wife, had borne Nahor eight sons. The oldest was named Uz, the next oldest was Buz, followed by Kemuel (the ancestor of the Arameans), Kesed, Hazo, Pildash, Jidlaph, and Bethuel. (Bethuel became the father of Rebekah.) In addition to these eight sons from Milcah, Nahor had four other children from his concubine Reumah. Their names were Tebah, Gaham, Tahash, and Maacah.

When Sarah was 127 years old, she died at Kiriath-arba (now called Hebron) in the land of Canaan. There Abraham mourned and wept for her.

Then, leaving her body, he said to the Hittite elders, "Here I am, a stranger and a foreigner among you. Please sell me a piece of land so I can give my wife a proper burial."

The Hittites replied to Abraham, "Listen, my lord, you are an honored prince among us. Choose the finest of our tombs and bury her there. No one here will refuse to help you in this way."

Then Abraham bowed low before the Hittites and said, "Since you are willing to help me in this way, be so kind as to ask Ephron son of Zohar to let me buy his cave at Machpelah, down at the end of his field. I will pay the full price in the presence of witnesses, so I will have a permanent burial place for my family."

Ephron was sitting there among the others, and he answered Abraham as the others listened, speaking publicly before all the Hittite elders of the town. "No, my lord," he said to Abraham, "please listen to me. I will give you the field and the cave. Here in the presence of my people, I give it to you. Go and bury your dead."

Abraham again bowed low before the citizens of the land, and he replied to Ephron as everyone listened. "No, listen to me. I will buy it from you. Let me pay the full price for the field so I can bury my dead there."

Ephron answered Abraham, "My lord, please listen to me. The land is worth 400 pieces of silver, but what is that between friends? Go ahead and bury your dead."

So Abraham agreed to Ephron's price and paid the amount he had suggested—400 pieces of silver, weighed according to the market standard. The Hittite elders witnessed the transaction.

So Abraham bought the plot of land belonging to Ephron at Machpelah, near Mamre. This included the field itself, the cave that was in it, and all the surrounding trees. It was transferred to Abraham as his permanent possession in the presence of the Hittite elders at the city gate. Then Abraham buried his wife, Sarah, there in Canaan, in the cave of Machpelah, near Mamre (also called Hebron). So the field and the cave were transferred from the Hittites to Abraham for use as a permanent burial place.

Abraham was now a very old man, and the LORD had blessed him in every way. One day Abraham said to his oldest servant, the man in charge of his household, "Take an oath by putting your hand under my thigh. Swear by the LORD, the God of heaven and earth, that you will not allow my son to marry one of these local Canaanite women. Go instead to my homeland, to my relatives, and find a wife there for my son Isaac."

The servant asked, "But what if I can't find a young woman who is willing to travel so far from home? Should I then take Isaac there to live among your relatives in the land you came from?"

"No!" Abraham responded. "Be careful never to take my son there. For the LORD, the God of heaven, who took me from my father's house and my native land, solemnly promised to give this land to my descendants. He will send his angel ahead of you, and he will see to it that you find a wife there for my son. If she is unwilling to come back with you, then you are free from this oath of mine. But under no circumstances are you to take my son there."

So the servant took an oath by putting his hand under the thigh of his master, Abraham. He swore to follow Abraham's instructions. Then he loaded ten of Abraham's camels with all kinds of expensive gifts from his master, and he traveled to distant Aram-naharaim. There he went to the town where Abraham's brother Nahor had settled. He made the camels kneel beside a well just outside the town. It was evening, and the women were coming out to draw water.

"O LORD, God of my master, Abraham," he prayed. "Please give me success today, and show unfailing love to my master, Abraham. See, I am standing here beside this spring, and the young women of the town are coming out to draw water. This is my request. I will ask one of them, 'Please give me a drink from your jug.' If she says, 'Yes, have a drink, and I will water your camels, too!'—let her be the one you have selected as Isaac's wife. This is how I will know that you have shown unfailing love to my master."

Before he had finished praying, he saw a young woman named Rebekah coming out with her water jug on her shoulder. She was the daughter of Bethuel, who was the son of Abraham's brother Nahor and his wife,

Milcah. Rebekah was very beautiful and old enough to be married, but she was still a virgin. She went down to the spring, filled her jug, and came up again. Running over to her, the servant said, "Please give me a little drink of water from your jug."

"Yes, my lord," she answered, "have a drink." And she quickly lowered her jug from her shoulder and gave him a drink. When she had given him a drink, she said, "I'll draw water for your camels, too, until they have had enough to drink." So she quickly emptied her jug into the watering trough and ran back to the well to draw water for all his camels.

The servant watched her in silence, wondering whether or not the LORD had given him success in his mission. Then at last, when the camels had finished drinking, he took out a gold ring for her nose and two large gold bracelets for her wrists.

"Whose daughter are you?" he asked. "And please tell me, would your father have any room to put us up for the night?"

"I am the daughter of Bethuel," she replied. "My grandparents are Nahor and Milcah. Yes, we have plenty of straw and feed for the camels, and we have room for guests."

The man bowed low and worshiped the LORD. "Praise the LORD, the God of my master, Abraham," he said. "The LORD has shown unfailing love and faithfulness to my master, for he has led me straight to my master's relatives."

The young woman ran home to tell her family everything that had happened. Now Rebekah had a brother named Laban, who ran out to meet the man at the spring. He had seen the nose-ring and the bracelets on his sister's wrists, and had heard Rebekah tell what the man had said. So he rushed out to the spring, where the man was still standing beside his camels. Laban said to him, "Come and stay with us, you who are blessed by the LORD! Why are you standing here outside the town when I have a room all ready for you and a place prepared for the camels?"

So the man went home with Laban, and Laban unloaded the camels, gave him straw for their bedding, fed them, and provided water for the man and the camel drivers to wash their feet. Then food was served. But Abraham's servant said, "I don't want to eat until I have told you why I have come."

"All right," Laban said, "tell us."

"I am Abraham's servant," he explained. "And the LORD has greatly blessed my master; he has become a wealthy man. The LORD has given him flocks of sheep and goats, herds of cattle, a fortune in silver and gold, and many male and female servants and camels and donkeys.

"When Sarah, my master's wife, was very old, she gave birth to my master's son, and my master has given him everything he owns. And my master made me take an oath. He said, 'Do not allow my son to marry one of these local Canaanite women. Go instead to my father's house, to my relatives, and find a wife there for my son.'

"But I said to my master, 'What if I can't find a young woman who is willing to go back with me?' He responded, 'The LORD, in whose presence I have lived, will send his angel with you and will make your mission successful. Yes, you must find a wife for my son from among my relatives, from my father's family. Then you will have fulfilled your obligation. But if you go to my relatives and they refuse to let her go with you, you will be free from my oath.'

"So today when I came to the spring, I prayed this prayer: 'O LORD, God of my master, Abraham, please give me success on this mission. See, I am standing here beside this spring. This is my request. When a young woman comes to draw water, I will say to her, "Please give me a little drink of water from your jug." If she says, "Yes, have a drink, and I will draw water for your camels, too," let her be the one you have selected to be the wife of my master's son.'

"Before I had finished praying in my heart, I saw Rebekah coming out with her water jug on her shoulder. She went down to the spring and drew water. So I said to her, 'Please give me a drink.' She quickly lowered her jug from her shoulder and said, 'Yes, have a drink, and I will water your camels, too!' So I drank, and then she watered the camels.

"Then I asked, 'Whose daughter are you?' She replied, 'I am the daughter of Bethuel, and my grandparents are Nahor and Milcah.' So I put the ring on her nose, and the bracelets on her wrists.

"Then I bowed low and worshiped the LORD. I praised the LORD, the God of my master, Abraham, because he had led me straight to my master's niece to be his son's wife. So tell me—will you or won't you show unfailing love and faithfulness to my master? Please tell me yes or no, and then I'll know what to do next."

Then Laban and Bethuel replied, "The LORD has obviously brought you here, so there is nothing we can say. Here is Rebekah; take her and go. Yes, let her be the wife of your master's son, as the LORD has directed."

When Abraham's servant heard their answer, he bowed down to the ground and worshiped the LORD. Then he brought out silver and gold jewelry and clothing and presented them to Rebekah. He also gave expensive presents to her brother and mother. Then they ate their meal, and the servant and the men with him stayed there overnight.

But early the next morning, Abraham's servant said, "Send me back to my master."

"But we want Rebekah to stay with us at least ten days," her brother and mother said. "Then she can go."

But he said, "Don't delay me. The LORD has made my mission success-ful; now send me back so I can return to my master."

"Well," they said, "we'll call Rebekah and ask her what she thinks." So they called Rebekah. "Are you willing to go with this man?" they asked her. And she replied, "Yes, I will go."

So they said good-bye to Rebekah and sent her away with Abraham's servant and his men. The woman who had been Rebekah's childhood nurse went along with her. They gave her this blessing as she parted:

"Our sister, may you become
    the mother of many millions!
May your descendants be strong
    and conquer the cities of their enemies."

Then Rebekah and her servant girls mounted the camels and followed the man. So Abraham's servant took Rebekah and went on his way.

Meanwhile, Isaac, whose home was in the Negev, had returned from Beer-lahai-roi. One evening as he was walking and meditating in the fields, he looked up and saw the camels coming. When Rebekah looked up and saw Isaac, she quickly dismounted from her camel. "Who is that man walk-ing through the fields to meet us?" she asked the servant.

And he replied, "It is my master." So Rebekah covered her face with her veil. Then the servant told Isaac everything he had done.

And Isaac brought Rebekah into his mother Sarah's tent, and she be-came his wife. He loved her deeply, and she was a special comfort to him after the death of his mother.

Abraham married another wife, whose name was Keturah. She gave birth to Zimran, Jokshan, Medan, Midian, Ishbak, and Shuah. Jokshan was the father of Sheba and Dedan. Dedan's descendants were the Asshurites, Le-tushites, and Leummites. Midian's sons were Ephah, Epher, Hanoch, Abida, and Eldaah. These were all descendants of Abraham through Keturah.

Abraham gave everything he owned to his son Isaac. But before he died, he gave gifts to the sons of his concubines and sent them off to a land in the east, away from Isaac.

Abraham lived for 175 years, and he died at a ripe old age, having lived a long and satisfying life. He breathed his last and joined his ancestors in death. His sons Isaac and Ishmael buried him in the cave of Machpelah, near Mamre, in the field of Ephron son of Zohar the Hittite. This was the field Abraham had purchased from the Hittites and where he had bur-ied his wife Sarah. After Abraham's death, God blessed his son Isaac, who settled near Beer-lahai-roi in the Negev.

+ + +

This is the account of the family of Ishmael, the son of Abraham through Hagar, Sarah's Egyptian servant.

Here is a list, by their names and clans, of Ishmael's descendants: The oldest was Nebaioth, followed by Kedar, Adbeel, Mibsam, Mishma, Dumah, Massa, Hadad, Tema, Jetur, Naphish, and Kedemah. These twelve sons of Ishmael became the founders of twelve tribes named after them, listed according to the places they settled and camped. Ishmael lived for 137 years. Then he breathed his last and joined his ancestors in death. Ishmael's descendants occupied the region from Havilah to Shur, which is east of Egypt in the direction of Asshur. There they lived in open hostility toward all their relatives.

+ + +

This is the account of the family of Isaac, the son of Abraham.

When Isaac was forty years old, he married Rebekah, the daughter of Bethuel the Aramean from Paddan-aram and the sister of Laban the Aramean.

Isaac pleaded with the LORD on behalf of his wife, because she was unable to have children. The LORD answered Isaac's prayer, and Rebekah became pregnant with twins. But the two children struggled with each other in her womb. So she went to ask the LORD about it. "Why is this happening to me?" she asked.

And the LORD told her, "The sons in your womb will become two nations. From the very beginning, the two nations will be rivals. One nation will be stronger than the other; and your older son will serve your younger son."

And when the time came to give birth, Rebekah discovered that she did indeed have twins! The first one was very red at birth and covered with thick hair like a fur coat. So they named him Esau. Then the other twin was born with his hand grasping Esau's heel. So they named him Jacob. Isaac was sixty years old when the twins were born.

As the boys grew up, Esau became a skillful hunter. He was an outdoorsman, but Jacob had a quiet temperament, preferring to stay at home. Isaac loved Esau because he enjoyed eating the wild game Esau brought home, but Rebekah loved Jacob.

One day when Jacob was cooking some stew, Esau arrived home from the wilderness exhausted and hungry. Esau said to Jacob, "I'm starved!

Give me some of that red stew!" (This is how Esau got his other name, Edom, which means "red.")

"All right," Jacob replied, "but trade me your rights as the firstborn son."

"Look, I'm dying of starvation!" said Esau. "What good is my birthright to me now?"

But Jacob said, "First you must swear that your birthright is mine." So Esau swore an oath, thereby selling all his rights as the firstborn to his brother, Jacob.

Then Jacob gave Esau some bread and lentil stew. Esau ate the meal, then got up and left. He showed contempt for his rights as the firstborn.

A severe famine now struck the land, as had happened before in Abraham's time. So Isaac moved to Gerar, where Abimelech, king of the Philistines, lived.

The LORD appeared to Isaac and said, "Do not go down to Egypt, but do as I tell you. Live here as a foreigner in this land, and I will be with you and bless you. I hereby confirm that I will give all these lands to you and your descendants, just as I solemnly promised Abraham, your father. I will cause your descendants to become as numerous as the stars of the sky, and I will give them all these lands. And through your descendants all the nations of the earth will be blessed. I will do this because Abraham listened to me and obeyed all my requirements, commands, decrees, and instructions." So Isaac stayed in Gerar.

When the men who lived there asked Isaac about his wife, Rebekah, he said, "She is my sister." He was afraid to say, "She is my wife." He thought, "They will kill me to get her, because she is so beautiful." But some time later, Abimelech, king of the Philistines, looked out his window and saw Isaac caressing Rebekah.

Immediately, Abimelech called for Isaac and exclaimed, "She is obviously your wife! Why did you say, 'She is my sister'?"

"Because I was afraid someone would kill me to get her from me," Isaac replied.

"How could you do this to us?" Abimelech exclaimed. "One of my people might easily have taken your wife and slept with her, and you would have made us guilty of great sin."

Then Abimelech issued a public proclamation: "Anyone who touches this man or his wife will be put to death!"

When Isaac planted his crops that year, he harvested a hundred times more grain than he planted, for the LORD blessed him. He became a very rich man, and his wealth continued to grow. He acquired so many flocks of sheep and goats, herds of cattle, and servants that the Philistines became jealous of him. So the Philistines filled up all of Isaac's wells with dirt. These were the wells that had been dug by the servants of his father, Abraham.

Finally, Abimelech ordered Isaac to leave the country. "Go somewhere else," he said, "for you have become too powerful for us."

So Isaac moved away to the Gerar Valley, where he set up their tents and settled down. He reopened the wells his father had dug, which the Philistines had filled in after Abraham's death. Isaac also restored the names Abraham had given them.

Isaac's servants also dug in the Gerar Valley and discovered a well of fresh water. But then the shepherds from Gerar came and claimed the spring. "This is our water," they said, and they argued over it with Isaac's herdsmen. So Isaac named the well Esek (which means "argument"). Isaac's men then dug another well, but again there was a dispute over it. So Isaac named it Sitnah (which means "hostility"). Abandoning that one, Isaac moved on and dug another well. This time there was no dispute over it, so Isaac named the place Rehoboth (which means "open space"), for he said, "At last the LORD has created enough space for us to prosper in this land."

From there Isaac moved to Beersheba, where the LORD appeared to him on the night of his arrival. "I am the God of your father, Abraham," he said. "Do not be afraid, for I am with you and will bless you. I will multiply your descendants, and they will become a great nation. I will do this because of my promise to Abraham, my servant." Then Isaac built an altar there and worshiped the LORD. He set up his camp at that place, and his servants dug another well.

One day King Abimelech came from Gerar with his adviser, Ahuzzath, and also Phicol, his army commander. "Why have you come here?" Isaac asked. "You obviously hate me, since you kicked me off your land."

They replied, "We can plainly see that the LORD is with you. So we want to enter into a sworn treaty with you. Let's make a covenant. Swear that you will not harm us, just as we have never troubled you. We have always treated you well, and we sent you away from us in peace. And now look how the LORD has blessed you!"

So Isaac prepared a covenant feast to celebrate the treaty, and they ate and drank together. Early the next morning, they each took a solemn oath not to interfere with each other. Then Isaac sent them home again, and they left him in peace.

That very day Isaac's servants came and told him about a new well they had dug. "We've found water!" they exclaimed. So Isaac named the well Shibah (which means "oath"). And to this day the town that grew up there is called Beersheba (which means "well of the oath").

+

At the age of forty, Esau married two Hittite wives: Judith, the daughter of Beeri, and Basemath, the daughter of Elon. But Esau's wives made life miserable for Isaac and Rebekah.

One day when Isaac was old and turning blind, he called for Esau, his older son, and said, "My son."

"Yes, Father?" Esau replied.

"I am an old man now," Isaac said, "and I don't know when I may die. Take your bow and a quiver full of arrows, and go out into the open country to hunt some wild game for me. Prepare my favorite dish, and bring it here for me to eat. Then I will pronounce the blessing that belongs to you, my firstborn son, before I die."

But Rebekah overheard what Isaac had said to his son Esau. So when Esau left to hunt for the wild game, she said to her son Jacob, "Listen. I overheard your father say to Esau, 'Bring me some wild game and prepare me a delicious meal. Then I will bless you in the LORD's presence before I die.' Now, my son, listen to me. Do exactly as I tell you. Go out to the flocks, and bring me two fine young goats. I'll use them to prepare your father's favorite dish. Then take the food to your father so he can eat it and bless you before he dies."

"But look," Jacob replied to Rebekah, "my brother, Esau, is a hairy man, and my skin is smooth. What if my father touches me? He'll see that I'm trying to trick him, and then he'll curse me instead of blessing me."

But his mother replied, "Then let the curse fall on me, my son! Just do what I tell you. Go out and get the goats for me!"

So Jacob went out and got the young goats for his mother. Rebekah took them and prepared a delicious meal, just the way Isaac liked it. Then she took Esau's favorite clothes, which were there in the house, and gave them to her younger son, Jacob. She covered his arms and the smooth part of his neck with the skin of the young goats. Then she gave Jacob the delicious meal, including freshly baked bread.

So Jacob took the food to his father. "My father?" he said.

"Yes, my son," Isaac answered. "Who are you—Esau or Jacob?"

Jacob replied, "It's Esau, your firstborn son. I've done as you told me. Here is the wild game. Now sit up and eat it so you can give me your blessing."

Isaac asked, "How did you find it so quickly, my son?"

"The LORD your God put it in my path!" Jacob replied.

Then Isaac said to Jacob, "Come closer so I can touch you and make sure that you really are Esau." So Jacob went closer to his father, and Isaac touched him. "The voice is Jacob's, but the hands are Esau's," Isaac said. But he did not recognize Jacob, because Jacob's hands felt hairy just like Esau's. So Isaac prepared to bless Jacob. "But are you really my son Esau?" he asked.

"Yes, I am," Jacob replied.

Then Isaac said, "Now, my son, bring me the wild game. Let me eat it, and then I will give you my blessing." So Jacob took the food to his father, and Isaac ate it. He also drank the wine that Jacob served him. Then Isaac said to Jacob, "Please come a little closer and kiss me, my son."

So Jacob went over and kissed him. And when Isaac caught the smell of his clothes, he was finally convinced, and he blessed his son. He said, "Ah! The smell of my son is like the smell of the outdoors, which the LORD has blessed!

> "From the dew of heaven
>   and the richness of the earth,
> may God always give you abundant harvests of grain
>   and bountiful new wine.
> May many nations become your servants,
>   and may they bow down to you.
> May you be the master over your brothers,
>   and may your mother's sons bow down to you.
> All who curse you will be cursed,
>   and all who bless you will be blessed."

As soon as Isaac had finished blessing Jacob, and almost before Jacob had left his father, Esau returned from his hunt. Esau prepared a delicious meal and brought it to his father. Then he said, "Sit up, my father, and eat my wild game so you can give me your blessing."

But Isaac asked him, "Who are you?"

Esau replied, "It's your son, your firstborn son, Esau."

Isaac began to tremble uncontrollably and said, "Then who just served me wild game? I have already eaten it, and I blessed him just before you came. And yes, that blessing must stand!"

When Esau heard his father's words, he let out a loud and bitter cry. "Oh my father, what about me? Bless me, too!" he begged.

But Isaac said, "Your brother was here, and he tricked me. He has taken away your blessing."

Esau exclaimed, "No wonder his name is Jacob, for now he has cheated me twice. First he took my rights as the firstborn, and now he has stolen my blessing. Oh, haven't you saved even one blessing for me?"

Isaac said to Esau, "I have made Jacob your master and have declared that all his brothers will be his servants. I have guaranteed him an abundance of grain and wine—what is left for me to give you, my son?"

Esau pleaded, "But do you have only one blessing? Oh my father, bless me, too!" Then Esau broke down and wept.

Finally, his father, Isaac, said to him,

"You will live away from the richness of the earth,
and away from the dew of the heaven above.
You will live by your sword,
and you will serve your brother.
But when you decide to break free,
you will shake his yoke from your neck."

From that time on, Esau hated Jacob because their father had given Jacob the blessing. And Esau began to scheme: "I will soon be mourning my father's death. Then I will kill my brother, Jacob."

But Rebekah heard about Esau's plans. So she sent for Jacob and told him, "Listen, Esau is consoling himself by plotting to kill you. So listen carefully, my son. Get ready and flee to my brother, Laban, in Haran. Stay there with him until your brother cools off. When he calms down and forgets what you have done to him, I will send for you to come back. Why should I lose both of you in one day?"

Then Rebekah said to Isaac, "I'm sick and tired of these local Hittite women! I would rather die than see Jacob marry one of them."

So Isaac called for Jacob, blessed him, and said, "You must not marry any of these Canaanite women. Instead, go at once to Paddan-aram, to the house of your grandfather Bethuel, and marry one of your uncle Laban's daughters. May God Almighty bless you and give you many children. And may your descendants multiply and become many nations! May God pass on to you and your descendants the blessings he promised to Abraham. May you own this land where you are now living as a foreigner, for God gave this land to Abraham."

So Isaac sent Jacob away, and he went to Paddan-aram to stay with his uncle Laban, his mother's brother, the son of Bethuel the Aramean.

Esau knew that his father, Isaac, had blessed Jacob and sent him to Paddan-aram to find a wife, and that he had warned Jacob, "You must not marry a Canaanite woman." He also knew that Jacob had obeyed his parents and gone to Paddan-aram. It was now very clear to Esau that his father did not like the local Canaanite women. So Esau visited his uncle Ishmael's family and married one of Ishmael's daughters, in addition to the wives he already had. His new wife's name was Mahalath. She was the sister of Nebaioth and the daughter of Ishmael, Abraham's son.

+

Meanwhile, Jacob left Beersheba and traveled toward Haran. At sundown he arrived at a good place to set up camp and stopped there for the night. Jacob found a stone to rest his head against and lay down to sleep. As he slept, he dreamed of a stairway that reached from the earth up to heaven. And he saw the angels of God going up and down the stairway.

At the top of the stairway stood the LORD, and he said, "I am the LORD, the God of your grandfather Abraham, and the God of your father, Isaac. The ground you are lying on belongs to you. I am giving it to you and your descendants. Your descendants will be as numerous as the dust of the earth! They will spread out in all directions—to the west and the east, to the north and the south. And all the families of the earth will be blessed through you and your descendants. What's more, I am with you, and I will protect you wherever you go. One day I will bring you back to this land. I will not leave you until I have finished giving you everything I have promised you."

Then Jacob awoke from his sleep and said, "Surely the LORD is in this place, and I wasn't even aware of it!" But he was also afraid and said, "What an awesome place this is! It is none other than the house of God, the very gateway to heaven!"

The next morning Jacob got up very early. He took the stone he had rested his head against, and he set it upright as a memorial pillar. Then he poured olive oil over it. He named that place Bethel (which means "house of God"), although it was previously called Luz.

Then Jacob made this vow: "If God will indeed be with me and protect me on this journey, and if he will provide me with food and clothing, and if I return safely to my father's home, then the LORD will certainly be my God. And this memorial pillar I have set up will become a place for worshiping God, and I will present to God a tenth of everything he gives me."

+

Then Jacob hurried on, finally arriving in the land of the east. He saw a well in the distance. Three flocks of sheep and goats lay in an open field beside it, waiting to be watered. But a heavy stone covered the mouth of the well.

It was the custom there to wait for all the flocks to arrive before removing the stone and watering the animals. Afterward the stone would be placed back over the mouth of the well. Jacob went over to the shepherds and asked, "Where are you from, my friends?"

"We are from Haran," they answered.

"Do you know a man there named Laban, the grandson of Nahor?" he asked.

"Yes, we do," they replied.

"Is he doing well?" Jacob asked.

"Yes, he's well," they answered. "Look, here comes his daughter Rachel with the flock now."

Jacob said, "Look, it's still broad daylight—too early to round up the animals. Why don't you water the sheep and goats so they can get back out to pasture?"

"We can't water the animals until all the flocks have arrived," they replied. "Then the shepherds move the stone from the mouth of the well, and we water all the sheep and goats."

Jacob was still talking with them when Rachel arrived with her father's flock, for she was a shepherd. And because Rachel was his cousin—the daughter of Laban, his mother's brother—and because the sheep and goats belonged to his uncle Laban, Jacob went over to the well and moved the stone from its mouth and watered his uncle's flock. Then Jacob kissed Rachel, and he wept aloud. He explained to Rachel that he was her cousin on her father's side—the son of her aunt Rebekah. So Rachel quickly ran and told her father, Laban.

As soon as Laban heard that his nephew Jacob had arrived, he ran out to meet him. He embraced and kissed him and brought him home. When Jacob had told him his story, Laban exclaimed, "You really are my own flesh and blood!"

✦

After Jacob had stayed with Laban for about a month, Laban said to him, "You shouldn't work for me without pay just because we are relatives. Tell me how much your wages should be."

Now Laban had two daughters. The older daughter was named Leah, and the younger one was Rachel. There was no sparkle in Leah's eyes, but Rachel had a beautiful figure and a lovely face. Since Jacob was in love with Rachel, he told her father, "I'll work for you for seven years if you'll give me Rachel, your younger daughter, as my wife."

"Agreed!" Laban replied. "I'd rather give her to you than to anyone else. Stay and work with me." So Jacob worked seven years to pay for Rachel. But his love for her was so strong that it seemed to him but a few days.

Finally, the time came for him to marry her. "I have fulfilled my agreement," Jacob said to Laban. "Now give me my wife so I can sleep with her."

So Laban invited everyone in the neighborhood and prepared a wedding feast. But that night, when it was dark, Laban took Leah to Jacob, and he slept with her. (Laban had given Leah a servant, Zilpah, to be her maid.)

But when Jacob woke up in the morning—it was Leah! "What have you done to me?" Jacob raged at Laban. "I worked seven years for Rachel! Why have you tricked me?"

"It's not our custom here to marry off a younger daughter ahead of the firstborn," Laban replied. "But wait until the bridal week is over; then we'll give you Rachel, too—provided you promise to work another seven years for me."

So Jacob agreed to work seven more years. A week after Jacob had married Leah, Laban gave him Rachel, too. (Laban gave Rachel a servant, Bilhah, to be her maid.) So Jacob slept with Rachel, too, and he loved her much more than Leah. He then stayed and worked for Laban the additional seven years.

+

When the LORD saw that Leah was unloved, he enabled her to have children, but Rachel could not conceive. So Leah became pregnant and gave birth to a son. She named him Reuben, for she said, "The LORD has noticed my misery, and now my husband will love me."

She soon became pregnant again and gave birth to another son. She named him Simeon, for she said, "The LORD heard that I was unloved and has given me another son."

Then she became pregnant a third time and gave birth to another son. He was named Levi, for she said, "Surely this time my husband will feel affection for me, since I have given him three sons!"

Once again Leah became pregnant and gave birth to another son. She named him Judah, for she said, "Now I will praise the LORD!" And then she stopped having children.

When Rachel saw that she wasn't having any children for Jacob, she became jealous of her sister. She pleaded with Jacob, "Give me children, or I'll die!"

Then Jacob became furious with Rachel. "Am I God?" he asked. "He's the one who has kept you from having children!"

Then Rachel told him, "Take my maid, Bilhah, and sleep with her. She will bear children for me, and through her I can have a family, too." So Rachel gave her servant, Bilhah, to Jacob as a wife, and he slept with her. Bilhah became pregnant and presented him with a son. Rachel named him Dan, for she said, "God has vindicated me! He has heard my request and given me a son." Then Bilhah became pregnant again and gave Jacob a second son. Rachel named him Naphtali, for she said, "I have struggled hard with my sister, and I'm winning!"

Meanwhile, Leah realized that she wasn't getting pregnant anymore, so she took her servant, Zilpah, and gave her to Jacob as a wife. Soon Zilpah presented him with a son. Leah named him Gad, for she said, "How fortunate I am!" Then Zilpah gave Jacob a second son. And Leah named him Asher, for she said, "What joy is mine! Now the other women will celebrate with me."

One day during the wheat harvest, Reuben found some mandrakes growing in a field and brought them to his mother, Leah. Rachel begged Leah, "Please give me some of your son's mandrakes."

But Leah angrily replied, "Wasn't it enough that you stole my husband? Now will you steal my son's mandrakes, too?"

Rachel answered, "I will let Jacob sleep with you tonight if you give me some of the mandrakes."

So that evening, as Jacob was coming home from the fields, Leah went out to meet him. "You must come and sleep with me tonight!" she said. "I have paid for you with some mandrakes that my son found." So that night he slept with Leah. And God answered Leah's prayers. She became pregnant again and gave birth to a fifth son for Jacob. She named him Issachar, for she said, "God has rewarded me for giving my servant to my husband as a wife." Then Leah became pregnant again and gave birth to a sixth son for Jacob. She named him Zebulun, for she said, "God has given me a good reward. Now my husband will treat me with respect, for I have given him six sons." Later she gave birth to a daughter and named her Dinah.

Then God remembered Rachel's plight and answered her prayers by enabling her to have children. She became pregnant and gave birth to a son. "God has removed my disgrace," she said. And she named him Joseph, for she said, "May the LORD add yet another son to my family."

✢

Soon after Rachel had given birth to Joseph, Jacob said to Laban, "Please release me so I can go home to my own country. Let me take my wives and children, for I have earned them by serving you, and let me be on my way. You certainly know how hard I have worked for you."

"Please listen to me," Laban replied. "I have become wealthy, for the LORD has blessed me because of you. Tell me how much I owe you. Whatever it is, I'll pay it."

Jacob replied, "You know how hard I've worked for you, and how your flocks and herds have grown under my care. You had little indeed before I came, but your wealth has increased enormously. The LORD has blessed you through everything I've done. But now, what about me? When can I start providing for my own family?"

"What wages do you want?" Laban asked again.

Jacob replied, "Don't give me anything. Just do this one thing, and I'll continue to tend and watch over your flocks. Let me inspect your flocks today and remove all the sheep and goats that are speckled or spotted, along with all the black sheep. Give these to me as my wages. In the future, when you check on the animals you have given me as my wages, you'll see that I have been honest. If you find in my flock any goats without speckles or spots, or any sheep that are not black, you will know that I have stolen them from you."

"All right," Laban replied. "It will be as you say." But that very day Laban went out and removed the male goats that were streaked and spotted, all the female goats that were speckled and spotted or had white patches, and all the black sheep. He placed them in the care of his own sons, who took them a three-days' journey from where Jacob was. Meanwhile, Jacob stayed and cared for the rest of Laban's flock.

Then Jacob took some fresh branches from poplar, almond, and plane trees and peeled off strips of bark, making white streaks on them. Then he placed these peeled branches in the watering troughs where the flocks came to drink, for that was where they mated. And when they mated in front of the white-streaked branches, they gave birth to young that were streaked, speckled, and spotted. Jacob separated those lambs from Laban's flock. And at mating time he turned the flock to face Laban's animals that were streaked or black. This is how he built his own flock instead of increasing Laban's.

Whenever the stronger females were ready to mate, Jacob would place the peeled branches in the watering troughs in front of them. Then they would mate in front of the branches. But he didn't do this with the weaker ones, so the weaker lambs belonged to Laban, and the stronger ones were Jacob's. As a result, Jacob became very wealthy, with large flocks of sheep and goats, female and male servants, and many camels and donkeys.

+

But Jacob soon learned that Laban's sons were grumbling about him. "Jacob has robbed our father of everything!" they said. "He has gained all his wealth at our father's expense." And Jacob began to notice a change in Laban's attitude toward him.

Then the LORD said to Jacob, "Return to the land of your father and grandfather and to your relatives there, and I will be with you."

So Jacob called Rachel and Leah out to the field where he was watching his flock. He said to them, "I have noticed that your father's attitude toward me has changed. But the God of my father has been with me. You know how hard I have worked for your father, but he has cheated me, changing my wages ten times. But God has not allowed him to do me any harm. For if he said, 'The speckled animals will be your wages,' the whole flock began to produce speckled young. And when he changed his mind and said, 'The striped animals will be your wages,' then the whole flock produced striped young. In this way, God has taken your father's animals and given them to me.

"One time during the mating season, I had a dream and saw that the male goats mating with the females were streaked, speckled, and spotted. Then in my dream, the angel of God said to me, 'Jacob!' And I replied, 'Yes, here I am.'

"The angel said, 'Look up, and you will see that only the streaked, speckled, and spotted males are mating with the females of your flock. For I have seen how Laban has treated you. I am the God who appeared to you at Bethel, the place where you anointed the pillar of stone and made your vow to me. Now get ready and leave this country and return to the land of your birth.'"

Rachel and Leah responded, "That's fine with us! We won't inherit any of our father's wealth anyway. He has reduced our rights to those of foreign women. And after he sold us, he wasted the money you paid him for us. All the wealth God has given you from our father legally belongs to us and our children. So go ahead and do whatever God has told you."

So Jacob put his wives and children on camels, and he drove all his livestock in front of him. He packed all the belongings he had acquired in Paddan-aram and set out for the land of Canaan, where his father, Isaac, lived. At the time they left, Laban was some distance away, shearing his sheep. Rachel stole her father's household idols and took them with her. Jacob outwitted Laban the Aramean, for they set out secretly and never told Laban they were leaving. So Jacob took all his possessions with him and crossed the Euphrates River, heading for the hill country of Gilead.

Three days later, Laban was told that Jacob had fled. So he gathered a group of his relatives and set out in hot pursuit. He caught up with Jacob seven days later in the hill country of Gilead. But the previous night God had appeared to Laban the Aramean in a dream and told him, "I'm warning you—leave Jacob alone!"

Laban caught up with Jacob as he was camped in the hill country of Gilead, and he set up his camp not far from Jacob's. "What do you mean by deceiving me like this?" Laban demanded. "How dare you drag my daughters away like prisoners of war? Why did you slip away secretly? Why did you deceive me? And why didn't you say you wanted to leave? I would have given you a farewell feast, with singing and music, accompanied by tambourines and harps. Why didn't you let me kiss my daughters and grandchildren and tell them good-bye? You have acted very foolishly! I could destroy you, but the God of your father appeared to me last night and warned me, 'Leave Jacob alone!' I can understand your feeling that you must go, and your intense longing for your father's home. But why have you stolen my gods?"

"I rushed away because I was afraid," Jacob answered. "I thought you would take your daughters from me by force. But as for your gods, see if you can find them, and let the person who has taken them die! And if you find anything else that belongs to you, identify it before all these relatives of ours, and I will give it back!" But Jacob did not know that Rachel had stolen the household idols.

Laban went first into Jacob's tent to search there, then into Leah's, and then the tents of the two servant wives—but he found nothing. Finally, he went into Rachel's tent. But Rachel had taken the household idols and hidden them in her camel saddle, and now she was sitting on them. When Laban had thoroughly searched her tent without finding them, she said to her father, "Please, sir, forgive me if I don't get up for you. I'm having my monthly period." So Laban continued his search, but he could not find the household idols.

Then Jacob became very angry, and he challenged Laban. "What's my crime?" he demanded. "What have I done wrong to make you chase after me as though I were a criminal? You have rummaged through everything I own. Now show me what you found that belongs to you! Set it out here in front of us, before our relatives, for all to see. Let them judge between us!

"For twenty years I have been with you, caring for your flocks. In all that time your sheep and goats never miscarried. In all those years I never used a single ram of yours for food. If any were attacked and killed by wild animals, I never showed you the carcass and asked you to reduce the count of your flock. No, I took the loss myself! You made me pay for every stolen animal, whether it was taken in broad daylight or in the dark of night.

"I worked for you through the scorching heat of the day and through cold and sleepless nights. Yes, for twenty years I slaved in your house! I worked for fourteen years earning your two daughters, and then six more years for your flock. And you changed my wages ten times! In fact, if the God of my father had not been on my side—the God of Abraham and the fearsome God of Isaac—you would have sent me away empty-handed. But God has seen your abuse and my hard work. That is why he appeared to you last night and rebuked you!"

Then Laban replied to Jacob, "These women are my daughters, these children are my grandchildren, and these flocks are my flocks—in fact, everything you see is mine. But what can I do now about my daughters and their children? So come, let's make a covenant, you and I, and it will be a witness to our commitment."

So Jacob took a stone and set it up as a monument. Then he told his family members, "Gather some stones." So they gathered stones and piled them in a heap. Then Jacob and Laban sat down beside the pile of stones to eat a covenant meal. To commemorate the event, Laban called the place Jegar-sahadutha (which means "witness pile" in Aramaic), and Jacob called it Galeed (which means "witness pile" in Hebrew).

Then Laban declared, "This pile of stones will stand as a witness to remind us of the covenant we have made today." This explains why it was called Galeed—"Witness Pile." But it was also called Mizpah (which means "watchtower"), for Laban said, "May the LORD keep watch between us to make sure that we keep this covenant when we are out of each other's sight. If you mistreat my daughters or if you marry other wives, God will see it even if no one else does. He is a witness to this covenant between us.

"See this pile of stones," Laban continued, "and see this monument I have set between us. They stand between us as witnesses of our vows. I will never pass this pile of stones to harm you, and you must never pass these stones or this monument to harm me. I call on the God of our ancestors—the God of your grandfather Abraham and the God of my grandfather Nahor—to serve as a judge between us."

So Jacob took an oath before the fearsome God of his father, Isaac, to respect the boundary line. Then Jacob offered a sacrifice to God there on the mountain and invited everyone to a covenant feast. After they had eaten, they spent the night on the mountain.

Laban got up early the next morning, and he kissed his grandchildren and his daughters and blessed them. Then he left and returned home.

As Jacob started on his way again, angels of God came to meet him. When Jacob saw them, he exclaimed, "This is God's camp!" So he named the place Mahanaim.

Then Jacob sent messengers ahead to his brother, Esau, who was living in the region of Seir in the land of Edom. He told them, "Give this message to my master Esau: 'Humble greetings from your servant Jacob. Until now I have been living with Uncle Laban, and now I own cattle, donkeys, flocks of sheep and goats, and many servants, both men and women. I have sent these messengers to inform my lord of my coming, hoping that you will be friendly to me.'"

After delivering the message, the messengers returned to Jacob and reported, "We met your brother, Esau, and he is already on his way to meet you—with an army of 400 men!" Jacob was terrified at the news. He divided his household, along with the flocks and herds and camels, into two groups. He thought, "If Esau meets one group and attacks it, perhaps the other group can escape."

Then Jacob prayed, "O God of my grandfather Abraham, and God of my father, Isaac—O LORD, you told me, 'Return to your own land and to your relatives.' And you promised me, 'I will treat you kindly.' I am not worthy of all the unfailing love and faithfulness you have shown to me, your servant. When I left home and crossed the Jordan River, I owned nothing except a walking stick. Now my household fills two large camps! O LORD, please rescue me from the hand of my brother, Esau. I am afraid that he is coming to attack me, along with my wives and children. But you promised me, 'I will surely treat you kindly, and I will multiply your descendants until they become as numerous as the sands along the seashore—too many to count.'"

Jacob stayed where he was for the night. Then he selected these gifts from his possessions to present to his brother, Esau: 200 female goats, 20 male goats, 200 ewes, 20 rams, 30 female camels with their young, 40 cows, 10 bulls, 20 female donkeys, and 10 male donkeys. He divided these animals into herds and assigned each to different servants. Then he told his servants, "Go ahead of me with the animals, but keep some distance between the herds."

He gave these instructions to the men leading the first group: "When my brother, Esau, meets you, he will ask, 'Whose servants are you? Where are you going? Who owns these animals?' You must reply, 'They belong to your servant Jacob, but they are a gift for his master Esau. Look, he is coming right behind us.'"

Jacob gave the same instructions to the second and third herdsmen and to all who followed behind the herds: "You must say the same thing to Esau when you meet him. And be sure to say, 'Look, your servant Jacob is right behind us.'"

Jacob thought, "I will try to appease him by sending gifts ahead of me. When I see him in person, perhaps he will be friendly to me." So the gifts were sent on ahead, while Jacob himself spent that night in the camp.

+

During the night Jacob got up and took his two wives, his two servant wives, and his eleven sons and crossed the Jabbok River with them. After taking them to the other side, he sent over all his possessions.

This left Jacob all alone in the camp, and a man came and wrestled with him until the dawn began to break. When the man saw that he would not win the match, he touched Jacob's hip and wrenched it out of its socket. Then the man said, "Let me go, for the dawn is breaking!"

But Jacob said, "I will not let you go unless you bless me."

"What is your name?" the man asked.

He replied, "Jacob."

"Your name will no longer be Jacob," the man told him. "From now on you will be called Israel, because you have fought with God and with men and have won."

"Please tell me your name," Jacob said.

"Why do you want to know my name?" the man replied. Then he blessed Jacob there.

Jacob named the place Peniel (which means "face of God"), for he said, "I have seen God face to face, yet my life has been spared." The sun was rising as Jacob left Peniel, and he was limping because of the injury to his hip. (Even today the people of Israel don't eat the tendon near the hip socket because of what happened that night when the man strained the tendon of Jacob's hip.)

+

Then Jacob looked up and saw Esau coming with his 400 men. So he divided the children among Leah, Rachel, and his two servant wives. He put the servant wives and their children at the front, Leah and her children next, and Rachel and Joseph last. Then Jacob went on ahead. As he approached his brother, he bowed to the ground seven times before him. Then Esau ran to meet him and embraced him, threw his arms around his neck, and kissed him. And they both wept.

Then Esau looked at the women and children and asked, "Who are these people with you?"

"These are the children God has graciously given to me, your servant," Jacob replied. Then the servant wives came forward with their children and bowed before him. Next came Leah with her children, and they bowed before him. Finally, Joseph and Rachel came forward and bowed before him.

"And what were all the flocks and herds I met as I came?" Esau asked.

Jacob replied, "They are a gift, my lord, to ensure your friendship."

"My brother, I have plenty," Esau answered. "Keep what you have for yourself."

But Jacob insisted, "No, if I have found favor with you, please accept this gift from me. And what a relief to see your friendly smile. It is like seeing the face of God! Please take this gift I have brought you, for God has been very gracious to me. I have more than enough." And because Jacob insisted, Esau finally accepted the gift.

"Well," Esau said, "let's be going. I will lead the way."

But Jacob replied, "You can see, my lord, that some of the children are very young, and the flocks and herds have their young, too. If they are driven too hard, even for one day, all the animals could die. Please, my lord, go ahead of your servant. We will follow slowly, at a pace that is comfortable for the livestock and the children. I will meet you at Seir."

"All right," Esau said, "but at least let me assign some of my men to guide and protect you."

Jacob responded, "That's not necessary. It's enough that you've received me warmly, my lord!"

So Esau turned around and started back to Seir that same day. Jacob, on the other hand, traveled on to Succoth. There he built himself a house and made shelters for his livestock. That is why the place was named Succoth (which means "shelters").

Later, having traveled all the way from Paddan-aram, Jacob arrived safely at the town of Shechem, in the land of Canaan. There he set up camp outside the town. Jacob bought the plot of land where he camped from the family of Hamor, the father of Shechem, for 100 pieces of silver. And there he built an altar and named it El-Elohe-Israel.

+

One day Dinah, the daughter of Jacob and Leah, went to visit some of the young women who lived in the area. But when the local prince, Shechem son of Hamor the Hivite, saw Dinah, he seized her and raped her. But then he fell in love with her, and he tried to win her affection with tender words. He said to his father, Hamor, "Get me this young girl. I want to marry her."

Soon Jacob heard that Shechem had defiled his daughter, Dinah. But since his sons were out in the fields herding his livestock, he said nothing until they returned. Hamor, Shechem's father, came to discuss the matter with Jacob. Meanwhile, Jacob's sons had come in from the field as soon as they heard what had happened. They were shocked and furious that their sister had been raped. Shechem had done a disgraceful thing against Jacob's family, something that should never be done.

Hamor tried to speak with Jacob and his sons. "My son Shechem is truly in love with your daughter," he said. "Please let him marry her. In fact, let's arrange other marriages, too. You give us your daughters for our sons, and we will give you our daughters for your sons. And you may live among us; the land is open to you! Settle here and trade with us. And feel free to buy property in the area."

Then Shechem himself spoke to Dinah's father and brothers. "Please be kind to me, and let me marry her," he begged. "I will give you whatever you ask. No matter what dowry or gift you demand, I will gladly pay it—just give me the girl as my wife."

But since Shechem had defiled their sister, Dinah, Jacob's sons responded deceitfully to Shechem and his father, Hamor. They said to them, "We couldn't possibly allow this, because you're not circumcised. It would be a disgrace for our sister to marry a man like you! But here is a solution. If every man among you will be circumcised like we are, then we will give you our daughters, and we'll take your daughters for ourselves. We will live among you and become one people. But if you don't agree to be circumcised, we will take her and be on our way."

Hamor and his son Shechem agreed to their proposal. Shechem wasted no time in acting on this request, for he wanted Jacob's daughter desperately. Shechem was a highly respected member of his family, and he went with his father, Hamor, to present this proposal to the leaders at the town gate.

"These men are our friends," they said. "Let's invite them to live here among us and trade freely. Look, the land is large enough to hold them. We can take their daughters as wives and let them marry ours. But they will consider staying here and becoming one people with us only if all of our men are circumcised, just as they are. But if we do this, all their livestock and possessions will eventually be ours. Come, let's agree to their terms and let them settle here among us."

So all the men in the town council agreed with Hamor and Shechem, and every male in the town was circumcised. But three days later, when their wounds were still sore, two of Jacob's sons, Simeon and Levi, who were Dinah's full brothers, took their swords and entered the town without opposition. Then they slaughtered every male there, including Hamor and his son Shechem. They killed them with their swords, then took Dinah from Shechem's house and returned to their camp.

Meanwhile, the rest of Jacob's sons arrived. Finding the men slaughtered, they plundered the town because their sister had been defiled there. They seized all the flocks and herds and donkeys—everything they could lay their hands on, both inside the town and outside in the fields. They looted all their wealth and plundered their houses. They also took all their little children and wives and led them away as captives.

Afterward Jacob said to Simeon and Levi, "You have ruined me! You've made me stink among all the people of this land—among all the Canaanites and Perizzites. We are so few that they will join forces and crush us. I will be ruined, and my entire household will be wiped out!"

"But why should we let him treat our sister like a prostitute?" they retorted angrily.

Then God said to Jacob, "Get ready and move to Bethel and settle there. Build an altar there to the God who appeared to you when you fled from your brother, Esau."

So Jacob told everyone in his household, "Get rid of all your pagan idols, purify yourselves, and put on clean clothing. We are now going to Bethel, where I will build an altar to the God who answered my prayers when I was in distress. He has been with me wherever I have gone."

So they gave Jacob all their pagan idols and earrings, and he buried them under the great tree near Shechem. As they set out, a terror from God spread over the people in all the towns of that area, so no one attacked Jacob's family.

Eventually, Jacob and his household arrived at Luz (also called Bethel) in Canaan. Jacob built an altar there and named the place El-bethel (which means "God of Bethel"), because God had appeared to him there when he was fleeing from his brother, Esau.

Soon after this, Rebekah's old nurse, Deborah, died. She was buried beneath the oak tree in the valley below Bethel. Ever since, the tree has been called Allon-bacuth (which means "oak of weeping").

Now that Jacob had returned from Paddan-aram, God appeared to him again at Bethel. God blessed him, saying, "Your name is Jacob, but you will not be called Jacob any longer. From now on your name will be Israel." So God renamed him Israel.

Then God said, "I am El-Shaddai—'God Almighty.' Be fruitful and multiply. You will become a great nation, even many nations. Kings will be among your descendants! And I will give you the land I once gave to Abraham and Isaac. Yes, I will give it to you and your descendants after you." Then God went up from the place where he had spoken to Jacob.

Jacob set up a stone pillar to mark the place where God had spoken to him. Then he poured wine over it as an offering to God and anointed the pillar with olive oil. And Jacob named the place Bethel (which means "house of God"), because God had spoken to him there.

Leaving Bethel, Jacob and his clan moved on toward Ephrath. But Rachel went into labor while they were still some distance away. Her labor pains were intense. After a very hard delivery, the midwife finally exclaimed, "Don't be afraid—you have another son!" Rachel was about to die, but with her last breath she named the baby Ben-oni (which means "son of my sorrow"). The baby's father, however, called him Benjamin (which means "son of my right hand"). So Rachel died and was buried on the way to Ephrath (that is, Bethlehem). Jacob set up a stone monument over Rachel's grave, and it can be seen there to this day.

Then Jacob traveled on and camped beyond Migdal-eder. While he was living there, Reuben had intercourse with Bilhah, his father's concubine, and Jacob soon heard about it.

These are the names of the twelve sons of Jacob:

The sons of Leah were Reuben (Jacob's oldest son), Simeon, Levi,
Judah, Issachar, and Zebulun.
The sons of Rachel were Joseph and Benjamin.
The sons of Bilhah, Rachel's servant, were Dan and Naphtali.
The sons of Zilpah, Leah's servant, were Gad and Asher.
These are the names of the sons who were born to Jacob at Paddan-aram.

So Jacob returned to his father, Isaac, in Mamre, which is near Kiriath-arba (now called Hebron), where Abraham and Isaac had both lived as foreigners. Isaac lived for 180 years. Then he breathed his last and died at a ripe old age, joining his ancestors in death. And his sons, Esau and Jacob, buried him.

+ + +

This is the account of the descendants of Esau (also known as Edom).

Esau married two young women from Canaan: Adah, the daughter of Elon the Hittite; and Oholibamah, the daughter of Anah and granddaughter of Zibeon the Hivite. He also married his cousin Basemath, who was the daughter of Ishmael and the sister of Nebaioth. Adah gave birth to a son named Eliphaz for Esau. Basemath gave birth to a son named Reuel. Oholibamah gave birth to sons named Jeush, Jalam, and Korah. All these sons were born to Esau in the land of Canaan.

Esau took his wives, his children, and his entire household, along with his livestock and cattle—all the wealth he had acquired in the land of Canaan—and moved away from his brother, Jacob. There was not enough land to support them both because of all the livestock and possessions they had acquired. So Esau (also known as Edom) settled in the hill country of Seir.

+ + +

This is the account of Esau's descendants, the Edomites, who lived in the hill country of Seir.

These are the names of Esau's sons: Eliphaz, the son of Esau's wife Adah; and Reuel, the son of Esau's wife Basemath.
The descendants of Eliphaz were Teman, Omar, Zepho, Gatam, and Kenaz. Timna, the concubine of Esau's son Eliphaz, gave birth to a son named Amalek. These are the descendants of Esau's wife Adah.
The descendants of Reuel were Nahath, Zerah, Shammah, and Mizzah. These are the descendants of Esau's wife Basemath.

Esau also had sons through Oholibamah, the daughter of Anah and
granddaughter of Zibeon. Their names were Jeush, Jalam, and Korah.

These are the descendants of Esau who became the leaders of various
clans:

The descendants of Esau's oldest son, Eliphaz, became the leaders of the
clans of Teman, Omar, Zepho, Kenaz, Korah, Gatam, and Amalek.
These are the clan leaders in the land of Edom who descended from
Eliphaz. All these were descendants of Esau's wife Adah.
The descendants of Esau's son Reuel became the leaders of the clans
of Nahath, Zerah, Shammah, and Mizzah. These are the clan leaders
in the land of Edom who descended from Reuel. All these were
descendants of Esau's wife Basemath.
The descendants of Esau and his wife Oholibamah became the leaders
of the clans of Jeush, Jalam, and Korah. These are the clan leaders who
descended from Esau's wife Oholibamah, the daughter of Anah.
These are the clans descended from Esau (also known as Edom), identified by their clan leaders.

These are the names of the tribes that descended from Seir the Horite.
They lived in the land of Edom: Lotan, Shobal, Zibeon, Anah, Dishon,
Ezer, and Dishan. These were the Horite clan leaders, the descendants of
Seir, who lived in the land of Edom.

The descendants of Lotan were Hori and Hemam. Lotan's sister was
named Timna.
The descendants of Shobal were Alvan, Manahath, Ebal, Shepho, and
Onam.
The descendants of Zibeon were Aiah and Anah. (This is the Anah who
discovered the hot springs in the wilderness while he was grazing his
father's donkeys.)
The descendants of Anah were his son, Dishon, and his daughter,
Oholibamah.
The descendants of Dishon were Hemdan, Eshban, Ithran, and Keran.
The descendants of Ezer were Bilhan, Zaavan, and Akan.
The descendants of Dishan were Uz and Aran.
So these were the leaders of the Horite clans: Lotan, Shobal, Zibeon,
Anah, Dishon, Ezer, and Dishan. The Horite clans are named after their
clan leaders, who lived in the land of Seir.

These are the kings who ruled in the land of Edom before any king ruled
over the Israelites:

Bela son of Beor, who ruled in Edom from his city of Dinhabah.

When Bela died, Jobab son of Zerah from Bozrah became king in his
place.

When Jobab died, Husham from the land of the Temanites became king
in his place.

When Husham died, Hadad son of Bedad became king in his place
and ruled from the city of Avith. He was the one who defeated the
Midianites in the land of Moab.

When Hadad died, Samlah from the city of Masrekah became king in his
place.

When Samlah died, Shaul from the city of Rehoboth-on-the-River
became king in his place.

When Shaul died, Baal-hanan son of Acbor became king in his place.

When Baal-hanan son of Acbor died, Hadad became king in his place
and ruled from the city of Pau. His wife was Mehetabel, the daughter
of Matred and granddaughter of Me-zahab.

These are the names of the leaders of the clans descended from Esau,
who lived in the places named for them: Timna, Alvah, Jetheth, Oholibamah, Elah, Pinon, Kenaz, Teman, Mibzar, Magdiel, and Iram. These are
the leaders of the clans of Edom, listed according to their settlements in
the land they occupied. They all descended from Esau, the ancestor of the
Edomites.

So Jacob settled again in the land of Canaan, where his father had lived
as a foreigner.

+ + +

This is the account of Jacob and his family.

When Joseph was seventeen years old, he often tended his father's flocks.
He worked for his half brothers, the sons of his father's wives Bilhah and
Zilpah. But Joseph reported to his father some of the bad things his broth-
ers were doing.

Jacob loved Joseph more than any of his other children because Joseph
had been born to him in his old age. So one day Jacob had a special gift
made for Joseph—a beautiful robe. But his brothers hated Joseph because
their father loved him more than the rest of them. They couldn't say a kind
word to him.

One night Joseph had a dream, and when he told his brothers about it,
they hated him more than ever. "Listen to this dream," he said. "We were
out in the field, tying up bundles of grain. Suddenly my bundle stood up,
and your bundles all gathered around and bowed low before mine!"

His brothers responded, "So you think you will be our king, do you? Do you actually think you will reign over us?" And they hated him all the more because of his dreams and the way he talked about them.

Soon Joseph had another dream, and again he told his brothers about it. "Listen, I have had another dream," he said. "The sun, moon, and eleven stars bowed low before me!"

This time he told the dream to his father as well as to his brothers, but his father scolded him. "What kind of dream is that?" he asked. "Will your mother and I and your brothers actually come and bow to the ground before you?" But while his brothers were jealous of Joseph, his father wondered what the dreams meant.

Soon after this, Joseph's brothers went to pasture their father's flocks at Shechem. When they had been gone for some time, Jacob said to Joseph, "Your brothers are pasturing the sheep at Shechem. Get ready, and I will send you to them."

"I'm ready to go," Joseph replied.

"Go and see how your brothers and the flocks are getting along," Jacob said. "Then come back and bring me a report." So Jacob sent him on his way, and Joseph traveled to Shechem from their home in the valley of Hebron.

When he arrived there, a man from the area noticed him wandering around the countryside. "What are you looking for?" he asked.

"I'm looking for my brothers," Joseph replied. "Do you know where they are pasturing their sheep?"

"Yes," the man told him. "They have moved on from here, but I heard them say, 'Let's go on to Dothan.'" So Joseph followed his brothers to Dothan and found them there.

When Joseph's brothers saw him coming, they recognized him in the distance. As he approached, they made plans to kill him. "Here comes the dreamer!" they said. "Come on, let's kill him and throw him into one of these cisterns. We can tell our father, 'A wild animal has eaten him.' Then we'll see what becomes of his dreams!"

But when Reuben heard of their scheme, he came to Joseph's rescue. "Let's not kill him," he said. "Why should we shed any blood? Let's just throw him into this empty cistern here in the wilderness. Then he'll die without our laying a hand on him." Reuben was secretly planning to rescue Joseph and return him to his father.

So when Joseph arrived, his brothers ripped off the beautiful robe he was wearing. Then they grabbed him and threw him into the cistern. Now the cistern was empty; there was no water in it. Then, just as they were sitting down to eat, they looked up and saw a caravan of camels in the distance coming toward them. It was a group of Ishmaelite traders taking a load of gum, balm, and aromatic resin from Gilead down to Egypt.

Judah said to his brothers, "What will we gain by killing our brother? We'd have to cover up the crime. Instead of hurting him, let's sell him to those Ishmaelite traders. After all, he is our brother—our own flesh and blood!" And his brothers agreed. So when the Ishmaelites, who were Midianite traders, came by, Joseph's brothers pulled him out of the cistern and sold him to them for twenty pieces of silver. And the traders took him to Egypt.

Some time later, Reuben returned to get Joseph out of the cistern. When he discovered that Joseph was missing, he tore his clothes in grief. Then he went back to his brothers and lamented, "The boy is gone! What will I do now?"

Then the brothers killed a young goat and dipped Joseph's robe in its blood. They sent the beautiful robe to their father with this message: "Look at what we found. Doesn't this robe belong to your son?"

Their father recognized it immediately. "Yes," he said, "it is my son's robe. A wild animal must have eaten him. Joseph has clearly been torn to pieces!" Then Jacob tore his clothes and dressed himself in burlap. He mourned deeply for his son for a long time. His family all tried to comfort him, but he refused to be comforted. "I will go to my grave mourning for my son," he would say, and then he would weep.

Meanwhile, the Midianite traders arrived in Egypt, where they sold Joseph to Potiphar, an officer of Pharaoh, the king of Egypt. Potiphar was captain of the palace guard.

About this time, Judah left home and moved to Adullam, where he stayed with a man named Hirah. There he saw a Canaanite woman, the daughter of Shua, and he married her. When he slept with her, she became pregnant and gave birth to a son, and he named the boy Er. Then she became pregnant again and gave birth to another son, and she named him Onan. And when she gave birth to a third son, she named him Shelah. At the time of Shelah's birth, they were living at Kezib.

In the course of time, Judah arranged for his firstborn son, Er, to marry a young woman named Tamar. But Er was a wicked man in the LORD's sight, so the LORD took his life. Then Judah said to Er's brother Onan, "Go and marry Tamar, as our law requires of the brother of a man who has died. You must produce an heir for your brother."

But Onan was not willing to have a child who would not be his own heir. So whenever he had intercourse with his brother's wife, he spilled the semen on the ground. This prevented her from having a child who would belong to his brother. But the LORD considered it evil for Onan to deny a child to his dead brother. So the LORD took Onan's life, too.

Then Judah said to Tamar, his daughter-in-law, "Go back to your parents' home and remain a widow until my son Shelah is old enough to marry you." (But Judah didn't really intend to do this because he was afraid Shelah would also die, like his two brothers.) So Tamar went back to live in her father's home.

Some years later Judah's wife died. After the time of mourning was over, Judah and his friend Hirah the Adullamite went up to Timnah to supervise the shearing of his sheep. Someone told Tamar, "Look, your father-in-law is going up to Timnah to shear his sheep."

Tamar was aware that Shelah had grown up, but no arrangements had been made for her to come and marry him. So she changed out of her widow's clothing and covered herself with a veil to disguise herself. Then she sat beside the road at the entrance to the village of Enaim, which is on the road to Timnah. Judah noticed her and thought she was a prostitute, since she had covered her face. So he stopped and propositioned her. "Let me have sex with you," he said, not realizing that she was his own daughter-in-law.

"How much will you pay to have sex with me?" Tamar asked.

"I'll send you a young goat from my flock," Judah promised.

"But what will you give me to guarantee that you will send the goat?" she asked.

"What kind of guarantee do you want?" he replied.

She answered, "Leave me your identification seal and its cord and the walking stick you are carrying." So Judah gave them to her. Then he had intercourse with her, and she became pregnant. Afterward she went back home, took off her veil, and put on her widow's clothing as usual.

Later Judah asked his friend Hirah the Adullamite to take the young goat to the woman and to pick up the things he had given her as his guarantee. But Hirah couldn't find her. So he asked the men who lived there, "Where can I find the shrine prostitute who was sitting beside the road at the entrance to Enaim?"

"We've never had a shrine prostitute here," they replied.

So Hirah returned to Judah and told him, "I couldn't find her anywhere, and the men of the village claim they've never had a shrine prostitute there."

"Then let her keep the things I gave her," Judah said. "I sent the young goat as we agreed, but you couldn't find her. We'd be the laughingstock of the village if we went back again to look for her."

About three months later, Judah was told, "Tamar, your daughter-in-law, has acted like a prostitute. And now, because of this, she's pregnant."

"Bring her out, and let her be burned!" Judah demanded.

But as they were taking her out to kill her, she sent this message to her father-in-law: "The man who owns these things made me pregnant. Look closely. Whose seal and cord and walking stick are these?"

Judah recognized them immediately and said, "She is more righteous than I am, because I didn't arrange for her to marry my son Shelah." And Judah never slept with Tamar again.

When the time came for Tamar to give birth, it was discovered that she was carrying twins. While she was in labor, one of the babies reached out his hand. The midwife grabbed it and tied a scarlet string around the child's wrist, announcing, "This one came out first." But then he pulled back his hand, and out came his brother! "What!" the midwife exclaimed. "How did you break out first?" So he was named Perez. Then the baby with the scarlet string on his wrist was born, and he was named Zerah.

When Joseph was taken to Egypt by the Ishmaelite traders, he was purchased by Potiphar, an Egyptian officer. Potiphar was captain of the guard for Pharaoh, the king of Egypt.

The LORD was with Joseph, so he succeeded in everything he did as he served in the home of his Egyptian master. Potiphar noticed this and realized that the LORD was with Joseph, giving him success in everything he did. This pleased Potiphar, so he soon made Joseph his personal attendant. He put him in charge of his entire household and everything he owned. From the day Joseph was put in charge of his master's household and property, the LORD began to bless Potiphar's household for Joseph's sake. All his household affairs ran smoothly, and his crops and livestock flourished. So Potiphar gave Joseph complete administrative responsibility over everything he owned. With Joseph there, he didn't worry about a thing—except what kind of food to eat!

Joseph was a very handsome and well-built young man, and Potiphar's wife soon began to look at him lustfully. "Come and sleep with me," she demanded.

But Joseph refused. "Look," he told her, "my master trusts me with everything in his entire household. No one here has more authority than I do. He has held back nothing from me except you, because you are his wife. How could I do such a wicked thing? It would be a great sin against God."

She kept putting pressure on Joseph day after day, but he refused to sleep with her, and he kept out of her way as much as possible. One day, however, no one else was around when he went in to do his work. She came and grabbed him by his cloak, demanding, "Come on, sleep with me!" Joseph tore himself away, but he left his cloak in her hand as he ran from the house.

When she saw that she was holding his cloak and he had fled, she called out to her servants. Soon all the men came running. "Look!" she said. "My husband has brought this Hebrew slave here to make fools of us! He came into my room to rape me, but I screamed. When he heard me scream, he ran outside and got away, but he left his cloak behind with me."

She kept the cloak with her until her husband came home. Then she told him her story. "That Hebrew slave you've brought into our house tried to come in and fool around with me," she said. "But when I screamed, he ran outside, leaving his cloak with me!"

Potiphar was furious when he heard his wife's story about how Joseph had treated her. So he took Joseph and threw him into the prison where the king's prisoners were held, and there he remained. But the LORD was with Joseph in the prison and showed him his faithful love. And the LORD made Joseph a favorite with the prison warden. Before long, the warden put Joseph in charge of all the other prisoners and over everything that happened in the prison. The warden had no more worries, because Joseph took care of everything. The LORD was with him and caused everything he did to succeed.

Some time later, Pharaoh's chief cup-bearer and chief baker offended their royal master. Pharaoh became angry with these two officials, and he put them in the prison where Joseph was, in the palace of the captain of the guard. They remained in prison for quite some time, and the captain of the guard assigned them to Joseph, who looked after them.

While they were in prison, Pharaoh's cup-bearer and baker each had a dream one night, and each dream had its own meaning. When Joseph saw them the next morning, he noticed that they both looked upset. "Why do you look so worried today?" he asked them.

And they replied, "We both had dreams last night, but no one can tell us what they mean."

"Interpreting dreams is God's business," Joseph replied. "Go ahead and tell me your dreams."

So the chief cup-bearer told Joseph his dream first. "In my dream," he said, "I saw a grapevine in front of me. The vine had three branches that began to bud and blossom, and soon it produced clusters of ripe grapes. I was holding Pharaoh's wine cup in my hand, so I took a cluster of grapes and squeezed the juice into the cup. Then I placed the cup in Pharaoh's hand."

"This is what the dream means," Joseph said. "The three branches represent three days. Within three days Pharaoh will lift you up and restore you to your position as his chief cup-bearer. And please remember me and do me a favor when things go well for you. Mention me to Pharaoh, so he might let me out of this place. For I was kidnapped from my homeland, the land of the Hebrews, and now I'm here in prison, but I did nothing to deserve it."

When the chief baker saw that Joseph had given the first dream such a positive interpretation, he said to Joseph, "I had a dream, too. In my dream there were three baskets of white pastries stacked on my head. The top basket contained all kinds of pastries for Pharaoh, but the birds came and ate them from the basket on my head."

"This is what the dream means," Joseph told him. "The three baskets also represent three days. Three days from now Pharaoh will lift you up and impale your body on a pole. Then birds will come and peck away at your flesh."

Pharaoh's birthday came three days later, and he prepared a banquet for all his officials and staff. He summoned his chief cup-bearer and chief baker to join the other officials. He then restored the chief cup-bearer to his former position, so he could again hand Pharaoh his cup. But Pharaoh impaled the chief baker, just as Joseph had predicted when he interpreted his dream. Pharaoh's chief cup-bearer, however, forgot all about Joseph, never giving him another thought.

Two full years later, Pharaoh dreamed that he was standing on the bank of the Nile River. In his dream he saw seven fat, healthy cows come up out of the river and begin grazing in the marsh grass. Then he saw seven more cows come up behind them from the Nile, but these were scrawny and thin. These cows stood beside the fat cows on the riverbank. Then the scrawny, thin cows ate the seven healthy, fat cows! At this point in the dream, Pharaoh woke up.

But he fell asleep again and had a second dream. This time he saw seven heads of grain, plump and beautiful, growing on a single stalk. Then seven more heads of grain appeared, but these were shriveled and withered by the east wind. And these thin heads swallowed up the seven plump, well-formed heads! Then Pharaoh woke up again and realized it was a dream.

The next morning Pharaoh was very disturbed by the dreams. So he called for all the magicians and wise men of Egypt. When Pharaoh told them his dreams, not one of them could tell him what they meant.

Finally, the king's chief cup-bearer spoke up. "Today I have been reminded of my failure," he told Pharaoh. "Some time ago, you were angry with the chief baker and me, and you imprisoned us in the palace of the captain of the guard. One night the chief baker and I each had a dream, and each dream had its own meaning. There was a young Hebrew man with us in the prison who was a slave of the captain of the guard. We told him our dreams, and he told us what each of our dreams meant. And everything happened just as he had predicted. I was restored to my position as cupbearer, and the chief baker was executed and impaled on a pole."

Pharaoh sent for Joseph at once, and he was quickly brought from the prison. After he shaved and changed his clothes, he went in and stood before Pharaoh. Then Pharaoh said to Joseph, "I had a dream last night, and no one here can tell me what it means. But I have heard that when you hear about a dream you can interpret it."

"It is beyond my power to do this," Joseph replied. "But God can tell you what it means and set you at ease."

So Pharaoh told Joseph his dream. "In my dream," he said, "I was standing on the bank of the Nile River, and I saw seven fat, healthy cows come up out of the river and begin grazing in the marsh grass. But then I saw seven sick-looking cows, scrawny and thin, come up after them. I've never seen such sorry-looking animals in all the land of Egypt. These thin, scrawny cows ate the seven fat cows. But afterward you wouldn't have known it, for they were still as thin and scrawny as before! Then I woke up.

"In my dream I also saw seven heads of grain, full and beautiful, growing on a single stalk. Then seven more heads of grain appeared, but these were blighted, shriveled, and withered by the east wind. And the shriveled heads swallowed the seven healthy heads. I told these dreams to the magicians, but no one could tell me what they mean."

Joseph responded, "Both of Pharaoh's dreams mean the same thing. God is telling Pharaoh in advance what he is about to do. The seven healthy cows and the seven healthy heads of grain both represent seven years of prosperity. The seven thin, scrawny cows that came up later and the seven thin heads of grain, withered by the east wind, represent seven years of famine.

"This will happen just as I have described it, for God has revealed to Pharaoh in advance what he is about to do. The next seven years will be a period of great prosperity throughout the land of Egypt. But afterward there will be seven years of famine so great that all the prosperity will be forgotten in Egypt. Famine will destroy the land. This famine will be so severe that even the memory of the good years will be erased. As for having two similar dreams, it means that these events have been decreed by God, and he will soon make them happen.

"Therefore, Pharaoh should find an intelligent and wise man and put him in charge of the entire land of Egypt. Then Pharaoh should appoint supervisors over the land and let them collect one-fifth of all the crops during the seven good years. Have them gather all the food produced in the good years that are just ahead and bring it to Pharaoh's storehouses. Store it away, and guard it so there will be food in the cities. That way there will be enough to eat when the seven years of famine come to the land of Egypt. Otherwise this famine will destroy the land."

Joseph's suggestions were well received by Pharaoh and his officials. So Pharaoh asked his officials, "Can we find anyone else like this man so obviously filled with the spirit of God?" Then Pharaoh said to Joseph, "Since God has revealed the meaning of the dreams to you, clearly no one else is as intelligent or wise as you are. You will be in charge of my court, and all my people will take orders from you. Only I, sitting on my throne, will have a rank higher than yours."

Pharaoh said to Joseph, "I hereby put you in charge of the entire land of Egypt." Then Pharaoh removed his signet ring from his hand and placed it on Joseph's finger. He dressed him in fine linen clothing and hung a gold chain around his neck. Then he had Joseph ride in the chariot reserved for his second-in-command. And wherever Joseph went, the command was shouted, "Kneel down!" So Pharaoh put Joseph in charge of all Egypt. And Pharaoh said to him, "I am Pharaoh, but no one will lift a hand or foot in the entire land of Egypt without your approval."

Then Pharaoh gave Joseph a new Egyptian name, Zaphenath-paneah. He also gave him a wife, whose name was Asenath. She was the daughter of Potiphera, the priest of On. So Joseph took charge of the entire land of Egypt. He was thirty years old when he began serving in the court of Pharaoh, the king of Egypt. And when Joseph left Pharaoh's presence, he inspected the entire land of Egypt.

As predicted, for seven years the land produced bumper crops. During those years, Joseph gathered all the crops grown in Egypt and stored the grain from the surrounding fields in the cities. He piled up huge amounts of grain like sand on the seashore. Finally, he stopped keeping records because there was too much to measure.

During this time, before the first of the famine years, two sons were born to Joseph and his wife, Asenath, the daughter of Potiphera, the priest of On. Joseph named his older son Manasseh, for he said, "God has made me forget all my troubles and everyone in my father's family." Joseph named his second son Ephraim, for he said, "God has made me fruitful in this land of my grief."

At last the seven years of bumper crops throughout the land of Egypt came to an end. Then the seven years of famine began, just as Joseph had predicted. The famine also struck all the surrounding countries, but throughout Egypt there was plenty of food. Eventually, however, the famine spread throughout the land of Egypt as well. And when the people cried out to Pharaoh for food, he told them, "Go to Joseph, and do whatever he tells you." So with severe famine everywhere, Joseph opened up the storehouses and distributed grain to the Egyptians, for the famine was severe throughout the land of Egypt. And people from all around came to Egypt to buy grain from Joseph because the famine was severe throughout the world.

+

When Jacob heard that grain was available in Egypt, he said to his sons, "Why are you standing around looking at one another? I have heard there is grain in Egypt. Go down there, and buy enough grain to keep us alive. Otherwise we'll die."

So Joseph's ten older brothers went down to Egypt to buy grain. But Jacob wouldn't let Joseph's younger brother, Benjamin, go with them, for fear some harm might come to him. So Jacob's sons arrived in Egypt along with others to buy food, for the famine was in Canaan as well.

Since Joseph was governor of all Egypt and in charge of selling grain to all the people, it was to him that his brothers came. When they arrived, they bowed before him with their faces to the ground. Joseph recognized his brothers instantly, but he pretended to be a stranger and spoke harshly to them. "Where are you from?" he demanded.

"From the land of Canaan," they replied. "We have come to buy food."

Although Joseph recognized his brothers, they didn't recognize him. And he remembered the dreams he'd had about them many years before. He said to them, "You are spies! You have come to see how vulnerable our land has become."

"No, my lord!" they exclaimed. "Your servants have simply come to buy food. We are all brothers—members of the same family. We are honest men, sir! We are not spies!"

"Yes, you are!" Joseph insisted. "You have come to see how vulnerable our land has become."

"Sir," they said, "there are actually twelve of us. We, your servants, are all brothers, sons of a man living in the land of Canaan. Our youngest brother is back there with our father right now, and one of our brothers is no longer with us."

But Joseph insisted, "As I said, you are spies! This is how I will test your story. I swear by the life of Pharaoh that you will never leave Egypt unless your youngest brother comes here! One of you must go and get your brother. I'll keep the rest of you here in prison. Then we'll find out whether or not your story is true. By the life of Pharaoh, if it turns out that you don't have a younger brother, then I'll know you are spies."

So Joseph put them all in prison for three days. On the third day Joseph said to them, "I am a God-fearing man. If you do as I say, you will live. If you really are honest men, choose one of your brothers to remain in prison. The rest of you may go home with grain for your starving families.

But you must bring your youngest brother back to me. This will prove that you are telling the truth, and you will not die." To this they agreed.

Speaking among themselves, they said, "Clearly we are being punished because of what we did to Joseph long ago. We saw his anguish when he pleaded for his life, but we wouldn't listen. That's why we're in this trouble."

"Didn't I tell you not to sin against the boy?" Reuben asked. "But you wouldn't listen. And now we have to answer for his blood!"

Of course, they didn't know that Joseph understood them, for he had been speaking to them through an interpreter. Now he turned away from them and began to weep. When he regained his composure, he spoke to them again. Then he chose Simeon from among them and had him tied up right before their eyes.

Joseph then ordered his servants to fill the men's sacks with grain, but he also gave secret instructions to return each brother's payment at the top of his sack. He also gave them supplies for their journey home. So the brothers loaded their donkeys with the grain and headed for home.

But when they stopped for the night and one of them opened his sack to get grain for his donkey, he found his money in the top of his sack. "Look!" he exclaimed to his brothers. "My money has been returned; it's here in my sack!" Then their hearts sank. Trembling, they said to each other, "What has God done to us?"

When the brothers came to their father, Jacob, in the land of Canaan, they told him everything that had happened to them. "The man who is governor of the land spoke very harshly to us," they told him. "He accused us of being spies scouting the land. But we said, 'We are honest men, not spies. We are twelve brothers, sons of one father. One brother is no longer with us, and the youngest is at home with our father in the land of Canaan.'

"Then the man who is governor of the land told us, 'This is how I will find out if you are honest men. Leave one of your brothers here with me, and take grain for your starving families and go on home. But you must bring your youngest brother back to me. Then I will know you are honest men and not spies. Then I will give you back your brother, and you may trade freely in the land.'"

As they emptied out their sacks, there in each man's sack was the bag of money he had paid for the grain! The brothers and their father were terrified when they saw the bags of money. Jacob exclaimed, "You are robbing me of my children! Joseph is gone! Simeon is gone! And now you want to take Benjamin, too. Everything is going against me!"

Then Reuben said to his father, "You may kill my two sons if I don't bring Benjamin back to you. I'll be responsible for him, and I promise to bring him back."

But Jacob replied, "My son will not go down with you. His brother Joseph is dead, and he is all I have left. If anything should happen to him on your journey, you would send this grieving, white-haired man to his grave."

But the famine continued to ravage the land of Canaan. When the grain they had brought from Egypt was almost gone, Jacob said to his sons, "Go back and buy us a little more food."

But Judah said, "The man was serious when he warned us, 'You won't see my face again unless your brother is with you.' If you send Benjamin with us, we will go down and buy more food. But if you don't let Benjamin go, we won't go either. Remember, the man said, 'You won't see my face again unless your brother is with you.'"

"Why were you so cruel to me?" Jacob moaned. "Why did you tell him you had another brother?"

"The man kept asking us questions about our family," they replied. "He asked, 'Is your father still alive? Do you have another brother?' So we answered his questions. How could we know he would say, 'Bring your brother down here'?"

Judah said to his father, "Send the boy with me, and we will be on our way. Otherwise we will all die of starvation—and not only we, but you and our little ones. I personally guarantee his safety. You may hold me responsible if I don't bring him back to you. Then let me bear the blame forever. If we hadn't wasted all this time, we could have gone and returned twice by now."

So their father, Jacob, finally said to them, "If it can't be avoided, then at least do this. Pack your bags with the best products of this land. Take them down to the man as gifts—balm, honey, gum, aromatic resin, pistachio nuts, and almonds. Also take double the money that was put back in your sacks, as it was probably someone's mistake. Then take your brother, and go back to the man. May God Almighty give you mercy as you go before the man, so that he will release Simeon and let Benjamin return. But if I must lose my children, so be it."

So the men packed Jacob's gifts and double the money and headed off with Benjamin. They finally arrived in Egypt and presented themselves to Joseph. When Joseph saw Benjamin with them, he said to the manager of his household, "These men will eat with me this noon. Take them inside the palace. Then go slaughter an animal, and prepare a big feast." So the man did as Joseph told him and took them into Joseph's palace.

The brothers were terrified when they saw that they were being taken into Joseph's house. "It's because of the money someone put in our sacks last time we were here," they said. "He plans to pretend that we stole it. Then he will seize us, make us slaves, and take our donkeys."

The brothers approached the manager of Joseph's household and spoke to him at the entrance to the palace. "Sir," they said, "we came to Egypt once before to buy food. But as we were returning home, we stopped for the night and opened our sacks. Then we discovered that each man's money—the exact amount paid—was in the top of his sack! Here it is; we have brought it back with us. We also have additional money to buy more food. We have no idea who put our money in our sacks."

"Relax. Don't be afraid," the household manager told them. "Your God, the God of your father, must have put this treasure into your sacks. I know I received your payment." Then he released Simeon and brought him out to them.

The manager then led the men into Joseph's palace. He gave them water to wash their feet and provided food for their donkeys. They were told they would be eating there, so they prepared their gifts for Joseph's arrival at noon.

When Joseph came home, they gave him the gifts they had brought him, then bowed low to the ground before him. After greeting them, he asked, "How is your father, the old man you spoke about? Is he still alive?"

"Yes," they replied. "Our father, your servant, is alive and well." And they bowed low again.

Then Joseph looked at his brother Benjamin, the son of his own mother. "Is this your youngest brother, the one you told me about?" Joseph asked. "May God be gracious to you, my son." Then Joseph hurried from the room because he was overcome with emotion for his brother. He went into his private room, where he broke down and wept. After washing his face, he came back out, keeping himself under control. Then he ordered, "Bring out the food!"

The waiters served Joseph at his own table, and his brothers were served at a separate table. The Egyptians who ate with Joseph sat at their own table, because Egyptians despise Hebrews and refuse to eat with them. Joseph told each of his brothers where to sit, and to their amazement, he seated them according to age, from oldest to youngest. And Joseph filled their plates with food from his own table, giving Benjamin five times as much as he gave the others. So they feasted and drank freely with him.

When his brothers were ready to leave, Joseph gave these instructions to his palace manager: "Fill each of their sacks with as much grain as they can carry, and put each man's money back into his sack. Then put my personal silver cup at the top of the youngest brother's sack, along with the money for his grain." So the manager did as Joseph instructed him.

The brothers were up at dawn and were sent on their journey with their loaded donkeys. But when they had gone only a short distance and were barely out of the city, Joseph said to his palace manager, "Chase after them and stop them. When you catch up with them, ask them, 'Why have you repaid my kindness with such evil? Why have you stolen my master's silver cup, which he uses to predict the future? What a wicked thing you have done!'"

When the palace manager caught up with the men, he spoke to them as he had been instructed.

"What are you talking about?" the brothers responded. "We are your servants and would never do such a thing! Didn't we return the money we found in our sacks? We brought it back all the way from the land of Canaan. Why would we steal silver or gold from your master's house? If you find his cup with any one of us, let that man die. And all the rest of us, my lord, will be your slaves."

"That's fair," the man replied. "But only the one who stole the cup will be my slave. The rest of you may go free."

They all quickly took their sacks from the backs of their donkeys and opened them. The palace manager searched the brothers' sacks, from the oldest to the youngest. And the cup was found in Benjamin's sack! When the brothers saw this, they tore their clothing in despair. Then they loaded their donkeys again and returned to the city.

Joseph was still in his palace when Judah and his brothers arrived, and they fell to the ground before him. "What have you done?" Joseph demanded. "Don't you know that a man like me can predict the future?"

Judah answered, "Oh, my lord, what can we say to you? How can we explain this? How can we prove our innocence? God is punishing us for our sins. My lord, we have all returned to be your slaves—all of us, not just our brother who had your cup in his sack."

"No," Joseph said. "I would never do such a thing! Only the man who stole the cup will be my slave. The rest of you may go back to your father in peace."

Then Judah stepped forward and said, "Please, my lord, let your servant say just one word to you. Please, do not be angry with me, even though you are as powerful as Pharaoh himself.

"My lord, previously you asked us, your servants, 'Do you have a father or a brother?' And we responded, 'Yes, my lord, we have a father who is an old man, and his youngest son is a child of his old age. His full brother is dead, and he alone is left of his mother's children, and his father loves him very much.'

"And you said to us, 'Bring him here so I can see him with my own eyes.' But we said to you, 'My lord, the boy cannot leave his father, for his father would die.' But you told us, 'Unless your youngest brother comes with you, you will never see my face again.'

"So we returned to your servant, our father, and told him what you had said. Later, when he said, 'Go back again and buy us more food,' we replied, 'We can't go unless you let our youngest brother go with us. We'll never get to see the man's face unless our youngest brother is with us.'

"Then my father said to us, 'As you know, my wife had two sons, and one of them went away and never returned. Doubtless he was torn to pieces by some wild animal. I have never seen him since. Now if you take his brother away from me, and any harm comes to him, you will send this grieving, white-haired man to his grave.'

"And now, my lord, I cannot go back to my father without the boy. Our father's life is bound up in the boy's life. If he sees that the boy is not with us, our father will die. We, your servants, will indeed be responsible for sending that grieving, white-haired man to his grave. My lord, I guaranteed to my father that I would take care of the boy. I told him, 'If I don't bring him back to you, I will bear the blame forever.'

"So please, my lord, let me stay here as a slave instead of the boy, and let the boy return with his brothers. For how can I return to my father if the boy is not with me? I couldn't bear to see the anguish this would cause my father!"

Joseph could stand it no longer. There were many people in the room, and he said to his attendants, "Out, all of you!" So he was alone with his brothers when he told them who he was. Then he broke down and wept. He wept so loudly the Egyptians could hear him, and word of it quickly carried to Pharaoh's palace.

"I am Joseph!" he said to his brothers. "Is my father still alive?" But his brothers were speechless! They were stunned to realize that Joseph was standing there in front of them. "Please, come closer," he said to them. So they came closer. And he said again, "I am Joseph, your brother, whom you sold into slavery in Egypt. But don't be upset, and don't be angry with yourselves for selling me to this place. It was God who sent me here ahead of you to preserve your lives. This famine that has ravaged the land for two years will last five more years, and there will be neither plowing nor harvesting. God has sent me ahead of you to keep you and your families alive and to preserve many survivors. So it was God who sent me here, not you! And he is the one who made me an adviser to Pharaoh—the manager of his entire palace and the governor of all Egypt.

"Now hurry back to my father and tell him, 'This is what your son Joseph says: God has made me master over all the land of Egypt. So come down to me immediately! You can live in the region of Goshen, where you can be near me with all your children and grandchildren, your flocks and herds, and everything you own. I will take care of you there, for there are still five years of famine ahead of us. Otherwise you, your household, and all your animals will starve.'"

Then Joseph added, "Look! You can see for yourselves, and so can my brother Benjamin, that I really am Joseph! Go tell my father of my honored position here in Egypt. Describe for him everything you have seen, and then bring my father here quickly." Weeping with joy, he embraced Benjamin, and Benjamin did the same. Then Joseph kissed each of his brothers and wept over them, and after that they began talking freely with him.

The news soon reached Pharaoh's palace: "Joseph's brothers have arrived!" Pharaoh and his officials were all delighted to hear this.

Pharaoh said to Joseph, "Tell your brothers, 'This is what you must do: Load your pack animals, and hurry back to the land of Canaan. Then get your father and all of your families, and return here to me. I will give you the very best land in Egypt, and you will eat from the best that the land produces.'"

Then Pharaoh said to Joseph, "Tell your brothers, 'Take wagons from the land of Egypt to carry your little children and your wives, and bring your father here. Don't worry about your personal belongings, for the best of all the land of Egypt is yours.'"

So the sons of Jacob did as they were told. Joseph provided them with wagons, as Pharaoh had commanded, and he gave them supplies for the journey. And he gave each of them new clothes—but to Benjamin he gave five changes of clothes and 300 pieces of silver. He also sent his father ten male donkeys loaded with the finest products of Egypt, and ten female donkeys loaded with grain and bread and other supplies he would need on his journey.

So Joseph sent his brothers off, and as they left, he called after them, "Don't quarrel about all this along the way!" And they left Egypt and returned to their father, Jacob, in the land of Canaan.

"Joseph is still alive!" they told him. "And he is governor of all the land of Egypt!" Jacob was stunned at the news—he couldn't believe it. But when they repeated to Jacob everything Joseph had told them, and when he saw the wagons Joseph had sent to carry him, their father's spirits revived.

Then Jacob exclaimed, "It must be true! My son Joseph is alive! I must go and see him before I die."

So Jacob set out for Egypt with all his possessions. And when he came to Beersheba, he offered sacrifices to the God of his father, Isaac. During the night God spoke to him in a vision. "Jacob! Jacob!" he called.

"Here I am," Jacob replied.

"I am God, the God of your father," the voice said. "Do not be afraid to go down to Egypt, for there I will make your family into a great nation. I will go with you down to Egypt, and I will bring you back again. You will die in Egypt, but Joseph will be with you to close your eyes."

So Jacob left Beersheba, and his sons took him to Egypt. They carried him and their little ones and their wives in the wagons Pharaoh had provided for them. They also took all their livestock and all the personal belongings they had acquired in the land of Canaan. So Jacob and his entire family went to Egypt—sons and grandsons, daughters and granddaughters—all his descendants.

These are the names of the descendants of Israel—the sons of Jacob—who went to Egypt:

Reuben was Jacob's oldest son. The sons of Reuben were Hanoch, Pallu, Hezron, and Carmi.
The sons of Simeon were Jemuel, Jamin, Ohad, Jakin, Zohar, and Shaul. (Shaul's mother was a Canaanite woman.)
The sons of Levi were Gershon, Kohath, and Merari.
The sons of Judah were Er, Onan, Shelah, Perez, and Zerah (though Er and Onan had died in the land of Canaan). The sons of Perez were Hezron and Hamul.
The sons of Issachar were Tola, Puah, Jashub, and Shimron.
The sons of Zebulun were Sered, Elon, and Jahleel.
These were the sons of Leah and Jacob who were born in Paddan-aram, in addition to their daughter, Dinah. The number of Jacob's descendants (male and female) through Leah was thirty-three.

The sons of Gad were Zephon, Haggi, Shuni, Ezbon, Eri, Arodi, and Areli.
The sons of Asher were Imnah, Ishvah, Ishvi, and Beriah. Their sister was Serah. Beriah's sons were Heber and Malkiel.
These were the sons of Zilpah, the servant given to Leah by her father, Laban. The number of Jacob's descendants through Zilpah was sixteen.

The sons of Jacob's wife Rachel were Joseph and Benjamin.
Joseph's sons, born in the land of Egypt, were Manasseh and Ephraim. Their mother was Asenath, daughter of Potiphera, the priest of On.
Benjamin's sons were Bela, Beker, Ashbel, Gera, Naaman, Ehi, Rosh, Muppim, Huppim, and Ard.
These were the sons of Rachel and Jacob. The number of Jacob's descendants through Rachel was fourteen.

The son of Dan was Hushim.
The sons of Naphtali were Jahzeel, Guni, Jezer, and Shillem.

These were the sons of Bilhah, the servant given to Rachel by her father, Laban. The number of Jacob's descendants through Bilhah was seven.

The total number of Jacob's direct descendants who went with him to Egypt, not counting his sons' wives, was sixty-six. In addition, Joseph had two sons who were born in Egypt. So altogether, there were seventy members of Jacob's family in the land of Egypt.

+

As they neared their destination, Jacob sent Judah ahead to meet Joseph and get directions to the region of Goshen. And when they finally arrived there, Joseph prepared his chariot and traveled to Goshen to meet his father, Jacob. When Joseph arrived, he embraced his father and wept, holding him for a long time. Finally, Jacob said to Joseph, "Now I am ready to die, since I have seen your face again and know you are still alive."

And Joseph said to his brothers and to his father's entire family, "I will go to Pharaoh and tell him, 'My brothers and my father's entire family have come to me from the land of Canaan. These men are shepherds, and they raise livestock. They have brought with them their flocks and herds and everything they own.'"

Then he said, "When Pharaoh calls for you and asks you about your occupation, you must tell him, 'We, your servants, have raised livestock all our lives, as our ancestors have always done.' When you tell him this, he will let you live here in the region of Goshen, for the Egyptians despise shepherds."

Then Joseph went to see Pharaoh and told him, "My father and my brothers have arrived from the land of Canaan. They have come with all their flocks and herds and possessions, and they are now in the region of Goshen."

Joseph took five of his brothers with him and presented them to Pharaoh. And Pharaoh asked the brothers, "What is your occupation?"

They replied, "We, your servants, are shepherds, just like our ancestors. We have come to live here in Egypt for a while, for there is no pasture for our flocks in Canaan. The famine is very severe there. So please, we request permission to live in the region of Goshen."

Then Pharaoh said to Joseph, "Now that your father and brothers have joined you here, choose any place in the entire land of Egypt for them to live. Give them the best land of Egypt. Let them live in the region of Goshen. And if any of them have special skills, put them in charge of my livestock, too."

Then Joseph brought in his father, Jacob, and presented him to Pharaoh. And Jacob blessed Pharaoh.

"How old are you?" Pharaoh asked him.

Jacob replied, "I have traveled this earth for 130 hard years. But my life has been short compared to the lives of my ancestors." Then Jacob blessed Pharaoh again before leaving his court.

So Joseph assigned the best land of Egypt—the region of Rameses—to his father and his brothers, and he settled them there, just as Pharaoh had commanded. And Joseph provided food for his father and his brothers in amounts appropriate to the number of their dependents, including the smallest children.

Meanwhile, the famine became so severe that all the food was used up, and people were starving throughout the lands of Egypt and Canaan. By selling grain to the people, Joseph eventually collected all the money in Egypt and Canaan, and he put the money in Pharaoh's treasury. When the people of Egypt and Canaan ran out of money, all the Egyptians came to Joseph. "Our money is gone!" they cried. "But please give us food, or we will die before your very eyes!"

Joseph replied, "Since your money is gone, bring me your livestock. I will give you food in exchange for your livestock." So they brought their livestock to Joseph in exchange for food. In exchange for their horses, flocks of sheep and goats, herds of cattle, and donkeys, Joseph provided them with food for another year.

But that year ended, and the next year they came again and said, "We cannot hide the truth from you, my lord. Our money is gone, and all our livestock and cattle are yours. We have nothing left to give but our bodies and our land. Why should we die before your very eyes? Buy us and our land in exchange for food; we offer our land and ourselves as slaves for Pharaoh. Just give us grain so we may live and not die, and so the land does not become empty and desolate."

So Joseph bought all the land of Egypt for Pharaoh. All the Egyptians sold him their fields because the famine was so severe, and soon all the land belonged to Pharaoh. As for the people, he made them all slaves, from one end of Egypt to the other. The only land he did not buy was the land belonging to the priests. They received an allotment of food directly from Pharaoh, so they didn't need to sell their land.

Then Joseph said to the people, "Look, today I have bought you and your land for Pharaoh. I will provide you with seed so you can plant the fields. Then when you harvest it, one-fifth of your crop will belong to Pharaoh. You may keep the remaining four-fifths as seed for your fields and as food for you, your households, and your little ones."

"You have saved our lives!" they exclaimed. "May it please you, my lord, to let us be Pharaoh's servants." Joseph then issued a decree still in effect in the land of Egypt, that Pharaoh should receive one-fifth of all the crops grown on his land. Only the land belonging to the priests was not given to Pharaoh.

Meanwhile, the people of Israel settled in the region of Goshen in Egypt. There they acquired property, and they were fruitful, and their population grew rapidly. Jacob lived for seventeen years after his arrival in Egypt, so he lived 147 years in all.

As the time of his death drew near, Jacob called for his son Joseph and said to him, "Please do me this favor. Put your hand under my thigh and swear that you will treat me with unfailing love by honoring this last request: Do not bury me in Egypt. When I die, please take my body out of Egypt and bury me with my ancestors."

So Joseph promised, "I will do as you ask."

"Swear that you will do it," Jacob insisted. So Joseph gave his oath, and Jacob bowed humbly at the head of his bed.

One day not long after this, word came to Joseph, "Your father is failing rapidly." So Joseph went to visit his father, and he took with him his two sons, Manasseh and Ephraim.

When Joseph arrived, Jacob was told, "Your son Joseph has come to see you." So Jacob gathered his strength and sat up in his bed.

Jacob said to Joseph, "God Almighty appeared to me at Luz in the land of Canaan and blessed me. He said to me, 'I will make you fruitful, and I will multiply your descendants. I will make you a multitude of nations. And I will give this land of Canaan to your descendants after you as an everlasting possession.'

"Now I am claiming as my own sons these two boys of yours, Ephraim and Manasseh, who were born here in the land of Egypt before I arrived. They will be my sons, just as Reuben and Simeon are. But any children born to you in the future will be your own, and they will inherit land within the territories of their brothers Ephraim and Manasseh.

"Long ago, as I was returning from Paddan-aram, Rachel died in the land of Canaan. We were still on the way, some distance from Ephrath (that is, Bethlehem). So with great sorrow I buried her there beside the road to Ephrath."

Then Jacob looked over at the two boys. "Are these your sons?" he asked.

"Yes," Joseph told him, "these are the sons God has given me here in Egypt."

And Jacob said, "Bring them closer to me, so I can bless them."

Jacob was half blind because of his age and could hardly see. So Joseph brought the boys close to him, and Jacob kissed and embraced them. Then

Jacob said to Joseph, "I never thought I would see your face again, but now God has let me see your children, too!"

Joseph moved the boys, who were at their grandfather's knees, and he bowed with his face to the ground. Then he positioned the boys in front of Jacob. With his right hand he directed Ephraim toward Jacob's left hand, and with his left hand he put Manasseh at Jacob's right hand. But Jacob crossed his arms as he reached out to lay his hands on the boys' heads. He put his right hand on the head of Ephraim, though he was the younger boy, and his left hand on the head of Manasseh, though he was the firstborn. Then he blessed Joseph and said,

> "May the God before whom my grandfather Abraham
>   and my father, Isaac, walked—
> the God who has been my shepherd
>   all my life, to this very day,
> the Angel who has redeemed me from all harm—
>   may he bless these boys.
> May they preserve my name
>   and the names of Abraham and Isaac.
> And may their descendants multiply greatly
>   throughout the earth."

But Joseph was upset when he saw that his father placed his right hand on Ephraim's head. So Joseph lifted it to move it from Ephraim's head to Manasseh's head. "No, my father," he said. "This one is the firstborn. Put your right hand on his head."

But his father refused. "I know, my son; I know," he replied. "Manasseh will also become a great people, but his younger brother will become even greater. And his descendants will become a multitude of nations."

So Jacob blessed the boys that day with this blessing: "The people of Israel will use your names when they give a blessing. They will say, 'May God make you as prosperous as Ephraim and Manasseh.'" In this way, Jacob put Ephraim ahead of Manasseh.

Then Jacob said to Joseph, "Look, I am about to die, but God will be with you and will take you back to Canaan, the land of your ancestors. And beyond what I have given your brothers, I am giving you an extra portion of the land that I took from the Amorites with my sword and bow."

Then Jacob called together all his sons and said, "Gather around me, and I will tell you what will happen to each of you in the days to come.

> "Come and listen, you sons of Jacob;
>   listen to Israel, your father.

"Reuben, you are my firstborn, my strength,
    the child of my vigorous youth.
    You are first in rank and first in power.
But you are as unruly as a flood,
    and you will be first no longer.
For you went to bed with my wife;
    you defiled my marriage couch.

"Simeon and Levi are two of a kind;
    their weapons are instruments of violence.
May I never join in their meetings;
    may I never be a party to their plans.
For in their anger they murdered men,
    and they crippled oxen just for sport.
A curse on their anger, for it is fierce;
    a curse on their wrath, for it is cruel.
I will scatter them among the descendants of Jacob;
    I will disperse them throughout Israel.

"Judah, your brothers will praise you.
    You will grasp your enemies by the neck.
    All your relatives will bow before you.
Judah, my son, is a young lion
    that has finished eating its prey.
Like a lion he crouches and lies down;
    like a lioness—who dares to rouse him?
The scepter will not depart from Judah,
    nor the ruler's staff from his descendants,
until the coming of the one to whom it belongs,
    the one whom all nations will honor.
He ties his foal to a grapevine,
    the colt of his donkey to a choice vine.
He washes his clothes in wine,
    his robes in the blood of grapes.
His eyes are darker than wine,
    and his teeth are whiter than milk.

"Zebulun will settle by the seashore
    and will be a harbor for ships;
    his borders will extend to Sidon.

"Issachar is a sturdy donkey,
    resting between two saddlepacks.

When he sees how good the countryside is
  and how pleasant the land,
he will bend his shoulder to the load
  and submit himself to hard labor.

"Dan will govern his people,
  like any other tribe in Israel.
Dan will be a snake beside the road,
  a poisonous viper along the path
that bites the horse's hooves
  so its rider is thrown off.
I trust in you for salvation, O LORD!

"Gad will be attacked by marauding bands,
  but he will attack them when they retreat.

"Asher will dine on rich foods
  and produce food fit for kings.

"Naphtali is a doe set free
  that bears beautiful fawns.

"Joseph is the foal of a wild donkey,
  the foal of a wild donkey at a spring—
  one of the wild donkeys on the ridge.
Archers attacked him savagely;
  they shot at him and harassed him.
But his bow remained taut,
  and his arms were strengthened
by the hands of the Mighty One of Jacob,
  by the Shepherd, the Rock of Israel.
May the God of your father help you;
  may the Almighty bless you
with the blessings of the heavens above,
  and blessings of the watery depths below,
  and blessings of the breasts and womb.
May my fatherly blessings on you
  surpass the blessings of my ancestors,
  reaching to the heights of the eternal hills.
May these blessings rest on the head of Joseph,
  who is a prince among his brothers.

"Benjamin is a ravenous wolf,
  devouring his enemies in the morning
  and dividing his plunder in the evening."

These are the twelve tribes of Israel, and this is what their father said as he told his sons good-bye. He blessed each one with an appropriate message.

Then Jacob instructed them, "Soon I will die and join my ancestors. Bury me with my father and grandfather in the cave in the field of Ephron the Hittite. This is the cave in the field of Machpelah, near Mamre in Canaan, that Abraham bought from Ephron the Hittite as a permanent burial site. There Abraham and his wife Sarah are buried. There Isaac and his wife, Rebekah, are buried. And there I buried Leah. It is the plot of land and the cave that my grandfather Abraham bought from the Hittites."

When Jacob had finished this charge to his sons, he drew his feet into the bed, breathed his last, and joined his ancestors in death.

Joseph threw himself on his father and wept over him and kissed him. Then Joseph told the physicians who served him to embalm his father's body; so Jacob was embalmed. The embalming process took the usual forty days. And the Egyptians mourned his death for seventy days.

When the period of mourning was over, Joseph approached Pharaoh's advisers and said, "Please do me this favor and speak to Pharaoh on my behalf. Tell him that my father made me swear an oath. He said to me, 'Listen, I am about to die. Take my body back to the land of Canaan, and bury me in the tomb I prepared for myself.' So please allow me to go and bury my father. After his burial, I will return without delay."

Pharaoh agreed to Joseph's request. "Go and bury your father, as he made you promise," he said. So Joseph went up to bury his father. He was accompanied by all of Pharaoh's officials, all the senior members of Pharaoh's household, and all the senior officers of Egypt. Joseph also took his entire household and his brothers and their households. But they left their little children and flocks and herds in the land of Goshen. A great number of chariots and charioteers accompanied Joseph.

When they arrived at the threshing floor of Atad, near the Jordan River, they held a very great and solemn memorial service, with a seven-day period of mourning for Joseph's father. The local residents, the Canaanites, watched them mourning at the threshing floor of Atad. Then they renamed that place (which is near the Jordan) Abel-mizraim, for they said, "This is a place of deep mourning for these Egyptians."

So Jacob's sons did as he had commanded them. They carried his body to the land of Canaan and buried him in the cave in the field of Machpelah, near Mamre. This is the cave that Abraham had bought as a permanent burial site from Ephron the Hittite.

After burying Jacob, Joseph returned to Egypt with his brothers and all who had accompanied him to his father's burial. But now that their father was dead, Joseph's brothers became fearful. "Now Joseph will show his anger and pay us back for all the wrong we did to him," they said.

So they sent this message to Joseph: "Before your father died, he instructed us to say to you: 'Please forgive your brothers for the great wrong they did to you—for their sin in treating you so cruelly.' So we, the servants of the God of your father, beg you to forgive our sin." When Joseph received the message, he broke down and wept. Then his brothers came and threw themselves down before Joseph. "Look, we are your slaves!" they said.

But Joseph replied, "Don't be afraid of me. Am I God, that I can punish you? You intended to harm me, but God intended it all for good. He brought me to this position so I could save the lives of many people. No, don't be afraid. I will continue to take care of you and your children." So he reassured them by speaking kindly to them.

So Joseph and his brothers and their families continued to live in Egypt. Joseph lived to the age of 110. He lived to see three generations of descendants of his son Ephraim, and he lived to see the birth of the children of Manasseh's son Makir, whom he claimed as his own.

"Soon I will die," Joseph told his brothers, "but God will surely come to help you and lead you out of this land of Egypt. He will bring you back to the land he solemnly promised to give to Abraham, to Isaac, and to Jacob."

Then Joseph made the sons of Israel swear an oath, and he said, "When God comes to help you and lead you back, you must take my bones with you." So Joseph died at the age of 110. The Egyptians embalmed him, and his body was placed in a coffin in Egypt.

IMMERSED IN EXODUS

THE BOOK OF EXODUS DESCRIBES HOW GOD makes his third covenant with humanity. Abraham's descendants multiply into the ancient nation of Israel, and God appoints Moses to serve as the mediator of Israel's covenant relationship with God. The Bible describes this covenant in such detail that its story and provisions make up the rest of the first five books, a sign of how crucial it is for what follows.

Exodus continues the story from the book of Genesis. It explains how the descendants of Jacob's sons, after settling in Egypt, multiply into a nation and become enslaved by Pharaoh, the ruler of Egypt. God sees the suffering of his people and intervenes to save them—a move that establishes the pattern for God's future acts of rescue. Moses is chosen as the leader who will deliver the Israelites from slavery and bring them to their own land. Through a series of terrible plagues, God convinces Pharaoh to release the people. The plagues represent the LORD's "judgment against all the gods of Egypt." God reveals his name to Moses (Yahweh, meaning "I AM WHO I AM"), and shows himself to be more powerful than these false gods and powers. (These stories are told in the same *chiastic* arrangement as many of the stories in Genesis.)

Once they are free from slavery, the Israelites set off toward Canaan, the land God had promised to Abraham. God goes with them along the way, and at Mount Sinai he renews his covenant with them. If the people obey God's instructions, they will be God's "special treasure from among all the peoples on earth," his "kingdom of priests," and his "holy nation." The implication of this covenant ceremony is that Israel is not being chosen merely for their own sake. They are being given a special vocation as part of God's mission to restore the world. At Mount Sinai, God begins to deliver the laws—starting with the Ten Commandments—that will shape the Israelites into his community.

Many of these laws teach the way of life that God intends for his people by explaining what to do in specific situations. For example, one law states: "If you see that the donkey of someone who hates you has collapsed under its load, do not walk by. Instead, stop and help" (and perhaps make a friend out of an enemy). Other laws speak in more general terms, for example: "You must not mistreat or oppress foreigners in any way. Remember, you yourselves were once foreigners in the land of Egypt."

Many more laws of both kinds are given in the books that follow. But Exodus, after presenting an initial collection of laws, then turns to describe the Tabernacle. This is a beautiful tent with a courtyard and furnishings where God will live in the midst of the people's encampment. The Tabernacle is filled with representations of different parts of the creation (earth, sea, lights in the sky, etc.), revealing that God intends for the world to be his home, with humanity living in close fellowship with him. The Tabernacle's description is actually recounted twice in detail: once as the plans for the Tabernacle are given and again when those plans are carried out. Then, the Tabernacle's construction is summarized three additional times. These repeated descriptions of the Tabernacle indicate the importance of God returning to live among his people.

This is one of the places in the Bible where it can feel like the story stops because there are practically no action episodes for a very long stretch. (Although Moses does put down a rebellion among the people between the two detailed descriptions of the Tabernacle.) But the story of God's covenant relationship with humanity continues to unfold as that relationship is given statutory expression through the Law and artistic expression through the craftsmanship of the Tabernacle. It's early in the Bible's story, but God is already working to create a new humanity and a new world.

EXODUS

✦

These are the names of the sons of Israel (that is, Jacob) who moved to Egypt with their father, each with his family: Reuben, Simeon, Levi, Judah, Issachar, Zebulun, Benjamin, Dan, Naphtali, Gad, and Asher. In all, Jacob had seventy descendants in Egypt, including Joseph, who was already there.

In time, Joseph and all of his brothers died, ending that entire generation. But their descendants, the Israelites, had many children and grandchildren. In fact, they multiplied so greatly that they became extremely powerful and filled the land.

Eventually, a new king came to power in Egypt who knew nothing about Joseph or what he had done. He said to his people, "Look, the people of Israel now outnumber us and are stronger than we are. We must make a plan to keep them from growing even more. If we don't, and if war breaks out, they will join our enemies and fight against us. Then they will escape from the country."

So the Egyptians made the Israelites their slaves. They appointed brutal slave drivers over them, hoping to wear them down with crushing labor. They forced them to build the cities of Pithom and Rameses as supply centers for the king. But the more the Egyptians oppressed them, the more the Israelites multiplied and spread, and the more alarmed the Egyptians became. So the Egyptians worked the people of Israel without mercy. They made their lives bitter, forcing them to mix mortar and make bricks and do all the work in the fields. They were ruthless in all their demands.

Then Pharaoh, the king of Egypt, gave this order to the Hebrew midwives, Shiphrah and Puah: "When you help the Hebrew women as they give birth, watch as they deliver. If the baby is a boy, kill him; if it is a girl, let her live." But because the midwives feared God, they refused to obey the king's orders. They allowed the boys to live, too.

So the king of Egypt called for the midwives. "Why have you done this?" he demanded. "Why have you allowed the boys to live?"

"The Hebrew women are not like the Egyptian women," the midwives replied. "They are more vigorous and have their babies so quickly that we cannot get there in time."

So God was good to the midwives, and the Israelites continued to multiply, growing more and more powerful. And because the midwives feared God, he gave them families of their own.

Then Pharaoh gave this order to all his people: "Throw every newborn Hebrew boy into the Nile River. But you may let the girls live."

About this time, a man and woman from the tribe of Levi got married. The woman became pregnant and gave birth to a son. She saw that he was a special baby and kept him hidden for three months. But when she could no longer hide him, she got a basket made of papyrus reeds and waterproofed it with tar and pitch. She put the baby in the basket and laid it among the reeds along the bank of the Nile River. The baby's sister then stood at a distance, watching to see what would happen to him.

Soon Pharaoh's daughter came down to bathe in the river, and her attendants walked along the riverbank. When the princess saw the basket among the reeds, she sent her maid to get it for her. When the princess opened it, she saw the baby. The little boy was crying, and she felt sorry for him. "This must be one of the Hebrew children," she said.

Then the baby's sister approached the princess. "Should I go and find one of the Hebrew women to nurse the baby for you?" she asked.

"Yes, do!" the princess replied. So the girl went and called the baby's mother.

"Take this baby and nurse him for me," the princess told the baby's mother. "I will pay you for your help." So the woman took her baby home and nursed him.

Later, when the boy was older, his mother brought him back to Pharaoh's daughter, who adopted him as her own son. The princess named him Moses, for she explained, "I lifted him out of the water."

Many years later, when Moses had grown up, he went out to visit his own people, the Hebrews, and he saw how hard they were forced to work. During his visit, he saw an Egyptian beating one of his fellow Hebrews. After looking in all directions to make sure no one was watching, Moses killed the Egyptian and hid the body in the sand.

The next day, when Moses went out to visit his people again, he saw two Hebrew men fighting. "Why are you beating up your friend?" Moses said to the one who had started the fight.

The man replied, "Who appointed you to be our prince and judge? Are you going to kill me as you killed that Egyptian yesterday?"

Then Moses was afraid, thinking, "Everyone knows what I did." And sure enough, Pharaoh heard what had happened, and he tried to kill Moses. But Moses fled from Pharaoh and went to live in the land of Midian.

When Moses arrived in Midian, he sat down beside a well. Now the priest of Midian had seven daughters who came as usual to draw water and fill the water troughs for their father's flocks. But some other shepherds came and chased them away. So Moses jumped up and rescued the girls from the shepherds. Then he drew water for their flocks.

When the girls returned to Reuel, their father, he asked, "Why are you back so soon today?"

"An Egyptian rescued us from the shepherds," they answered. "And then he drew water for us and watered our flocks."

"Then where is he?" their father asked. "Why did you leave him there? Invite him to come and eat with us."

Moses accepted the invitation, and he settled there with him. In time, Reuel gave Moses his daughter Zipporah to be his wife. Later she gave birth to a son, and Moses named him Gershom, for he explained, "I have been a foreigner in a foreign land."

+ + +

Years passed, and the king of Egypt died. But the Israelites continued to groan under their burden of slavery. They cried out for help, and their cry rose up to God. God heard their groaning, and he remembered his covenant promise to Abraham, Isaac, and Jacob. He looked down on the people of Israel and knew it was time to act.

One day Moses was tending the flock of his father-in-law, Jethro, the priest of Midian. He led the flock far into the wilderness and came to Sinai, the mountain of God. There the angel of the LORD appeared to him in a blazing fire from the middle of a bush. Moses stared in amazement. Though the bush was engulfed in flames, it didn't burn up. "This is amazing," Moses said to himself. "Why isn't that bush burning up? I must go see it."

When the LORD saw Moses coming to take a closer look, God called to him from the middle of the bush, "Moses! Moses!"

"Here I am!" Moses replied.

"Do not come any closer," the LORD warned. "Take off your sandals, for you are standing on holy ground. I am the God of your father—the God of Abraham, the God of Isaac, and the God of Jacob." When Moses heard this, he covered his face because he was afraid to look at God.

Then the LORD told him, "I have certainly seen the oppression of my people in Egypt. I have heard their cries of distress because of their harsh slave drivers. Yes, I am aware of their suffering. So I have come down to rescue them from the power of the Egyptians and lead them out of Egypt into their own fertile and spacious land. It is a land flowing with milk and honey—the land where the Canaanites, Hittites, Amorites, Perizzites, Hivites, and Jebusites now live. Look! The cry of the people of Israel has reached me, and I have seen how harshly the Egyptians abuse them. Now go, for I am sending you to Pharaoh. You must lead my people Israel out of Egypt."

But Moses protested to God, "Who am I to appear before Pharaoh? Who am I to lead the people of Israel out of Egypt?"

God answered, "I will be with you. And this is your sign that I am the one who has sent you: When you have brought the people out of Egypt, you will worship God at this very mountain."

But Moses protested, "If I go to the people of Israel and tell them, 'The God of your ancestors has sent me to you,' they will ask me, 'What is his name?' Then what should I tell them?"

God replied to Moses, "I AM WHO I AM. Say this to the people of Israel: I AM has sent me to you." God also said to Moses, "Say this to the people of Israel: Yahweh, the God of your ancestors—the God of Abraham, the God of Isaac, and the God of Jacob—has sent me to you.

This is my eternal name,
my name to remember for all generations.

"Now go and call together all the elders of Israel. Tell them, 'Yahweh, the God of your ancestors—the God of Abraham, Isaac, and Jacob—has appeared to me. He told me, "I have been watching closely, and I see how the Egyptians are treating you. I have promised to rescue you from your oppression in Egypt. I will lead you to a land flowing with milk and honey—the land where the Canaanites, Hittites, Amorites, Perizzites, Hivites, and Jebusites now live."'

"The elders of Israel will accept your message. Then you and the elders must go to the king of Egypt and tell him, 'The LORD, the God of the Hebrews, has met with us. So please let us take a three-day journey into the wilderness to offer sacrifices to the LORD, our God.'

"But I know that the king of Egypt will not let you go unless a mighty hand forces him. So I will raise my hand and strike the Egyptians, performing all kinds of miracles among them. Then at last he will let you go. And I will cause the Egyptians to look favorably on you. They will give you gifts when you go so you will not leave empty-handed. Every Israelite woman will ask for articles of silver and gold and fine clothing from her Egyptian neighbors and from the foreign women in their houses. You will dress your sons and daughters with these, stripping the Egyptians of their wealth."

But Moses protested again, "What if they won't believe me or listen to me? What if they say, 'The LORD never appeared to you'?"

Then the LORD asked him, "What is that in your hand?"

"A shepherd's staff," Moses replied.

"Throw it down on the ground," the LORD told him. So Moses threw down the staff, and it turned into a snake! Moses jumped back.

Then the LORD told him, "Reach out and grab its tail." So Moses reached out and grabbed it, and it turned back into a shepherd's staff in his hand.

"Perform this sign," the LORD told him. "Then they will believe that the LORD, the God of their ancestors—the God of Abraham, the God of Isaac, and the God of Jacob—really has appeared to you."

Then the LORD said to Moses, "Now put your hand inside your cloak." So Moses put his hand inside his cloak, and when he took it out again, his hand was white as snow with a severe skin disease. "Now put your hand back into your cloak," the LORD said. So Moses put his hand back in, and when he took it out again, it was as healthy as the rest of his body.

The LORD said to Moses, "If they do not believe you and are not convinced by the first miraculous sign, they will be convinced by the second sign. And if they don't believe you or listen to you even after these two signs, then take some water from the Nile River and pour it out on the dry ground. When you do, the water from the Nile will turn to blood on the ground."

But Moses pleaded with the LORD, "O Lord, I'm not very good with words. I never have been, and I'm not now, even though you have spoken to me. I get tongue-tied, and my words get tangled."

Then the LORD asked Moses, "Who makes a person's mouth? Who decides whether people speak or do not speak, hear or do not hear, see or do not see? Is it not I, the LORD? Now go! I will be with you as you speak, and I will instruct you in what to say."

But Moses again pleaded, "Lord, please! Send anyone else."

Then the LORD became angry with Moses. "All right," he said. "What about your brother, Aaron the Levite? I know he speaks well. And look! He is on his way to meet you now. He will be delighted to see you. Talk to him, and put the words in his mouth. I will be with both of you as you speak, and I will instruct you both in what to do. Aaron will be your spokesman to the people. He will be your mouthpiece, and you will stand in the place of God for him, telling him what to say. And take your shepherd's staff with you, and use it to perform the miraculous signs I have shown you."

So Moses went back home to Jethro, his father-in-law. "Please let me return to my relatives in Egypt," Moses said. "I don't even know if they are still alive."

"Go in peace," Jethro replied.

Before Moses left Midian, the LORD said to him, "Return to Egypt, for all those who wanted to kill you have died."

So Moses took his wife and sons, put them on a donkey, and headed back to the land of Egypt. In his hand he carried the staff of God.

And the LORD told Moses, "When you arrive back in Egypt, go to Pharaoh and perform all the miracles I have empowered you to do. But I will harden his heart so he will refuse to let the people go. Then you will tell him, 'This is what the LORD says: Israel is my firstborn son. I commanded you, "Let my son go, so he can worship me." But since you have refused, I will now kill your firstborn son!'"

On the way to Egypt, at a place where Moses and his family had stopped for the night, the LORD confronted him and was about to kill him. But Moses' wife, Zipporah, took a flint knife and circumcised her son. She touched his feet with the foreskin and said, "Now you are a bridegroom of blood to me." (When she said "a bridegroom of blood," she was referring to the circumcision.) After that, the LORD left him alone.

Now the LORD had said to Aaron, "Go out into the wilderness to meet Moses." So Aaron went and met Moses at the mountain of God, and he embraced him. Moses then told Aaron everything the LORD had commanded him to say. And he told him about the miraculous signs the LORD had commanded him to perform.

Then Moses and Aaron returned to Egypt and called all the elders of Israel together. Aaron told them everything the LORD had told Moses, and Moses performed the miraculous signs as they watched. Then the people of Israel were convinced that the LORD had sent Moses and Aaron. When they heard that the LORD was concerned about them and had seen their misery, they bowed down and worshiped.

After this presentation to Israel's leaders, Moses and Aaron went and spoke to Pharaoh. They told him, "This is what the LORD, the God of Israel, says: Let my people go so they may hold a festival in my honor in the wilderness."

"Is that so?" retorted Pharaoh. "And who is the LORD? Why should I listen to him and let Israel go? I don't know the LORD, and I will not let Israel go."

But Aaron and Moses persisted. "The God of the Hebrews has met with us," they declared. "So let us take a three-day journey into the wilderness so we can offer sacrifices to the LORD our God. If we don't, he will kill us with a plague or with the sword."

Pharaoh replied, "Moses and Aaron, why are you distracting the people from their tasks? Get back to work! Look, there are many of your people in the land, and you are stopping them from their work."

That same day Pharaoh sent this order to the Egyptian slave drivers and the Israelite foremen: "Do not supply any more straw for making bricks. Make the people get it themselves! But still require them to make the same number of bricks as before. Don't reduce the quota. They are lazy. That's why they are crying out, 'Let us go and offer sacrifices to our God.' Load them down with more work. Make them sweat! That will teach them to listen to lies!"

So the slave drivers and foremen went out and told the people: "This is what Pharaoh says: I will not provide any more straw for you. Go and get it yourselves. Find it wherever you can. But you must produce just as many bricks as before!" So the people scattered throughout the land of Egypt in search of stubble to use as straw.

Meanwhile, the Egyptian slave drivers continued to push hard. "Meet your daily quota of bricks, just as you did when we provided you with straw!" they demanded. Then they whipped the Israelite foremen they had put in charge of the work crews. "Why haven't you met your quotas either yesterday or today?" they demanded.

So the Israelite foremen went to Pharaoh and pleaded with him. "Please don't treat your servants like this," they begged. "We are given no straw, but the slave drivers still demand, 'Make bricks!' We are being beaten, but it isn't our fault! Your own people are to blame!"

But Pharaoh shouted, "You're just lazy! Lazy! That's why you're saying, 'Let us go and offer sacrifices to the LORD.' Now get back to work! No straw will be given to you, but you must still produce the full quota of bricks."

The Israelite foremen could see that they were in serious trouble when they were told, "You must not reduce the number of bricks you make each day." As they left Pharaoh's court, they confronted Moses and Aaron, who were waiting outside for them. The foremen said to them, "May the LORD judge and punish you for making us stink before Pharaoh and his officials. You have put a sword into their hands, an excuse to kill us!"

Then Moses went back to the LORD and protested, "Why have you brought all this trouble on your own people, Lord? Why did you send me? Ever since I came to Pharaoh as your spokesman, he has been even more brutal to your people. And you have done nothing to rescue them!"

Then the LORD told Moses, "Now you will see what I will do to Pharaoh. When he feels the force of my strong hand, he will let the people go. In fact, he will force them to leave his land!"

And God said to Moses, "I am Yahweh—'the LORD.' I appeared to Abraham, to Isaac, and to Jacob as El-Shaddai—'God Almighty'—but I did not reveal my name, Yahweh, to them. And I reaffirmed my covenant with them. Under its terms, I promised to give them the land of Canaan, where they were living as foreigners. You can be sure that I have heard the groans of the people of Israel, who are now slaves to the Egyptians. And I am well aware of my covenant with them.

"Therefore, say to the people of Israel: 'I am the LORD. I will free you from your oppression and will rescue you from your slavery in Egypt. I will redeem you with a powerful arm and great acts of judgment. I will claim you as my own people, and I will be your God. Then you will know that I am the LORD your God who has freed you from your oppression in Egypt. I will bring you into the land I swore to give to Abraham, Isaac, and Jacob. I will give it to you as your very own possession. I am the LORD!'"

So Moses told the people of Israel what the LORD had said, but they refused to listen anymore. They had become too discouraged by the brutality of their slavery.

Then the LORD said to Moses, "Go back to Pharaoh, the king of Egypt, and tell him to let the people of Israel leave his country."

"But LORD!" Moses objected. "My own people won't listen to me anymore. How can I expect Pharaoh to listen? I'm such a clumsy speaker!"

But the LORD spoke to Moses and Aaron and gave them orders for the Israelites and for Pharaoh, the king of Egypt. The LORD commanded Moses and Aaron to lead the people of Israel out of Egypt.

+ + +

These are the ancestors of some of the clans of Israel:

The sons of Reuben, Israel's oldest son, were Hanoch, Pallu, Hezron, and Carmi. Their descendants became the clans of Reuben.

The sons of Simeon were Jemuel, Jamin, Ohad, Jakin, Zohar, and Shaul. (Shaul's mother was a Canaanite woman.) Their descendants became the clans of Simeon.

These are the descendants of Levi, as listed in their family records: The sons of Levi were Gershon, Kohath, and Merari. (Levi lived to be 137 years old.)

   The descendants of Gershon included Libni and Shimei, each of whom became the ancestor of a clan.

The descendants of Kohath included Amram, Izhar, Hebron, and Uzziel. (Kohath lived to be 133 years old.)

The descendants of Merari included Mahli and Mushi.

These are the clans of the Levites, as listed in their family records.

Amram married his father's sister Jochebed, and she gave birth to his sons, Aaron and Moses. (Amram lived to be 137 years old.)

The sons of Izhar were Korah, Nepheg, and Zicri.

The sons of Uzziel were Mishael, Elzaphan, and Sithri.

Aaron married Elisheba, the daughter of Amminadab and sister of Nahshon, and she gave birth to his sons, Nadab, Abihu, Eleazar, and Ithamar.

The sons of Korah were Assir, Elkanah, and Abiasaph. Their descendants became the clans of Korah.

Eleazar son of Aaron married one of the daughters of Putiel, and she gave birth to his son, Phinehas.

These are the ancestors of the Levite families, listed according to their clans.

The Aaron and Moses named in this list are the same ones to whom the LORD said, "Lead the people of Israel out of the land of Egypt like an army." It was Moses and Aaron who spoke to Pharaoh, the king of Egypt, about leading the people of Israel out of Egypt.

When the LORD spoke to Moses in the land of Egypt, he said to him, "I am the LORD! Tell Pharaoh, the king of Egypt, everything I am telling you." But Moses argued with the LORD, saying, "I can't do it! I'm such a clumsy speaker! Why should Pharaoh listen to me?"

+ + +

Then the LORD said to Moses, "Pay close attention to this. I will make you seem like God to Pharaoh, and your brother, Aaron, will be your prophet. Tell Aaron everything I command you, and Aaron must command Pharaoh to let the people of Israel leave his country. But I will make Pharaoh's heart stubborn so I can multiply my miraculous signs and wonders in the land of Egypt. Even then Pharaoh will refuse to listen to you. So I will bring down my fist on Egypt. Then I will rescue my forces—my people, the Israelites—from the land of Egypt with great acts of judgment. When I raise my powerful hand and bring out the Israelites, the Egyptians will know that I am the LORD."

So Moses and Aaron did just as the LORD had commanded them. Moses was eighty years old, and Aaron was eighty-three when they made their demands to Pharaoh.

Then the LORD said to Moses and Aaron, "Pharaoh will demand, 'Show me a miracle.' When he does this, say to Aaron, 'Take your staff and throw it down in front of Pharaoh, and it will become a serpent.'"

So Moses and Aaron went to Pharaoh and did what the LORD had commanded them. Aaron threw down his staff before Pharaoh and his officials, and it became a serpent! Then Pharaoh called in his own wise men and sorcerers, and these Egyptian magicians did the same thing with their magic. They threw down their staffs, which also became serpents! But then Aaron's staff swallowed up their staffs. Pharaoh's heart, however, remained hard. He still refused to listen, just as the LORD had predicted.

Then the LORD said to Moses, "Pharaoh's heart is stubborn, and he still refuses to let the people go. So go to Pharaoh in the morning as he goes down to the river. Stand on the bank of the Nile and meet him there. Be sure to take along the staff that turned into a snake. Then announce to him, 'The LORD, the God of the Hebrews, has sent me to tell you, "Let my people go, so they can worship me in the wilderness." Until now, you have refused to listen to him. So this is what the LORD says: "I will show you that I am the LORD." Look! I will strike the water of the Nile with this staff in my hand, and the river will turn to blood. The fish in it will die, and the river will stink. The Egyptians will not be able to drink any water from the Nile.'"

Then the LORD said to Moses: "Tell Aaron, 'Take your staff and raise your hand over the waters of Egypt—all its rivers, canals, ponds, and all the reservoirs. Turn all the water to blood. Everywhere in Egypt the water will turn to blood, even the water stored in wooden bowls and stone pots.'"

So Moses and Aaron did just as the LORD commanded them. As Pharaoh and all of his officials watched, Aaron raised his staff and struck the water of the Nile. Suddenly, the whole river turned to blood! The fish in the river died, and the water became so foul that the Egyptians couldn't drink it. There was blood everywhere throughout the land of Egypt. But again the magicians of Egypt used their magic, and they, too, turned water into blood. So Pharaoh's heart remained hard. He refused to listen to Moses and Aaron, just as the LORD had predicted. Pharaoh returned to his palace and put the whole thing out of his mind. Then all the Egyptians dug along the riverbank to find drinking water, for they couldn't drink the water from the Nile.

Seven days passed from the time the LORD struck the Nile.

Then the LORD said to Moses, "Go back to Pharaoh and announce to him, 'This is what the LORD says: Let my people go, so they can worship me. If you refuse to let them go, I will send a plague of frogs across your entire land. The Nile River will swarm with frogs. They will come up out of the river and into your palace, even into your bedroom and onto your bed! They will enter the houses of your officials and your people. They will even jump into your ovens and your kneading bowls. Frogs will jump on you, your people, and all your officials.'"

Then the LORD said to Moses, "Tell Aaron, 'Raise the staff in your hand over all the rivers, canals, and ponds of Egypt, and bring up frogs over all the land.'" So Aaron raised his hand over the waters of Egypt, and frogs came up and covered the whole land! But the magicians were able to do the same thing with their magic. They, too, caused frogs to come up on the land of Egypt.

Then Pharaoh summoned Moses and Aaron and begged, "Plead with the LORD to take the frogs away from me and my people. I will let your people go, so they can offer sacrifices to the LORD."

"You set the time!" Moses replied. "Tell me when you want me to pray for you, your officials, and your people. Then you and your houses will be rid of the frogs. They will remain only in the Nile River."

"Do it tomorrow," Pharaoh said.

"All right," Moses replied, "it will be as you have said. Then you will know that there is no one like the LORD our God. The frogs will leave you and your houses, your officials, and your people. They will remain only in the Nile River."

So Moses and Aaron left Pharaoh's palace, and Moses cried out to the LORD about the frogs he had inflicted on Pharaoh. And the LORD did just what Moses had predicted. The frogs in the houses, the courtyards, and the fields all died. The Egyptians piled them into great heaps, and a terrible stench filled the land. But when Pharaoh saw that relief had come, he became stubborn. He refused to listen to Moses and Aaron, just as the LORD had predicted.

So the LORD said to Moses, "Tell Aaron, 'Raise your staff and strike the ground. The dust will turn into swarms of gnats throughout the land of Egypt.'" So Moses and Aaron did just as the LORD had commanded them. When Aaron raised his hand and struck the ground with his staff, gnats infested the entire land, covering the Egyptians and their animals. All the dust in the land of Egypt turned into gnats. Pharaoh's magicians tried to do the same thing with their secret arts, but this time they failed. And the gnats covered everyone, people and animals alike.

"This is the finger of God!" the magicians exclaimed to Pharaoh. But Pharaoh's heart remained hard. He wouldn't listen to them, just as the LORD had predicted.

Then the Lord told Moses, "Get up early in the morning and stand in Pharaoh's way as he goes down to the river. Say to him, 'This is what the Lord says: Let my people go, so they can worship me. If you refuse, then I will send swarms of flies on you, your officials, your people, and all the houses. The Egyptian homes will be filled with flies, and the ground will be covered with them. But this time I will spare the region of Goshen, where my people live. No flies will be found there. Then you will know that I am the Lord and that I am present even in the heart of your land. I will make a clear distinction between my people and your people. This miraculous sign will happen tomorrow.'"

And the Lord did just as he had said. A thick swarm of flies filled Pharaoh's palace and the houses of his officials. The whole land of Egypt was thrown into chaos by the flies.

Pharaoh called for Moses and Aaron. "All right! Go ahead and offer sacrifices to your God," he said. "But do it here in this land."

But Moses replied, "That wouldn't be right. The Egyptians detest the sacrifices that we offer to the Lord our God. Look, if we offer our sacrifices here where the Egyptians can see us, they will stone us. We must take a three-day trip into the wilderness to offer sacrifices to the Lord our God, just as he has commanded us."

"All right, go ahead," Pharaoh replied. "I will let you go into the wilderness to offer sacrifices to the Lord your God. But don't go too far away. Now hurry and pray for me."

Moses answered, "As soon as I leave you, I will pray to the Lord, and tomorrow the swarms of flies will disappear from you and your officials and all your people. But I am warning you, Pharaoh, don't lie to us again and refuse to let the people go to sacrifice to the Lord."

So Moses left Pharaoh's palace and pleaded with the Lord to remove all the flies. And the Lord did as Moses asked and caused the swarms of flies to disappear from Pharaoh, his officials, and his people. Not a single fly remained. But Pharaoh again became stubborn and refused to let the people go.

"Go back to Pharaoh," the Lord commanded Moses. "Tell him, 'This is what the Lord, the God of the Hebrews, says: Let my people go, so they can worship me. If you continue to hold them and refuse to let them go, the hand of the Lord will strike all your livestock—your horses, donkeys, camels, cattle, sheep, and goats—with a deadly plague. But the Lord will again make a distinction between the livestock of the Israelites and that of the Egyptians. Not a single one of Israel's animals will die! The Lord has already set the time for the plague to begin. He has declared that he will strike the land tomorrow.'"

And the LORD did just as he had said. The next morning all the livestock of the Egyptians died, but the Israelites didn't lose a single animal. Pharaoh sent his officials to investigate, and they discovered that the Israelites had not lost a single animal! But even so, Pharaoh's heart remained stubborn, and he still refused to let the people go.

Then the LORD said to Moses and Aaron, "Take handfuls of soot from a brick kiln, and have Moses toss it into the air while Pharaoh watches. The ashes will spread like fine dust over the whole land of Egypt, causing festering boils to break out on people and animals throughout the land."

So they took soot from a brick kiln and went and stood before Pharaoh. As Pharaoh watched, Moses threw the soot into the air, and boils broke out on people and animals alike. Even the magicians were unable to stand before Moses, because the boils had broken out on them and all the Egyptians. But the LORD hardened Pharaoh's heart, and just as the LORD had predicted to Moses, Pharaoh refused to listen.

Then the LORD said to Moses, "Get up early in the morning and stand before Pharaoh. Tell him, 'This is what the LORD, the God of the Hebrews, says: Let my people go, so they can worship me. If you don't, I will send more plagues on you and your officials and your people. Then you will know that there is no one like me in all the earth. By now I could have lifted my hand and struck you and your people with a plague to wipe you off the face of the earth. But I have spared you for a purpose—to show you my power and to spread my fame throughout the earth. But you still lord it over my people and refuse to let them go. So tomorrow at this time I will send a hailstorm more devastating than any in all the history of Egypt. Quick! Order your livestock and servants to come in from the fields to find shelter. Any person or animal left outside will die when the hail falls.'"

Some of Pharaoh's officials were afraid because of what the LORD had said. They quickly brought their servants and livestock in from the fields. But those who paid no attention to the word of the LORD left theirs out in the open.

Then the LORD said to Moses, "Lift your hand toward the sky so hail may fall on the people, the livestock, and all the plants throughout the land of Egypt."

So Moses lifted his staff toward the sky, and the LORD sent thunder and hail, and lightning flashed toward the earth. The LORD sent a tremendous hailstorm against all the land of Egypt. Never in all the history of Egypt had there been a storm like that, with such devastating hail and continuous lightning. It left all of Egypt in ruins. The hail struck down everything in the open field—people, animals, and plants alike. Even the trees were destroyed. The only place without hail was the region of Goshen, where the people of Israel lived.

Then Pharaoh quickly summoned Moses and Aaron. "This time I have sinned," he confessed. "The LORD is the righteous one, and my people and I are wrong. Please beg the LORD to end this terrifying thunder and hail. We've had enough. I will let you go; you don't need to stay any longer."

"All right," Moses replied. "As soon as I leave the city, I will lift my hands and pray to the LORD. Then the thunder and hail will stop, and you will know that the earth belongs to the LORD. But I know that you and your officials still do not fear the LORD God."

(All the flax and barley were ruined by the hail, because the barley had formed heads and the flax was budding. But the wheat and the emmer wheat were spared, because they had not yet sprouted from the ground.)

So Moses left Pharaoh's court and went out of the city. When he lifted his hands to the LORD, the thunder and hail stopped, and the downpour ceased. But when Pharaoh saw that the rain, hail, and thunder had stopped, he and his officials sinned again, and Pharaoh again became stubborn. Because his heart was hard, Pharaoh refused to let the people leave, just as the LORD had predicted through Moses.

Then the LORD said to Moses, "Return to Pharaoh and make your demands again. I have made him and his officials stubborn so I can display my miraculous signs among them. I've also done it so you can tell your children and grandchildren about how I made a mockery of the Egyptians and about the signs I displayed among them—and so you will know that I am the LORD."

So Moses and Aaron went to Pharaoh and said, "This is what the LORD, the God of the Hebrews, says: How long will you refuse to submit to me? Let my people go, so they can worship me. If you refuse, watch out! For tomorrow I will bring a swarm of locusts on your country. They will cover the land so that you won't be able to see the ground. They will devour what little is left of your crops after the hailstorm, including all the trees growing in the fields. They will overrun your palaces and the homes of your officials and all the houses in Egypt. Never in the history of Egypt have your ancestors seen a plague like this one!" And with that, Moses turned and left Pharaoh.

Pharaoh's officials now came to Pharaoh and appealed to him. "How long will you let this man hold us hostage? Let the men go to worship the LORD their God! Don't you realize that Egypt lies in ruins?"

So Moses and Aaron were brought back to Pharaoh. "All right," he told them, "go and worship the LORD your God. But who exactly will be going with you?"

Moses replied, "We will all go—young and old, our sons and daughters, and our flocks and herds. We must all join together in celebrating a festival to the LORD."

Pharaoh retorted, "The LORD will certainly need to be with you if I let you take your little ones! I can see through your evil plan. Never! Only the men may go and worship the LORD, since that is what you requested." And Pharaoh threw them out of the palace.

Then the LORD said to Moses, "Raise your hand over the land of Egypt to bring on the locusts. Let them cover the land and devour every plant that survived the hailstorm."

So Moses raised his staff over Egypt, and the LORD caused an east wind to blow over the land all that day and through the night. When morning arrived, the east wind had brought the locusts. And the locusts swarmed over the whole land of Egypt, settling in dense swarms from one end of the country to the other. It was the worst locust plague in Egyptian history, and there has never been another one like it. For the locusts covered the whole country and darkened the land. They devoured every plant in the fields and all the fruit on the trees that had survived the hailstorm. Not a single leaf was left on the trees and plants throughout the land of Egypt.

Pharaoh quickly summoned Moses and Aaron. "I have sinned against the LORD your God and against you," he confessed. "Forgive my sin, just this once, and plead with the LORD your God to take away this death from me."

So Moses left Pharaoh's court and pleaded with the LORD. The LORD responded by shifting the wind, and the strong west wind blew the locusts into the Red Sea. Not a single locust remained in all the land of Egypt. But the LORD hardened Pharaoh's heart again, so he refused to let the people go.

Then the LORD said to Moses, "Lift your hand toward heaven, and the land of Egypt will be covered with a darkness so thick you can feel it." So Moses lifted his hand to the sky, and a deep darkness covered the entire land of Egypt for three days. During all that time the people could not see each other, and no one moved. But there was light as usual where the people of Israel lived.

Finally, Pharaoh called for Moses. "Go and worship the LORD," he said. "But leave your flocks and herds here. You may even take your little ones with you."

"No," Moses said, "you must provide us with animals for sacrifices and burnt offerings to the LORD our God. All our livestock must go with us, too; not a hoof can be left behind. We must choose our sacrifices for the LORD our God from among these animals. And we won't know how we are to worship the LORD until we get there."

But the LORD hardened Pharaoh's heart once more, and he would not let them go. "Get out of here!" Pharaoh shouted at Moses. "I'm warning you. Never come back to see me again! The day you see my face, you will die!"

"Very well," Moses replied. "I will never see your face again."

+

Then the LORD said to Moses, "I will strike Pharaoh and the land of Egypt with one more blow. After that, Pharaoh will let you leave this country. In fact, he will be so eager to get rid of you that he will force you all to leave. Tell all the Israelite men and women to ask their Egyptian neighbors for articles of silver and gold." (Now the LORD had caused the Egyptians to look favorably on the people of Israel. And Moses was considered a very great man in the land of Egypt, respected by Pharaoh's officials and the Egyptian people alike.)

Moses had announced to Pharaoh, "This is what the LORD says: At midnight tonight I will pass through the heart of Egypt. All the firstborn sons will die in every family in Egypt, from the oldest son of Pharaoh, who sits on his throne, to the oldest son of his lowliest servant girl who grinds the flour. Even the firstborn of all the livestock will die. Then a loud wail will rise throughout the land of Egypt, a wail like no one has heard before or will ever hear again. But among the Israelites it will be so peaceful that not even a dog will bark. Then you will know that the LORD makes a distinction between the Egyptians and the Israelites. All the officials of Egypt will run to me and fall to the ground before me. 'Please leave!' they will beg. 'Hurry! And take all your followers with you.' Only then will I go!" Then, burning with anger, Moses left Pharaoh.

Now the LORD had told Moses earlier, "Pharaoh will not listen to you, but then I will do even more mighty miracles in the land of Egypt." Moses and Aaron performed these miracles in Pharaoh's presence, but the LORD hardened Pharaoh's heart, and he wouldn't let the Israelites leave the country.

While the Israelites were still in the land of Egypt, the LORD gave the following instructions to Moses and Aaron: "From now on, this month will be the first month of the year for you. Announce to the whole community of Israel that on the tenth day of this month each family must choose a lamb or a young goat for a sacrifice, one animal for each household. If a family is too small to eat a whole animal, let them share with another family in the neighborhood. Divide the animal according to the size of each family and how much they can eat. The animal you select must be a one-year-old male, either a sheep or a goat, with no defects.

"Take special care of this chosen animal until the evening of the fourteenth day of this first month. Then the whole assembly of the community of Israel must slaughter their lamb or young goat at twilight. They are to take some of the blood and smear it on the sides and top of the doorframes of the houses where they eat the animal. That same night they must roast the meat over a fire and eat it along with bitter salad greens and bread made without yeast. Do not eat any of the meat raw or boiled in water. The whole animal—including the head, legs, and internal organs—must be roasted over a fire. Do not leave any of it until the next morning. Burn whatever is not eaten before morning.

"These are your instructions for eating this meal: Be fully dressed, wear your sandals, and carry your walking stick in your hand. Eat the meal with urgency, for this is the LORD's Passover. On that night I will pass through the land of Egypt and strike down every firstborn son and firstborn male animal in the land of Egypt. I will execute judgment against all the gods of Egypt, for I am the LORD! But the blood on your doorposts will serve as a sign, marking the houses where you are staying. When I see the blood, I will pass over you. This plague of death will not touch you when I strike the land of Egypt.

"This is a day to remember. Each year, from generation to generation, you must celebrate it as a special festival to the LORD. This is a law for all time. For seven days the bread you eat must be made without yeast. On the first day of the festival, remove every trace of yeast from your homes. Anyone who eats bread made with yeast during the seven days of the festival will be cut off from the community of Israel. On the first day of the festival and again on the seventh day, all the people must observe an official day for holy assembly. No work of any kind may be done on these days except in the preparation of food.

"Celebrate this Festival of Unleavened Bread, for it will remind you that I brought your forces out of the land of Egypt on this very day. This festival will be a permanent law for you; celebrate this day from generation to generation. The bread you eat must be made without yeast from the evening of the fourteenth day of the first month until the evening of the twenty-first day of that month. During those seven days, there must be no trace of yeast in your homes. Anyone who eats anything made with yeast during this week will be cut off from the community of Israel. These regulations apply both to the foreigners living among you and to the native-born Israelites. During those days you must not eat anything made with yeast. Wherever you live, eat only bread made without yeast."

Then Moses called all the elders of Israel together and said to them, "Go, pick out a lamb or young goat for each of your families, and slaughter the Passover animal. Drain the blood into a basin. Then take a bundle of hyssop branches and dip it into the blood. Brush the hyssop across the top and sides of the doorframes of your houses. And no one may go out through the door until morning. For the LORD will pass through the land to strike down the Egyptians. But when he sees the blood on the top and sides of the doorframe, the LORD will pass over your home. He will not permit his death angel to enter your house and strike you down.

"Remember, these instructions are a permanent law that you and your descendants must observe forever. When you enter the land the LORD has promised to give you, you will continue to observe this ceremony. Then your children will ask, 'What does this ceremony mean?' And you will reply, 'It is the Passover sacrifice to the LORD, for he passed over the houses of the Israelites in Egypt. And though he struck the Egyptians, he spared our families.'" When Moses had finished speaking, all the people bowed down to the ground and worshiped.

So the people of Israel did just as the LORD had commanded through Moses and Aaron.

And that night at midnight, the LORD struck down all the firstborn sons in the land of Egypt, from the firstborn son of Pharaoh, who sat on his throne, to the firstborn son of the prisoner in the dungeon. Even the firstborn of their livestock were killed. Pharaoh and all his officials and all the people of Egypt woke up during the night, and loud wailing was heard throughout the land of Egypt. There was not a single house where someone had not died.

Pharaoh sent for Moses and Aaron during the night. "Get out!" he ordered. "Leave my people—and take the rest of the Israelites with you! Go and worship the LORD as you have requested. Take your flocks and herds, as you said, and be gone. Go, but bless me as you leave." All the Egyptians urged the people of Israel to get out of the land as quickly as possible, for they thought, "We will all die!"

The Israelites took their bread dough before yeast was added. They wrapped their kneading boards in their cloaks and carried them on their shoulders. And the people of Israel did as Moses had instructed; they asked the Egyptians for clothing and articles of silver and gold. The LORD caused the Egyptians to look favorably on the Israelites, and they gave the Israelites whatever they asked for. So they stripped the Egyptians of their wealth!

That night the people of Israel left Rameses and started for Succoth. There were about 600,000 men, plus all the women and children. A rabble of non-Israelites went with them, along with great flocks and herds of livestock. For bread they baked flat cakes from the dough without yeast they had brought from Egypt. It was made without yeast because the people were driven out of Egypt in such a hurry that they had no time to prepare the bread or other food.

+ + +

The people of Israel had lived in Egypt for 430 years. In fact, it was on the last day of the 430th year that all the LORD's forces left the land. On this night the LORD kept his promise to bring his people out of the land of Egypt. So this night belongs to him, and it must be commemorated every year by all the Israelites, from generation to generation.

Then the LORD said to Moses and Aaron, "These are the instructions for the festival of Passover. No outsiders are allowed to eat the Passover meal. But any slave who has been purchased may eat it if he has been circumcised. Temporary residents and hired servants may not eat it. Each Passover lamb must be eaten in one house. Do not carry any of its meat outside, and do not break any of its bones. The whole community of Israel must celebrate this Passover festival.

"If there are foreigners living among you who want to celebrate the LORD's Passover, let all their males be circumcised. Only then may they celebrate the Passover with you like any native-born Israelite. But no uncircumcised male may ever eat the Passover meal. This instruction applies to everyone, whether a native-born Israelite or a foreigner living among you."

So all the people of Israel followed all the LORD's commands to Moses and Aaron. On that very day the LORD brought the people of Israel out of the land of Egypt like an army.

Then the LORD said to Moses, "Dedicate to me every firstborn among the Israelites. The first offspring to be born, of both humans and animals, belongs to me."

So Moses said to the people, "This is a day to remember forever—the day you left Egypt, the place of your slavery. Today the LORD has brought you out by the power of his mighty hand. (Remember, eat no food containing yeast.) On this day in early spring, in the month of Abib, you have been set free. You must celebrate this event in this month each year after the LORD brings you into the land of the Canaanites, Hittites, Amorites, Hivites, and Jebusites. (He swore to your ancestors that he would give you this land—a land flowing with milk and honey.) For seven days the bread you eat must be made without yeast. Then on the seventh day, celebrate a feast to the LORD. Eat bread without yeast during those seven days. In fact, there must be no yeast bread or any yeast at all found within the borders of your land during this time.

"On the seventh day you must explain to your children, 'I am celebrating what the LORD did for me when I left Egypt.' This annual festival will be a visible sign to you, like a mark branded on your hand or your forehead. Let it remind you always to recite this teaching of the LORD: 'With a strong hand, the LORD rescued you from Egypt.' So observe the decree of this festival at the appointed time each year.

"This is what you must do when the LORD fulfills the promise he swore to you and to your ancestors. When he gives you the land where the Canaanites now live, you must present all firstborn sons and firstborn male animals to the LORD, for they belong to him. A firstborn donkey may be bought back from the LORD by presenting a lamb or young goat in its place. But if you do not buy it back, you must break its neck. However, you must buy back every firstborn son.

"And in the future, your children will ask you, 'What does all this mean?' Then you will tell them, 'With the power of his mighty hand, the LORD brought us out of Egypt, the place of our slavery. Pharaoh stubbornly refused to let us go, so the LORD killed all the firstborn males throughout the land of Egypt, both people and animals. That is why I now sacrifice all the firstborn males to the LORD—except that the firstborn sons are always bought back.' This ceremony will be like a mark branded on your hand or your forehead. It is a reminder that the power of the LORD's mighty hand brought us out of Egypt."

+

When Pharaoh finally let the people go, God did not lead them along the main road that runs through Philistine territory, even though that was the shortest route to the Promised Land. God said, "If the people are faced with a battle, they might change their minds and return to Egypt." So God led them in a roundabout way through the wilderness toward the Red Sea. Thus the Israelites left Egypt like an army ready for battle.

Moses took the bones of Joseph with him, for Joseph had made the sons of Israel swear to do this. He said, "God will certainly come to help you. When he does, you must take my bones with you from this place."

The Israelites left Succoth and camped at Etham on the edge of the wilderness. The LORD went ahead of them. He guided them during the day with a pillar of cloud, and he provided light at night with a pillar of fire. This allowed them to travel by day or by night. And the LORD did not remove the pillar of cloud or pillar of fire from its place in front of the people.

+

Then the LORD gave these instructions to Moses: "Order the Israelites to turn back and camp by Pi-hahiroth between Migdol and the sea. Camp there along the shore, across from Baal-zephon. Then Pharaoh will think, 'The Israelites are confused. They are trapped in the wilderness!' And once again I will harden Pharaoh's heart, and he will chase after you. I have planned this in order to display my glory through Pharaoh and his whole army. After this the Egyptians will know that I am the LORD!" So the Israelites camped there as they were told.

When word reached the king of Egypt that the Israelites had fled, Pharaoh and his officials changed their minds. "What have we done, letting all those Israelite slaves get away?" they asked. So Pharaoh harnessed his chariot and called up his troops. He took with him 600 of Egypt's best chariots, along with the rest of the chariots of Egypt, each with its commander. The LORD hardened the heart of Pharaoh, the king of Egypt, so he chased after the people of Israel, who had left with fists raised in defiance. The Egyptians chased after them with all the forces in Pharaoh's army—all his horses and chariots, his charioteers, and his troops. The Egyptians caught up with the people of Israel as they were camped beside the shore near Pi-hahiroth, across from Baal-zephon.

As Pharaoh approached, the people of Israel looked up and panicked when they saw the Egyptians overtaking them. They cried out to the LORD, and they said to Moses, "Why did you bring us out here to die in the wilderness? Weren't there enough graves for us in Egypt? What have you done to us? Why did you make us leave Egypt? Didn't we tell you this would happen while we were still in Egypt? We said, 'Leave us alone! Let us be slaves to the Egyptians. It's better to be a slave in Egypt than a corpse in the wilderness!'"

But Moses told the people, "Don't be afraid. Just stand still and watch the LORD rescue you today. The Egyptians you see today will never be seen again. The LORD himself will fight for you. Just stay calm."

Then the LORD said to Moses, "Why are you crying out to me? Tell the people to get moving! Pick up your staff and raise your hand over the sea. Divide the water so the Israelites can walk through the middle of the sea on dry ground. And I will harden the hearts of the Egyptians, and they will charge in after the Israelites. My great glory will be displayed through Pharaoh and his troops, his chariots, and his charioteers. When my glory is displayed through them, all Egypt will see my glory and know that I am the LORD!"

Then the angel of God, who had been leading the people of Israel, moved to the rear of the camp. The pillar of cloud also moved from the front and stood behind them. The cloud settled between the Egyptian and Israelite camps. As darkness fell, the cloud turned to fire, lighting up the night. But the Egyptians and Israelites did not approach each other all night.

Then Moses raised his hand over the sea, and the LORD opened up a path through the water with a strong east wind. The wind blew all that night, turning the seabed into dry land. So the people of Israel walked through the middle of the sea on dry ground, with walls of water on each side!

Then the Egyptians—all of Pharaoh's horses, chariots, and charioteers—chased them into the middle of the sea. But just before dawn the LORD looked down on the Egyptian army from the pillar of fire and cloud, and he threw their forces into total confusion. He twisted their chariot wheels, making their chariots difficult to drive. "Let's get out of here—away from these Israelites!" the Egyptians shouted. "The LORD is fighting for them against Egypt!"

When all the Israelites had reached the other side, the LORD said to Moses, "Raise your hand over the sea again. Then the waters will rush back and cover the Egyptians and their chariots and charioteers." So as the sun began to rise, Moses raised his hand over the sea, and the water rushed back into its usual place. The Egyptians tried to escape, but the LORD swept them into the sea. Then the waters returned and covered all the chariots and charioteers—the entire army of Pharaoh. Of all the Egyptians who had chased the Israelites into the sea, not a single one survived.

But the people of Israel had walked through the middle of the sea on dry ground, as the water stood up like a wall on both sides. That is how the LORD rescued Israel from the hand of the Egyptians that day. And the Israelites saw the bodies of the Egyptians washed up on the seashore. When the people of Israel saw the mighty power that the LORD had unleashed against the Egyptians, they were filled with awe before him. They put their faith in the LORD and in his servant Moses.

Then Moses and the people of Israel sang this song to the LORD:

"I will sing to the LORD,
    for he has triumphed gloriously;
he has hurled both horse and rider
    into the sea.
The LORD is my strength and my song;
    he has given me victory.
This is my God, and I will praise him—
    my father's God, and I will exalt him!
The LORD is a warrior;
    Yahweh is his name!

Pharaoh's chariots and army
   he has hurled into the sea.
The finest of Pharaoh's officers
   are drowned in the Red Sea.
The deep waters gushed over them;
   they sank to the bottom like a stone.

"Your right hand, O Lord,
   is glorious in power.
Your right hand, O Lord,
   smashes the enemy.
In the greatness of your majesty,
   you overthrow those who rise against you.
You unleash your blazing fury;
   it consumes them like straw.
At the blast of your breath,
   the waters piled up!
The surging waters stood straight like a wall;
   in the heart of the sea the deep waters became hard.

"The enemy boasted, 'I will chase them
   and catch up with them.
I will plunder them
   and consume them.
I will flash my sword;
   my powerful hand will destroy them.'
But you blew with your breath,
   and the sea covered them.
They sank like lead
   in the mighty waters.

"Who is like you among the gods, O Lord—
   glorious in holiness,
awesome in splendor,
   performing great wonders?
You raised your right hand,
   and the earth swallowed our enemies.

"With your unfailing love you lead
   the people you have redeemed.
In your might, you guide them
   to your sacred home.
The peoples hear and tremble;
   anguish grips those who live in Philistia.

The leaders of Edom are terrified;
    the nobles of Moab tremble.
All who live in Canaan melt away;
    terror and dread fall upon them.
The power of your arm
    makes them lifeless as stone
until your people pass by, O Lord,
    until the people you purchased pass by.
You will bring them in and plant them on your own mountain—
    the place, O Lord, reserved for your own dwelling,
    the sanctuary, O Lord, that your hands have established.
The Lord will reign forever and ever!"

When Pharaoh's horses, chariots, and charioteers rushed into the sea, the Lord brought the water crashing down on them. But the people of Israel had walked through the middle of the sea on dry ground!

Then Miriam the prophet, Aaron's sister, took a tambourine and led all the women as they played their tambourines and danced. And Miriam sang this song:

"Sing to the Lord,
    for he has triumphed gloriously;
he has hurled both horse and rider
    into the sea."

+

Then Moses led the people of Israel away from the Red Sea, and they moved out into the desert of Shur. They traveled in this desert for three days without finding any water. When they came to the oasis of Marah, the water was too bitter to drink. So they called the place Marah (which means "bitter").

Then the people complained and turned against Moses. "What are we going to drink?" they demanded. So Moses cried out to the Lord for help, and the Lord showed him a piece of wood. Moses threw it into the water, and this made the water good to drink.

It was there at Marah that the Lord set before them the following decree as a standard to test their faithfulness to him. He said, "If you will listen carefully to the voice of the Lord your God and do what is right in his sight, obeying his commands and keeping all his decrees, then I will not make you suffer any of the diseases I sent on the Egyptians; for I am the Lord who heals you."

+

After leaving Marah, the Israelites traveled on to the oasis of Elim, where they found twelve springs and seventy palm trees. They camped there beside the water.

+

Then the whole community of Israel set out from Elim and journeyed into the wilderness of Sin, between Elim and Mount Sinai. They arrived there on the fifteenth day of the second month, one month after leaving the land of Egypt. There, too, the whole community of Israel complained about Moses and Aaron.

"If only the LORD had killed us back in Egypt," they moaned. "There we sat around pots filled with meat and ate all the bread we wanted. But now you have brought us into this wilderness to starve us all to death."

Then the LORD said to Moses, "Look, I'm going to rain down food from heaven for you. Each day the people can go out and pick up as much food as they need for that day. I will test them in this to see whether or not they will follow my instructions. On the sixth day they will gather food, and when they prepare it, there will be twice as much as usual."

So Moses and Aaron said to all the people of Israel, "By evening you will realize it was the LORD who brought you out of the land of Egypt. In the morning you will see the glory of the LORD, because he has heard your complaints, which are against him, not against us. What have we done that you should complain about us?" Then Moses added, "The LORD will give you meat to eat in the evening and bread to satisfy you in the morning, for he has heard all your complaints against him. What have we done? Yes, your complaints are against the LORD, not against us."

Then Moses said to Aaron, "Announce this to the entire community of Israel: 'Present yourselves before the LORD, for he has heard your complaining.'" And as Aaron spoke to the whole community of Israel, they looked out toward the wilderness. There they could see the awesome glory of the LORD in the cloud.

Then the LORD said to Moses, "I have heard the Israelites' complaints. Now tell them, 'In the evening you will have meat to eat, and in the morning you will have all the bread you want. Then you will know that I am the LORD your God.'"

That evening vast numbers of quail flew in and covered the camp. And the next morning the area around the camp was wet with dew. When the dew evaporated, a flaky substance as fine as frost blanketed the ground. The Israelites were puzzled when they saw it. "What is it?" they asked each other. They had no idea what it was.

And Moses told them, "It is the food the LORD has given you to eat.

These are the LORD's instructions: Each household should gather as much as it needs. Pick up two quarts for each person in your tent."

So the people of Israel did as they were told. Some gathered a lot, some only a little. But when they measured it out, everyone had just enough. Those who gathered a lot had nothing left over, and those who gathered only a little had enough. Each family had just what it needed.

Then Moses told them, "Do not keep any of it until morning." But some of them didn't listen and kept some of it until morning. But by then it was full of maggots and had a terrible smell. Moses was very angry with them.

After this the people gathered the food morning by morning, each family according to its need. And as the sun became hot, the flakes they had not picked up melted and disappeared. On the sixth day, they gathered twice as much as usual—four quarts for each person instead of two. Then all the leaders of the community came and asked Moses for an explanation. He told them, "This is what the LORD commanded: Tomorrow will be a day of complete rest, a holy Sabbath day set apart for the LORD. So bake or boil as much as you want today, and set aside what is left for tomorrow."

So they put some aside until morning, just as Moses had commanded. And in the morning the leftover food was wholesome and good, without maggots or odor. Moses said, "Eat this food today, for today is a Sabbath day dedicated to the LORD. There will be no food on the ground today. You may gather the food for six days, but the seventh day is the Sabbath. There will be no food on the ground that day."

Some of the people went out anyway on the seventh day, but they found no food. The LORD asked Moses, "How long will these people refuse to obey my commands and instructions? They must realize that the Sabbath is the LORD's gift to you. That is why he gives you a two-day supply on the sixth day, so there will be enough for two days. On the Sabbath day you must each stay in your place. Do not go out to pick up food on the seventh day." So the people did not gather any food on the seventh day.

The Israelites called the food manna. It was white like coriander seed, and it tasted like honey wafers.

Then Moses said, "This is what the LORD has commanded: Fill a two-quart container with manna to preserve it for your descendants. Then later generations will be able to see the food I gave you in the wilderness when I set you free from Egypt."

Moses said to Aaron, "Get a jar and fill it with two quarts of manna. Then put it in a sacred place before the LORD to preserve it for all future generations." Aaron did just as the LORD had commanded Moses. He eventually placed it in the Ark of the Covenant—in front of the stone tablets inscribed with the terms of the covenant. So the people of Israel ate manna for forty years until they arrived at the land where they would settle. They ate manna until they came to the border of the land of Canaan.

The container used to measure the manna was an omer, which was one-tenth of an ephah; it held about two quarts.

+

At the LORD's command, the whole community of Israel left the wilderness of Sin and moved from place to place. Eventually they camped at Rephidim, but there was no water there for the people to drink. So once more the people complained against Moses. "Give us water to drink!" they demanded.

"Quiet!" Moses replied. "Why are you complaining against me? And why are you testing the LORD?"

But tormented by thirst, they continued to argue with Moses. "Why did you bring us out of Egypt? Are you trying to kill us, our children, and our livestock with thirst?"

Then Moses cried out to the LORD, "What should I do with these people? They are ready to stone me!"

The LORD said to Moses, "Walk out in front of the people. Take your staff, the one you used when you struck the water of the Nile, and call some of the elders of Israel to join you. I will stand before you on the rock at Mount Sinai. Strike the rock, and water will come gushing out. Then the people will be able to drink." So Moses struck the rock as he was told, and water gushed out as the elders looked on.

Moses named the place Massah (which means "test") and Meribah (which means "arguing") because the people of Israel argued with Moses and tested the LORD by saying, "Is the LORD here with us or not?"

While the people of Israel were still at Rephidim, the warriors of Amalek attacked them. Moses commanded Joshua, "Choose some men to go out and fight the army of Amalek for us. Tomorrow, I will stand at the top of the hill, holding the staff of God in my hand."

So Joshua did what Moses had commanded and fought the army of Amalek. Meanwhile, Moses, Aaron, and Hur climbed to the top of a nearby hill. As long as Moses held up the staff in his hand, the Israelites had the advantage. But whenever he dropped his hand, the Amalekites gained the advantage. Moses' arms soon became so tired he could no longer hold them up. So Aaron and Hur found a stone for him to sit on. Then they stood on each side of Moses, holding up his hands. So his hands held steady until sunset. As a result, Joshua overwhelmed the army of Amalek in battle.

After the victory, the LORD instructed Moses, "Write this down on a scroll as a permanent reminder, and read it aloud to Joshua: I will erase the memory of Amalek from under heaven." Moses built an altar there and named it Yahweh-Nissi (which means "the LORD is my banner"). He said, "They have raised their fist against the LORD's throne, so now the LORD will be at war with Amalek generation after generation."

Moses' father-in-law, Jethro, the priest of Midian, heard about everything God had done for Moses and his people, the Israelites. He heard especially about how the LORD had rescued them from Egypt.

Earlier, Moses had sent his wife, Zipporah, and his two sons back to Jethro, who had taken them in. (Moses' first son was named Gershom, for Moses had said when the boy was born, "I have been a foreigner in a foreign land." His second son was named Eliezer, for Moses had said, "The God of my ancestors was my helper; he rescued me from the sword of Pharaoh.") Jethro, Moses' father-in-law, now came to visit Moses in the wilderness. He brought Moses' wife and two sons with him, and they arrived while Moses and the people were camped near the mountain of God. Jethro had sent a message to Moses, saying, "I, Jethro, your father-in-law, am coming to see you with your wife and your two sons."

So Moses went out to meet his father-in-law. He bowed low and kissed him. They asked about each other's welfare and then went into Moses' tent. Moses told his father-in-law everything the LORD had done to Pharaoh and Egypt on behalf of Israel. He also told about all the hardships they had experienced along the way and how the LORD had rescued his people from all their troubles. Jethro was delighted when he heard about all the good things the LORD had done for Israel as he rescued them from the hand of the Egyptians.

"Praise the LORD," Jethro said, "for he has rescued you from the Egyptians and from Pharaoh. Yes, he has rescued Israel from the powerful hand of Egypt! I know now that the LORD is greater than all other gods, because he rescued his people from the oppression of the proud Egyptians."

Then Jethro, Moses' father-in-law, brought a burnt offering and sacrifices to God. Aaron and all the elders of Israel came out and joined him in a sacrificial meal in God's presence.

The next day, Moses took his seat to hear the people's disputes against each other. They waited before him from morning till evening.

When Moses' father-in-law saw all that Moses was doing for the people, he asked, "What are you really accomplishing here? Why are you trying to do all this alone while everyone stands around you from morning till evening?"

Moses replied, "Because the people come to me to get a ruling from God. When a dispute arises, they come to me, and I am the one who settles the case between the quarreling parties. I inform the people of God's decrees and give them his instructions."

"This is not good!" Moses' father-in-law exclaimed. "You're going to wear yourself out—and the people, too. This job is too heavy a burden for you to handle all by yourself. Now listen to me, and let me give you a word of advice, and may God be with you. You should continue to be the people's representative before God, bringing their disputes to him. Teach them God's decrees, and give them his instructions. Show them how to conduct their lives. But select from all the people some capable, honest men who fear God and hate bribes. Appoint them as leaders over groups of one thousand, one hundred, fifty, and ten. They should always be available to solve the people's common disputes, but have them bring the major cases to you. Let the leaders decide the smaller matters themselves. They will help you carry the load, making the task easier for you. If you follow this advice, and if God commands you to do so, then you will be able to endure the pressures, and all these people will go home in peace."

Moses listened to his father-in-law's advice and followed his suggestions. He chose capable men from all over Israel and appointed them as leaders over the people. He put them in charge of groups of one thousand, one hundred, fifty, and ten. These men were always available to solve the people's common disputes. They brought the major cases to Moses, but they took care of the smaller matters themselves.

Soon after this, Moses said good-bye to his father-in-law, who returned to his own land.

+ + +

Exactly two months after the Israelites left Egypt, they arrived in the wilderness of Sinai. After breaking camp at Rephidim, they came to the wilderness of Sinai and set up camp there at the base of Mount Sinai.

Then Moses climbed the mountain to appear before God. The LORD called to him from the mountain and said, "Give these instructions to the family of Jacob; announce it to the descendants of Israel: 'You have seen what I did to the Egyptians. You know how I carried you on eagles' wings and brought you to myself. Now if you will obey me and keep my covenant, you will be my own special treasure from among all the peoples on earth; for all the earth belongs to me. And you will be my kingdom of priests, my holy nation.' This is the message you must give to the people of Israel."

So Moses returned from the mountain and called together the elders of the people and told them everything the LORD had commanded him. And all the people responded together, "We will do everything the LORD has commanded." So Moses brought the people's answer back to the LORD.

Then the LORD said to Moses, "I will come to you in a thick cloud, Moses, so the people themselves can hear me when I speak with you. Then they will always trust you."

Moses told the LORD what the people had said. Then the LORD told Moses, "Go down and prepare the people for my arrival. Consecrate them today and tomorrow, and have them wash their clothing. Be sure they are ready on the third day, for on that day the LORD will come down on Mount Sinai as all the people watch. Mark off a boundary all around the mountain. Warn the people, 'Be careful! Do not go up on the mountain or even touch its boundaries. Anyone who touches the mountain will certainly be put to death. No hand may touch the person or animal that crosses the boundary; instead, stone them or shoot them with arrows. They must be put to death.' However, when the ram's horn sounds a long blast, then the people may go up on the mountain."

So Moses went down to the people. He consecrated them for worship, and they washed their clothes. He told them, "Get ready for the third day, and until then abstain from having sexual intercourse."

On the morning of the third day, thunder roared and lightning flashed, and a dense cloud came down on the mountain. There was a long, loud blast from a ram's horn, and all the people trembled. Moses led them out from the camp to meet with God, and they stood at the foot of the mountain. All of Mount Sinai was covered with smoke because the LORD had descended on it in the form of fire. The smoke billowed into the sky like smoke from a brick kiln, and the whole mountain shook violently. As the blast of the ram's horn grew louder and louder, Moses spoke, and God thundered his reply. The LORD came down on the top of Mount Sinai and called Moses to the top of the mountain. So Moses climbed the mountain.

Then the LORD told Moses, "Go back down and warn the people not to break through the boundaries to see the LORD, or they will die. Even the priests who regularly come near to the LORD must purify themselves so that the LORD does not break out and destroy them."

"But LORD," Moses protested, "the people cannot come up to Mount Sinai. You already warned us. You told me, 'Mark off a boundary all around the mountain to set it apart as holy.'"

But the LORD said, "Go down and bring Aaron back up with you. In the meantime, do not let the priests or the people break through to approach the LORD, or he will break out and destroy them."

So Moses went down to the people and told them what the LORD had said.

Then God gave the people all these instructions:

"I am the LORD your God, who rescued you from the land of Egypt, the place of your slavery.

"You must not have any other god but me.

"You must not make for yourself an idol of any kind or an image of anything in the heavens or on the earth or in the sea. You must not bow down to them or worship them, for I, the LORD your God, am a jealous God who will not tolerate your affection for any other gods. I lay the sins of the parents upon their children; the entire family is affected—even children in the third and fourth generations of those who reject me. But I lavish unfailing love for a thousand generations on those who love me and obey my commands.

"You must not misuse the name of the LORD your God. The LORD will not let you go unpunished if you misuse his name.

"Remember to observe the Sabbath day by keeping it holy. You have six days each week for your ordinary work, but the seventh day is a Sabbath day of rest dedicated to the LORD your God. On that day no one in your household may do any work. This includes you, your sons and daughters, your male and female servants, your livestock, and any foreigners living among you. For in six days the LORD made the heavens, the earth, the sea, and everything in them; but on the seventh day he rested. That is why the LORD blessed the Sabbath day and set it apart as holy.

"Honor your father and mother. Then you will live a long, full life in the land the LORD your God is giving you.

"You must not murder.

"You must not commit adultery.

"You must not steal.

"You must not testify falsely against your neighbor.

"You must not covet your neighbor's house. You must not covet your neighbor's wife, male or female servant, ox or donkey, or anything else that belongs to your neighbor."

When the people heard the thunder and the loud blast of the ram's horn, and when they saw the flashes of lightning and the smoke billowing from the mountain, they stood at a distance, trembling with fear.

And they said to Moses, "You speak to us, and we will listen. But don't let God speak directly to us, or we will die!"

"Don't be afraid," Moses answered them, "for God has come in this way to test you, and so that your fear of him will keep you from sinning!"

As the people stood in the distance, Moses approached the dark cloud where God was.

And the LORD said to Moses, "Say this to the people of Israel: You saw for yourselves that I spoke to you from heaven. Remember, you must not make any idols of silver or gold to rival me.

"Build for me an altar made of earth, and offer your sacrifices to me—your burnt offerings and peace offerings, your sheep and goats, and your cattle. Build my altar wherever I cause my name to be remembered, and I will come to you and bless you. If you use stones to build my altar, use only natural, uncut stones. Do not shape the stones with a tool, for that would make the altar unfit for holy use. And do not approach my altar by going up steps. If you do, someone might look up under your clothing and see your nakedness.

"These are the regulations you must present to Israel.

"If you buy a Hebrew slave, he may serve for no more than six years. Set him free in the seventh year, and he will owe you nothing for his freedom. If he was single when he became your slave, he shall leave single. But if he was married before he became a slave, then his wife must be freed with him.

"If his master gave him a wife while he was a slave and they had sons or daughters, then only the man will be free in the seventh year, but his wife and children will still belong to his master. But the slave may declare, 'I love my master, my wife, and my children. I don't want to go free.' If he does this, his master must present him before God. Then his master must take him to the door or doorpost and publicly pierce his ear with an awl. After that, the slave will serve his master for life.

"When a man sells his daughter as a slave, she will not be freed at the end of six years as the men are. If she does not satisfy her owner, he must allow her to be bought back again. But he is not allowed to sell her to foreigners, since he is the one who broke the contract with her. But if the slave's owner arranges for her to marry his son, he may no longer treat her as a slave but as a daughter.

"If a man who has married a slave wife takes another wife for himself, he must not neglect the rights of the first wife to food, clothing, and sexual intimacy. If he fails in any of these three obligations, she may leave as a free woman without making any payment.

"Anyone who assaults and kills another person must be put to death. But if it was simply an accident permitted by God, I will appoint a place of refuge where the slayer can run for safety. However, if someone deliberately kills another person, then the slayer must be dragged even from my altar and be put to death.

"Anyone who strikes father or mother must be put to death.

"Kidnappers must be put to death, whether they are caught in possession of their victims or have already sold them as slaves.

"Anyone who dishonors father or mother must be put to death.

"Now suppose two men quarrel, and one hits the other with a stone or fist, and the injured person does not die but is confined to bed. If he is later able to walk outside again, even with a crutch, the assailant will not be punished but must compensate his victim for lost wages and provide for his full recovery.

"If a man beats his male or female slave with a club and the slave dies as a result, the owner must be punished. But if the slave recovers within a day or two, then the owner shall not be punished, since the slave is his property.

"Now suppose two men are fighting, and in the process they accidentally strike a pregnant woman so she gives birth prematurely. If no further injury results, the man who struck the woman must pay the amount of compensation the woman's husband demands and the judges approve. But if there is further injury, the punishment must match the injury: a life for a life, an eye for an eye, a tooth for a tooth, a hand for a hand, a foot for a foot, a burn for a burn, a wound for a wound, a bruise for a bruise.

"If a man hits his male or female slave in the eye and the eye is blinded, he must let the slave go free to compensate for the eye. And if a man knocks out the tooth of his male or female slave, he must let the slave go free to compensate for the tooth.

"If an ox gores a man or woman to death, the ox must be stoned, and its flesh may not be eaten. In such a case, however, the owner will not be held liable. But suppose the ox had a reputation for goring, and the owner had been informed but failed to keep it under control. If the ox then kills someone, it must be stoned, and the owner must also be put to death. However, the dead person's relatives may accept payment to compensate for the loss of life. The owner of the ox may redeem his life by paying whatever is demanded.

"The same regulation applies if the ox gores a boy or a girl. But if the ox gores a slave, either male or female, the animal's owner must pay the slave's owner thirty silver coins, and the ox must be stoned.

"Suppose someone digs or uncovers a pit and fails to cover it, and then an ox or a donkey falls into it. The owner of the pit must pay full compensation to the owner of the animal, but then he gets to keep the dead animal.

"If someone's ox injures a neighbor's ox and the injured ox dies, then the two owners must sell the live ox and divide the price equally between them. They must also divide the dead animal. But if the ox had a reputation for goring, yet its owner failed to keep it under control, he must pay full compensation—a live ox for the dead one—but he may keep the dead ox.

"If someone steals an ox or sheep and then kills or sells it, the thief must pay back five oxen for each ox stolen, and four sheep for each sheep stolen.

"If a thief is caught in the act of breaking into a house and is struck and killed in the process, the person who killed the thief is not guilty of murder. But if it happens in daylight, the one who killed the thief is guilty of murder.

"A thief who is caught must pay in full for everything he stole. If he cannot pay, he must be sold as a slave to pay for his theft. If someone steals an ox or a donkey or a sheep and it is found in the thief's possession, then the thief must pay double the value of the stolen animal.

"If an animal is grazing in a field or vineyard and the owner lets it stray into someone else's field to graze, then the animal's owner must pay compensation from the best of his own grain or grapes.

"If you are burning thornbushes and the fire gets out of control and spreads into another person's field, destroying the sheaves or the uncut grain or the whole crop, the one who started the fire must pay for the lost crop.

"Suppose someone leaves money or goods with a neighbor for safekeeping, and they are stolen from the neighbor's house. If the thief is caught, the compensation is double the value of what was stolen. But if the thief is not caught, the neighbor must appear before God, who will determine if he stole the property.

"Suppose there is a dispute between two people who both claim to own a particular ox, donkey, sheep, article of clothing, or any lost property. Both parties must come before God, and the person whom God declares guilty must pay double compensation to the other.

"Now suppose someone leaves a donkey, ox, sheep, or any other animal with a neighbor for safekeeping, but it dies or is injured or is taken away, and no one sees what happened. The neighbor must then take an oath in the presence of the LORD. If the LORD confirms that the neighbor did not steal the property, the owner must accept the verdict, and no payment will be required. But if the animal was indeed stolen, the guilty person must pay compensation to the owner. If it was torn to pieces by a wild animal, the remains of the carcass must be shown as evidence, and no compensation will be required.

"If someone borrows an animal from a neighbor and it is injured or dies when the owner is absent, the person who borrowed it must pay full compensation. But if the owner was present, no compensation is required.

And no compensation is required if the animal was rented, for this loss is covered by the rental fee.

"If a man seduces a virgin who is not engaged to anyone and has sex with her, he must pay the customary bride price and marry her. But if her father refuses to let him marry her, the man must still pay him an amount equal to the bride price of a virgin.

"You must not allow a sorceress to live.

"Anyone who has sexual relations with an animal must certainly be put to death.

"Anyone who sacrifices to any god other than the LORD must be destroyed.

"You must not mistreat or oppress foreigners in any way. Remember, you yourselves were once foreigners in the land of Egypt.

"You must not exploit a widow or an orphan. If you exploit them in any way and they cry out to me, then I will certainly hear their cry. My anger will blaze against you, and I will kill you with the sword. Then your wives will be widows and your children fatherless.

"If you lend money to any of my people who are in need, do not charge interest as a money lender would. If you take your neighbor's cloak as security for a loan, you must return it before sunset. This coat may be the only blanket your neighbor has. How can a person sleep without it? If you do not return it and your neighbor cries out to me for help, then I will hear, for I am merciful.

"You must not dishonor God or curse any of your rulers.

"You must not hold anything back when you give me offerings from your crops and your wine.

"You must give me your firstborn sons.

"You must also give me the firstborn of your cattle, sheep, and goats. But leave the newborn animal with its mother for seven days; then give it to me on the eighth day.

"You must be my holy people. Therefore, do not eat any animal that has been torn up and killed by wild animals. Throw it to the dogs.

"You must not pass along false rumors. You must not cooperate with evil people by lying on the witness stand.

"You must not follow the crowd in doing wrong. When you are called to testify in a dispute, do not be swayed by the crowd to twist justice. And do not slant your testimony in favor of a person just because that person is poor.

"If you come upon your enemy's ox or donkey that has strayed away, take it back to its owner. If you see that the donkey of someone who hates you has collapsed under its load, do not walk by. Instead, stop and help.

"In a lawsuit, you must not deny justice to the poor.

"Be sure never to charge anyone falsely with evil. Never sentence an innocent or blameless person to death, for I never declare a guilty person to be innocent.

"Take no bribes, for a bribe makes you ignore something that you clearly see. A bribe makes even a righteous person twist the truth.

"You must not oppress foreigners. You know what it's like to be a foreigner, for you yourselves were once foreigners in the land of Egypt.

"Plant and harvest your crops for six years, but let the land be renewed and lie uncultivated during the seventh year. Then let the poor among you harvest whatever grows on its own. Leave the rest for wild animals to eat. The same applies to your vineyards and olive groves.

"You have six days each week for your ordinary work, but on the seventh day you must stop working. This gives your ox and your donkey a chance to rest. It also allows your slaves and the foreigners living among you to be refreshed.

"Pay close attention to all my instructions. You must not call on the name of any other gods. Do not even speak their names.

"Each year you must celebrate three festivals in my honor. First, celebrate the Festival of Unleavened Bread. For seven days the bread you eat must be made without yeast, just as I commanded you. Celebrate this festival annually at the appointed time in early spring, in the month of Abib, for that is the anniversary of your departure from Egypt. No one may appear before me without an offering.

"Second, celebrate the Festival of Harvest, when you bring me the first crops of your harvest.

"Finally, celebrate the Festival of the Final Harvest at the end of the harvest season, when you have harvested all the crops from your fields. At these three times each year, every man in Israel must appear before the Sovereign, the LORD.

"You must not offer the blood of my sacrificial offerings together with any baked goods containing yeast. And do not leave the fat from the festival offerings until the next morning.

"As you harvest your crops, bring the very best of the first harvest to the house of the LORD your God.

"You must not cook a young goat in its mother's milk.

"See, I am sending an angel before you to protect you on your journey and lead you safely to the place I have prepared for you. Pay close attention to him, and obey his instructions. Do not rebel against him, for he is my representative, and he will not forgive your rebellion. But if you are careful to obey him, following all my instructions, then I will be an enemy to your enemies, and I will oppose those who oppose you. For my angel will go before you and bring you into the land of the Amorites, Hittites, Perizzites, Canaanites, Hivites, and Jebusites, so you may live there. And I will destroy them completely. You must not worship the gods of these nations or serve them in any way or imitate their evil practices. Instead, you must utterly destroy them and smash their sacred pillars.

"You must serve only the LORD your God. If you do, I will bless you with food and water, and I will protect you from illness. There will be no miscarriages or infertility in your land, and I will give you long, full lives.

"I will send my terror ahead of you and create panic among all the people whose lands you invade. I will make all your enemies turn and run. I will send terror ahead of you to drive out the Hivites, Canaanites, and Hittites. But I will not drive them out in a single year, because the land would become desolate and the wild animals would multiply and threaten you. I will drive them out a little at a time until your population has increased enough to take possession of the land. And I will fix your boundaries from the Red Sea to the Mediterranean Sea, and from the eastern wilderness to the Euphrates River. I will hand over to you the people now living in the land, and you will drive them out ahead of you.

"Make no treaties with them or their gods. They must not live in your land, or they will cause you to sin against me. If you serve their gods, you will be caught in the trap of idolatry."

Then the LORD instructed Moses: "Come up here to me, and bring along Aaron, Nadab, Abihu, and seventy of Israel's elders. All of you must worship from a distance. Only Moses is allowed to come near to the LORD. The others must not come near, and none of the other people are allowed to climb up the mountain with him."

Then Moses went down to the people and repeated all the instructions and regulations the LORD had given him. All the people answered with one voice, "We will do everything the LORD has commanded."

Then Moses carefully wrote down all the LORD's instructions. Early the next morning Moses got up and built an altar at the foot of the mountain. He also set up twelve pillars, one for each of the twelve tribes of Israel. Then he sent some of the young Israelite men to present burnt offerings and to sacrifice bulls as peace offerings to the LORD. Moses drained half the blood from these animals into basins. The other half he splattered against the altar.

Then he took the Book of the Covenant and read it aloud to the people.

Again they all responded, "We will do everything the LORD has commanded. We will obey."

Then Moses took the blood from the basins and splattered it over the people, declaring, "Look, this blood confirms the covenant the LORD has made with you in giving you these instructions."

Then Moses, Aaron, Nadab, Abihu, and the seventy elders of Israel climbed up the mountain. There they saw the God of Israel. Under his feet there seemed to be a surface of brilliant blue lapis lazuli, as clear as the sky itself. And though these nobles of Israel gazed upon God, he did not destroy them. In fact, they ate a covenant meal, eating and drinking in his presence!

Then the LORD said to Moses, "Come up to me on the mountain. Stay there, and I will give you the tablets of stone on which I have inscribed the instructions and commands so you can teach the people." So Moses and his assistant Joshua set out, and Moses climbed up the mountain of God.

Moses told the elders, "Stay here and wait for us until we come back. Aaron and Hur are here with you. If anyone has a dispute while I am gone, consult with them."

Then Moses climbed up the mountain, and the cloud covered it. And the glory of the LORD settled down on Mount Sinai, and the cloud covered it for six days. On the seventh day the LORD called to Moses from inside the cloud. To the Israelites at the foot of the mountain, the glory of the LORD appeared at the summit like a consuming fire. Then Moses disappeared into the cloud as he climbed higher up the mountain. He remained on the mountain forty days and forty nights.

+ + +

The LORD said to Moses, "Tell the people of Israel to bring me their sacred offerings. Accept the contributions from all whose hearts are moved to offer them. Here is a list of sacred offerings you may accept from them:

gold, silver, and bronze;
blue, purple, and scarlet thread;
fine linen and goat hair for cloth;
tanned ram skins and fine goatskin leather;
acacia wood;
olive oil for the lamps;
spices for the anointing oil and the fragrant incense;
onyx stones, and other gemstones to be set in the ephod and the
priest's chestpiece.

"Have the people of Israel build me a holy sanctuary so I can live among them. You must build this Tabernacle and its furnishings exactly according to the pattern I will show you.

"Have the people make an Ark of acacia wood—a sacred chest 45 inches long, 27 inches wide, and 27 inches high. Overlay it inside and outside with pure gold, and run a molding of gold all around it. Cast four gold rings and attach them to its four feet, two rings on each side. Make poles from acacia wood, and overlay them with gold. Insert the poles into the rings at the sides of the Ark to carry it. These carrying poles must stay inside the rings; never remove them. When the Ark is finished, place inside it the stone tablets inscribed with the terms of the covenant, which I will give to you.

"Then make the Ark's cover—the place of atonement—from pure gold. It must be 45 inches long and 27 inches wide. Then make two cherubim from hammered gold, and place them on the two ends of the atonement cover. Mold the cherubim on each end of the atonement cover, making it all of one piece of gold. The cherubim will face each other and look down on the atonement cover. With their wings spread above it, they will protect it. Place inside the Ark the stone tablets inscribed with the terms of the covenant, which I will give to you. Then put the atonement cover on top of the Ark. I will meet with you there and talk to you from above the atonement cover between the gold cherubim that hover over the Ark of the Covenant. From there I will give you my commands for the people of Israel.

"Then make a table of acacia wood, 36 inches long, 18 inches wide, and 27 inches high. Overlay it with pure gold and run a gold molding around the edge. Decorate it with a 3-inch border all around, and run a gold molding along the border. Make four gold rings for the table and attach them at the four corners next to the four legs. Attach the rings near the border to hold the poles that are used to carry the table. Make these poles from acacia wood, and overlay them with gold. Make special containers of pure gold for the table—bowls, ladles, pitchers, and jars—to be used in pouring out liquid offerings. Place the Bread of the Presence on the table to remain before me at all times.

"Make a lampstand of pure, hammered gold. Make the entire lampstand and its decorations of one piece—the base, center stem, lamp cups, buds, and petals. Make it with six branches going out from the center stem, three on each side. Each of the six branches will have three lamp cups shaped like almond blossoms, complete with buds and petals. Craft the center stem of the lampstand with four lamp cups shaped like almond blossoms, complete with buds and petals. There will also be an almond bud beneath each pair of branches where the six branches extend from the center stem. The almond buds and branches must all be of one piece with the center stem, and they must be hammered from pure gold. Then make the seven lamps for the lampstand, and set them so they reflect their light forward. The lamp snuffers and trays must also be made of pure gold. You will need 75 pounds of pure gold for the lampstand and its accessories.

"Be sure that you make everything according to the pattern I have shown you here on the mountain.

"Make the Tabernacle from ten curtains of finely woven linen. Decorate the curtains with blue, purple, and scarlet thread and with skillfully embroidered cherubim. These ten curtains must all be exactly the same size—42 feet long and 6 feet wide. Join five of these curtains together to make one long curtain, then join the other five into a second long curtain. Put loops of blue yarn along the edge of the last curtain in each set. The fifty loops along the edge of one curtain are to match the fifty loops along the edge of the other curtain. Then make fifty gold clasps and fasten the long curtains together with the clasps. In this way, the Tabernacle will be made of one continuous piece.

"Make eleven curtains of goat-hair cloth to serve as a tent covering for the Tabernacle. These eleven curtains must all be exactly the same size—45 feet long and 6 feet wide. Join five of these curtains together to make one long curtain, and join the other six into a second long curtain. Allow 3 feet of material from the second set of curtains to hang over the front of the sacred tent. Make fifty loops for one edge of each large curtain. Then make fifty bronze clasps, and fasten the loops of the long curtains with the clasps. In this way, the tent covering will be made of one continuous piece. The remaining 3 feet of this tent covering will be left to hang over the back of the Tabernacle. Allow 18 inches of remaining material to hang down over each side, so the Tabernacle is completely covered. Complete the tent covering with a protective layer of tanned ram skins and a layer of fine goatskin leather.

"For the framework of the Tabernacle, construct frames of acacia wood. Each frame must be 15 feet high and 27 inches wide, with two pegs under each frame. Make all the frames identical. Make twenty of these frames to support the curtains on the south side of the Tabernacle. Also make forty silver bases—two bases under each frame, with the pegs fitting securely into the bases. For the north side of the Tabernacle, make another twenty frames, with their forty silver bases, two bases under each frame. Make six frames for the rear—the west side of the Tabernacle—along with two additional frames to reinforce the rear corners of the Tabernacle. These corner frames will be matched at the bottom and firmly attached at the top with a single ring, forming a single corner unit. Make both of these corner units the same way. So there will be eight frames at the rear of the Tabernacle, set in sixteen silver bases—two bases under each frame.

"Make crossbars of acacia wood to link the frames, five crossbars for the north side of the Tabernacle and five for the south side. Also make five crossbars for the rear of the Tabernacle, which will face west. The middle crossbar, attached halfway up the frames, will run all the way from one end of the Tabernacle to the other. Overlay the frames with gold, and make gold rings to hold the crossbars. Overlay the crossbars with gold as well.

"Set up this Tabernacle according to the pattern you were shown on the mountain.

"For the inside of the Tabernacle, make a special curtain of finely woven linen. Decorate it with blue, purple, and scarlet thread and with skillfully embroidered cherubim. Hang this curtain on gold hooks attached to four posts of acacia wood. Overlay the posts with gold, and set them in four silver bases. Hang the inner curtain from clasps, and put the Ark of the Covenant in the room behind it. This curtain will separate the Holy Place from the Most Holy Place.

"Then put the Ark's cover—the place of atonement—on top of the Ark of the Covenant inside the Most Holy Place. Place the table outside the inner curtain on the north side of the Tabernacle, and place the lampstand across the room on the south side.

"Make another curtain for the entrance to the sacred tent. Make it of finely woven linen and embroider it with exquisite designs, using blue, purple, and scarlet thread. Craft five posts from acacia wood. Overlay them with gold, and hang the curtain from them with gold hooks. Cast five bronze bases for the posts.

"Using acacia wood, construct a square altar 7½ feet wide, 7½ feet long, and 4½ feet high. Make horns for each of its four corners so that the horns and altar are all one piece. Overlay the altar with bronze. Make ash buckets, shovels, basins, meat forks, and firepans, all of bronze. Make a bronze grating for it, and attach four bronze rings at its four corners. Install the grating halfway down the side of the altar, under the ledge. For carrying the altar, make poles from acacia wood, and overlay them with bronze. Insert the poles through the rings on the two sides of the altar. The altar must be hollow, made from planks. Build it just as you were shown on the mountain.

"Then make the courtyard for the Tabernacle, enclosed with curtains made of finely woven linen. On the south side, make the curtains 150 feet long. They will be held up by twenty posts set securely in twenty bronze bases. Hang the curtains with silver hooks and rings. Make the curtains the same on the north side—150 feet of curtains held up by twenty posts set securely in bronze bases. Hang the curtains with silver hooks and rings. The curtains on the west end of the courtyard will be 75 feet long, supported by ten posts set into ten bases. The east end of the courtyard, the front, will also be 75 feet long. The courtyard entrance will be on the east end, flanked by two curtains. The curtain on the right side will be 22½ feet long, supported by three posts set into three bases. The curtain on the left side will also be 22½ feet long, supported by three posts set into three bases.

"For the entrance to the courtyard, make a curtain that is 30 feet long. Make it from finely woven linen, and decorate it with beautiful embroidery in blue, purple, and scarlet thread. Support it with four posts, each securely set in its own base. All the posts around the courtyard must have silver rings and hooks and bronze bases. So the entire courtyard will be 150 feet long and 75 feet wide, with curtain walls 7½ feet high, made from finely woven linen. The bases for the posts will be made of bronze.

"All the articles used in the rituals of the Tabernacle, including all the tent pegs used to support the Tabernacle and the courtyard curtains, must be made of bronze.

"Command the people of Israel to bring you pure oil of pressed olives for the light, to keep the lamps burning continually. The lampstand will stand in the Tabernacle, in front of the inner curtain that shields the Ark of the Covenant. Aaron and his sons must keep the lamps burning in the LORD's presence all night. This is a permanent law for the people of Israel, and it must be observed from generation to generation.

+

"Call for your brother, Aaron, and his sons, Nadab, Abihu, Eleazar, and Ithamar. Set them apart from the rest of the people of Israel so they may minister to me and be my priests. Make sacred garments for Aaron that are glorious and beautiful. Instruct all the skilled craftsmen whom I have filled with the spirit of wisdom. Have them make garments for Aaron that will distinguish him as a priest set apart for my service. These are the garments they are to make: a chestpiece, an ephod, a robe, a patterned tunic, a turban, and a sash. They are to make these sacred garments for your brother, Aaron, and his sons to wear when they serve me as priests. So give them fine linen cloth, gold thread, and blue, purple, and scarlet thread.

"The craftsmen must make the ephod of finely woven linen and skillfully embroider it with gold and with blue, purple, and scarlet thread. It will consist of two pieces, front and back, joined at the shoulders with two shoulder-pieces. The decorative sash will be made of the same materials: finely woven linen embroidered with gold and with blue, purple, and scarlet thread.

"Take two onyx stones, and engrave on them the names of the tribes of Israel. Six names will be on each stone, arranged in the order of the births of the original sons of Israel. Engrave these names on the two stones in the same way a jeweler engraves a seal. Then mount the stones in settings of gold filigree. Fasten the two stones on the shoulder-pieces of the ephod as a reminder that Aaron represents the people of Israel. Aaron will carry these names on his shoulders as a constant reminder whenever he goes before the LORD. Make the settings of gold filigree, then braid two cords of pure gold and attach them to the filigree settings on the shoulders of the ephod.

"Then, with great skill and care, make a chestpiece to be worn for seeking a decision from God. Make it to match the ephod, using finely woven linen embroidered with gold and with blue, purple, and scarlet thread. Make the chestpiece of a single piece of cloth folded to form a pouch nine inches square. Mount four rows of gemstones on it. The first row will contain a red carnelian, a pale-green peridot, and an emerald. The second row will contain a turquoise, a blue lapis lazuli, and a white moonstone. The third row will contain an orange jacinth, an agate, and a purple amethyst. The fourth row will contain a blue-green beryl, an onyx, and a green jasper. All these stones will be set in gold filigree. Each stone will represent one of the twelve sons of Israel, and the name of that tribe will be engraved on it like a seal.

"To attach the chestpiece to the ephod, make braided cords of pure gold thread. Then make two gold rings and attach them to the top corners of the chestpiece. Tie the two gold cords to the two rings on the chestpiece. Tie the other ends of the cords to the gold settings on the shoulder-pieces of the ephod. Then make two more gold rings and attach them to the inside edges of the chestpiece next to the ephod. And make two more gold rings and attach them to the front of the ephod, below the shoulder-pieces, just above the knot where the decorative sash is fastened to the ephod. Then attach the bottom rings of the chestpiece to the rings on the ephod with blue cords. This will hold the chestpiece securely to the ephod above the decorative sash.

"In this way, Aaron will carry the names of the tribes of Israel on the sacred chestpiece over his heart when he goes into the Holy Place. This will be a continual reminder that he represents the people when he comes before the LORD. Insert the Urim and Thummim into the sacred chestpiece so they will be carried over Aaron's heart when he goes into the LORD's presence. In this way, Aaron will always carry over his heart the objects used to determine the LORD's will for his people whenever he goes in before the LORD.

"Make the robe that is worn with the ephod from a single piece of blue cloth, with an opening for Aaron's head in the middle of it. Reinforce the opening with a woven collar so it will not tear. Make pomegranates out of blue, purple, and scarlet yarn, and attach them to the hem of the robe, with gold bells between them. The gold bells and pomegranates are to alternate all around the hem. Aaron will wear this robe whenever he ministers before the LORD, and the bells will tinkle as he goes in and out of the LORD's presence in the Holy Place. If he wears it, he will not die.

"Next make a medallion of pure gold, and engrave it like a seal with these words: HOLY TO THE LORD. Attach the medallion with a blue cord to the front of Aaron's turban, where it must remain. Aaron must wear it on his forehead so he may take on himself any guilt of the people of Israel when they consecrate their sacred offerings. He must always wear it on his forehead so the LORD will accept the people.

"Weave Aaron's patterned tunic from fine linen cloth. Fashion the turban from this linen as well. Also make a sash, and decorate it with colorful embroidery.

"For Aaron's sons, make tunics, sashes, and special head coverings that are glorious and beautiful. Clothe your brother, Aaron, and his sons with these garments, and then anoint and ordain them. Consecrate them so they can serve as my priests. Also make linen undergarments for them, to be worn next to their bodies, reaching from their hips to their thighs. These must be worn whenever Aaron and his sons enter the Tabernacle or approach the altar in the Holy Place to perform their priestly duties. Then they will not incur guilt and die. This is a permanent law for Aaron and all his descendants after him.

"This is the ceremony you must follow when you consecrate Aaron and his sons to serve me as priests: Take a young bull and two rams with no defects. Then, using choice wheat flour and no yeast, make loaves of bread, thin cakes mixed with olive oil, and wafers spread with oil. Place them all in a single basket, and present them at the entrance of the Tabernacle, along with the young bull and the two rams.

"Present Aaron and his sons at the entrance of the Tabernacle, and wash them with water. Dress Aaron in his priestly garments—the tunic, the robe worn with the ephod, the ephod itself, and the chestpiece. Then wrap the decorative sash of the ephod around him. Place the turban on his head, and fasten the sacred medallion to the turban. Then anoint him by pouring the anointing oil over his head. Next present his sons, and dress them in their tunics. Wrap the sashes around the waists of Aaron and his sons, and put their special head coverings on them. Then the right to the priesthood will be theirs by law forever. In this way, you will ordain Aaron and his sons.

"Bring the young bull to the entrance of the Tabernacle, where Aaron and his sons will lay their hands on its head. Then slaughter the bull in the LORD's presence at the entrance of the Tabernacle. Put some of its blood on the horns of the altar with your finger, and pour out the rest at the base of the altar. Take all the fat around the internal organs, the long lobe of the liver, and the two kidneys and the fat around them, and burn it all on the altar. Then take the rest of the bull, including its hide, meat, and dung, and burn it outside the camp as a sin offering.

"Next Aaron and his sons must lay their hands on the head of one of the rams. Then slaughter the ram, and splatter its blood against all sides of the altar. Cut the ram into pieces, and wash off the internal organs and the legs. Set them alongside the head and the other pieces of the body, then burn the entire animal on the altar. This is a burnt offering to the LORD; it is a pleasing aroma, a special gift presented to the LORD.

"Now take the other ram, and have Aaron and his sons lay their hands on its head. Then slaughter it, and apply some of its blood to the right earlobes of Aaron and his sons. Also put it on the thumbs of their right hands and the big toes of their right feet. Splatter the rest of the blood against all sides of the altar. Then take some of the blood from the altar and some of the anointing oil, and sprinkle it on Aaron and his sons and on their garments. In this way, they and their garments will be set apart as holy.

"Since this is the ram for the ordination of Aaron and his sons, take the fat of the ram, including the fat of the broad tail, the fat around the internal organs, the long lobe of the liver, and the two kidneys and the fat around them, along with the right thigh. Then take one round loaf of bread, one thin cake mixed with olive oil, and one wafer from the basket of bread without yeast that was placed in the LORD's presence. Put all these in the hands of Aaron and his sons to be lifted up as a special offering to the LORD. Afterward take the various breads from their hands, and burn them on the altar along with the burnt offering. It is a pleasing aroma to the LORD, a special gift for him. Then take the breast of Aaron's ordination ram, and lift it up in the LORD's presence as a special offering to him. Then keep it as your own portion.

"Set aside the portions of the ordination ram that belong to Aaron and his sons. This includes the breast and the thigh that were lifted up before the LORD as a special offering. In the future, whenever the people of Israel lift up a peace offering, a portion of it must be set aside for Aaron and his descendants. This is their permanent right, and it is a sacred offering from the Israelites to the LORD.

"Aaron's sacred garments must be preserved for his descendants who succeed him, and they will wear them when they are anointed and ordained. The descendant who succeeds him as high priest will wear these clothes for seven days as he ministers in the Tabernacle and the Holy Place.

"Take the ram used in the ordination ceremony, and boil its meat in a sacred place. Then Aaron and his sons will eat this meat, along with the bread in the basket, at the Tabernacle entrance. They alone may eat the meat and bread used for their purification in the ordination ceremony. No one else may eat them, for these things are set apart and holy. If any of the ordination meat or bread remains until the morning, it must be burned. It may not be eaten, for it is holy.

"This is how you will ordain Aaron and his sons to their offices, just as I have commanded you. The ordination ceremony will go on for seven days. Each day you must sacrifice a young bull as a sin offering to purify them, making them right with the LORD. Afterward, cleanse the altar by purifying it; make it holy by anointing it with oil. Purify the altar, and consecrate it every day for seven days. After that, the altar will be absolutely holy, and whatever touches it will become holy.

"These are the sacrifices you are to offer regularly on the altar. Each day, offer two lambs that are a year old, one in the morning and the other in the evening. With one of them, offer two quarts of choice flour mixed with one quart of pure oil of pressed olives; also, offer one quart of wine as a liquid offering. Offer the other lamb in the evening, along with the same offerings of flour and wine as in the morning. It will be a pleasing aroma, a special gift presented to the LORD.

"These burnt offerings are to be made each day from generation to generation. Offer them in the LORD's presence at the Tabernacle entrance; there I will meet with you and speak with you. I will meet the people of Israel there, in the place made holy by my glorious presence. Yes, I will consecrate the Tabernacle and the altar, and I will consecrate Aaron and his sons to serve me as priests. Then I will live among the people of Israel and be their God, and they will know that I am the LORD their God. I am the one who brought them out of the land of Egypt so that I could live among them. I am the LORD their God.

+

"Then make another altar of acacia wood for burning incense. Make it 18 inches square and 36 inches high, with horns at the corners carved from the same piece of wood as the altar itself. Overlay the top, sides, and horns of the altar with pure gold, and run a gold molding around the entire altar. Make two gold rings, and attach them on opposite sides of the altar below the gold molding to hold the carrying poles. Make the poles of acacia wood and overlay them with gold. Place the incense altar just outside the inner curtain that shields the Ark of the Covenant, in front of the Ark's cover—the place of atonement—that covers the tablets inscribed with the terms of the covenant. I will meet with you there.

"Every morning when Aaron maintains the lamps, he must burn fragrant incense on the altar. And each evening when he lights the lamps, he must again burn incense in the LORD's presence. This must be done from generation to generation. Do not offer any unholy incense on this altar, or any burnt offerings, grain offerings, or liquid offerings.

"Once a year Aaron must purify the altar by smearing its horns with blood from the offering made to purify the people from their sin. This will be a regular, annual event from generation to generation, for this is the LORD's most holy altar."

Then the LORD said to Moses, "Whenever you take a census of the people of Israel, each man who is counted must pay a ransom for himself to the LORD. Then no plague will strike the people as you count them. Each person who is counted must give a small piece of silver as a sacred offering to the LORD. (This payment is half a shekel, based on the sanctuary shekel, which equals twenty gerahs.) All who have reached their twentieth birthday must give this sacred offering to the LORD. When this offering is given to the LORD to purify your lives, making you right with him, the rich must not give more than the specified amount, and the poor must not give less. Receive this ransom money from the Israelites, and use it for the care of the Tabernacle. It will bring the Israelites to the LORD's attention, and it will purify your lives."

Then the LORD said to Moses, "Make a bronze washbasin with a bronze stand. Place it between the Tabernacle and the altar, and fill it with water. Aaron and his sons will wash their hands and feet there. They must wash with water whenever they go into the Tabernacle to appear before the LORD and when they approach the altar to burn up their special gifts to the LORD—or they will die! They must always wash their hands and feet, or they will die. This is a permanent law for Aaron and his descendants, to be observed from generation to generation."

Then the LORD said to Moses, "Collect choice spices—12½ pounds of pure myrrh, 6¼ pounds of fragrant cinnamon, 6¼ pounds of fragrant calamus, and 12½ pounds of cassia—as measured by the weight of the sanctuary shekel. Also get one gallon of olive oil. Like a skilled incense maker, blend these ingredients to make a holy anointing oil. Use this sacred oil to anoint the Tabernacle, the Ark of the Covenant, the table and all its utensils, the lampstand and all its accessories, the incense altar, the altar of burnt offering and all its utensils, and the washbasin with its stand. Consecrate them to make them absolutely holy. After this, whatever touches them will also become holy.

"Anoint Aaron and his sons also, consecrating them to serve me as priests. And say to the people of Israel, 'This holy anointing oil is reserved for me from generation to generation. It must never be used to anoint anyone else, and you must never make any blend like it for yourselves. It is holy, and you must treat it as holy. Anyone who makes a blend like it or anoints someone other than a priest will be cut off from the community.'"

Then the LORD said to Moses, "Gather fragrant spices—resin droplets, mollusk shell, and galbanum—and mix these fragrant spices with pure frankincense, weighed out in equal amounts. Using the usual techniques of the incense maker, blend the spices together and sprinkle them with salt to produce a pure and holy incense. Grind some of the mixture into a very fine powder and put it in front of the Ark of the Covenant, where I will meet with you in the Tabernacle. You must treat this incense as most holy. Never use this formula to make this incense for yourselves. It is reserved for the LORD, and you must treat it as holy. Anyone who makes incense like this for personal use will be cut off from the community."

+

Then the LORD said to Moses, "Look, I have specifically chosen Bezalel son of Uri, grandson of Hur, of the tribe of Judah. I have filled him with the Spirit of God, giving him great wisdom, ability, and expertise in all kinds of crafts. He is a master craftsman, expert in working with gold, silver, and bronze. He is skilled in engraving and mounting gemstones and in carving wood. He is a master at every craft!

"And I have personally appointed Oholiab son of Ahisamach, of the tribe of Dan, to be his assistant. Moreover, I have given special skill to all the gifted craftsmen so they can make all the things I have commanded you to make:

the Tabernacle;
the Ark of the Covenant;

the Ark's cover—the place of atonement;
all the furnishings of the Tabernacle;
the table and its utensils;
the pure gold lampstand with all its accessories;
the incense altar;
the altar of burnt offering with all its utensils;
the washbasin with its stand;
the beautifully stitched garments—the sacred garments for Aaron
   the priest, and the garments for his sons to wear as they minister as
   priests;
the anointing oil;
the fragrant incense for the Holy Place.

The craftsmen must make everything as I have commanded you."

The LORD then gave these instructions to Moses: "Tell the people of Israel: 'Be careful to keep my Sabbath day, for the Sabbath is a sign of the covenant between me and you from generation to generation. It is given so you may know that I am the LORD, who makes you holy. You must keep the Sabbath day, for it is a holy day for you. Anyone who desecrates it must be put to death; anyone who works on that day will be cut off from the community. You have six days each week for your ordinary work, but the seventh day must be a Sabbath day of complete rest, a holy day dedicated to the LORD. Anyone who works on the Sabbath must be put to death. The people of Israel must keep the Sabbath day by observing it from generation to generation. This is a covenant obligation for all time. It is a permanent sign of my covenant with the people of Israel. For in six days the LORD made heaven and earth, but on the seventh day he stopped working and was refreshed.'"

When the LORD finished speaking with Moses on Mount Sinai, he gave him the two stone tablets inscribed with the terms of the covenant, written by the finger of God.

✢ ✢ ✢

When the people saw how long it was taking Moses to come back down the mountain, they gathered around Aaron. "Come on," they said, "make us some gods who can lead us. We don't know what happened to this fellow Moses, who brought us here from the land of Egypt."

So Aaron said, "Take the gold rings from the ears of your wives and sons and daughters, and bring them to me."

All the people took the gold rings from their ears and brought them to Aaron. Then Aaron took the gold, melted it down, and molded it into the shape of a calf. When the people saw it, they exclaimed, "O Israel, these are the gods who brought you out of the land of Egypt!"

Aaron saw how excited the people were, so he built an altar in front of the calf. Then he announced, "Tomorrow will be a festival to the LORD!"

The people got up early the next morning to sacrifice burnt offerings and peace offerings. After this, they celebrated with feasting and drinking, and they indulged in pagan revelry.

The LORD told Moses, "Quick! Go down the mountain! Your people whom you brought from the land of Egypt have corrupted themselves. How quickly they have turned away from the way I commanded them to live! They have melted down gold and made a calf, and they have bowed down and sacrificed to it. They are saying, 'These are your gods, O Israel, who brought you out of the land of Egypt.'"

Then the LORD said, "I have seen how stubborn and rebellious these people are. Now leave me alone so my fierce anger can blaze against them, and I will destroy them. Then I will make you, Moses, into a great nation."

But Moses tried to pacify the LORD his God. "O LORD!" he said. "Why are you so angry with your own people whom you brought from the land of Egypt with such great power and such a strong hand? Why let the Egyptians say, 'Their God rescued them with the evil intention of slaughtering them in the mountains and wiping them from the face of the earth'? Turn away from your fierce anger. Change your mind about this terrible disaster you have threatened against your people! Remember your servants Abraham, Isaac, and Jacob. You bound yourself with an oath to them, saying, 'I will make your descendants as numerous as the stars of heaven. And I will give them all of this land that I have promised to your descendants, and they will possess it forever.'"

So the LORD changed his mind about the terrible disaster he had threatened to bring on his people.

Then Moses turned and went down the mountain. He held in his hands the two stone tablets inscribed with the terms of the covenant. They were inscribed on both sides, front and back. These tablets were God's work; the words on them were written by God himself.

When Joshua heard the boisterous noise of the people shouting below them, he exclaimed to Moses, "It sounds like war in the camp!"

But Moses replied, "No, it's not a shout of victory nor the wailing of defeat. I hear the sound of a celebration."

When they came near the camp, Moses saw the calf and the dancing, and he burned with anger. He threw the stone tablets to the ground, smashing them at the foot of the mountain. He took the calf they had made and burned it. Then he ground it into powder, threw it into the water, and forced the people to drink it.

Finally, he turned to Aaron and demanded, "What did these people do to you to make you bring such terrible sin upon them?"

"Don't get so upset, my lord," Aaron replied. "You yourself know how evil these people are. They said to me, 'Make us gods who will lead us. We don't know what happened to this fellow Moses, who brought us here from the land of Egypt.' So I told them, 'Whoever has gold jewelry, take it off.' When they brought it to me, I simply threw it into the fire—and out came this calf!"

Moses saw that Aaron had let the people get completely out of control, much to the amusement of their enemies. So he stood at the entrance to the camp and shouted, "All of you who are on the LORD's side, come here and join me." And all the Levites gathered around him.

Moses told them, "This is what the LORD, the God of Israel, says: Each of you, take your swords and go back and forth from one end of the camp to the other. Kill everyone—even your brothers, friends, and neighbors." The Levites obeyed Moses' command, and about 3,000 people died that day.

Then Moses told the Levites, "Today you have ordained yourselves for the service of the LORD, for you obeyed him even though it meant killing your own sons and brothers. Today you have earned a blessing."

The next day Moses said to the people, "You have committed a terrible sin, but I will go back up to the LORD on the mountain. Perhaps I will be able to obtain forgiveness for your sin."

So Moses returned to the LORD and said, "Oh, what a terrible sin these people have committed. They have made gods of gold for themselves. But now, if you will only forgive their sin—but if not, erase my name from the record you have written!"

But the LORD replied to Moses, "No, I will erase the name of everyone who has sinned against me. Now go, lead the people to the place I told you about. Look! My angel will lead the way before you. And when I come to call the people to account, I will certainly hold them responsible for their sins."

Then the LORD sent a great plague upon the people because they had worshiped the calf Aaron had made.

The LORD said to Moses, "Get going, you and the people you brought up from the land of Egypt. Go up to the land I swore to give to Abraham, Isaac, and Jacob. I told them, 'I will give this land to your descendants.' And I will send an angel before you to drive out the Canaanites, Amorites, Hittites, Perizzites, Hivites, and Jebusites. Go up to this land that flows with milk and honey. But I will not travel among you, for you are a stubborn and rebellious people. If I did, I would surely destroy you along the way."

When the people heard these stern words, they went into mourning and stopped wearing their jewelry and fine clothes. For the LORD had told Moses to tell them, "You are a stubborn and rebellious people. If I were to travel with you for even a moment, I would destroy you. Remove your jewelry and fine clothes while I decide what to do with you." So from the time they left Mount Sinai, the Israelites wore no more jewelry or fine clothes.

It was Moses' practice to take the Tent of Meeting and set it up some distance from the camp. Everyone who wanted to make a request of the LORD would go to the Tent of Meeting outside the camp.

Whenever Moses went out to the Tent of Meeting, all the people would get up and stand in the entrances of their own tents. They would all watch Moses until he disappeared inside. As he went into the tent, the pillar of cloud would come down and hover at its entrance while the LORD spoke with Moses. When the people saw the cloud standing at the entrance of the tent, they would stand and bow down in front of their own tents. Inside the Tent of Meeting, the LORD would speak to Moses face to face, as one speaks to a friend. Afterward Moses would return to the camp, but the young man who assisted him, Joshua son of Nun, would remain behind in the Tent of Meeting.

One day Moses said to the LORD, "You have been telling me, 'Take these people up to the Promised Land.' But you haven't told me whom you will send with me. You have told me, 'I know you by name, and I look favorably on you.' If it is true that you look favorably on me, let me know your ways so I may understand you more fully and continue to enjoy your favor. And remember that this nation is your very own people."

The LORD replied, "I will personally go with you, Moses, and I will give you rest—everything will be fine for you."

Then Moses said, "If you don't personally go with us, don't make us leave this place. How will anyone know that you look favorably on me—on me and on your people—if you don't go with us? For your presence among us sets your people and me apart from all other people on the earth."

The LORD replied to Moses, "I will indeed do what you have asked, for I look favorably on you, and I know you by name."

Moses responded, "Then show me your glorious presence."

The LORD replied, "I will make all my goodness pass before you, and I will call out my name, Yahweh, before you. For I will show mercy to anyone I choose, and I will show compassion to anyone I choose. But you may not look directly at my face, for no one may see me and live." The LORD continued, "Look, stand near me on this rock. As my glorious presence passes by, I will hide you in the crevice of the rock and cover you with my hand until I have passed by. Then I will remove my hand and let you see me from behind. But my face will not be seen."

Then the LORD told Moses, "Chisel out two stone tablets like the first ones. I will write on them the same words that were on the tablets you smashed. Be ready in the morning to climb up Mount Sinai and present yourself to me on the top of the mountain. No one else may come with you. In fact, no one is to appear anywhere on the mountain. Do not even let the flocks or herds graze near the mountain."

So Moses chiseled out two tablets of stone like the first ones. Early in the morning he climbed Mount Sinai as the LORD had commanded him, and he carried the two stone tablets in his hands.

Then the LORD came down in a cloud and stood there with him; and he called out his own name, Yahweh. The LORD passed in front of Moses, calling out,

"Yahweh! The LORD!
    The God of compassion and mercy!
I am slow to anger
    and filled with unfailing love and faithfulness.
I lavish unfailing love to a thousand generations.
    I forgive iniquity, rebellion, and sin.
But I do not excuse the guilty.
    I lay the sins of the parents upon their children and grandchildren;
    the entire family is affected—
    even children in the third and fourth generations."

Moses immediately threw himself to the ground and worshiped. And he said, "O Lord, if it is true that I have found favor with you, then please travel with us. Yes, this is a stubborn and rebellious people, but please forgive our iniquity and our sins. Claim us as your own special possession."

The LORD replied, "Listen, I am making a covenant with you in the presence of all your people. I will perform miracles that have never been performed anywhere in all the earth or in any nation. And all the people around you will see the power of the LORD—the awesome power I will display for you. But listen carefully to everything I command you today. Then I will go ahead of you and drive out the Amorites, Canaanites, Hittites, Perizzites, Hivites, and Jebusites.

"Be very careful never to make a treaty with the people who live in the land where you are going. If you do, you will follow their evil ways and be

trapped. Instead, you must break down their pagan altars, smash their sacred pillars, and cut down their Asherah poles. You must worship no other
gods, for the LORD, whose very name is Jealous, is a God who is jealous
about his relationship with you.

"You must not make a treaty of any kind with the people living in the
land. They lust after their gods, offering sacrifices to them. They will invite you to join them in their sacrificial meals, and you will go with them.
Then you will accept their daughters, who sacrifice to other gods, as wives
for your sons. And they will seduce your sons to commit adultery against
me by worshiping other gods. You must not make any gods of molten
metal for yourselves.

"You must celebrate the Festival of Unleavened Bread. For seven days
the bread you eat must be made without yeast, just as I commanded you.
Celebrate this festival annually at the appointed time in early spring, in the
month of Abib, for that is the anniversary of your departure from Egypt.

"The firstborn of every animal belongs to me, including the firstborn
males from your herds of cattle and your flocks of sheep and goats. A firstborn donkey may be bought back from the LORD by presenting a lamb or
young goat in its place. But if you do not buy it back, you must break its
neck. However, you must buy back every firstborn son.

"No one may appear before me without an offering.

"You have six days each week for your ordinary work, but on the seventh day you must stop working, even during the seasons of plowing and
harvest.

"You must celebrate the Festival of Harvest with the first crop of the
wheat harvest, and celebrate the Festival of the Final Harvest at the end
of the harvest season. Three times each year every man in Israel must appear before the Sovereign, the LORD, the God of Israel. I will drive out the
other nations ahead of you and expand your territory, so no one will covet
and conquer your land while you appear before the LORD your God three
times each year.

"You must not offer the blood of my sacrificial offerings together with
any baked goods containing yeast. And none of the meat of the Passover
sacrifice may be kept over until the next morning.

"As you harvest your crops, bring the very best of the first harvest to the
house of the LORD your God.

"You must not cook a young goat in its mother's milk."

Then the LORD said to Moses, "Write down all these instructions, for
they represent the terms of the covenant I am making with you and with
Israel."

Moses remained there on the mountain with the LORD forty days and
forty nights. In all that time he ate no bread and drank no water. And the

LORD wrote the terms of the covenant—the Ten Commandments—on the stone tablets.

When Moses came down Mount Sinai carrying the two stone tablets inscribed with the terms of the covenant, he wasn't aware that his face had become radiant because he had spoken to the LORD. So when Aaron and the people of Israel saw the radiance of Moses' face, they were afraid to come near him.

But Moses called out to them and asked Aaron and all the leaders of the community to come over, and he talked with them. Then all the people of Israel approached him, and Moses gave them all the instructions the LORD had given him on Mount Sinai. When Moses finished speaking with them, he covered his face with a veil. But whenever he went into the Tent of Meeting to speak with the LORD, he would remove the veil until he came out again. Then he would give the people whatever instructions the LORD had given him, and the people of Israel would see the radiant glow of his face. So he would put the veil over his face until he returned to speak with the LORD.

✛ ✛ ✛

Then Moses called together the whole community of Israel and told them, "These are the instructions the LORD has commanded you to follow. You have six days each week for your ordinary work, but the seventh day must be a Sabbath day of complete rest, a holy day dedicated to the LORD. Anyone who works on that day must be put to death. You must not even light a fire in any of your homes on the Sabbath."

Then Moses said to the whole community of Israel, "This is what the LORD has commanded: Take a sacred offering for the LORD. Let those with generous hearts present the following gifts to the LORD:

gold, silver, and bronze;
blue, purple, and scarlet thread;
fine linen and goat hair for cloth;
tanned ram skins and fine goatskin leather;
acacia wood;
olive oil for the lamps;
spices for the anointing oil and the fragrant incense;
onyx stones, and other gemstones to be set in the ephod and the
    priest's chestpiece.

"Come, all of you who are gifted craftsmen. Construct everything that the LORD has commanded:

the Tabernacle and its sacred tent, its covering, clasps, frames,
    crossbars, posts, and bases;
the Ark and its carrying poles;
the Ark's cover—the place of atonement;
the inner curtain to shield the Ark;
the table, its carrying poles, and all its utensils;
the Bread of the Presence;
for light, the lampstand, its accessories, the lamp cups, and the olive
    oil for lighting;
the incense altar and its carrying poles;
the anointing oil and fragrant incense;
the curtain for the entrance of the Tabernacle;
the altar of burnt offering;
the bronze grating of the altar and its carrying poles and utensils;
the washbasin with its stand;
the curtains for the walls of the courtyard;
the posts and their bases;
the curtain for the entrance to the courtyard;
the tent pegs of the Tabernacle and courtyard and their ropes;
the beautifully stitched garments for the priests to wear while
    ministering in the Holy Place—the sacred garments for Aaron the
    priest, and the garments for his sons to wear as they minister as
    priests."

So the whole community of Israel left Moses and returned to their tents.
All whose hearts were stirred and whose spirits were moved came and
brought their sacred offerings to the Lord. They brought all the materials
needed for the Tabernacle, for the performance of its rituals, and for the
sacred garments. Both men and women came, all whose hearts were willing. They brought to the Lord their offerings of gold—brooches, earrings, rings from their fingers, and necklaces. They presented gold objects
of every kind as a special offering to the Lord. All those who owned the
following items willingly brought them: blue, purple, and scarlet thread;
fine linen and goat hair for cloth; and tanned ram skins and fine goatskin
leather. And all who had silver and bronze objects gave them as a sacred
offering to the Lord. And those who had acacia wood brought it for use
in the project.

All the women who were skilled in sewing and spinning prepared blue,
purple, and scarlet thread, and fine linen cloth. All the women who were
willing used their skills to spin the goat hair into yarn. The leaders brought
onyx stones and the special gemstones to be set in the ephod and the
priest's chestpiece. They also brought spices and olive oil for the light, the

anointing oil, and the fragrant incense. So the people of Israel—every man and woman who was eager to help in the work the LORD had given them through Moses—brought their gifts and gave them freely to the LORD.

Then Moses told the people of Israel, "The LORD has specifically chosen Bezalel son of Uri, grandson of Hur, of the tribe of Judah. The LORD has filled Bezalel with the Spirit of God, giving him great wisdom, ability, and expertise in all kinds of crafts. He is a master craftsman, expert in working with gold, silver, and bronze. He is skilled in engraving and mounting gemstones and in carving wood. He is a master at every craft. And the LORD has given both him and Oholiab son of Ahisamach, of the tribe of Dan, the ability to teach their skills to others. The LORD has given them special skills as engravers, designers, embroiderers in blue, purple, and scarlet thread on fine linen cloth, and weavers. They excel as craftsmen and as designers.

"The LORD has gifted Bezalel, Oholiab, and the other skilled craftsmen with wisdom and ability to perform any task involved in building the sanctuary. Let them construct and furnish the Tabernacle, just as the LORD has commanded."

So Moses summoned Bezalel and Oholiab and all the others who were specially gifted by the LORD and were eager to get to work. Moses gave them the materials donated by the people of Israel as sacred offerings for the completion of the sanctuary. But the people continued to bring additional gifts each morning. Finally the craftsmen who were working on the sanctuary left their work. They went to Moses and reported, "The people have given more than enough materials to complete the job the LORD has commanded us to do!"

So Moses gave the command, and this message was sent throughout the camp: "Men and women, don't prepare any more gifts for the sanctuary. We have enough!" So the people stopped bringing their sacred offerings. Their contributions were more than enough to complete the whole project.

The skilled craftsmen made ten curtains of finely woven linen for the Tabernacle. Then Bezalel decorated the curtains with blue, purple, and scarlet thread and with skillfully embroidered cherubim. All ten curtains were exactly the same size—42 feet long and 6 feet wide. Five of these curtains were joined together to make one long curtain, and the other five were joined to make a second long curtain. He made fifty loops of blue yarn and put them along the edge of the last curtain in each set. The fifty loops along the edge of one curtain matched the fifty loops along the edge of the other curtain. Then he made fifty gold clasps and fastened the long curtains together with the clasps. In this way, the Tabernacle was made of one continuous piece.

He made eleven curtains of goat-hair cloth to serve as a tent covering for the Tabernacle. These eleven curtains were all exactly the same size—45 feet long and 6 feet wide. Bezalel joined five of these curtains together to make one long curtain, and the other six were joined to make a second long curtain. He made fifty loops for the edge of each large curtain. He also made fifty bronze clasps to fasten the long curtains together. In this way, the tent covering was made of one continuous piece. He completed the tent covering with a layer of tanned ram skins and a layer of fine goatskin leather.

For the framework of the Tabernacle, Bezalel constructed frames of acacia wood. Each frame was 15 feet high and 27 inches wide, with two pegs under each frame. All the frames were identical. He made twenty of these frames to support the curtains on the south side of the Tabernacle. He also made forty silver bases—two bases under each frame, with the pegs fitting securely into the bases. For the north side of the Tabernacle, he made another twenty frames, with their forty silver bases, two bases under each frame. He made six frames for the rear—the west side of the Tabernacle—along with two additional frames to reinforce the rear corners of the Tabernacle. These corner frames were matched at the bottom and firmly attached at the top with a single ring, forming a single corner unit. Both of these corner units were made the same way. So there were eight frames at the rear of the Tabernacle, set in sixteen silver bases—two bases under each frame.

Then he made crossbars of acacia wood to link the frames, five crossbars for the north side of the Tabernacle and five for the south side. He also made five crossbars for the rear of the Tabernacle, which faced west. He made the middle crossbar to attach halfway up the frames; it ran all the way from one end of the Tabernacle to the other. He overlaid the frames with gold and made gold rings to hold the crossbars. Then he overlaid the crossbars with gold as well.

For the inside of the Tabernacle, Bezalel made a special curtain of finely woven linen. He decorated it with blue, purple, and scarlet thread and with skillfully embroidered cherubim. For the curtain, he made four posts of acacia wood and four gold hooks. He overlaid the posts with gold and set them in four silver bases.

Then he made another curtain for the entrance to the sacred tent. He made it of finely woven linen and embroidered it with exquisite designs using blue, purple, and scarlet thread. This curtain was hung on gold hooks attached to five posts. The posts with their decorated tops and hooks were overlaid with gold, and the five bases were cast from bronze.

Next Bezalel made the Ark of acacia wood—a sacred chest 45 inches long, 27 inches wide, and 27 inches high. He overlaid it inside and outside with pure gold, and he ran a molding of gold all around it. He cast four gold rings and attached them to its four feet, two rings on each side. Then he made poles from acacia wood and overlaid them with gold. He inserted the poles into the rings at the sides of the Ark to carry it.

Then he made the Ark's cover—the place of atonement—from pure gold. It was 45 inches long and 27 inches wide. He made two cherubim from hammered gold and placed them on the two ends of the atonement cover. He molded the cherubim on each end of the atonement cover, making it all of one piece of gold. The cherubim faced each other and looked down on the atonement cover. With their wings spread above it, they protected it.

Then Bezalel made the table of acacia wood, 36 inches long, 18 inches wide, and 27 inches high. He overlaid it with pure gold and ran a gold molding around the edge. He decorated it with a 3-inch border all around, and he ran a gold molding along the border. Then he cast four gold rings for the table and attached them at the four corners next to the four legs. The rings were attached near the border to hold the poles that were used to carry the table. He made these poles from acacia wood and overlaid them with gold. Then he made special containers of pure gold for the table—bowls, ladles, jars, and pitchers—to be used in pouring out liquid offerings.

Then Bezalel made the lampstand of pure, hammered gold. He made the entire lampstand and its decorations of one piece—the base, center stem, lamp cups, buds, and petals. The lampstand had six branches going out from the center stem, three on each side. Each of the six branches had three lamp cups shaped like almond blossoms, complete with buds and petals. The center stem of the lampstand was crafted with four lamp cups shaped like almond blossoms, complete with buds and petals. There was an almond bud beneath each pair of branches where the six branches extended from the center stem, all made of one piece. The almond buds and branches were all of one piece with the center stem, and they were hammered from pure gold.

He also made seven lamps for the lampstand, lamp snuffers, and trays, all of pure gold. The entire lampstand, along with its accessories, was made from 75 pounds of pure gold.

Then Bezalel made the incense altar of acacia wood. It was 18 inches square and 36 inches high, with horns at the corners carved from the same piece of wood as the altar itself. He overlaid the top, sides, and horns of the altar with pure gold, and he ran a gold molding around the entire altar. He made two gold rings and attached them on opposite sides of the altar below the gold molding to hold the carrying poles. He made the poles of acacia wood and overlaid them with gold.

Then he made the sacred anointing oil and the fragrant incense, using the techniques of a skilled incense maker.

Next Bezalel used acacia wood to construct the square altar of burnt offering. It was 7½ feet wide, 7½ feet long, and 4½ feet high. He made horns for each of its four corners so that the horns and altar were all one piece. He overlaid the altar with bronze. Then he made all the altar utensils of bronze—the ash buckets, shovels, basins, meat forks, and firepans. Next he made a bronze grating and installed it halfway down the side of the altar, under the ledge. He cast four rings and attached them to the corners of the bronze grating to hold the carrying poles. He made the poles from acacia wood and overlaid them with bronze. He inserted the poles through the rings on the sides of the altar. The altar was hollow and was made from planks.

Bezalel made the bronze washbasin and its bronze stand from bronze mirrors donated by the women who served at the entrance of the Tabernacle.

Then Bezalel made the courtyard, which was enclosed with curtains made of finely woven linen. On the south side the curtains were 150 feet long. They were held up by twenty posts set securely in twenty bronze bases. He hung the curtains with silver hooks and rings. He made a similar set of curtains for the north side—150 feet of curtains held up by twenty posts set securely in bronze bases. He hung the curtains with silver hooks and rings. The curtains on the west end of the courtyard were 75 feet long, hung with silver hooks and rings and supported by ten posts set into ten bases. The east end, the front, was also 75 feet long.

The courtyard entrance was on the east end, flanked by two curtains. The curtain on the right side was 22½ feet long and was supported by three posts set into three bases. The curtain on the left side was also 22½ feet long and was supported by three posts set into three bases. All the curtains used in the courtyard were made of finely woven linen. Each post had a bronze base, and all the hooks and rings were silver. The tops of the posts of the courtyard were overlaid with silver, and the rings to hold up the curtains were made of silver.

He made the curtain for the entrance to the courtyard of finely woven linen, and he decorated it with beautiful embroidery in blue, purple, and scarlet thread. It was 30 feet long, and its height was 7½ feet, just like the curtains of the courtyard walls. It was supported by four posts, each set securely in its own bronze base. The tops of the posts were overlaid with silver, and the hooks and rings were also made of silver.

All the tent pegs used in the Tabernacle and courtyard were made of bronze.

This is an inventory of the materials used in building the Tabernacle of the Covenant. The Levites compiled the figures, as Moses directed, and Ithamar son of Aaron the priest served as recorder. Bezalel son of Uri, grandson of Hur, of the tribe of Judah, made everything just as the LORD had commanded Moses. He was assisted by Oholiab son of Ahisamach, of the tribe of Dan, a craftsman expert at engraving, designing, and embroidering with blue, purple, and scarlet thread on fine linen cloth.

The people brought special offerings of gold totaling 2,193 pounds, as measured by the weight of the sanctuary shekel. This gold was used throughout the Tabernacle.

The whole community of Israel gave 7,545 pounds of silver, as measured by the weight of the sanctuary shekel. This silver came from the tax collected from each man registered in the census. (The tax is one beka, which is half a shekel, based on the sanctuary shekel.) The tax was collected from 603,550 men who had reached their twentieth birthday. The hundred bases for the frames of the sanctuary walls and for the posts supporting the inner curtain required 7,500 pounds of silver, about 75 pounds for each base. The remaining 45 pounds of silver was used to make the hooks and rings and to overlay the tops of the posts.

The people also brought as special offerings 5,310 pounds of bronze, which was used for casting the bases for the posts at the entrance to the Tabernacle, and for the bronze altar with its bronze grating and all the altar utensils. Bronze was also used to make the bases for the posts that supported the curtains around the courtyard, the bases for the curtain at the entrance of the courtyard, and all the tent pegs for the Tabernacle and the courtyard.

+

The craftsmen made beautiful sacred garments of blue, purple, and scarlet cloth—clothing for Aaron to wear while ministering in the Holy Place, just as the LORD had commanded Moses.

Bezalel made the ephod of finely woven linen and embroidered it with gold and with blue, purple, and scarlet thread. He made gold thread by hammering out thin sheets of gold and cutting it into fine strands. With great skill and care, he worked it into the fine linen with the blue, purple, and scarlet thread.

The ephod consisted of two pieces, front and back, joined at the shoulders with two shoulder-pieces. The decorative sash was made of the same materials: finely woven linen embroidered with gold and with blue, purple, and scarlet thread, just as the LORD had commanded Moses. They mounted the two onyx stones in settings of gold filigree. The stones were engraved with the names of the tribes of Israel, just as a seal is engraved. He fastened these stones on the shoulder-pieces of the ephod as a reminder that the priest represents the people of Israel. All this was done just as the LORD had commanded Moses.

Bezalel made the chestpiece with great skill and care. He made it to match the ephod, using finely woven linen embroidered with gold and with blue, purple, and scarlet thread. He made the chestpiece of a single piece of cloth folded to form a pouch nine inches square. They mounted four rows of gemstones on it. The first row contained a red carnelian, a pale-green peridot, and an emerald. The second row contained a turquoise, a blue lapis lazuli, and a white moonstone. The third row contained an orange jacinth, an agate, and a purple amethyst. The fourth row contained a blue-green beryl, an onyx, and a green jasper. All these stones were set in gold filigree. Each stone represented one of the twelve sons of Israel, and the name of that tribe was engraved on it like a seal.

To attach the chestpiece to the ephod, they made braided cords of pure gold thread. They also made two settings of gold filigree and two gold rings and attached them to the top corners of the chestpiece. They tied the two gold cords to the rings on the chestpiece. They tied the other ends of the cords to the gold settings on the shoulder-pieces of the ephod. Then they made two more gold rings and attached them to the inside edges of the chestpiece next to the ephod. Then they made two more gold rings and attached them to the front of the ephod, below the shoulder-pieces, just above the knot where the decorative sash was fastened to the ephod. They attached the bottom rings of the chestpiece to the rings on the ephod with blue cords. In this way, the chestpiece was held securely to the ephod above the decorative sash. All this was done just as the LORD had commanded Moses.

Bezalel made the robe that is worn with the ephod from a single piece of blue woven cloth, with an opening for Aaron's head in the middle of it. The opening was reinforced with a woven collar so it would not tear. They made pomegranates of blue, purple, and scarlet yarn, and attached them to the hem of the robe. They also made bells of pure gold and placed them between the pomegranates along the hem of the robe, with bells and pomegranates alternating all around the hem. This robe was to be worn whenever the priest ministered before the LORD, just as the LORD had commanded Moses.

They made tunics for Aaron and his sons from fine linen cloth. The turban and the special head coverings were made of fine linen, and the undergarments were also made of finely woven linen. The sashes were made of finely woven linen and embroidered with blue, purple, and scarlet thread, just as the LORD had commanded Moses.

Finally, they made the sacred medallion—the badge of holiness—of pure gold. They engraved it like a seal with these words: HOLY TO THE LORD. They attached the medallion with a blue cord to Aaron's turban, just as the LORD had commanded Moses.

✛ ✛ ✛

And so at last the Tabernacle was finished. The Israelites had done everything just as the LORD had commanded Moses. And they brought the entire Tabernacle to Moses:

the sacred tent with all its furnishings, clasps, frames, crossbars, posts, and bases;
the tent coverings of tanned ram skins and fine goatskin leather;
the inner curtain to shield the Ark;
the Ark of the Covenant and its carrying poles;
the Ark's cover—the place of atonement;
the table and all its utensils;
the Bread of the Presence;
the pure gold lampstand with its symmetrical lamp cups, all its accessories, and the olive oil for lighting;
the gold altar;
the anointing oil and fragrant incense;
the curtain for the entrance of the sacred tent;
the bronze altar;
the bronze grating and its carrying poles and utensils;
the washbasin with its stand;
the curtains for the walls of the courtyard;
the posts and their bases;
the curtain for the entrance to the courtyard;
the ropes and tent pegs;
all the furnishings to be used in worship at the Tabernacle;
the beautifully stitched garments for the priests to wear while

ministering in the Holy Place—the sacred garments for Aaron the priest, and the garments for his sons to wear as they minister as priests.

So the people of Israel followed all of the LORD's instructions to Moses. Then Moses inspected all their work. When he found it had been done just as the LORD had commanded him, he blessed them.

Then the LORD said to Moses, "Set up the Tabernacle on the first day of the new year. Place the Ark of the Covenant inside, and install the inner curtain to enclose the Ark within the Most Holy Place. Then bring in the table, and arrange the utensils on it. And bring in the lampstand, and set up the lamps.

"Place the gold incense altar in front of the Ark of the Covenant. Then hang the curtain at the entrance of the Tabernacle. Place the altar of burnt offering in front of the Tabernacle entrance. Set the washbasin between the Tabernacle and the altar, and fill it with water. Then set up the courtyard around the outside of the tent, and hang the curtain for the courtyard entrance.

"Take the anointing oil and anoint the Tabernacle and all its furnishings to consecrate them and make them holy. Anoint the altar of burnt offering and its utensils to consecrate them. Then the altar will become absolutely holy. Next anoint the washbasin and its stand to consecrate them.

"Present Aaron and his sons at the entrance of the Tabernacle, and wash them with water. Dress Aaron with the sacred garments and anoint him, consecrating him to serve me as a priest. Then present his sons and dress them in their tunics. Anoint them as you did their father, so they may also serve me as priests. With their anointing, Aaron's descendants are set apart for the priesthood forever, from generation to generation."

Moses proceeded to do everything just as the LORD had commanded him.

So the Tabernacle was set up on the first day of the first month of the second year. Moses erected the Tabernacle by setting down its bases, inserting the frames, attaching the crossbars, and setting up the posts. Then he spread the coverings over the Tabernacle framework and put on the protective layers, just as the LORD had commanded him.

He took the stone tablets inscribed with the terms of the covenant and placed them inside the Ark. Then he attached the carrying poles to the Ark, and he set the Ark's cover—the place of atonement—on top of it. Then he brought the Ark of the Covenant into the Tabernacle and hung the inner curtain to shield it from view, just as the LORD had commanded him.

Next Moses placed the table in the Tabernacle, along the north side of the Holy Place, just outside the inner curtain. And he arranged the Bread of the Presence on the table before the LORD, just as the LORD had commanded him.

He set the lampstand in the Tabernacle across from the table on the south side of the Holy Place. Then he lit the lamps in the LORD's presence, just as the LORD had commanded him. He also placed the gold incense altar in the Tabernacle, in the Holy Place in front of the inner curtain. On it he burned the fragrant incense, just as the LORD had commanded him.

He hung the curtain at the entrance of the Tabernacle, and he placed the altar of burnt offering near the Tabernacle entrance. On it he offered a burnt offering and a grain offering, just as the LORD had commanded him.

Next Moses placed the washbasin between the Tabernacle and the altar. He filled it with water so the priests could wash themselves. Moses and Aaron and Aaron's sons used water from it to wash their hands and feet. Whenever they approached the altar and entered the Tabernacle, they washed themselves, just as the LORD had commanded Moses.

Then he hung the curtains forming the courtyard around the Tabernacle and the altar. And he set up the curtain at the entrance of the courtyard. So at last Moses finished the work.

Then the cloud covered the Tabernacle, and the glory of the LORD filled the Tabernacle. Moses could no longer enter the Tabernacle because the cloud had settled down over it, and the glory of the LORD filled the Tabernacle.

Now whenever the cloud lifted from the Tabernacle, the people of Israel would set out on their journey, following it. But if the cloud did not rise, they remained where they were until it lifted. The cloud of the LORD hovered over the Tabernacle during the day, and at night fire glowed inside the cloud so the whole family of Israel could see it. This continued throughout all their journeys.

IMMERSED IN LEVITICUS

IN THE BOOK OF EXODUS, the Israelites traveled from Egypt to Mount Sinai, where the Tabernacle was created and set up. The book of Leviticus continues the story, as it records the instructions God gives to Moses on Mount Sinai before the people continue their journey to Canaan. Many of these instructions may seem strange because the ancient cultures to which they belong are so different from our own. We must be careful to read these instructions to Israel in the context of their own time, not as written directly to us. Within the context of Israel's covenant, these laws provided cleansing and restoration for the people, allowing them to remain in a close relationship with God in order to fulfill their calling as a light to the world.

The instructions are based on careful distinctions between what is "clean" and "unclean" and between what is "common" and "holy." Unclean here does not mean dirty or bad but rather that something has been compromised or tainted in some way. As long as something remains clean, it may be set apart for a special purpose, and thus become holy. The Israelites are to observe these distinctions to demonstrate how they have been set apart for a special purpose by God: to live out the life he intends as an example to all nations. The laws collected here distinguish God's people from the surrounding cultures and move the story forward, closer to God's ultimate vision for humanity.

Leviticus presents four major groups of instructions. The first gives direction for the various types of *offerings* that will be used to cleanse people and objects that have become unclean and to set apart common people and common objects to make them holy.

The second section of the book explains what can cause a person or thing to lose its state of *cleanness*. These laws express a specific concern for an unclean person to be restored to physical integrity and then to community.

In its third section of laws, Leviticus describes how the Israelites are to pursue *holiness* in their everyday lives and in their worship of God. The various regulations pertaining to holiness, including issues related to blood, celebrating festivals, and even the holy bread in the Tabernacle, all represent how God has designated the people of Israel to be holy—set apart for a special purpose.

Central to this section on holiness is a collection of ethical commands. These commands embody the essence of why the Israelites have been set apart—to demonstrate the just and compassionate character of God. This collection includes commands on showing generosity to the poor, treating the elderly and handicapped with dignity, paying fair wages and on time, freeing people from exploitation, caring for foreigners, and so forth. These practices would identify the covenant community as God's new model for humanity. They are meant to overcome the exhibitions of pride and selfishness that so often mark human rebellion.

The fourth and final section of Leviticus explores a process known as *redemption*, which means "buying back." Redemption addresses the critical issue of recovering something that has lost its holy status. If something that was supposed to be "set apart" has been treated as common, can it be reclaimed for its special purpose? The answer is yes. Ancestral land, for example, can be reclaimed during a special time of freedom called the Year of Jubilee. A possession given to God in a vow may be repurchased. Israelites who were sold into slavery can obtain their release.

At the end of the book, an important question is raised with regard to the issue of redemption. If the Israelites forfeit their role as a holy people through disobedience and are exiled from the Land of Promise, can they ever be brought back? Again we find that restoration is possible: God declares that Israel can and will be brought back from punishment and exile. This final section of Leviticus assures the nation that God would never forget his covenant with them.

Repeatedly in Leviticus, God tells his people, "You must be holy because I, the LORD your God, am holy." Just as God is set apart, high above anything in creation, he calls his people to be set apart in this world. He chooses to accomplish his purposes for the world through his people, and if necessary, God himself will redeem his people so they can complete their work.

LEVITICUS

✝

The LORD called to Moses from the Tabernacle and said to him, "Give the following instructions to the people of Israel. When you present an animal as an offering to the LORD, you may take it from your herd of cattle or your flock of sheep and goats.

"If the animal you present as a burnt offering is from the herd, it must be a male with no defects. Bring it to the entrance of the Tabernacle so you may be accepted by the LORD. Lay your hand on the animal's head, and the LORD will accept its death in your place to purify you, making you right with him. Then slaughter the young bull in the LORD's presence, and Aaron's sons, the priests, will present the animal's blood by splattering it against all sides of the altar that stands at the entrance to the Tabernacle. Then skin the animal and cut it into pieces. The sons of Aaron the priest will build a wood fire on the altar. They will arrange the pieces of the offering, including the head and fat, on the wood burning on the altar. But the internal organs and the legs must first be washed with water. Then the priest will burn the entire sacrifice on the altar as a burnt offering. It is a special gift, a pleasing aroma to the LORD.

"If the animal you present as a burnt offering is from the flock, it may be either a sheep or a goat, but it must be a male with no defects. Slaughter the animal on the north side of the altar in the LORD's presence, and Aaron's sons, the priests, will splatter its blood against all sides of the altar. Then cut the animal in pieces, and the priests will arrange the pieces of the offering, including the head and fat, on the wood burning on the altar. But the internal organs and the legs must first be washed with water. Then the priest will burn the entire sacrifice on the altar as a burnt offering. It is a special gift, a pleasing aroma to the LORD.

"If you present a bird as a burnt offering to the LORD, choose either a turtledove or a young pigeon. The priest will take the bird to the altar, wring off its head, and burn it on the altar. But first he must drain its blood against the side of the altar. The priest must also remove the crop and the feathers and throw them in the ashes on the east side of the altar. Then, grasping the bird by its wings, the priest will tear the bird open, but without tearing it apart. Then he will burn it as a burnt offering on the wood burning on the altar. It is a special gift, a pleasing aroma to the LORD.

+

"When you present grain as an offering to the LORD, the offering must consist of choice flour. You are to pour olive oil on it, sprinkle it with frankincense, and bring it to Aaron's sons, the priests. The priest will scoop out a handful of the flour moistened with oil, together with all the frankincense, and burn this representative portion on the altar. It is a special gift, a pleasing aroma to the LORD. The rest of the grain offering will then be given to Aaron and his sons. This offering will be considered a most holy part of the special gifts presented to the LORD.

"If your offering is a grain offering baked in an oven, it must be made of choice flour, but without any yeast. It may be presented in the form of thin cakes mixed with olive oil or wafers spread with olive oil. If your grain offering is cooked on a griddle, it must be made of choice flour mixed with olive oil but without any yeast. Break it in pieces and pour olive oil on it; it is a grain offering. If your grain offering is prepared in a pan, it must be made of choice flour and olive oil.

"No matter how a grain offering for the LORD has been prepared, bring it to the priest, who will present it at the altar. The priest will take a representative portion of the grain offering and burn it on the altar. It is a special gift, a pleasing aroma to the LORD. The rest of the grain offering will then be given to Aaron and his sons as their food. This offering will be considered a most holy part of the special gifts presented to the LORD.

"Do not use yeast in preparing any of the grain offerings you present to the LORD, because no yeast or honey may be burned as a special gift presented to the LORD. You may add yeast and honey to an offering of the first crops of your harvest, but these must never be offered on the altar as a pleasing aroma to the LORD. Season all your grain offerings with salt to remind you of God's eternal covenant. Never forget to add salt to your grain offerings.

"If you present a grain offering to the LORD from the first portion of your harvest, bring fresh grain that is coarsely ground and roasted on a fire. Put olive oil on this grain offering, and sprinkle it with frankincense. The priest will take a representative portion of the grain moistened with oil, together with all the frankincense, and burn it as a special gift presented to the LORD.

+

"If you present an animal from the herd as a peace offering to the LORD, it may be a male or a female, but it must have no defects. Lay your hand on the animal's head, and slaughter it at the entrance of the Tabernacle. Then Aaron's sons, the priests, will splatter its blood against all sides of the altar. The priest must present part of this peace offering as a special gift to the LORD. This includes all the fat around the internal organs, the two kidneys and the fat around them near the loins, and the long lobe of the liver. These must be removed with the kidneys, and Aaron's sons will burn them on top of the burnt offering on the wood burning on the altar. It is a special gift, a pleasing aroma to the LORD.

"If you present an animal from the flock as a peace offering to the LORD, it may be a male or a female, but it must have no defects. If you present a sheep as your offering, bring it to the LORD, lay your hand on its head, and slaughter it in front of the Tabernacle. Aaron's sons will then splatter the sheep's blood against all sides of the altar. The priest must present the fat of this peace offering as a special gift to the LORD. This includes the fat of the broad tail cut off near the backbone, all the fat around the internal organs, the two kidneys and the fat around them near the loins, and the long lobe of the liver. These must be removed with the kidneys, and the priest will burn them on the altar. It is a special gift of food presented to the LORD.

"If you present a goat as your offering, bring it to the LORD, lay your hand on its head, and slaughter it in front of the Tabernacle. Aaron's sons will then splatter the goat's blood against all sides of the altar. The priest must present part of this offering as a special gift to the LORD. This includes all the fat around the internal organs, the two kidneys and the fat around them near the loins, and the long lobe of the liver. These must be removed with the kidneys, and the priest will burn them on the altar. It is a special gift of food, a pleasing aroma to the LORD. All the fat belongs to the LORD.

"You must never eat any fat or blood. This is a permanent law for you, and it must be observed from generation to generation, wherever you live."

+

Then the LORD said to Moses, "Give the following instructions to the people of Israel. This is how you are to deal with those who sin unintentionally by doing anything that violates one of the LORD's commands.

"If the high priest sins, bringing guilt upon the entire community, he must give a sin offering for the sin he has committed. He must present to the LORD a young bull with no defects. He must bring the bull to the LORD at the entrance of the Tabernacle, lay his hand on the bull's head, and slaughter it before the LORD. The high priest will then take some of the bull's blood into the Tabernacle, dip his finger in the blood, and sprinkle it seven times before the LORD in front of the inner curtain of the sanctuary. The priest will then put some of the blood on the horns of the altar for fragrant incense that stands in the LORD's presence inside the Tabernacle. He will pour out the rest of the bull's blood at the base of the altar for burnt offerings at the entrance of the Tabernacle. Then the priest must remove all the fat of the bull to be offered as a sin offering. This includes all the fat around the internal organs, the two kidneys and the fat around them near the loins, and the long lobe of the liver. He must remove these along with the kidneys, just as he does with cattle offered as a peace offering, and burn them on the altar of burnt offerings. But he must take whatever is left of the bull—its hide, meat, head, legs, internal organs, and dung—and carry it away to a place outside the camp that is ceremonially clean, the place where the ashes are dumped. There, on the ash heap, he will burn it on a wood fire.

"If the entire Israelite community sins by violating one of the LORD's commands, but the people don't realize it, they are still guilty. When they become aware of their sin, the people must bring a young bull as an offering for their sin and present it before the Tabernacle. The elders of the community must then lay their hands on the bull's head and slaughter it before the LORD. The high priest will then take some of the bull's blood into the Tabernacle, dip his finger in the blood, and sprinkle it seven times before the LORD in front of the inner curtain. He will then put some of the blood on the horns of the altar for fragrant incense that stands in the LORD's presence inside the Tabernacle. He will pour out the rest of the blood at the base of the altar for burnt offerings at the entrance of the Tabernacle. Then the priest must remove all the animal's fat and burn it on the altar, just as he does with the bull offered as a sin offering for the high priest. Through this process, the priest will purify the people, making them right with the LORD, and they will be forgiven. Then the priest must take what is left of the bull and carry it outside the camp and burn it there, just as is done with the sin offering for the high priest. This offering is for the sin of the entire congregation of Israel.

"If one of Israel's leaders sins by violating one of the commands of the LORD his God but doesn't realize it, he is still guilty. When he becomes aware of his sin, he must bring as his offering a male goat with no defects. He must lay his hand on the goat's head and slaughter it at the place where burnt offerings are slaughtered before the LORD. This is an offering for his sin. Then the priest will dip his finger in the blood of the sin offering and put it on the horns of the altar for burnt offerings. He will pour out the rest of the blood at the base of the altar. Then he must burn all the goat's fat on the altar, just as he does with the peace offering. Through this process, the priest will purify the leader from his sin, making him right with the LORD, and he will be forgiven.

"If any of the common people sin by violating one of the LORD's commands, but they don't realize it, they are still guilty. When they become aware of their sin, they must bring as an offering for their sin a female goat with no defects. They must lay a hand on the head of the sin offering and slaughter it at the place where burnt offerings are slaughtered. Then the priest will dip his finger in the blood and put it on the horns of the altar for burnt offerings. He will pour out the rest of the blood at the base of the altar. Then he must remove all the goat's fat, just as he does with the fat of the peace offering. He will burn the fat on the altar, and it will be a pleasing aroma to the LORD. Through this process, the priest will purify the people, making them right with the LORD, and they will be forgiven.

"If the people bring a sheep as their sin offering, it must be a female with no defects. They must lay a hand on the head of the sin offering and slaughter it at the place where burnt offerings are slaughtered. Then the priest will dip his finger in the blood of the sin offering and put it on the horns of the altar for burnt offerings. He will pour out the rest of the blood at the base of the altar. Then he must remove all the sheep's fat, just as he does with the fat of a sheep presented as a peace offering. He will burn the fat on the altar on top of the special gifts presented to the LORD. Through this process, the priest will purify the people from their sin, making them right with the LORD, and they will be forgiven.

"If you are called to testify about something you have seen or that you know about, it is sinful to refuse to testify, and you will be punished for your sin.

"Or suppose you unknowingly touch something that is ceremonially unclean, such as the carcass of an unclean animal. When you realize what you have done, you must admit your defilement and your guilt. This is true whether it is a wild animal, a domestic animal, or an animal that scurries along the ground.

"Or suppose you unknowingly touch something that makes a person unclean. When you realize what you have done, you must admit your guilt.

"Or suppose you make a foolish vow of any kind, whether its purpose is for good or for bad. When you realize its foolishness, you must admit your guilt.

"When you become aware of your guilt in any of these ways, you must confess your sin. Then you must bring to the LORD as the penalty for your sin a female from the flock, either a sheep or a goat. This is a sin offering with which the priest will purify you from your sin, making you right with the LORD.

"But if you cannot afford to bring a sheep, you may bring to the LORD two turtledoves or two young pigeons as the penalty for your sin. One of the birds will be for a sin offering, and the other for a burnt offering. You must bring them to the priest, who will present the first bird as the sin offering. He will wring its neck but without severing its head from the body. Then he will sprinkle some of the blood of the sin offering against the sides of the altar, and the rest of the blood will be drained out at the base of the altar. This is an offering for sin. The priest will then prepare the second bird as a burnt offering, following all the procedures that have been prescribed. Through this process the priest will purify you from your sin, making you right with the LORD, and you will be forgiven.

"If you cannot afford to bring two turtledoves or two young pigeons, you may bring two quarts of choice flour for your sin offering. Since it is an offering for sin, you must not moisten it with olive oil or put any frankincense on it. Take the flour to the priest, who will scoop out a handful as a representative portion. He will burn it on the altar on top of the special gifts presented to the LORD. It is an offering for sin. Through this process, the priest will purify those who are guilty of any of these sins, making them right with the LORD, and they will be forgiven. The rest of the flour will belong to the priest, just as with the grain offering."

Then the LORD said to Moses, "If one of you commits a sin by unintentionally defiling the LORD's sacred property, you must bring a guilt offering to the LORD. The offering must be your own ram with no defects, or you may buy one of equal value with silver, as measured by the weight of the sanctuary shekel. You must make restitution for the sacred property you have harmed by paying for the loss, plus an additional 20 percent. When you give the payment to the priest, he will purify you with the ram sacrificed as a guilt offering, making you right with the LORD, and you will be forgiven.

"Suppose you sin by violating one of the LORD's commands. Even if you are unaware of what you have done, you are guilty and will be punished for your sin. For a guilt offering, you must bring to the priest your own ram with no defects, or you may buy one of equal value. Through this process the priest will purify you from your unintentional sin, making you right with the LORD, and you will be forgiven. This is a guilt offering, for you have been guilty of an offense against the LORD."

Then the LORD said to Moses, "Suppose one of you sins against your associate and is unfaithful to the LORD. Suppose you cheat in a deal involving a security deposit, or you steal or commit fraud, or you find lost property and lie about it, or you lie while swearing to tell the truth, or you commit any other such sin. If you have sinned in any of these ways, you are guilty.

You must give back whatever you stole, or the money you took by extortion, or the security deposit, or the lost property you found, or anything obtained by swearing falsely. You must make restitution by paying the full price plus an additional 20 percent to the person you have harmed. On the same day you must present a guilt offering. As a guilt offering to the LORD, you must bring to the priest your own ram with no defects, or you may buy one of equal value. Through this process, the priest will purify you before the LORD, making you right with him, and you will be forgiven for any of these sins you have committed."

+

Then the LORD said to Moses, "Give Aaron and his sons the following instructions regarding the burnt offering. The burnt offering must be left on top of the altar until the next morning, and the fire on the altar must be kept burning all night. In the morning, after the priest on duty has put on his official linen clothing and linen undergarments, he must clean out the ashes of the burnt offering and put them beside the altar. Then he must take off these garments, change back into his regular clothes, and carry the ashes outside the camp to a place that is ceremonially clean. Meanwhile, the fire on the altar must be kept burning; it must never go out. Each morning the priest will add fresh wood to the fire and arrange the burnt offering on it. He will then burn the fat of the peace offerings on it. Remember, the fire must be kept burning on the altar at all times. It must never go out.

"These are the instructions regarding the grain offering. Aaron's sons must present this offering to the LORD in front of the altar. The priest on duty will take from the grain offering a handful of the choice flour moistened with olive oil, together with all the frankincense. He will burn this representative portion on the altar as a pleasing aroma to the LORD. Aaron and his sons may eat the rest of the flour, but it must be baked without yeast and eaten in a sacred place within the courtyard of the Tabernacle. Remember, it must never be prepared with yeast. I have given it to the priests as their share of the special gifts presented to me. Like the sin offering and the guilt offering, it is most holy. Any of Aaron's male descendants may eat from the special gifts presented to the LORD. This is their permanent right from generation to generation. Anyone or anything that touches these offerings will become holy."

Then the LORD said to Moses, "On the day Aaron and his sons are anointed, they must present to the LORD the standard grain offering of two quarts of choice flour, half to be offered in the morning and half to be offered in the evening. It must be carefully mixed with olive oil and cooked on a griddle. Then slice this grain offering and present it as a pleasing aroma to the LORD. In each generation, the high priest who succeeds Aaron must prepare this same offering. It belongs to the LORD and must be burned up completely. This is a permanent law. All such grain offerings of a priest must be burned up entirely. None of it may be eaten."

Then the LORD said to Moses, "Give Aaron and his sons the following instructions regarding the sin offering. The animal given as an offering for sin is a most holy offering, and it must be slaughtered in the LORD's presence at the place where the burnt offerings are slaughtered. The priest who offers the sacrifice as a sin offering must eat his portion in a sacred place within the courtyard of the Tabernacle. Anyone or anything that touches the sacrificial meat will become holy. If any of the sacrificial blood spatters on a person's clothing, the soiled garment must be washed in a sacred place. If a clay pot is used to boil the sacrificial meat, it must then be broken. If a bronze pot is used, it must be scoured and thoroughly rinsed with water. Any male from a priest's family may eat from this offering; it is most holy. But the offering for sin may not be eaten if its blood was brought into the Tabernacle as an offering for purification in the Holy Place. It must be completely burned with fire.

"These are the instructions for the guilt offering. It is most holy. The animal sacrificed as a guilt offering must be slaughtered at the place where the burnt offerings are slaughtered, and its blood must be splattered against all sides of the altar. The priest will then offer all its fat on the altar, including the fat of the broad tail, the fat around the internal organs, the two kidneys and the fat around them near the loins, and the long lobe of the liver. These are to be removed with the kidneys, and the priests will burn them on the altar as a special gift presented to the LORD. This is the guilt offering. Any male from a priest's family may eat the meat. It must be eaten in a sacred place, for it is most holy.

"The same instructions apply to both the guilt offering and the sin offering. Both belong to the priest who uses them to purify someone, making that person right with the LORD. In the case of the burnt offering, the priest may keep the hide of the sacrificed animal. Any grain offering that has been baked in an oven, prepared in a pan, or cooked on a griddle belongs to the priest who presents it. All other grain offerings, whether made of dry flour or flour moistened with olive oil, are to be shared equally among all the priests, the descendants of Aaron.

"These are the instructions regarding the different kinds of peace offerings that may be presented to the LORD. If you present your peace offering as an expression of thanksgiving, the usual animal sacrifice must be accompanied by various kinds of bread made without yeast—thin cakes mixed with olive oil, wafers spread with oil, and cakes made of choice flour mixed with olive oil. This peace offering of thanksgiving must also be accompanied by loaves of bread made with yeast. One of each kind of bread must be presented as a gift to the LORD. It will then belong to the priest who splatters the blood of the peace offering against the altar. The meat of the peace offering of thanksgiving must be eaten on the same day it is offered. None of it may be saved for the next morning.

"If you bring an offering to fulfill a vow or as a voluntary offering, the meat must be eaten on the same day the sacrifice is offered, but whatever is left over may be eaten on the second day. Any meat left over until the third day must be completely burned up. If any of the meat from the peace offering is eaten on the third day, the person who presented it will not be accepted by the LORD. You will receive no credit for offering it. By then the meat will be contaminated; if you eat it, you will be punished for your sin.

"Meat that touches anything ceremonially unclean may not be eaten; it must be completely burned up. The rest of the meat may be eaten, but only by people who are ceremonially clean. If you are ceremonially unclean and you eat meat from a peace offering that was presented to the LORD, you will be cut off from the community. If you touch anything that is unclean (whether it is human defilement or an unclean animal or any other unclean, detestable thing) and then eat meat from a peace offering presented to the LORD, you will be cut off from the community."

Then the LORD said to Moses, "Give the following instructions to the people of Israel. You must never eat fat, whether from cattle, sheep, or goats. The fat of an animal found dead or torn to pieces by wild animals must never be eaten, though it may be used for any other purpose. Anyone who eats fat from an animal presented as a special gift to the LORD will be cut off from the community. No matter where you live, you must never consume the blood of any bird or animal. Anyone who consumes blood will be cut off from the community."

Then the LORD said to Moses, "Give the following instructions to the people of Israel. When you present a peace offering to the LORD, bring part of it as a gift to the LORD. Present it to the LORD with your own hands as a special gift to the LORD. Bring the fat of the animal, together with the breast, and lift up the breast as a special offering to the LORD. Then the priest will burn the fat on the altar, but the breast will belong to

Aaron and his descendants. Give the right thigh of your peace offering to the priest as a gift. The right thigh must always be given to the priest who offers the blood and the fat of the peace offering. For I have reserved the breast of the special offering and the right thigh of the sacred offering for the priests. It is the permanent right of Aaron and his descendants to share in the peace offerings brought by the people of Israel. This is their rightful share. The special gifts presented to the Lord have been reserved for Aaron and his descendants from the time they were set apart to serve the Lord as priests. On the day they were anointed, the Lord commanded the Israelites to give these portions to the priests as their permanent share from generation to generation."

These are the instructions for the burnt offering, the grain offering, the sin offering, and the guilt offering, as well as the ordination offering and the peace offering. The Lord gave these instructions to Moses on Mount Sinai when he commanded the Israelites to present their offerings to the Lord in the wilderness of Sinai.

+ + +

Then the Lord said to Moses, "Bring Aaron and his sons, along with their sacred garments, the anointing oil, the bull for the sin offering, the two rams, and the basket of bread made without yeast, and call the entire community of Israel together at the entrance of the Tabernacle."

So Moses followed the Lord's instructions, and the whole community assembled at the Tabernacle entrance. Moses announced to them, "This is what the Lord has commanded us to do!" Then he presented Aaron and his sons and washed them with water. He put the official tunic on Aaron and tied the sash around his waist. He dressed him in the robe, placed the ephod on him, and attached the ephod securely with its decorative sash. Then Moses placed the chestpiece on Aaron and put the Urim and the Thummim inside it. He placed the turban on Aaron's head and attached the gold medallion—the badge of holiness—to the front of the turban, just as the Lord had commanded him.

Then Moses took the anointing oil and anointed the Tabernacle and everything in it, making them holy. He sprinkled the oil on the altar seven times, anointing it and all its utensils, as well as the washbasin and its stand, making them holy. Then he poured some of the anointing oil on Aaron's head, anointing him and making him holy for his work. Next Moses presented Aaron's sons. He clothed them in their tunics, tied their sashes around them, and put their special head coverings on them, just as the Lord had commanded him.

Then Moses presented the bull for the sin offering. Aaron and his sons laid their hands on the bull's head, and Moses slaughtered it. Moses took some of the blood, and with his finger he put it on the four horns of the altar to purify it. He poured out the rest of the blood at the base of the altar. Through this process, he made the altar holy by purifying it. Then Moses took all the fat around the internal organs, the long lobe of the liver, and the two kidneys and the fat around them, and he burned it all on the altar. He took the rest of the bull, including its hide, meat, and dung, and burned it on a fire outside the camp, just as the LORD had commanded him.

Then Moses presented the ram for the burnt offering. Aaron and his sons laid their hands on the ram's head, and Moses slaughtered it. Then Moses took the ram's blood and splattered it against all sides of the altar. Then he cut the ram into pieces, and he burned the head, some of its pieces, and the fat on the altar. After washing the internal organs and the legs with water, Moses burned the entire ram on the altar as a burnt offering. It was a pleasing aroma, a special gift presented to the LORD, just as the LORD had commanded him.

Then Moses presented the other ram, which was the ram of ordination. Aaron and his sons laid their hands on the ram's head, and Moses slaughtered it. Then Moses took some of its blood and applied it to the lobe of Aaron's right ear, the thumb of his right hand, and the big toe of his right foot. Next Moses presented Aaron's sons and applied some of the blood to the lobes of their right ears, the thumbs of their right hands, and the big toes of their right feet. He then splattered the rest of the blood against all sides of the altar.

Next Moses took the fat, including the fat of the broad tail, the fat around the internal organs, the long lobe of the liver, and the two kidneys and the fat around them, along with the right thigh. On top of these he placed a thin cake of bread made without yeast, a cake of bread mixed with olive oil, and a wafer spread with olive oil. All these were taken from the basket of bread made without yeast that was placed in the LORD's presence. He put all these in the hands of Aaron and his sons, and he lifted these gifts as a special offering to the LORD. Moses then took all the offerings back from them and burned them on the altar on top of the burnt offering. This was the ordination offering. It was a pleasing aroma, a special gift presented to the LORD. Then Moses took the breast and lifted it up as a special offering to the LORD. This was Moses' portion of the ram of ordination, just as the LORD had commanded him.

Next Moses took some of the anointing oil and some of the blood that was on the altar, and he sprinkled them on Aaron and his garments and on his sons and their garments. In this way, he made Aaron and his sons and their garments holy.

Then Moses said to Aaron and his sons, "Boil the remaining meat of the offerings at the Tabernacle entrance, and eat it there, along with the bread that is in the basket of offerings for the ordination, just as I commanded when I said, 'Aaron and his sons will eat it.' Any meat or bread that is left over must then be burned up. You must not leave the Tabernacle entrance for seven days, for that is when the ordination ceremony will be completed. Everything we have done today was commanded by the LORD in order to purify you, making you right with him. Now stay at the entrance of the Tabernacle day and night for seven days, and do everything the LORD requires. If you fail to do this, you will die, for this is what the LORD has commanded." So Aaron and his sons did everything the LORD had commanded through Moses.

After the ordination ceremony, on the eighth day, Moses called together Aaron and his sons and the elders of Israel. He said to Aaron, "Take a young bull for a sin offering and a ram for a burnt offering, both without defects, and present them to the LORD. Then tell the Israelites, 'Take a male goat for a sin offering, and take a calf and a lamb, both a year old and without defects, for a burnt offering. Also take a bull and a ram for a peace offering and flour moistened with olive oil for a grain offering. Present all these offerings to the LORD because the LORD will appear to you today.'"

So the people presented all these things at the entrance of the Tabernacle, just as Moses had commanded. Then the whole community came forward and stood before the LORD. And Moses said, "This is what the LORD has commanded you to do so that the glory of the LORD may appear to you."

Then Moses said to Aaron, "Come to the altar and sacrifice your sin offering and your burnt offering to purify yourself and the people. Then present the offerings of the people to purify them, making them right with the LORD, just as he has commanded."

So Aaron went to the altar and slaughtered the calf as a sin offering for himself. His sons brought him the blood, and he dipped his finger in it and put it on the horns of the altar. He poured out the rest of the blood at the base of the altar. Then he burned on the altar the fat, the kidneys, and the long lobe of the liver from the sin offering, just as the LORD had commanded Moses. The meat and the hide, however, he burned outside the camp.

Next Aaron slaughtered the animal for the burnt offering. His sons brought him the blood, and he splattered it against all sides of the altar. Then they handed him each piece of the burnt offering, including the head, and he burned them on the altar. Then he washed the internal organs and the legs and burned them on the altar along with the rest of the burnt offering.

Next Aaron presented the offerings of the people. He slaughtered the people's goat and presented it as an offering for their sin, just as he had first done with the offering for his own sin. Then he presented the burnt offering and sacrificed it in the prescribed way. He also presented the grain offering, burning a handful of the flour mixture on the altar, in addition to the regular burnt offering for the morning.

Then Aaron slaughtered the bull and the ram for the people's peace offering. His sons brought him the blood, and he splattered it against all sides of the altar. Then he took the fat of the bull and the ram—the fat of the broad tail and from around the internal organs—along with the kidneys and the long lobes of the livers. He placed these fat portions on top of the breasts of these animals and burned them on the altar. Aaron then lifted up the breasts and right thighs as a special offering to the LORD, just as Moses had commanded.

After that, Aaron raised his hands toward the people and blessed them. Then, after presenting the sin offering, the burnt offering, and the peace offering, he stepped down from the altar. Then Moses and Aaron went into the Tabernacle, and when they came back out, they blessed the people again, and the glory of the LORD appeared to the whole community. Fire blazed forth from the LORD's presence and consumed the burnt offering and the fat on the altar. When the people saw this, they shouted with joy and fell face down on the ground.

Aaron's sons Nadab and Abihu put coals of fire in their incense burners and sprinkled incense over them. In this way, they disobeyed the LORD by burning before him the wrong kind of fire, different than he had commanded. So fire blazed forth from the LORD's presence and burned them up, and they died there before the LORD.

Then Moses said to Aaron, "This is what the LORD meant when he said,

'I will display my holiness
    through those who come near me.
I will display my glory
    before all the people.'"

And Aaron was silent.

Then Moses called for Mishael and Elzaphan, Aaron's cousins, the sons of Aaron's uncle Uzziel. He said to them, "Come forward and carry away the bodies of your relatives from in front of the sanctuary to a place outside the camp." So they came forward and picked them up by their garments and carried them out of the camp, just as Moses had commanded.

Then Moses said to Aaron and his sons Eleazar and Ithamar, "Do not show grief by leaving your hair uncombed or by tearing your clothes. If you do, you will die, and the LORD's anger will strike the whole community of Israel. However, the rest of the Israelites, your relatives, may mourn because of the LORD's fiery destruction of Nadab and Abihu. But you must not leave the entrance of the Tabernacle or you will die, for you have been anointed with the LORD's anointing oil." So they did as Moses commanded.

Then the LORD said to Aaron, "You and your descendants must never drink wine or any other alcoholic drink before going into the Tabernacle. If you do, you will die. This is a permanent law for you, and it must be observed from generation to generation. You must distinguish between what is sacred and what is common, between what is ceremonially unclean and what is clean. And you must teach the Israelites all the decrees that the LORD has given them through Moses."

Then Moses said to Aaron and his remaining sons, Eleazar and Ithamar, "Take what is left of the grain offering after a portion has been presented as a special gift to the LORD, and eat it beside the altar. Make sure it contains no yeast, for it is most holy. You must eat it in a sacred place, for it has been given to you and your descendants as your portion of the special gifts presented to the LORD. These are the commands I have been given. But the breast and thigh that were lifted up as a special offering may be eaten in any place that is ceremonially clean. These parts have been given to you and your descendants as your portion of the peace offerings presented by the people of Israel. You must lift up the thigh and breast as a special offering to the LORD, along with the fat of the special gifts. These parts will belong to you and your descendants as your permanent right, just as the LORD has commanded."

Moses then asked them what had happened to the goat of the sin offering. When he discovered it had been burned up, he became very angry with Eleazar and Ithamar, Aaron's remaining sons. "Why didn't you eat the sin offering in the sacred area?" he demanded. "It is a holy offering! The LORD has given it to you to remove the guilt of the community and to purify the people, making them right with the LORD. Since the animal's blood was not brought into the Holy Place, you should have eaten the meat in the sacred area as I ordered you."

Then Aaron answered Moses, "Today my sons presented both their sin offering and their burnt offering to the LORD. And yet this tragedy has happened to me. If I had eaten the people's sin offering on such a tragic day as this, would the LORD have been pleased?" And when Moses heard this, he was satisfied.

✦ ✦ ✦

Then the LORD said to Moses and Aaron, "Give the following instructions to the people of Israel.

"Of all the land animals, these are the ones you may use for food. You may eat any animal that has completely split hooves and chews the cud. You may not, however, eat the following animals that have split hooves or that chew the cud, but not both. The camel chews the cud but does not have split hooves, so it is ceremonially unclean for you. The hyrax chews the cud but does not have split hooves, so it is unclean. The hare chews the cud but does not have split hooves, so it is unclean. The pig has evenly split hooves but does not chew the cud, so it is unclean. You may not eat the meat of these animals or even touch their carcasses. They are ceremonially unclean for you.

"Of all the marine animals, these are ones you may use for food. You may eat anything from the water if it has both fins and scales, whether taken from salt water or from streams. But you must never eat animals from the sea or from rivers that do not have both fins and scales. They are detestable to you. This applies both to little creatures that live in shallow water and to all creatures that live in deep water. They will always be detestable to you. You must never eat their meat or even touch their dead bodies. Any marine animal that does not have both fins and scales is detestable to you.

"These are the birds that are detestable to you. You must never eat them: the griffon vulture, the bearded vulture, the black vulture, the kite, falcons of all kinds, ravens of all kinds, the eagle owl, the short-eared owl, the seagull, hawks of all kinds, the little owl, the cormorant, the great owl, the barn owl, the desert owl, the Egyptian vulture, the stork, herons of all kinds, the hoopoe, and the bat.

"You must not eat winged insects that walk along the ground; they are detestable to you. You may, however, eat winged insects that walk along the ground and have jointed legs so they can jump. The insects you are permitted to eat include all kinds of locusts, bald locusts, crickets, and grasshoppers. All other winged insects that walk along the ground are detestable to you.

"The following creatures will make you ceremonially unclean. If any of you touch their carcasses, you will be defiled until evening. If you pick up their carcasses, you must wash your clothes, and you will remain defiled until evening.

"Any animal that has split hooves that are not evenly divided or that does not chew the cud is unclean for you. If you touch the carcass of such an animal, you will be defiled. Of the animals that walk on all fours, those that have paws are unclean. If you touch the carcass of such an animal, you will be defiled until evening. If you pick up its carcass, you must wash your clothes, and you will remain defiled until evening. These animals are unclean for you.

"Of the small animals that scurry along the ground, these are unclean for you: the mole rat, the rat, large lizards of all kinds, the gecko, the monitor lizard, the common lizard, the sand lizard, and the chameleon. All these small animals are unclean for you. If any of you touch the dead body of such an animal, you will be defiled until evening. If such an animal dies and falls on something, that object will be unclean. This is true whether the object is made of wood, cloth, leather, or burlap. Whatever its use, you must dip it in water, and it will remain defiled until evening. After that, it will be ceremonially clean and may be used again.

"If such an animal falls into a clay pot, everything in the pot will be defiled, and the pot must be smashed. If the water from such a container spills on any food, the food will be defiled. And any beverage in such a container will be defiled. Any object on which the carcass of such an animal falls will be defiled. If it is an oven or hearth, it must be destroyed, for it is defiled, and you must treat it accordingly.

"However, if the carcass of such an animal falls into a spring or a cistern, the water will still be clean. But anyone who touches the carcass will be defiled. If the carcass falls on seed grain to be planted in the field, the seed will still be considered clean. But if the seed is wet when the carcass falls on it, the seed will be defiled.

"If an animal you are permitted to eat dies and you touch its carcass, you will be defiled until evening. If you eat any of its meat or carry away its carcass, you must wash your clothes, and you will remain defiled until evening.

"All small animals that scurry along the ground are detestable, and you must never eat them. This includes all animals that slither along on their bellies, as well as those with four legs and those with many feet. All such animals that scurry along the ground are detestable, and you must never eat them. Do not defile yourselves by touching them. You must not make yourselves ceremonially unclean because of them. For I am the LORD your God. You must consecrate yourselves and be holy, because I am holy. So do not defile yourselves with any of these small animals that scurry along the ground. For I, the LORD, am the one who brought you up from the land of Egypt, that I might be your God. Therefore, you must be holy because I am holy.

"These are the instructions regarding land animals, birds, marine creatures, and animals that scurry along the ground. By these instructions you will know what is unclean and clean, and which animals may be eaten and which may not be eaten."

+

The LORD said to Moses, "Give the following instructions to the people of Israel. If a woman becomes pregnant and gives birth to a son, she will be ceremonially unclean for seven days, just as she is unclean during her menstrual period. On the eighth day the boy's foreskin must be circumcised. After waiting thirty-three days, she will be purified from the bleeding of childbirth. During this time of purification, she must not touch anything that is set apart as holy. And she must not enter the sanctuary until her time of purification is over. If a woman gives birth to a daughter, she will be ceremonially unclean for two weeks, just as she is unclean during her menstrual period. After waiting sixty-six days, she will be purified from the bleeding of childbirth.

"When the time of purification is completed for either a son or a daughter, the woman must bring a one-year-old lamb for a burnt offering and a young pigeon or turtledove for a purification offering. She must bring her offerings to the priest at the entrance of the Tabernacle. The priest will then present them to the LORD to purify her. Then she will be ceremonially clean again after her bleeding at childbirth. These are the instructions for a woman after the birth of a son or a daughter.

"If a woman cannot afford to bring a lamb, she must bring two turtledoves or two young pigeons. One will be for the burnt offering and the other for the purification offering. The priest will sacrifice them to purify her, and she will be ceremonially clean."

+

The LORD said to Moses and Aaron, "If anyone has a swelling or a rash or discolored skin that might develop into a serious skin disease, that person must be brought to Aaron the priest or to one of his sons. The priest will examine the affected area of the skin. If the hair in the affected area has turned white and the problem appears to be more than skin-deep, it is a serious skin disease, and the priest who examines it must pronounce the person ceremonially unclean.

"But if the affected area of the skin is only a white discoloration and does not appear to be more than skin-deep, and if the hair on the spot has not turned white, the priest will quarantine the person for seven days. On the seventh day the priest will make another examination. If he finds the affected area has not changed and the problem has not spread on the skin, the priest will quarantine the person for seven more days. On the seventh day the priest will make another examination. If he finds the affected area has faded and has not spread, the priest will pronounce the person ceremonially clean. It was only a rash. The person's clothing must be washed, and the person will be ceremonially clean. But if the rash continues to spread after the person has been examined by the priest and has been pronounced clean, the infected person must return to be examined again. If the priest finds that the rash has spread, he must pronounce the person ceremonially unclean, for it is indeed a skin disease.

"Anyone who develops a serious skin disease must go to the priest for an examination. If the priest finds a white swelling on the skin, and some hair on the spot has turned white, and there is an open sore in the affected area, it is a chronic skin disease, and the priest must pronounce the person ceremonially unclean. In such cases the person need not be quarantined, for it is obvious that the skin is defiled by the disease.

"Now suppose the disease has spread all over the person's skin, covering the body from head to foot. When the priest examines the infected person and finds that the disease covers the entire body, he will pronounce the person ceremonially clean. Since the skin has turned completely white, the person is clean. But if any open sores appear, the infected person will be pronounced ceremonially unclean. The priest must make this pronouncement as soon as he sees an open sore, since open sores indicate the presence of a skin disease. However, if the open sores heal and turn white like the rest of the skin, the person must return to the priest for another examination. If the affected areas have indeed turned white, the priest will then pronounce the person ceremonially clean by declaring, 'You are clean!'

"If anyone has a boil on the skin that has started to heal, but a white swelling or a reddish white spot develops in its place, that person must go to the priest to be examined. If the priest examines it and finds it to be more than skin-deep, and if the hair in the affected area has turned white, the priest must pronounce the person ceremonially unclean. The boil has become a serious skin disease. But if the priest finds no white hair on the affected area and the problem appears to be no more than skin-deep and has faded, the priest must quarantine the person for seven days. If during that time the affected area spreads on the skin, the priest must pronounce the person ceremonially unclean, because it is a serious disease. But if the area grows no larger and does not spread, it is merely the scar from the boil, and the priest will pronounce the person ceremonially clean.

"If anyone has suffered a burn on the skin and the burned area changes color, becoming either reddish white or shiny white, the priest must examine it. If he finds that the hair in the affected area has turned white and the problem appears to be more than skin-deep, a skin disease has broken out in the burn. The priest must then pronounce the person ceremonially unclean, for it is clearly a serious skin disease. But if the priest finds no white hair on the affected area and the problem appears to be no more than skin-deep and has faded, the priest must quarantine the infected person for seven days. On the seventh day the priest must examine the person again. If the affected area has spread on the skin, the priest must pronounce that person ceremonially unclean, for it is clearly a serious skin disease. But if the affected area has not changed or spread on the skin and has faded, it is simply a swelling from the burn. The priest will then pronounce the person ceremonially clean, for it is only the scar from the burn.

"If anyone, either a man or woman, has a sore on the head or chin, the priest must examine it. If he finds it is more than skin-deep and has fine yellow hair on it, the priest must pronounce the person ceremonially unclean. It is a scabby sore of the head or chin. If the priest examines the scabby sore and finds that it is only skin-deep but there is no black hair on it, he must quarantine the person for seven days. On the seventh day the priest must examine the sore again. If he finds that the scabby sore has not spread, and there is no yellow hair on it, and it appears to be only skin-deep, the person must shave off all hair except the hair on the affected area. Then the priest must quarantine the person for another seven days. On the seventh day he will examine the sore again. If it has not spread and appears to be no more than skin-deep, the priest will pronounce the person ceremonially clean. The person's clothing must be washed, and the person will be ceremonially clean. But if the scabby sore begins to spread after the person is pronounced clean, the priest must do another examination. If he finds that the sore has spread, the priest does not need to look for yellow hair. The infected person is ceremonially unclean. But if the color of the scabby sore does not change and black hair has grown on it, it has healed. The priest will then pronounce the person ceremonially clean.

"If anyone, either a man or woman, has shiny white patches on the skin, the priest must examine the affected area. If he finds that the shiny patches are only pale white, this is a harmless skin rash, and the person is ceremonially clean.

"If a man loses his hair and his head becomes bald, he is still ceremonially clean. And if he loses hair on his forehead, he simply has a bald forehead; he is still clean. However, if a reddish white sore appears on the bald area on top of his head or on his forehead, this is a skin disease. The priest must examine him, and if he finds swelling around the reddish white sore anywhere on the man's head and it looks like a skin disease, the man is indeed infected with a skin disease and is unclean. The priest must pronounce him ceremonially unclean because of the sore on his head.

"Those who suffer from a serious skin disease must tear their clothing and leave their hair uncombed. They must cover their mouth and call out, 'Unclean! Unclean!' As long as the serious disease lasts, they will be ceremonially unclean. They must live in isolation in their place outside the camp.

"Now suppose mildew contaminates some woolen or linen clothing, woolen or linen fabric, the hide of an animal, or anything made of leather. If the contaminated area in the clothing, the animal hide, the fabric, or the leather article has turned greenish or reddish, it is contaminated with mildew and must be shown to the priest. After examining the affected spot, the priest will put the article in quarantine for seven days. On the seventh day the priest must inspect it again. If the contaminated area has spread, the clothing or fabric or leather is clearly contaminated by a serious mildew and is ceremonially unclean. The priest must burn the item—the clothing, the woolen or linen fabric, or piece of leather—for it has been contaminated by a serious mildew. It must be completely destroyed by fire.

"But if the priest examines it and finds that the contaminated area has not spread in the clothing, the fabric, or the leather, the priest will order the object to be washed and then quarantined for seven more days. Then the priest must examine the object again. If he finds that the contaminated area has not changed color after being washed, even if it did not spread, the object is defiled. It must be completely burned up, whether the contaminated spot is on the inside or outside. But if the priest examines it and finds that the contaminated area has faded after being washed, he must cut the spot from the clothing, the fabric, or the leather. If the spot later reappears on the clothing, the fabric, or the leather article, the mildew is clearly spreading, and the contaminated object must be burned up. But if the spot disappears from the clothing, the fabric, or the leather article after it has been washed, it must be washed again; then it will be ceremonially clean.

"These are the instructions for dealing with mildew that contaminates woolen or linen clothing or fabric or anything made of leather. This is how the priest will determine whether these items are ceremonially clean or unclean."

And the LORD said to Moses, "The following instructions are for those seeking ceremonial purification from a skin disease. Those who have been healed must be brought to the priest, who will examine them at a place outside the camp. If the priest finds that someone has been healed of a serious skin disease, he will perform a purification ceremony, using two live birds that are ceremonially clean, a stick of cedar, some scarlet yarn, and a hyssop branch. The priest will order that one bird be slaughtered over a clay pot filled with fresh water. He will take the live bird, the cedar stick, the scarlet yarn, and the hyssop branch, and dip them into the blood of the bird that was slaughtered over the fresh water. The priest will then sprinkle the blood of the dead bird seven times on the person being puri-fied of the skin disease. When the priest has purified the person, he will release the live bird in the open field to fly away.

"The persons being purified must then wash their clothes, shave off all their hair, and bathe themselves in water. Then they will be ceremonially clean and may return to the camp. However, they must remain outside their tents for seven days. On the seventh day they must again shave all the hair from their heads, including the hair of the beard and eyebrows. They must also wash their clothes and bathe themselves in water. Then they will be ceremonially clean.

"On the eighth day each person being purified must bring two male lambs and a one-year-old female lamb, all with no defects, along with a grain offering of six quarts of choice flour moistened with olive oil, and a cup of olive oil. Then the officiating priest will present that person for purification, along with the offerings, before the LORD at the entrance of the Tabernacle. The priest will take one of the male lambs and the olive oil and present them as a guilt offering, lifting them up as a special offering before the LORD. He will then slaughter the male lamb in the sacred area where sin offerings and burnt offerings are slaughtered. As with the sin offering, the guilt offering belongs to the priest. It is a most holy offering. The priest will then take some of the blood of the guilt offering and apply it to the lobe of the right ear, the thumb of the right hand, and the big toe of the right foot of the person being purified.

"Then the priest will pour some of the olive oil into the palm of his own left hand. He will dip his right finger into the oil in his palm and sprinkle some of it with his finger seven times before the LORD. The priest will then apply some of the oil in his palm over the blood from the guilt offering that is on the lobe of the right ear, the thumb of the right hand, and the big toe of the right foot of the person being purified. The priest will apply the oil remaining in his hand to the head of the person being purified. Through this process, the priest will purify the person before the LORD.

"Then the priest must present the sin offering to purify the person who was cured of the skin disease. After that, the priest will slaughter the burnt offering and offer it on the altar along with the grain offering. Through this process, the priest will purify the person who was healed, and the person will be ceremonially clean.

"But anyone who is too poor and cannot afford these offerings may bring one male lamb for a guilt offering, to be lifted up as a special offer-ing for purification. The person must also bring two quarts of choice flour moistened with olive oil for the grain offering and a cup of olive oil. The offering must also include two turtledoves or two young pigeons, which-ever the person can afford. One of the pair must be used for the sin offering and the other for a burnt offering. On the eighth day of the purification ceremony, the person being purified must bring the offerings to the priest in the LORD's presence at the entrance of the Tabernacle. The priest will take the lamb for the guilt offering, along with the olive oil, and lift them up as a special offering to the LORD. Then the priest will slaughter the lamb for the guilt offering. He will take some of its blood and apply it to the lobe of the right ear, the thumb of the right hand, and the big toe of the right foot of the person being purified.

"The priest will also pour some of the olive oil into the palm of his own left hand. He will dip his right finger into the oil in his palm and sprinkle some of it seven times before the LORD. The priest will then apply some of the oil in his palm over the blood from the guilt offering that is on the lobe of the right ear, the thumb of the right hand, and the big toe of the right foot of the person being purified. The priest will apply the oil remaining in his hand to the head of the person being purified. Through this process, the priest will purify the person before the LORD.

"Then the priest will offer the two turtledoves or the two young pigeons, whichever the person can afford. One of them is for a sin offering and the other for a burnt offering, to be presented along with the grain offering. Through this process, the priest will purify the person before the LORD. These are the instructions for purification for those who have recovered from a serious skin disease but who cannot afford to bring the offerings normally required for the ceremony of purification."

Then the LORD said to Moses and Aaron, "When you arrive in Canaan, the land I am giving you as your own possession, I may contaminate some of the houses in your land with mildew. The owner of such a house must then go to the priest and say, 'It appears that my house has some kind of mildew.' Before the priest goes in to inspect the house, he must have the house emptied so nothing inside will be pronounced ceremonially unclean. Then the priest will go in and examine the mildew on the walls. If he finds greenish or reddish streaks and the contamination appears to go deeper than the wall's surface, the priest will step outside the door and put the house in quarantine for seven days. On the seventh day the priest must return for another inspection. If he finds that the mildew on the walls of the house has spread, the priest must order that the stones from those areas be removed. The contaminated material will then be taken outside the town to an area designated as ceremonially unclean. Next the inside walls of the entire house must be scraped thoroughly and the scrapings dumped in the unclean place outside the town. Other stones will be brought in to replace the ones that were removed, and the walls will be replastered.

"But if the mildew reappears after all the stones have been replaced and the house has been scraped and replastered, the priest must return and inspect the house again. If he finds that the mildew has spread, the walls are clearly contaminated with a serious mildew, and the house is defiled. It must be torn down, and all its stones, timbers, and plaster must be carried out of town to the place designated as ceremonially unclean. Those who enter the house during the period of quarantine will be ceremonially unclean until evening, and all who sleep or eat in the house must wash their clothing.

"But if the priest returns for his inspection and finds that the mildew has not reappeared in the house after the fresh plastering, he will pronounce it clean because the mildew is clearly gone. To purify the house the priest must take two birds, a stick of cedar, some scarlet yarn, and a hyssop branch. He will slaughter one of the birds over a clay pot filled with fresh water. He will take the cedar stick, the hyssop branch, the scarlet yarn, and the live bird, and dip them into the blood of the slaughtered bird and into the fresh water. Then he will sprinkle the house seven times. When the priest has purified the house in exactly this way, he will release the live bird in the open fields outside the town. Through this process, the priest will purify the house, and it will be ceremonially clean.

"These are the instructions for dealing with serious skin diseases, including scabby sores; and mildew, whether on clothing or in a house; and a swelling on the skin, a rash, or discolored skin. This procedure will determine whether a person or object is ceremonially clean or unclean.

"These are the instructions regarding skin diseases and mildew."

+

The LORD said to Moses and Aaron, "Give the following instructions to the people of Israel.

"Any man who has a bodily discharge is ceremonially unclean. This defilement is caused by his discharge, whether the discharge continues or stops. In either case the man is unclean. Any bed on which the man with the discharge lies and anything on which he sits will be ceremonially unclean. So if you touch the man's bed, you must wash your clothes and bathe yourself in water, and you will remain unclean until evening. If you sit where the man with the discharge has sat, you must wash your clothes and bathe yourself in water, and you will remain unclean until evening. If you touch the man with the discharge, you must wash your clothes and bathe yourself in water, and you will remain unclean until evening. If the man spits on you, you must wash your clothes and bathe yourself in water, and you will remain unclean until evening. Any saddle blanket on which the man rides will be ceremonially unclean. If you touch anything that was under the man, you will be unclean until evening. You must wash your clothes and bathe yourself in water, and you will remain unclean until evening. If the man touches you without first rinsing his hands, you must wash your clothes and bathe yourself in water, and you will remain unclean until evening. Any clay pot the man touches must be broken, and any wooden utensil he touches must be rinsed with water.

"When the man with the discharge is healed, he must count off seven days for the period of purification. Then he must wash his clothes and bathe himself in fresh water, and he will be ceremonially clean. On the eighth day he must get two turtledoves or two young pigeons and come before the LORD at the entrance of the Tabernacle and give his offerings to the priest. The priest will offer one bird for a sin offering and the other for a burnt offering. Through this process, the priest will purify the man before the LORD for his discharge.

"Whenever a man has an emission of semen, he must bathe his entire body in water, and he will remain ceremonially unclean until the next evening. Any clothing or leather with semen on it must be washed in water, and it will remain unclean until evening. After a man and a woman have sexual intercourse, they must each bathe in water, and they will remain unclean until the next evening.

"Whenever a woman has her menstrual period, she will be ceremonially unclean for seven days. Anyone who touches her during that time will be unclean until evening. Anything on which the woman lies or sits during the time of her period will be unclean. If any of you touch her bed, you must wash your clothes and bathe yourself in water, and you will remain unclean until evening. If you touch any object she has sat on, you must wash your clothes and bathe yourself in water, and you will remain unclean until evening. This includes her bed or any other object she has sat on; you will be unclean until evening if you touch it. If a man has sexual intercourse with her and her blood touches him, her menstrual impurity will be transmitted to him. He will remain unclean for seven days, and any bed on which he lies will be unclean.

"If a woman has a flow of blood for many days that is unrelated to her menstrual period, or if the blood continues beyond the normal period, she is ceremonially unclean. As during her menstrual period, the woman will be unclean as long as the discharge continues. Any bed she lies on and any object she sits on during that time will be unclean, just as during her normal menstrual period. If any of you touch these things, you will be ceremonially unclean. You must wash your clothes and bathe yourself in water, and you will remain unclean until evening.

"When the woman's bleeding stops, she must count off seven days. Then she will be ceremonially clean. On the eighth day she must bring two turtledoves or two young pigeons and present them to the priest at the entrance of the Tabernacle. The priest will offer one for a sin offering and the other for a burnt offering. Through this process, the priest will purify her before the LORD for the ceremonial impurity caused by her bleeding.

"This is how you will guard the people of Israel from ceremonial uncleanness. Otherwise they would die, for their impurity would defile my Tabernacle that stands among them. These are the instructions for dealing with anyone who has a bodily discharge—a man who is unclean because of an emission of semen or a woman during her menstrual period. It applies to any man or woman who has a bodily discharge, and to a man who has sexual intercourse with a woman who is ceremonially unclean."

✛ ✛ ✛

The LORD spoke to Moses after the death of Aaron's two sons, who died after they entered the LORD's presence and burned the wrong kind of fire before him. The LORD said to Moses, "Warn your brother, Aaron, not to enter the Most Holy Place behind the inner curtain whenever he chooses; if he does, he will die. For the Ark's cover—the place of atonement—is there, and I myself am present in the cloud above the atonement cover.

"When Aaron enters the sanctuary area, he must follow these instructions fully. He must bring a young bull for a sin offering and a ram for a burnt offering. He must put on his linen tunic and the linen undergarments worn next to his body. He must tie the linen sash around his waist and put the linen turban on his head. These are sacred garments, so he must bathe himself in water before he puts them on. Aaron must take from the community of Israel two male goats for a sin offering and a ram for a burnt offering.

"Aaron will present his own bull as a sin offering to purify himself and his family, making them right with the LORD. Then he must take the two male goats and present them to the LORD at the entrance of the Tabernacle. He is to cast sacred lots to determine which goat will be reserved as an offering to the LORD and which will carry the sins of the people to the wilderness of Azazel. Aaron will then present as a sin offering the goat chosen by lot for the LORD. The other goat, the scapegoat chosen by lot to be sent away, will be kept alive, standing before the LORD. When it is sent away to Azazel in the wilderness, the people will be purified and made right with the LORD.

"Aaron will present his own bull as a sin offering to purify himself and his family, making them right with the LORD. After he has slaughtered the bull as a sin offering, he will fill an incense burner with burning coals from the altar that stands before the LORD. Then he will take two handfuls of fragrant powdered incense and will carry the burner and the incense behind the inner curtain. There in the LORD's presence he will put the incense on the burning coals so that a cloud of incense will rise over the Ark's cover—the place of atonement—that rests on the Ark of the Covenant. If he follows these instructions, he will not die. Then he must take some of the blood of the bull, dip his finger in it, and sprinkle it on the east side of the atonement cover. He must sprinkle blood seven times with his finger in front of the atonement cover.

"Then Aaron must slaughter the first goat as a sin offering for the people and carry its blood behind the inner curtain. There he will sprinkle the goat's blood over the atonement cover and in front of it, just as he did with the bull's blood. Through this process, he will purify the Most Holy Place, and he will do the same for the entire Tabernacle, because of the defiling sin and rebellion of the Israelites. No one else is allowed inside the Tabernacle when Aaron enters it for the purification ceremony in the Most Holy Place. No one may enter until he comes out again after purifying himself, his family, and all the congregation of Israel, making them right with the LORD.

"Then Aaron will come out to purify the altar that stands before the LORD. He will do this by taking some of the blood from the bull and the goat and putting it on each of the horns of the altar. Then he must sprinkle the blood with his finger seven times over the altar. In this way, he will cleanse it from Israel's defilement and make it holy.

"When Aaron has finished purifying the Most Holy Place and the Tabernacle and the altar, he must present the live goat. He will lay both of his hands on the goat's head and confess over it all the wickedness, rebellion, and sins of the people of Israel. In this way, he will transfer the people's sins to the head of the goat. Then a man specially chosen for the task will drive the goat into the wilderness. As the goat goes into the wilderness, it will carry all the people's sins upon itself into a desolate land.

"When Aaron goes back into the Tabernacle, he must take off the linen garments he was wearing when he entered the Most Holy Place, and he must leave the garments there. Then he must bathe himself with water in a sacred place, put on his regular garments, and go out to sacrifice a burnt offering for himself and a burnt offering for the people. Through this process, he will purify himself and the people, making them right with the LORD. He must then burn all the fat of the sin offering on the altar.

"The man chosen to drive the scapegoat into the wilderness of Azazel must wash his clothes and bathe himself in water. Then he may return to the camp.

"The bull and the goat presented as sin offerings, whose blood Aaron takes into the Most Holy Place for the purification ceremony, will be carried outside the camp. The animals' hides, internal organs, and dung are all to be burned. The man who burns them must wash his clothes and bathe himself in water before returning to the camp.

"On the tenth day of the appointed month in early autumn, you must deny yourselves. Neither native-born Israelites nor foreigners living among you may do any kind of work. This is a permanent law for you. On that day offerings of purification will be made for you, and you will be purified in the Lord's presence from all your sins. It will be a Sabbath day of complete rest for you, and you must deny yourselves. This is a permanent law for you. In future generations, the purification ceremony will be performed by the priest who has been anointed and ordained to serve as high priest in place of his ancestor Aaron. He will put on the holy linen garments and purify the Most Holy Place, the Tabernacle, the altar, the priests, and the entire congregation. This is a permanent law for you, to purify the people of Israel from their sins, making them right with the Lord once each year."

Moses followed all these instructions exactly as the Lord had commanded him.

+ + +

Then the Lord said to Moses, "Give the following instructions to Aaron and his sons and all the people of Israel. This is what the Lord has commanded.

"If any native Israelite sacrifices a bull or a lamb or a goat anywhere inside or outside the camp instead of bringing it to the entrance of the Tabernacle to present it as an offering to the Lord, that person will be as guilty as a murderer. Such a person has shed blood and will be cut off from the community. The purpose of this rule is to stop the Israelites from sacrificing animals in the open fields. It will ensure that they bring their sacrifices to the priest at the entrance of the Tabernacle, so he can present them to the Lord as peace offerings. Then the priest will be able to splatter the blood against the Lord's altar at the entrance of the Tabernacle, and he will burn the fat as a pleasing aroma to the Lord. The people must no longer be unfaithful to the Lord by offering sacrifices to the goat idols. This is a permanent law for them, to be observed from generation to generation.

"Give them this command as well. If any native Israelite or foreigner living among you offers a burnt offering or a sacrifice but does not bring it to the entrance of the Tabernacle to offer it to the Lord, that person will be cut off from the community.

"And if any native Israelite or foreigner living among you eats or drinks blood in any form, I will turn against that person and cut him off from the community of your people, for the life of the body is in its blood. I have given you the blood on the altar to purify you, making you right with the LORD. It is the blood, given in exchange for a life, that makes purification possible. That is why I have said to the people of Israel, 'You must never eat or drink blood—neither you nor the foreigners living among you.'

"And if any native Israelite or foreigner living among you goes hunting and kills an animal or bird that is approved for eating, he must drain its blood and cover it with earth. The life of every creature is in its blood. That is why I have said to the people of Israel, 'You must never eat or drink blood, for the life of any creature is in its blood.' So whoever consumes blood will be cut off from the community.

"And if any native-born Israelites or foreigners eat the meat of an animal that died naturally or was torn up by wild animals, they must wash their clothes and bathe themselves in water. They will remain ceremonially unclean until evening, but then they will be clean. But if they do not wash their clothes and bathe themselves, they will be punished for their sin."

+

Then the LORD said to Moses, "Give the following instructions to the people of Israel. I am the LORD your God. So do not act like the people in Egypt, where you used to live, or like the people of Canaan, where I am taking you. You must not imitate their way of life. You must obey all my regulations and be careful to obey my decrees, for I am the LORD your God. If you obey my decrees and my regulations, you will find life through them. I am the LORD.

"You must never have sexual relations with a close relative, for I am the LORD.

"Do not violate your father by having sexual relations with your mother. She is your mother; you must not have sexual relations with her.

"Do not have sexual relations with any of your father's wives, for this would violate your father.

"Do not have sexual relations with your sister or half sister, whether she is your father's daughter or your mother's daughter, whether she was born into your household or someone else's.

"Do not have sexual relations with your granddaughter, whether she is your son's daughter or your daughter's daughter, for this would violate yourself.

"Do not have sexual relations with your stepsister, the daughter of any of your father's wives, for she is your sister.

"Do not have sexual relations with your father's sister, for she is your father's close relative.

"Do not have sexual relations with your mother's sister, for she is your mother's close relative.

"Do not violate your uncle, your father's brother, by having sexual relations with his wife, for she is your aunt.

"Do not have sexual relations with your daughter-in-law; she is your son's wife, so you must not have sexual relations with her.

"Do not have sexual relations with your brother's wife, for this would violate your brother.

"Do not have sexual relations with both a woman and her daughter. And do not take her granddaughter, whether her son's daughter or her daughter's daughter, and have sexual relations with her. They are close relatives, and this would be a wicked act.

"While your wife is living, do not marry her sister and have sexual relations with her, for they would be rivals.

"Do not have sexual relations with a woman during her period of menstrual impurity.

"Do not defile yourself by having sexual intercourse with your neighbor's wife.

"Do not permit any of your children to be offered as a sacrifice to Molech, for you must not bring shame on the name of your God. I am the LORD.

"Do not practice homosexuality, having sex with another man as with a woman. It is a detestable sin.

"A man must not defile himself by having sex with an animal. And a woman must not offer herself to a male animal to have intercourse with it. This is a perverse act.

"Do not defile yourselves in any of these ways, for the people I am driving out before you have defiled themselves in all these ways. Because the entire land has become defiled, I am punishing the people who live there. I will cause the land to vomit them out. You must obey all my decrees and regulations. You must not commit any of these detestable sins. This applies both to native-born Israelites and to the foreigners living among you.

"All these detestable activities are practiced by the people of the land where I am taking you, and this is how the land has become defiled. So do not defile the land and give it a reason to vomit you out, as it will vomit out the people who live there now. Whoever commits any of these detestable sins will be cut off from the community of Israel. So obey my instructions, and do not defile yourselves by committing any of these detestable practices that were committed by the people who lived in the land before you. I am the LORD your God."

+

The LORD also said to Moses, "Give the following instructions to the entire community of Israel. You must be holy because I, the LORD your God, am holy.

"Each of you must show great respect for your mother and father, and you must always observe my Sabbath days of rest. I am the LORD your God.

"Do not put your trust in idols or make metal images of gods for yourselves. I am the LORD your God.

"When you sacrifice a peace offering to the LORD, offer it properly so you will be accepted by God. The sacrifice must be eaten on the same day you offer it or on the next day. Whatever is left over until the third day must be completely burned up. If any of the sacrifice is eaten on the third day, it will be contaminated, and I will not accept it. Anyone who eats it on the third day will be punished for defiling what is holy to the LORD and will be cut off from the community.

"When you harvest the crops of your land, do not harvest the grain along the edges of your fields, and do not pick up what the harvesters drop. It is the same with your grape crop—do not strip every last bunch of grapes from the vines, and do not pick up the grapes that fall to the ground. Leave them for the poor and the foreigners living among you. I am the LORD your God.

"Do not steal.

"Do not deceive or cheat one another.

"Do not bring shame on the name of your God by using it to swear falsely. I am the LORD.

"Do not defraud or rob your neighbor.

"Do not make your hired workers wait until the next day to receive their pay.

"Do not insult the deaf or cause the blind to stumble. You must fear your God; I am the LORD.

"Do not twist justice in legal matters by favoring the poor or being partial to the rich and powerful. Always judge people fairly.

"Do not spread slanderous gossip among your people.

"Do not stand idly by when your neighbor's life is threatened. I am the LORD.

"Do not nurse hatred in your heart for any of your relatives. Confront people directly so you will not be held guilty for their sin.

"Do not seek revenge or bear a grudge against a fellow Israelite, but love your neighbor as yourself. I am the LORD.

"You must obey all my decrees.

"Do not mate two different kinds of animals. Do not plant your field with two different kinds of seed. Do not wear clothing woven from two different kinds of thread.

"If a man has sex with a slave girl whose freedom has never been purchased but who is committed to become another man's wife, he must pay full compensation to her master. But since she is not a free woman, neither the man nor the woman will be put to death. The man, however, must bring a ram as a guilt offering and present it to the LORD at the entrance of the Tabernacle. The priest will then purify him before the LORD with the ram of the guilt offering, and the man's sin will be forgiven.

"When you enter the land and plant fruit trees, leave the fruit unharvested for the first three years and consider it forbidden. Do not eat it. In the fourth year the entire crop must be consecrated to the LORD as a celebration of praise. Finally, in the fifth year you may eat the fruit. If you follow this pattern, your harvest will increase. I am the LORD your God.

"Do not eat meat that has not been drained of its blood.

"Do not practice fortune-telling or witchcraft.

"Do not trim off the hair on your temples or trim your beards.

"Do not cut your bodies for the dead, and do not mark your skin with tattoos. I am the LORD.

"Do not defile your daughter by making her a prostitute, or the land will be filled with prostitution and wickedness.

"Keep my Sabbath days of rest, and show reverence toward my sanctuary. I am the LORD.

"Do not defile yourselves by turning to mediums or to those who consult the spirits of the dead. I am the LORD your God.

"Stand up in the presence of the elderly, and show respect for the aged. Fear your God. I am the LORD.

"Do not take advantage of foreigners who live among you in your land. Treat them like native-born Israelites, and love them as you love yourself. Remember that you were once foreigners living in the land of Egypt. I am the LORD your God.

"Do not use dishonest standards when measuring length, weight, or volume. Your scales and weights must be accurate. Your containers for measuring dry materials or liquids must be accurate. I am the LORD your God who brought you out of the land of Egypt.

"You must be careful to keep all of my decrees and regulations by putting them into practice. I am the LORD."

+

The LORD said to Moses, "Give the people of Israel these instructions, which apply both to native Israelites and to the foreigners living in Israel.

"If any of them offer their children as a sacrifice to Molech, they must be put to death. The people of the community must stone them to death. I myself will turn against them and cut them off from the community, because they have defiled my sanctuary and brought shame on my holy name by offering their children to Molech. And if the people of the community ignore those who offer their children to Molech and refuse to execute them, I myself will turn against them and their families and will cut them off from the community. This will happen to all who commit spiritual prostitution by worshiping Molech.

"I will also turn against those who commit spiritual prostitution by putting their trust in mediums or in those who consult the spirits of the dead. I will cut them off from the community. So set yourselves apart to be holy, for I am the LORD your God. Keep all my decrees by putting them into practice, for I am the LORD who makes you holy.

"Anyone who dishonors father or mother must be put to death. Such a person is guilty of a capital offense.

"If a man commits adultery with his neighbor's wife, both the man and the woman who have committed adultery must be put to death.

"If a man violates his father by having sex with one of his father's wives, both the man and the woman must be put to death, for they are guilty of a capital offense.

"If a man has sex with his daughter-in-law, both must be put to death. They have committed a perverse act and are guilty of a capital offense.

"If a man practices homosexuality, having sex with another man as with a woman, both men have committed a detestable act. They must both be put to death, for they are guilty of a capital offense.

"If a man marries both a woman and her mother, he has committed a wicked act. The man and both women must be burned to death to wipe out such wickedness from among you.

"If a man has sex with an animal, he must be put to death, and the animal must be killed.

"If a woman presents herself to a male animal to have intercourse with it, she and the animal must both be put to death. You must kill both, for they are guilty of a capital offense.

"If a man marries his sister, the daughter of either his father or his mother, and they have sexual relations, it is a shameful disgrace. They must be publicly cut off from the community. Since the man has violated his sister, he will be punished for his sin.

"If a man has sexual relations with a woman during her menstrual period, both of them must be cut off from the community, for together they have exposed the source of her blood flow.

"Do not have sexual relations with your aunt, whether your mother's sister or your father's sister. This would dishonor a close relative. Both parties are guilty and will be punished for their sin.

"If a man has sex with his uncle's wife, he has violated his uncle. Both the man and woman will be punished for their sin, and they will die childless.

"If a man marries his brother's wife, it is an act of impurity. He has violated his brother, and the guilty couple will remain childless.

"You must keep all my decrees and regulations by putting them into practice; otherwise the land to which I am bringing you as your new home will vomit you out. Do not live according to the customs of the people I am driving out before you. It is because they do these shameful things that I detest them. But I have promised you, 'You will possess their land because I will give it to you as your possession—a land flowing with milk and honey.' I am the LORD your God, who has set you apart from all other people.

"You must therefore make a distinction between ceremonially clean and unclean animals, and between clean and unclean birds. You must not defile yourselves by eating any unclean animal or bird or creature that scurries along the ground. I have identified them as being unclean for you. You must be holy because I, the LORD, am holy. I have set you apart from all other people to be my very own.

"Men and women among you who act as mediums or who consult the spirits of the dead must be put to death by stoning. They are guilty of a capital offense."

+

The LORD said to Moses, "Give the following instructions to the priests, the descendants of Aaron.

"A priest must not make himself ceremonially unclean by touching the dead body of a relative. The only exceptions are his closest relatives—his mother or father, son or daughter, brother, or his virgin sister who depends on him because she has no husband. But a priest must not defile himself and make himself unclean for someone who is related to him only by marriage.

"The priests must not shave their heads or trim their beards or cut their bodies. They must be set apart as holy to their God and must never bring shame on the name of God. They must be holy, for they are the ones who present the special gifts to the LORD, gifts of food for their God.

"Priests may not marry a woman defiled by prostitution, and they may not marry a woman who is divorced from her husband, for the priests are set apart as holy to their God. You must treat them as holy because they offer up food to your God. You must consider them holy because I, the LORD, am holy, and I make you holy.

"If a priest's daughter defiles herself by becoming a prostitute, she also defiles her father's holiness, and she must be burned to death.

"The high priest has the highest rank of all the priests. The anointing oil has been poured on his head, and he has been ordained to wear the priestly garments. He must never leave his hair uncombed or tear his clothing. He must not defile himself by going near a dead body. He may not make himself ceremonially unclean even for his father or mother. He must not defile the sanctuary of his God by leaving it to attend to a dead person, for he has been made holy by the anointing oil of his God. I am the LORD.

"The high priest may marry only a virgin. He may not marry a widow, a woman who is divorced, or a woman who has defiled herself by prostitution. She must be a virgin from his own clan, so that he will not dishonor his descendants among his clan, for I am the LORD who makes him holy."

Then the LORD said to Moses, "Give the following instructions to Aaron: In all future generations, none of your descendants who has any defect will qualify to offer food to his God. No one who has a defect qualifies, whether he is blind, lame, disfigured, deformed, or has a broken foot or arm, or is hunchbacked or dwarfed, or has a defective eye, or skin sores or scabs, or damaged testicles. No descendant of Aaron who has a defect may approach the altar to present special gifts to the LORD. Since he has a defect, he may not approach the altar to offer food to his God. However, he may eat from the food offered to God, including the holy offerings and the most holy offerings. Yet because of his physical defect, he may not enter the room behind the inner curtain or approach the altar, for this would defile my holy places. I am the LORD who makes them holy."

So Moses gave these instructions to Aaron and his sons and to all the Israelites.

+

The LORD said to Moses, "Tell Aaron and his sons to be very careful with the sacred gifts that the Israelites set apart for me, so they do not bring shame on my holy name. I am the LORD. Give them the following instructions.

"In all future generations, if any of your descendants is ceremonially unclean when he approaches the sacred offerings that the people of Israel consecrate to the LORD, he must be cut off from my presence. I am the LORD.

"If any of Aaron's descendants has a skin disease or any kind of discharge that makes him ceremonially unclean, he may not eat from the sacred offerings until he has been pronounced clean. He also becomes unclean by touching a corpse, or by having an emission of semen, or by touching a small animal that is unclean, or by touching someone who is ceremonially unclean for any reason. The man who is defiled in any of these ways will remain unclean until evening. He may not eat from the sacred offerings until he has bathed himself in water. When the sun goes down, he will be ceremonially clean again and may eat from the sacred offerings, for this is his food. He may not eat an animal that has died a natural death or has been torn apart by wild animals, for this would defile him. I am the LORD.

"The priests must follow my instructions carefully. Otherwise they will be punished for their sin and will die for violating my instructions. I am the LORD who makes them holy.

"No one outside a priest's family may eat the sacred offerings. Even guests and hired workers in a priest's home are not allowed to eat them. However, if the priest buys a slave for himself, the slave may eat from the sacred offerings. And if his slaves have children, they also may share his food. If a priest's daughter marries someone outside the priestly family, she may no longer eat the sacred offerings. But if she becomes a widow or is divorced and has no children to support her, and she returns to live in her father's home as in her youth, she may eat her father's food again. Otherwise, no one outside a priest's family may eat the sacred offerings.

"Any such person who eats the sacred offerings without realizing it must pay the priest for the amount eaten, plus an additional 20 percent. The priests must not let the Israelites defile the sacred offerings brought to the LORD by allowing unauthorized people to eat them. This would bring guilt upon them and require them to pay compensation. I am the LORD who makes them holy."

✛

And the LORD said to Moses, "Give Aaron and his sons and all the Israelites these instructions, which apply both to native Israelites and to the foreigners living among you.

"If you present a gift as a burnt offering to the LORD, whether it is to fulfill a vow or is a voluntary offering, you will be accepted only if your offering is a male animal with no defects. It may be a bull, a ram, or a male goat. Do not present an animal with defects, because the LORD will not accept it on your behalf.

"If you present a peace offering to the LORD from the herd or the flock, whether it is to fulfill a vow or is a voluntary offering, you must offer a perfect animal. It may have no defect of any kind. You must not offer an animal that is blind, crippled, or injured, or that has a wart, a skin sore, or scabs. Such animals must never be offered on the altar as special gifts to the LORD. If a bull or lamb has a leg that is too long or too short, it may be offered as a voluntary offering, but it may not be offered to fulfill a vow. If an animal has damaged testicles or is castrated, you may not offer it to the

LORD. You must never do this in your own land, and you must not accept such an animal from foreigners and then offer it as a sacrifice to your God. Such animals will not be accepted on your behalf, for they are mutilated or defective."

And the LORD said to Moses, "When a calf or lamb or goat is born, it must be left with its mother for seven days. From the eighth day on, it will be acceptable as a special gift to the LORD. But you must not slaughter a mother animal and her offspring on the same day, whether from the herd or the flock. When you bring a thanksgiving offering to the LORD, sacrifice it properly so you will be accepted. Eat the entire sacrificial animal on the day it is presented. Do not leave any of it until the next morning. I am the LORD.

"You must faithfully keep all my commands by putting them into practice, for I am the LORD. Do not bring shame on my holy name, for I will display my holiness among the people of Israel. I am the LORD who makes you holy. It was I who rescued you from the land of Egypt, that I might be your God. I am the LORD."

+

The LORD said to Moses, "Give the following instructions to the people of Israel. These are the LORD's appointed festivals, which you are to proclaim as official days for holy assembly.

"You have six days each week for your ordinary work, but the seventh day is a Sabbath day of complete rest, an official day for holy assembly. It is the LORD's Sabbath day, and it must be observed wherever you live.

"In addition to the Sabbath, these are the LORD's appointed festivals, the official days for holy assembly that are to be celebrated at their proper times each year.

"The LORD's Passover begins at sundown on the fourteenth day of the first month. On the next day, the fifteenth day of the month, you must begin celebrating the Festival of Unleavened Bread. This festival to the LORD continues for seven days, and during that time the bread you eat must be made without yeast. On the first day of the festival, all the people must stop their ordinary work and observe an official day for holy assembly. For seven days you must present special gifts to the LORD. On the seventh day the people must again stop all their ordinary work to observe an official day for holy assembly."

Then the LORD said to Moses, "Give the following instructions to the people of Israel. When you enter the land I am giving you and you harvest its first crops, bring the priest a bundle of grain from the first cutting of your grain harvest. On the day after the Sabbath, the priest will lift it up before the LORD so it may be accepted on your behalf. On that same day you must sacrifice a one-year-old male lamb with no defects as a burnt offering to the LORD. With it you must present a grain offering consisting of four quarts of choice flour moistened with olive oil. It will be a special gift, a pleasing aroma to the LORD. You must also offer one quart of wine as a liquid offering. Do not eat any bread or roasted grain or fresh kernels on that day until you bring this offering to your God. This is a permanent law for you, and it must be observed from generation to generation wherever you live.

"From the day after the Sabbath—the day you bring the bundle of grain to be lifted up as a special offering—count off seven full weeks. Keep counting until the day after the seventh Sabbath, fifty days later. Then present an offering of new grain to the LORD. From wherever you live, bring two loaves of bread to be lifted up before the LORD as a special offering. Make these loaves from four quarts of choice flour, and bake them with yeast. They will be an offering to the LORD from the first of your crops. Along with the bread, present seven one-year-old male lambs with no defects, one young bull, and two rams as burnt offerings to the LORD. These burnt offerings, together with the grain offerings and liquid offerings, will be a special gift, a pleasing aroma to the LORD. Then you must offer one male goat as a sin offering and two one-year-old male lambs as a peace offering.

"The priest will lift up the two lambs as a special offering to the LORD, together with the loaves representing the first of your crops. These offerings, which are holy to the LORD, belong to the priests. That same day will be proclaimed an official day for holy assembly, a day on which you do no ordinary work. This is a permanent law for you, and it must be observed from generation to generation wherever you live.

"When you harvest the crops of your land, do not harvest the grain along the edges of your fields, and do not pick up what the harvesters drop. Leave it for the poor and the foreigners living among you. I am the LORD your God."

The LORD said to Moses, "Give the following instructions to the people of Israel. On the first day of the appointed month in early autumn, you are to observe a day of complete rest. It will be an official day for holy assembly, a day commemorated with loud blasts of a trumpet. You must do no ordinary work on that day. Instead, you are to present special gifts to the LORD."

Then the LORD said to Moses, "Be careful to celebrate the Day of Atonement on the tenth day of that same month—nine days after the Festival of Trumpets. You must observe it as an official day for holy assembly, a day to deny yourselves and present special gifts to the LORD. Do no work during that entire day because it is the Day of Atonement, when offerings of purification are made for you, making you right with the LORD your God. All who do not deny themselves that day will be cut off from God's people. And I will destroy anyone among you who does any work on that day. You must not do any work at all! This is a permanent law for you, and it must be observed from generation to generation wherever you live. This will be a Sabbath day of complete rest for you, and on that day you must deny yourselves. This day of rest will begin at sundown on the ninth day of the month and extend until sundown on the tenth day."

And the LORD said to Moses, "Give the following instructions to the people of Israel. Begin celebrating the Festival of Shelters on the fifteenth day of the appointed month—five days after the Day of Atonement. This festival to the LORD will last for seven days. On the first day of the festival you must proclaim an official day for holy assembly, when you do no ordinary work. For seven days you must present special gifts to the LORD. The eighth day is another holy day on which you present your special gifts to the LORD. This will be a solemn occasion, and no ordinary work may be done that day.

("These are the LORD's appointed festivals. Celebrate them each year as official days for holy assembly by presenting special gifts to the LORD— burnt offerings, grain offerings, sacrifices, and liquid offerings—each on its proper day. These festivals must be observed in addition to the LORD's regular Sabbath days, and the offerings are in addition to your personal gifts, the offerings you give to fulfill your vows, and the voluntary offerings you present to the LORD.)

"Remember that this seven-day festival to the LORD—the Festival of Shelters—begins on the fifteenth day of the appointed month, after you have harvested all the produce of the land. The first day and the eighth day of the festival will be days of complete rest. On the first day gather branches from magnificent trees—palm fronds, boughs from leafy trees, and willows that grow by the streams. Then celebrate with joy before the LORD your God for seven days. You must observe this festival to the LORD for seven days every year. This is a permanent law for you, and it must be observed in the appointed month from generation to generation. For seven days you must live outside in little shelters. All native-born Israelites must live in shelters. This will remind each new generation of Israelites that I made their ancestors live in shelters when I rescued them from the land of Egypt. I am the LORD your God."

So Moses gave the Israelites these instructions regarding the annual festivals of the LORD.

+

The LORD said to Moses, "Command the people of Israel to bring you pure oil of pressed olives for the light, to keep the lamps burning continually. This is the lampstand that stands in the Tabernacle, in front of the inner curtain that shields the Ark of the Covenant. Aaron must keep the lamps burning in the LORD's presence all night. This is a permanent law for you, and it must be observed from generation to generation. Aaron and the priests must tend the lamps on the pure gold lampstand continually in the LORD's presence.

"You must bake twelve flat loaves of bread from choice flour, using four quarts of flour for each loaf. Place the bread before the LORD on the pure gold table, and arrange the loaves in two stacks, with six loaves in each stack. Put some pure frankincense near each stack to serve as a representative offering, a special gift presented to the LORD. Every Sabbath day this bread must be laid out before the LORD as a gift from the Israelites; it is an ongoing expression of the eternal covenant. The loaves of bread will belong to Aaron and his descendants, who must eat them in a sacred place, for they are most holy. It is the permanent right of the priests to claim this portion of the special gifts presented to the LORD."

+ + +

One day a man who had an Israelite mother and an Egyptian father came out of his tent and got into a fight with one of the Israelite men. During the fight, this son of an Israelite woman blasphemed the Name of the LORD with a curse. So the man was brought to Moses for judgment. His mother was Shelomith, the daughter of Dibri of the tribe of Dan. They kept the man in custody until the LORD's will in the matter should become clear to them.

Then the LORD said to Moses, "Take the blasphemer outside the camp, and tell all those who heard the curse to lay their hands on his head. Then let the entire community stone him to death. Say to the people of Israel: Those who curse their God will be punished for their sin. Anyone who blasphemes the Name of the LORD must be stoned to death by the whole community of Israel. Any native-born Israelite or foreigner among you who blasphemes the Name of the LORD must be put to death.

"Anyone who takes another person's life must be put to death.

"Anyone who kills another person's animal must pay for it in full—a live animal for the animal that was killed.

"Anyone who injures another person must be dealt with according to the injury inflicted—a fracture for a fracture, an eye for an eye, a tooth for a tooth. Whatever anyone does to injure another person must be paid back in kind.

"Whoever kills an animal must pay for it in full, but whoever kills another person must be put to death.

"This same standard applies both to native-born Israelites and to the foreigners living among you. I am the LORD your God."

After Moses gave all these instructions to the Israelites, they took the blasphemer outside the camp and stoned him to death. The Israelites did just as the LORD had commanded Moses.

+ + +

While Moses was on Mount Sinai, the LORD said to him, "Give the following instructions to the people of Israel. When you have entered the land I am giving you, the land itself must observe a Sabbath rest before the LORD every seventh year. For six years you may plant your fields and prune your vineyards and harvest your crops, but during the seventh year the land must have a Sabbath year of complete rest. It is the LORD's Sabbath. Do not plant your fields or prune your vineyards during that year. And don't store away the crops that grow on their own or gather the grapes from your unpruned vines. The land must have a year of complete rest. But you may eat whatever the land produces on its own during its Sabbath. This applies to you, your male and female servants, your hired workers, and the temporary residents who live with you. Your livestock and the wild animals in your land will also be allowed to eat what the land produces.

"In addition, you must count off seven Sabbath years, seven sets of seven years, adding up to forty-nine years in all. Then on the Day of Atonement in the fiftieth year, blow the ram's horn loud and long throughout the land. Set this year apart as holy, a time to proclaim freedom throughout the land for all who live there. It will be a jubilee year for you, when each of you may return to the land that belonged to your ancestors and return to your own clan. This fiftieth year will be a jubilee for you. During that year you must not plant your fields or store away any of the crops that grow on their own, and don't gather the grapes from your unpruned vines. It will be a jubilee year for you, and you must keep it holy. But you may eat whatever the land produces on its own. In the Year of Jubilee each of you may return to the land that belonged to your ancestors.

"When you make an agreement with your neighbor to buy or sell property, you must not take advantage of each other. When you buy land from your neighbor, the price you pay must be based on the number of years since the last jubilee. The seller must set the price by taking into account the number of years remaining until the next Year of Jubilee. The more years until the next jubilee, the higher the price; the fewer years, the lower the price. After all, the person selling the land is actually selling you a certain number of harvests. Show your fear of God by not taking advantage of each other. I am the LORD your God.

"If you want to live securely in the land, follow my decrees and obey my regulations. Then the land will yield large crops, and you will eat your fill and live securely in it. But you might ask, 'What will we eat during the seventh year, since we are not allowed to plant or harvest crops that year?' Be assured that I will send my blessing for you in the sixth year, so the land will produce a crop large enough for three years. When you plant your fields in the eighth year, you will still be eating from the large crop of the sixth year. In fact, you will still be eating from that large crop when the new crop is harvested in the ninth year.

"The land must never be sold on a permanent basis, for the land belongs to me. You are only foreigners and tenant farmers working for me.

"With every purchase of land you must grant the seller the right to buy it back. If one of your fellow Israelites falls into poverty and is forced to sell some family land, then a close relative should buy it back for him. If there is no close relative to buy the land, but the person who sold it gets enough money to buy it back, he then has the right to redeem it from the one who bought it. The price of the land will be discounted according to the number of years until the next Year of Jubilee. In this way the original owner can then return to the land. But if the original owner cannot afford to buy back the land, it will remain with the new owner until the next Year of Jubilee. In the jubilee year, the land must be returned to the original owners so they can return to their family land.

"Anyone who sells a house inside a walled town has the right to buy it back for a full year after its sale. During that year, the seller retains the right to buy it back. But if it is not bought back within a year, the sale of the house within the walled town cannot be reversed. It will become the permanent property of the buyer. It will not be returned to the original owner in the Year of Jubilee. But a house in a village—a settlement without fortified walls—will be treated like property in the countryside. Such a house may be bought back at any time, and it must be returned to the original owner in the Year of Jubilee.

"The Levites always have the right to buy back a house they have sold within the towns allotted to them. And any property that is sold by the Levites—all houses within the Levitical towns—must be returned in the Year of Jubilee. After all, the houses in the towns reserved for the Levites are the only property they own in all Israel. The open pastureland around the Levitical towns may never be sold. It is their permanent possession.

"If one of your fellow Israelites falls into poverty and cannot support himself, support him as you would a foreigner or a temporary resident and allow him to live with you. Do not charge interest or make a profit at his expense. Instead, show your fear of God by letting him live with you as your relative. Remember, do not charge interest on money you lend him or make a profit on food you sell him. I am the LORD your God, who brought you out of the land of Egypt to give you the land of Canaan and to be your God.

"If one of your fellow Israelites falls into poverty and is forced to sell himself to you, do not treat him as a slave. Treat him instead as a hired worker or as a temporary resident who lives with you, and he will serve you only until the Year of Jubilee. At that time he and his children will no longer be obligated to you, and they will return to their clans and go back to the land originally allotted to their ancestors. The people of Israel are my servants, whom I brought out of the land of Egypt, so they must never be sold as slaves. Show your fear of God by not treating them harshly.

"However, you may purchase male and female slaves from among the nations around you. You may also purchase the children of temporary residents who live among you, including those who have been born in your land. You may treat them as your property, passing them on to your children as a permanent inheritance. You may treat them as slaves, but you must never treat your fellow Israelites this way.

"Suppose a foreigner or temporary resident becomes rich while living among you. If any of your fellow Israelites fall into poverty and are forced to sell themselves to such a foreigner or to a member of his family, they still retain the right to be bought back, even after they have been purchased. They may be bought back by a brother, an uncle, or a cousin. In fact, anyone from the extended family may buy them back. They may also redeem themselves if they have prospered. They will negotiate the price of their freedom with the person who bought them. The price will be based on the number of years from the time they were sold until the next Year of Jubilee—whatever it would cost to hire a worker for that period of time. If many years still remain until the jubilee, they will repay the proper proportion of what they received when they sold themselves. If only a few years remain until the Year of Jubilee, they will repay a small amount for their redemption. The foreigner must treat them as workers hired on a yearly basis. You must not allow a foreigner to treat any of your fellow Israelites harshly. If any Israelites have not been bought back by the time the Year of Jubilee arrives, they and their children must be set free at that time. For the people of Israel belong to me. They are my servants, whom I brought out of the land of Egypt. I am the LORD your God.

+

"Do not make idols or set up carved images, or sacred pillars, or sculptured stones in your land so you may worship them. I am the LORD your God. You must keep my Sabbath days of rest and show reverence for my sanctuary. I am the LORD.

"If you follow my decrees and are careful to obey my commands, I will send you the seasonal rains. The land will then yield its crops, and the trees of the field will produce their fruit. Your threshing season will overlap with the grape harvest, and your grape harvest will overlap with the season of planting grain. You will eat your fill and live securely in your own land.

"I will give you peace in the land, and you will be able to sleep with no cause for fear. I will rid the land of wild animals and keep your enemies out of your land. In fact, you will chase down your enemies and slaughter them with your swords. Five of you will chase a hundred, and a hundred of you will chase ten thousand! All your enemies will fall beneath your sword.

"I will look favorably upon you, making you fertile and multiplying your people. And I will fulfill my covenant with you. You will have such a surplus of crops that you will need to clear out the old grain to make room for the new harvest! I will live among you, and I will not despise you. I will walk among you; I will be your God, and you will be my people. I am the LORD your God, who brought you out of the land of Egypt so you would no longer be their slaves. I broke the yoke of slavery from your neck so you can walk with your heads held high.

"However, if you do not listen to me or obey all these commands, and if you break my covenant by rejecting my decrees, treating my regulations with contempt, and refusing to obey my commands, I will punish you. I will bring sudden terrors upon you—wasting diseases and burning fevers that will cause your eyes to fail and your life to ebb away. You will plant your crops in vain because your enemies will eat them. I will turn against you, and you will be defeated by your enemies. Those who hate you will rule over you, and you will run even when no one is chasing you!

"And if, in spite of all this, you still disobey me, I will punish you seven times over for your sins. I will break your proud spirit by making the skies as unyielding as iron and the earth as hard as bronze. All your work will be for nothing, for your land will yield no crops, and your trees will bear no fruit.

"If even then you remain hostile toward me and refuse to obey me, I will inflict disaster on you seven times over for your sins. I will send wild animals that will rob you of your children and destroy your livestock. Your numbers will dwindle, and your roads will be deserted.

"And if you fail to learn the lesson and continue your hostility toward me, then I myself will be hostile toward you. I will personally strike you with calamity seven times over for your sins. I will send armies against you to carry out the curse of the covenant you have broken. When you run to your towns for safety, I will send a plague to destroy you there, and you will be handed over to your enemies. I will destroy your food supply, so that ten women will need only one oven to bake bread for their families. They will ration your food by weight, and though you have food to eat, you will not be satisfied.

"If in spite of all this you still refuse to listen and still remain hostile toward me, then I will give full vent to my hostility. I myself will punish you seven times over for your sins. Then you will eat the flesh of your own sons and daughters. I will destroy your pagan shrines and knock down your places of worship. I will leave your lifeless corpses piled on top of your lifeless idols, and I will despise you. I will make your cities desolate and destroy your places of pagan worship. I will take no pleasure in your offerings that should be a pleasing aroma to me. Yes, I myself will devastate your land, and your enemies who come to occupy it will be appalled at what they see. I will scatter you among the nations and bring out my sword against you. Your land will become desolate, and your cities will lie in ruins. Then at last the land will enjoy its neglected Sabbath years as it lies desolate while you are in exile in the land of your enemies. Then the land will finally rest and enjoy the Sabbaths it missed. As long as the land lies in ruins, it will enjoy the rest you never allowed it to take every seventh year while you lived in it.

"And for those of you who survive, I will demoralize you in the land of your enemies. You will live in such fear that the sound of a leaf driven by the wind will send you fleeing. You will run as though fleeing from a sword, and you will fall even when no one pursues you. Though no one is chasing you, you will stumble over each other as though fleeing from a sword. You will have no power to stand up against your enemies. You will die among the foreign nations and be devoured in the land of your enemies. Those of you who survive will waste away in your enemies' lands because of their sins and the sins of their ancestors.

"But at last my people will confess their sins and the sins of their ancestors for betraying me and being hostile toward me. When I have turned their hostility back on them and brought them to the land of their enemies, then at last their stubborn hearts will be humbled, and they will pay for their sins. Then I will remember my covenant with Jacob and my covenant with Isaac and my covenant with Abraham, and I will remember the land. For the land must be abandoned to enjoy its years of Sabbath rest as it lies deserted. At last the people will pay for their sins, for they have continually rejected my regulations and despised my decrees.

"But despite all this, I will not utterly reject or despise them while they are in exile in the land of their enemies. I will not cancel my covenant with them by wiping them out, for I am the LORD their God. For their sakes I will remember my ancient covenant with their ancestors, whom I brought out of the land of Egypt in the sight of all the nations, that I might be their God. I am the LORD."

These are the decrees, regulations, and instructions that the LORD gave through Moses on Mount Sinai as evidence of the relationship between himself and the Israelites.

+

The LORD said to Moses, "Give the following instructions to the people of Israel. If anyone makes a special vow to dedicate someone to the LORD by paying the value of that person, here is the scale of values to be used. A man between the ages of twenty and sixty is valued at fifty shekels of silver, as measured by the sanctuary shekel. A woman of that age is valued at thirty shekels of silver. A boy between the ages of five and twenty is valued at twenty shekels of silver; a girl of that age is valued at ten shekels of silver. A boy between the ages of one month and five years is valued at five shekels of silver; a girl of that age is valued at three shekels of silver. A man older than sixty is valued at fifteen shekels of silver; a woman of that age is valued at ten shekels of silver. If you desire to make such a vow but cannot afford to pay the required amount, take the person to the priest. He will determine the amount for you to pay based on what you can afford.

"If your vow involves giving an animal that is acceptable as an offering to the LORD, any gift to the LORD will be considered holy. You may not exchange or substitute it for another animal—neither a good animal for a bad one nor a bad animal for a good one. But if you do exchange one animal for another, then both the original animal and its substitute will be considered holy. If your vow involves an unclean animal—one that is not acceptable as an offering to the LORD—then you must bring the animal to the priest. He will assess its value, and his assessment will be final, whether high or low. If you want to buy back the animal, you must pay the value set by the priest, plus 20 percent.

"If someone dedicates a house to the LORD, the priest will come to assess its value. The priest's assessment will be final, whether high or low. If the person who dedicated the house wants to buy it back, he must pay the value set by the priest, plus 20 percent. Then the house will again be his.

"If someone dedicates to the LORD a piece of his family property, its value will be assessed according to the amount of seed required to plant it—fifty shekels of silver for a field planted with five bushels of barley seed. If the field is dedicated to the LORD in the Year of Jubilee, then the entire assessment will apply. But if the field is dedicated after the Year of Jubilee, the priest will assess the land's value in proportion to the number of years left until the next Year of Jubilee. Its assessed value is reduced each year. If the person who dedicated the field wants to buy it back, he must pay the value set by the priest, plus 20 percent. Then the field will again be legally his. But if he does not want to buy it back, and it is sold to someone else, the field can no longer be bought back. When the field is released in the Year of Jubilee, it will be holy, a field specially set apart for the LORD. It will become the property of the priests.

"If someone dedicates to the LORD a field he has purchased but which is not part of his family property, the priest will assess its value based on the number of years left until the next Year of Jubilee. On that day he must give the assessed value of the land as a sacred donation to the LORD. In the Year of Jubilee the field must be returned to the person from whom he purchased it, the one who inherited it as family property. (All the payments must be measured by the weight of the sanctuary shekel, which equals twenty gerahs.)

"You may not dedicate a firstborn animal to the LORD, for the firstborn of your cattle, sheep, and goats already belong to him. However, you may buy back the firstborn of a ceremonially unclean animal by paying the priest's assessment of its worth, plus 20 percent. If you do not buy it back, the priest will sell it at its assessed value.

"However, anything specially set apart for the LORD—whether a person, an animal, or family property—must never be sold or bought back. Anything devoted in this way has been set apart as holy, and it belongs to the LORD. No person specially set apart for destruction may be bought back. Such a person must be put to death.

"One-tenth of the produce of the land, whether grain from the fields or fruit from the trees, belongs to the LORD and must be set apart to him as holy. If you want to buy back the LORD's tenth of the grain or fruit, you must pay its value, plus 20 percent. Count off every tenth animal from your herds and flocks and set them apart for the LORD as holy. You may not pick and choose between good and bad animals, and you may not substitute one for another. But if you do exchange one animal for another, then both the original animal and its substitute will be considered holy and cannot be bought back."

These are the commands that the LORD gave through Moses on Mount Sinai for the Israelites.

IMMERSED IN NUMBERS

THE FOURTH BOOK IN *BEGINNINGS*—Numbers—marks an important advance in Israel's story. The book begins with the Exodus generation (the people God freed from slavery in Egypt) but ends with the Conquest generation (the people God will lead into the Promised Land). The Exodus generation isn't allowed to enter the land because of their lack of faith in God's power and their disobedience to his directions. This is one of many examples of Israel's disloyalty to their covenant with God. Numbers helps us understand that Israel suffered from the same flaw as all of humanity—rebellion and disobedience. If God is going to use Israel to bless all peoples, then he is also going to have to overcome this flaw within his own people.

The literary structure of Numbers alternates back and forth between story and law, showing how these two elements of Israel's history are intertwined. Much of the nation's law is given "on the way" because this is a people with a destiny. The law and story sections in Numbers have distinct characteristics, but their interrelated nature shows how God's presence and word are living among his people.

Law sections begin with the LORD speaking to Moses, Aaron, or both. The laws given are typically to be kept in the future ("When you finally settle in the land I am giving you"). The account gives no description of how anyone obeyed or disobeyed the laws. No places and no people besides Moses and Aaron are named in these sections. They typically end with a standard phrase, such as "This is a permanent law for the people" or "I am the LORD your God."

Story sections are situated in place and time, and they name all who are involved (for example, "In the first month of the year, the whole community of Israel arrived in the wilderness of Zin"). People respond to the LORD either in obedience or disobedience and subsequently receive the consequences. Stories often end by explaining how a place was named (for example, "After that, the area was known as Taberah [which means 'the place of burning'], because fire from the LORD had burned among them there").

These different law and story sections in Numbers relate to one another in intricate ways. Each law section is tied to the preceding story section. For example, at the end of the book's second story section, it is announced that when the cloud (signifying the LORD's presence) moves, the Israelites must break camp. The subsequent law section commands trumpets to be made to signal when this should happen. We also see in these sections the same kind of *chiastic* pattern we've already seen in Genesis and Exodus (the first item in a series paired with the last one, and so on). In Numbers, each of the six law sections are paired together, as are the six story sections.

As it concludes, Numbers pulls together both strands—story and law—to show their inseparability in forming the identity of God's covenant people. It also brings the people to the edge of the Promised Land. The book does not just describe the journey; it also reveals the significance of what happens along the way. God's Story with the world is moving forward, but as we are learning, it is not an easy journey. God will continuously wrestle with his people, and his own commitment to the covenant will be tested.

However, as we read of the travels of Israel, we can see clear hints that the LORD's promise to bring blessing to Abraham's family will prevail. Note, for example, the words that God gives Moses for the high priest Aaron and his sons to share with the people of Israel as a special blessing:

"May the LORD bless you
    and protect you.
May the LORD smile on you
    and be gracious to you.
May the LORD show you his favor
    and give you his peace."

These words begin with blessing and end with peace. While the Bible's story is not a straightforward path to the fulfillment of God's intention—as there are ups and downs in the journey—he is faithful and true to his word. And his last word will be peace.

NUMBERS

✦

A year after Israel's departure from Egypt, the LORD spoke to Moses in the Tabernacle in the wilderness of Sinai. On the first day of the second month of that year he said, "From the whole community of Israel, record the names of all the warriors by their clans and families. List all the men twenty years old or older who are able to go to war. You and Aaron must register the troops, and you will be assisted by one family leader from each tribe.

"These are the tribes and the names of the leaders who will assist you:

Tribe	Leader
Reuben	Elizur son of Shedeur
Simeon	Shelumiel son of Zurishaddai
Judah	Nahshon son of Amminadab
Issachar	Nethanel son of Zuar
Zebulun	Eliab son of Helon
Ephraim son of Joseph	Elishama son of Ammihud
Manasseh son of Joseph	Gamaliel son of Pedahzur
Benjamin	Abidan son of Gideoni
Dan	Ahiezer son of Ammishaddai
Asher	Pagiel son of Ocran
Gad	Eliasaph son of Deuel
Naphtali	Ahira son of Enan

These are the chosen leaders of the community, the leaders of their ancestral tribes, the heads of the clans of Israel."

So Moses and Aaron called together these chosen leaders, and they assembled the whole community of Israel on that very day. All the people were registered according to their ancestry by their clans and families. The men of Israel who were twenty years old or older were listed one by one, just as the LORD had commanded Moses. So Moses recorded their names in the wilderness of Sinai.

This is the number of men twenty years old or older who were able to go to war, as their names were listed in the records of their clans and families:

Tribe	Number
Reuben (Jacob's oldest son)	46,500
Simeon	59,300
Gad	45,650
Judah	74,600
Issachar	54,400
Zebulun	57,400
Ephraim son of Joseph	40,500
Manasseh son of Joseph	32,200
Benjamin	35,400
Dan	62,700
Asher	41,500
Naphtali	53,400

These were the men registered by Moses and Aaron and the twelve leaders of Israel, all listed according to their ancestral descent. They were registered by families—all the men of Israel who were twenty years old or older and able to go to war. The total number was 603,550.

But this total did not include the Levites. For the LORD had said to Moses, "Do not include the tribe of Levi in the registration; do not count them with the rest of the Israelites. Put the Levites in charge of the Tabernacle of the Covenant, along with all its furnishings and equipment. They must carry the Tabernacle and all its furnishings as you travel, and they must take care of it and camp around it. Whenever it is time for the Tabernacle to move, the Levites will take it down. And when it is time to stop, they will set it up again. But any unauthorized person who goes too near the Tabernacle must be put to death. Each tribe of Israel will camp in a designated area with its own family banner. But the Levites will camp around the Tabernacle of the Covenant to protect the community of Israel from the LORD's anger. The Levites are responsible to stand guard around the Tabernacle."

So the Israelites did everything just as the LORD had commanded Moses.

+

Then the LORD gave these instructions to Moses and Aaron: "When the Israelites set up camp, each tribe will be assigned its own area. The tribal divisions will camp beneath their family banners on all four sides of the Tabernacle, but at some distance from it.

"The divisions of Judah, Issachar, and Zebulun are to camp toward the sunrise on the east side of the Tabernacle, beneath their family banners. These are the names of the tribes, their leaders, and the numbers of their registered troops:

Tribe	Leader	Number
Judah	Nahshon son of Amminadab	74,600
Issachar	Nethanel son of Zuar	54,400
Zebulun	Eliab son of Helon	57,400

So the total of all the troops on Judah's side of the camp is 186,400. These three tribes are to lead the way whenever the Israelites travel to a new campsite.

"The divisions of Reuben, Simeon, and Gad are to camp on the south side of the Tabernacle, beneath their family banners. These are the names of the tribes, their leaders, and the numbers of their registered troops:

Tribe	Leader	Number
Reuben	Elizur son of Shedeur	46,500
Simeon	Shelumiel son of Zurishaddai	59,300
Gad	Eliasaph son of Deuel	45,650

So the total of all the troops on Reuben's side of the camp is 151,450. These three tribes will be second in line whenever the Israelites travel.

"Then the Tabernacle, carried by the Levites, will set out from the middle of the camp. All the tribes are to travel in the same order that they camp, each in position under the appropriate family banner.

"The divisions of Ephraim, Manasseh, and Benjamin are to camp on the west side of the Tabernacle, beneath their family banners. These are the names of the tribes, their leaders, and the numbers of their registered troops:

Tribe	Leader	Number
Ephraim	Elishama son of Ammihud	40,500
Manasseh	Gamaliel son of Pedahzur	32,200
Benjamin	Abidan son of Gideoni	35,400

So the total of all the troops on Ephraim's side of the camp is 108,100. These three tribes will be third in line whenever the Israelites travel.

"The divisions of Dan, Asher, and Naphtali are to camp on the north side of the Tabernacle, beneath their family banners. These are the names of the tribes, their leaders, and the numbers of their registered troops:

Tribe	Leader	Number
Dan	Ahiezer son of Ammishaddai	62,700
Asher	Pagiel son of Ocran	41,500
Naphtali	Ahira son of Enan	53,400

So the total of all the troops on Dan's side of the camp is 157,600. These three tribes will be last, marching under their banners whenever the Israelites travel."

In summary, the troops of Israel listed by their families totaled 603,550. But as the LORD had commanded, the Levites were not included in this registration. So the people of Israel did everything as the LORD had commanded Moses. Each clan and family set up camp and marched under their banners exactly as the LORD had instructed them.

+

This is the family line of Aaron and Moses as it was recorded when the LORD spoke to Moses on Mount Sinai: The names of Aaron's sons were Nadab (the oldest), Abihu, Eleazar, and Ithamar. These sons of Aaron were anointed and ordained to minister as priests. But Nadab and Abihu died in the LORD's presence in the wilderness of Sinai when they burned before the LORD the wrong kind of fire, different than he had commanded. Since they had no sons, this left only Eleazar and Ithamar to serve as priests with their father, Aaron.

Then the LORD said to Moses, "Call forward the tribe of Levi, and present them to Aaron the priest to serve as his assistants. They will serve Aaron and the whole community, performing their sacred duties in and around the Tabernacle. They will also maintain all the furnishings of the sacred tent, serving in the Tabernacle on behalf of all the Israelites. Assign the Levites to Aaron and his sons. They have been given from among all the people of Israel to serve as their assistants. Appoint Aaron and his sons to carry out the duties of the priesthood. But any unauthorized person who goes too near the sanctuary must be put to death."

And the LORD said to Moses, "Look, I have chosen the Levites from among the Israelites to serve as substitutes for all the firstborn sons of the people of Israel. The Levites belong to me, for all the firstborn males are mine. On the day I struck down all the firstborn sons of the Egyptians, I set apart for myself all the firstborn in Israel, both of people and of animals. They are mine; I am the LORD."

The LORD spoke again to Moses in the wilderness of Sinai. He said, "Record the names of the members of the tribe of Levi by their families and clans. List every male who is one month old or older." So Moses listed them, just as the LORD had commanded.

Levi had three sons, whose names were Gershon, Kohath, and Merari.
The clans descended from Gershon were named after two of his
    descendants, Libni and Shimei.
The clans descended from Kohath were named after four of his
    descendants, Amram, Izhar, Hebron, and Uzziel.

The clans descended from Merari were named after two of his descendants, Mahli and Mushi.

These were the Levite clans, listed according to their family groups.

The descendants of Gershon were composed of the clans descended from Libni and Shimei. There were 7,500 males one month old or older among these Gershonite clans. They were assigned the area to the west of the Tabernacle for their camp. The leader of the Gershonite clans was Eliasaph son of Lael. These two clans were responsible to care for the Tabernacle, including the sacred tent with its layers of coverings, the curtain at its entrance, the curtains of the courtyard that surrounded the Tabernacle and altar, the curtain at the courtyard entrance, the ropes, and all the equipment related to their use.

The descendants of Kohath were composed of the clans descended from Amram, Izhar, Hebron, and Uzziel. There were 8,600 males one month old or older among these Kohathite clans. They were responsible for the care of the sanctuary, and they were assigned the area south of the Tabernacle for their camp. The leader of the Kohathite clans was Elizaphan son of Uzziel. These four clans were responsible for the care of the Ark, the table, the lampstand, the altars, the various articles used in the sanctuary, the inner curtain, and all the equipment related to their use. Eleazar, son of Aaron the priest, was the chief administrator over all the Levites, with special responsibility for the oversight of the sanctuary.

The descendants of Merari were composed of the clans descended from Mahli and Mushi. There were 6,200 males one month old or older among these Merarite clans. They were assigned the area north of the Tabernacle for their camp. The leader of the Merarite clans was Zuriel son of Abihail. These two clans were responsible for the care of the frames supporting the Tabernacle, the crossbars, the pillars, the bases, and all the equipment related to their use. They were also responsible for the posts of the courtyard and all their bases, pegs, and ropes.

The area in front of the Tabernacle, in the east toward the sunrise, was reserved for the tents of Moses and of Aaron and his sons, who had the final responsibility for the sanctuary on behalf of the people of Israel. Anyone other than a priest or Levite who went too near the sanctuary was to be put to death.

When Moses and Aaron counted the Levite clans at the LORD's command, the total number was 22,000 males one month old or older.

Then the LORD said to Moses, "Now count all the firstborn sons in Israel who are one month old or older, and make a list of their names. The Levites must be reserved for me as substitutes for the firstborn sons of Israel; I am the LORD. And the Levites' livestock must be reserved for me as substitutes for the firstborn livestock of the whole nation of Israel."

So Moses counted the firstborn sons of the people of Israel, just as the LORD had commanded. The number of firstborn sons who were one month old or older was 22,273.

Then the LORD said to Moses, "Take the Levites as substitutes for the firstborn sons of the people of Israel. And take the livestock of the Levites as substitutes for the firstborn livestock of the people of Israel. The Levites belong to me; I am the LORD. There are 273 more firstborn sons of Israel than there are Levites. To redeem these extra firstborn sons, collect five pieces of silver for each of them (each piece weighing the same as the sanctuary shekel, which equals twenty gerahs). Give the silver to Aaron and his sons as the redemption price for the extra firstborn sons."

So Moses collected the silver for redeeming the firstborn sons of Israel who exceeded the number of Levites. He collected 1,365 pieces of silver on behalf of these firstborn sons of Israel (each piece weighing the same as the sanctuary shekel). And Moses gave the silver for the redemption to Aaron and his sons, just as the LORD had commanded.

+

Then the LORD said to Moses and Aaron, "Record the names of the members of the clans and families of the Kohathite division of the tribe of Levi. List all the men between the ages of thirty and fifty who are eligible to serve in the Tabernacle.

"The duties of the Kohathites at the Tabernacle will relate to the most sacred objects. When the camp moves, Aaron and his sons must enter the Tabernacle first to take down the inner curtain and cover the Ark of the Covenant with it. Then they must cover the inner curtain with fine goatskin leather and spread over that a single piece of blue cloth. Finally, they must put the carrying poles of the Ark in place.

"Next they must spread a blue cloth over the table where the Bread of the Presence is displayed, and on the cloth they will place the bowls, ladles, jars, pitchers, and the special bread. They must spread a scarlet cloth over all of this, and finally a covering of fine goatskin leather on top of the scarlet cloth. Then they must insert the carrying poles into the table.

"Next they must cover the lampstand with a blue cloth, along with its lamps, lamp snuffers, trays, and special jars of olive oil. Then they must cover the lampstand and its accessories with fine goatskin leather and place the bundle on a carrying frame.

"Next they must spread a blue cloth over the gold incense altar and cover this cloth with fine goatskin leather. Then they must attach the carrying poles to the altar. They must take all the remaining furnishings of the sanctuary and wrap them in a blue cloth, cover them with fine goatskin leather, and place them on the carrying frame.

"They must remove the ashes from the altar for sacrifices and cover the altar with a purple cloth. All the altar utensils—the firepans, meat forks, shovels, basins, and all the containers—must be placed on the cloth, and a covering of fine goatskin leather must be spread over them. Finally, they must put the carrying poles in place. The camp will be ready to move when Aaron and his sons have finished covering the sanctuary and all the sacred articles. The Kohathites will come and carry these things to the next destination. But they must not touch the sacred objects, or they will die. So these are the things from the Tabernacle that the Kohathites must carry.

"Eleazar son of Aaron the priest will be responsible for the oil of the lampstand, the fragrant incense, the daily grain offering, and the anointing oil. In fact, Eleazar will be responsible for the entire Tabernacle and everything in it, including the sanctuary and its furnishings."

Then the LORD said to Moses and Aaron, "Do not let the Kohathite clans be destroyed from among the Levites! This is what you must do so they will live and not die when they approach the most sacred objects. Aaron and his sons must always go in with them and assign a specific duty or load to each person. The Kohathites must never enter the sanctuary to look at the sacred objects for even a moment, or they will die."

And the LORD said to Moses, "Record the names of the members of the clans and families of the Gershonite division of the tribe of Levi. List all the men between the ages of thirty and fifty who are eligible to serve in the Tabernacle.

"These Gershonite clans will be responsible for general service and carrying loads. They must carry the curtains of the Tabernacle, the Tabernacle itself with its coverings, the outer covering of fine goatskin leather, and the curtain for the Tabernacle entrance. They are also to carry the curtains for the courtyard walls that surround the Tabernacle and altar, the curtain across the courtyard entrance, the ropes, and all the equipment related to their use. The Gershonites are responsible for all these items. Aaron and his sons will direct the Gershonites regarding all their duties, whether it involves moving the equipment or doing other work. They must assign the Gershonites responsibility for the loads they are to carry. So these are the duties assigned to the Gershonite clans at the Tabernacle. They will be directly responsible to Ithamar son of Aaron the priest.

"Now record the names of the members of the clans and families of the Merarite division of the tribe of Levi. List all the men between the ages of thirty and fifty who are eligible to serve in the Tabernacle.

"Their only duty at the Tabernacle will be to carry loads. They will carry the frames of the Tabernacle, the crossbars, the posts, and the bases; also the posts for the courtyard walls with their bases, pegs, and ropes; and all the accessories and everything else related to their use. Assign the various loads to each man by name. So these are the duties of the Merarite clans at the Tabernacle. They are directly responsible to Ithamar son of Aaron the priest."

So Moses, Aaron, and the other leaders of the community listed the members of the Kohathite division by their clans and families. The list included all the men between thirty and fifty years of age who were eligible for service in the Tabernacle, and the total number came to 2,750. So this was the total of all those from the Kohathite clans who were eligible to serve at the Tabernacle. Moses and Aaron listed them, just as the Lord had commanded through Moses.

The Gershonite division was also listed by its clans and families. The list included all the men between thirty and fifty years of age who were eligible for service in the Tabernacle, and the total number came to 2,630. So this was the total of all those from the Gershonite clans who were eligible to serve at the Tabernacle. Moses and Aaron listed them, just as the Lord had commanded.

The Merarite division was also listed by its clans and families. The list included all the men between thirty and fifty years of age who were eligible for service in the Tabernacle, and the total number came to 3,200. So this was the total of all those from the Merarite clans who were eligible for service. Moses and Aaron listed them, just as the Lord had commanded through Moses.

So Moses, Aaron, and the leaders of Israel listed all the Levites by their clans and families. All the men between thirty and fifty years of age who were eligible for service in the Tabernacle and for its transportation numbered 8,580. When their names were recorded, as the Lord had commanded through Moses, each man was assigned his task and told what to carry.

And so the registration was completed, just as the Lord had commanded Moses.

+ + +

The Lord gave these instructions to Moses: "Command the people of Israel to remove from the camp anyone who has a skin disease or a discharge, or who has become ceremonially unclean by touching a dead person. This command applies to men and women alike. Remove them so they will not defile the camp in which I live among them." So the Israelites did as the LORD had commanded Moses and removed such people from the camp.

+

Then the LORD said to Moses, "Give the following instructions to the people of Israel: If any of the people—men or women—betray the LORD by doing wrong to another person, they are guilty. They must confess their sin and make full restitution for what they have done, adding an additional 20 percent and returning it to the person who was wronged. But if the person who was wronged is dead, and there are no near relatives to whom restitution can be made, the payment belongs to the LORD and must be given to the priest. Those who are guilty must also bring a ram as a sacrifice, and they will be purified and made right with the LORD. All the sacred offerings that the Israelites bring to a priest will belong to him. Each priest may keep all the sacred donations that he receives."

+

And the LORD said to Moses, "Give the following instructions to the people of Israel.

"Suppose a man's wife goes astray, and she is unfaithful to her husband and has sex with another man, but neither her husband nor anyone else knows about it. She has defiled herself, even though there was no witness and she was not caught in the act. If her husband becomes jealous and is suspicious of his wife and needs to know whether or not she has defiled herself, the husband must bring his wife to the priest. He must also bring an offering of two quarts of barley flour to be presented on her behalf. Do not mix it with olive oil or frankincense, for it is a jealousy offering—an offering to prove whether or not she is guilty.

"The priest will then present her to stand trial before the LORD. He must take some holy water in a clay jar and pour into it dust he has taken from the Tabernacle floor. When the priest has presented the woman before the LORD, he must unbind her hair and place in her hands the offering of proof—the jealousy offering to determine whether her husband's suspicions are justified. The priest will stand before her, holding the jar of bitter water that brings a curse to those who are guilty. The priest will then put the woman under oath and say to her, 'If no other man has had sex with you, and you have not gone astray and defiled yourself while under your husband's authority, may you be immune from the effects of this bitter water that brings on the curse. But if you have gone astray by being unfaithful to your husband, and have defiled yourself by having sex with another man—'

"At this point the priest must put the woman under oath by saying, 'May the people know that the LORD's curse is upon you when he makes you infertile, causing your womb to shrivel and your abdomen to swell. Now may this water that brings the curse enter your body and cause your abdomen to swell and your womb to shrivel.' And the woman will be required to say, 'Yes, let it be so.' And the priest will write these curses on a piece of leather and wash them off into the bitter water. He will make the woman drink the bitter water that brings on the curse. When the water enters her body, it will cause bitter suffering if she is guilty.

"The priest will take the jealousy offering from the woman's hand, lift it up before the LORD, and carry it to the altar. He will take a handful of the flour as a token portion and burn it on the altar, and he will require the woman to drink the water. If she has defiled herself by being unfaithful to her husband, the water that brings on the curse will cause bitter suffering. Her abdomen will swell and her womb will shrink, and her name will become a curse among her people. But if she has not defiled herself and is pure, then she will be unharmed and will still be able to have children.

"This is the ritual law for dealing with suspicion. If a woman goes astray and defiles herself while under her husband's authority, or if a man becomes jealous and is suspicious that his wife has been unfaithful, the husband must present his wife before the LORD, and the priest will apply this entire ritual law to her. The husband will be innocent of any guilt in this matter, but his wife will be held accountable for her sin."

+

Then the LORD said to Moses, "Give the following instructions to the people of Israel.

"If any of the people, either men or women, take the special vow of a Nazirite, setting themselves apart to the LORD in a special way, they must give up wine and other alcoholic drinks. They must not use vinegar made from wine or from other alcoholic drinks, they must not drink fresh grape juice, and they must not eat grapes or raisins. As long as they are bound by their Nazirite vow, they are not allowed to eat or drink anything that comes from a grapevine—not even the grape seeds or skins.

"They must never cut their hair throughout the time of their vow, for they are holy and set apart to the LORD. Until the time of their vow has been fulfilled, they must let their hair grow long. And they must not go near a dead body during the entire period of their vow to the LORD. Even if the dead person is their own father, mother, brother, or sister, they must not defile themselves, for the hair on their head is the symbol of their separation to God. This requirement applies as long as they are set apart to the LORD.

"If someone falls dead beside them, the hair they have dedicated will be defiled. They must wait for seven days and then shave their heads. Then they will be cleansed from their defilement. On the eighth day they must bring two turtledoves or two young pigeons to the priest at the entrance of the Tabernacle. The priest will offer one of the birds for a sin offering and the other for a burnt offering. In this way, he will purify them from the guilt they incurred through contact with the dead body. Then they must reaffirm their commitment and let their hair begin to grow again. The days of their vow that were completed before their defilement no longer count. They must rededicate themselves to the LORD as a Nazirite for the full term of their vow, and each must bring a one-year-old male lamb for a guilt offering.

"This is the ritual law for Nazirites. At the conclusion of their time of separation as Nazirites, they must each go to the entrance of the Tabernacle and offer their sacrifices to the LORD: a one-year-old male lamb without defect for a burnt offering, a one-year-old female lamb without defect for a sin offering, a ram without defect for a peace offering, a basket of bread made without yeast—cakes of choice flour mixed with olive oil and wafers spread with olive oil—along with their prescribed grain offerings and liquid offerings. The priest will present these offerings before the LORD: first the sin offering and the burnt offering; then the ram for a peace offering, along with the basket of bread made without yeast. The priest must also present the prescribed grain offering and liquid offering to the LORD.

"Then the Nazirites will shave their heads at the entrance of the Tabernacle. They will take the hair that had been dedicated and place it on the fire beneath the peace-offering sacrifice. After the Nazirite's head has been shaved, the priest will take for each of them the boiled shoulder of the ram, and he will take from the basket a cake and a wafer made without yeast. He will put them all into the Nazirite's hands. Then the priest will lift them up as a special offering before the LORD. These are holy portions for the priest, along with the breast of the special offering and the thigh of the sacred offering that are lifted up before the LORD. After this ceremony the Nazirites may again drink wine.

"This is the ritual law of the Nazirites, who vow to bring these offerings to the LORD. They may also bring additional offerings if they can afford it. And they must be careful to do whatever they vowed when they set themselves apart as Nazirites."

+

Then the Lord said to Moses, "Tell Aaron and his sons to bless the people of Israel with this special blessing:

'May the Lord bless you
    and protect you.
May the Lord smile on you
    and be gracious to you.
May the Lord show you his favor
    and give you his peace.'

Whenever Aaron and his sons bless the people of Israel in my name, I myself will bless them."

+ + +

On the day Moses set up the Tabernacle, he anointed it and set it apart as holy. He also anointed and set apart all its furnishings and the altar with its utensils. Then the leaders of Israel—the tribal leaders who had registered the troops—came and brought their offerings. Together they brought six large wagons and twelve oxen. There was a wagon for every two leaders and an ox for each leader. They presented these to the Lord in front of the Tabernacle.

Then the Lord said to Moses, "Receive their gifts, and use these oxen and wagons for transporting the Tabernacle. Distribute them among the Levites according to the work they have to do." So Moses took the wagons and oxen and presented them to the Levites. He gave two wagons and four oxen to the Gershonite division for their work, and he gave four wagons and eight oxen to the Merarite division for their work. All their work was done under the leadership of Ithamar son of Aaron the priest. But he gave none of the wagons or oxen to the Kohathite division, since they were required to carry the sacred objects of the Tabernacle on their shoulders.

The leaders also presented dedication gifts for the altar at the time it was anointed. They each placed their gifts before the altar. The Lord said to Moses, "Let one leader bring his gift each day for the dedication of the altar."

On the first day Nahshon son of Amminadab, leader of the tribe of Judah, presented his offering.

His offering consisted of a silver platter weighing 3¼ pounds and a silver basin weighing 1¾ pounds (as measured by the weight of the sanctuary shekel). These were both filled with grain offerings of choice flour moistened with olive oil. He also brought a gold container weighing four ounces, which was filled with incense. He brought a young bull, a ram, and a one-year-old male lamb for a burnt offering, and a male goat for a sin offering. For a peace offering he brought two bulls, five rams, five male goats, and five one-year-old male lambs. This was the offering brought by Nahshon son of Amminadab.

On the second day Nethanel son of Zuar, leader of the tribe of Issachar, presented his offering.

His offering consisted of a silver platter weighing 3¼ pounds and a silver basin weighing 1¾ pounds (as measured by the weight of the sanctuary shekel). These were both filled with grain offerings of choice flour moistened with olive oil. He also brought a gold container weighing four ounces, which was filled with incense. He brought a young bull, a ram, and a one-year-old male lamb for a burnt offering, and a male goat for a sin offering. For a peace offering he brought two bulls, five rams, five male goats, and five one-year-old male lambs. This was the offering brought by Nethanel son of Zuar.

On the third day Eliab son of Helon, leader of the tribe of Zebulun, presented his offering.

His offering consisted of a silver platter weighing 3¼ pounds and a silver basin weighing 1¾ pounds (as measured by the weight of the sanctuary shekel). These were both filled with grain offerings of choice flour moistened with olive oil. He also brought a gold container weighing four ounces, which was filled with incense. He brought a young bull, a ram, and a one-year-old male lamb for a burnt offering, and a male goat for a sin offering. For a peace offering he brought two bulls, five rams, five male goats, and five one-year-old male lambs. This was the offering brought by Eliab son of Helon.

On the fourth day Elizur son of Shedeur, leader of the tribe of Reuben, presented his offering.

His offering consisted of a silver platter weighing 3¼ pounds and a silver basin weighing 1¾ pounds (as measured by the weight of the sanctuary shekel). These were both filled with grain offerings of choice flour moistened with olive oil. He also brought a gold container weighing four ounces, which was filled with incense. He brought a young bull, a ram, and a one-year-old male lamb for a burnt offering, and a male goat for a sin offering. For a peace offering he brought two bulls, five rams, five male goats, and five one-year-old male lambs. This was the offering brought by Elizur son of Shedeur.

On the fifth day Shelumiel son of Zurishaddai, leader of the tribe of Simeon, presented his offering.

His offering consisted of a silver platter weighing 3¼ pounds and a silver basin weighing 1¾ pounds (as measured by the weight of the sanctuary shekel). These were both filled with grain offerings of choice flour moistened with olive oil. He also brought a gold container weighing four ounces, which was filled with incense. He brought a young bull, a ram, and a one-year-old male lamb for a burnt offering, and a male goat for a sin offering. For a peace offering he brought two bulls, five rams, five male goats, and five one-year-old male lambs. This was the offering brought by Shelumiel son of Zurishaddai.

On the sixth day Eliasaph son of Deuel, leader of the tribe of Gad, presented his offering.

His offering consisted of a silver platter weighing 3¼ pounds and a silver basin weighing 1¾ pounds (as measured by the weight of the sanctuary shekel). These were both filled with grain offerings of choice flour moistened with olive oil. He also brought a gold container weighing four ounces, which was filled with incense. He brought a young bull, a ram, and a one-year-old male lamb for a burnt offering, and a male goat for a sin offering. For a peace offering he brought two bulls, five rams, five male goats, and five one-year-old male lambs. This was the offering brought by Eliasaph son of Deuel.

On the seventh day Elishama son of Ammihud, leader of the tribe of Ephraim, presented his offering.

His offering consisted of a silver platter weighing 3¼ pounds and a silver basin weighing 1¾ pounds (as measured by the weight of the sanctuary shekel). These were both filled with grain offerings of choice flour moistened with olive oil. He also brought a gold container weighing four ounces, which was filled with incense. He brought a young bull, a ram, and a one-year-old male lamb for a burnt offering, and a male goat for a sin offering. For a peace offering he brought two bulls, five rams, five male goats, and five one-year-old male lambs. This was the offering brought by Elishama son of Ammihud.

On the eighth day Gamaliel son of Pedahzur, leader of the tribe of Manasseh, presented his offering.

His offering consisted of a silver platter weighing 3¼ pounds and a silver basin weighing 1¾ pounds (as measured by the weight of the sanctuary shekel). These were both filled with grain offerings of choice flour moistened with olive oil. He also brought a gold container weighing four ounces, which was filled with incense. He brought a young bull, a ram, and a one-year-old male lamb for a burnt offering, and a male goat for a sin offering. For a peace offering he brought two bulls, five rams, five male goats, and five one-year-old male lambs. This was the offering brought by Gamaliel son of Pedahzur.

On the ninth day Abidan son of Gideoni, leader of the tribe of Benjamin, presented his offering.

His offering consisted of a silver platter weighing 3¼ pounds and a silver basin weighing 1¾ pounds (as measured by the weight of the sanctuary shekel). These were both filled with grain offerings of choice flour moistened with olive oil. He also brought a gold container weighing four ounces, which was filled with incense. He brought a young bull, a ram, and a one-year-old male lamb for a burnt offering, and a male goat for a sin offering. For a peace offering he brought two bulls, five rams, five male goats, and five one-year-old male lambs. This was the offering brought by Abidan son of Gideoni.

On the tenth day Ahiezer son of Ammishaddai, leader of the tribe of Dan, presented his offering.

His offering consisted of a silver platter weighing 3¼ pounds and a silver basin weighing 1¾ pounds (as measured by the weight of the sanctuary shekel). These were both filled with grain offerings of choice flour moistened with olive oil. He also brought a gold container weighing four ounces, which was filled with incense. He brought a young bull, a ram, and a one-year-old male lamb for a burnt offering, and a male goat for a sin offering. For a peace offering he brought two bulls, five rams, five male goats, and five one-year-old male lambs. This was the offering brought by Ahiezer son of Ammishaddai.

On the eleventh day Pagiel son of Ocran, leader of the tribe of Asher, presented his offering.

His offering consisted of a silver platter weighing 3¼ pounds and a silver basin weighing 1¾ pounds (as measured by the weight of the sanctuary shekel). These were both filled with grain offerings of choice flour moistened with olive oil. He also brought a gold container weighing four ounces, which was filled with incense. He brought a young bull, a ram, and a one-year-old male lamb for a burnt offering, and a male goat for a sin offering. For a peace offering he brought two bulls, five rams, five male goats, and five one-year-old male lambs. This was the offering brought by Pagiel son of Ocran.

On the twelfth day Ahira son of Enan, leader of the tribe of Naphtali, presented his offering.

His offering consisted of a silver platter weighing 3¼ pounds and a silver basin weighing 1¾ pounds (as measured by the weight of the sanctuary shekel). These were both filled with grain offerings of choice flour moistened with olive oil. He also brought a gold container weighing four ounces, which was filled with incense. He brought a young bull, a ram, and a one-year-old male lamb for a burnt offering, and a male goat for a sin offering. For a peace offering he brought two bulls, five rams, five male goats, and five one-year-old male lambs. This was the offering brought by Ahira son of Enan.

So this was the dedication offering brought by the leaders of Israel at the time the altar was anointed: twelve silver platters, twelve silver basins, and twelve gold incense containers. Each silver platter weighed 3¼ pounds, and each silver basin weighed 1¾ pounds. The total weight of the silver was 60 pounds (as measured by the weight of the sanctuary shekel). Each of the twelve gold containers that was filled with incense weighed four ounces (as measured by the weight of the sanctuary shekel). The total weight of the gold was three pounds. Twelve young bulls, twelve rams, and twelve one-year-old male lambs were donated for the burnt offerings, along with their prescribed grain offerings. Twelve male goats were brought for the sin offerings. Twenty-four bulls, sixty rams, sixty male goats, and sixty one-year-old male lambs were donated for the peace offerings. This was the dedication offering for the altar after it was anointed.

+

Whenever Moses went into the Tabernacle to speak with the LORD, he heard the voice speaking to him from between the two cherubim above the Ark's cover—the place of atonement—that rests on the Ark of the Covenant. The LORD spoke to him from there.

+

The LORD said to Moses, "Give Aaron the following instructions: When you set up the seven lamps in the lampstand, place them so their light shines forward in front of the lampstand." So Aaron did this. He set up the seven lamps so they reflected their light forward, just as the LORD had commanded Moses. The entire lampstand, from its base to its decorative blossoms, was made of beaten gold. It was built according to the exact design the LORD had shown Moses.

+

Then the LORD said to Moses, "Now set the Levites apart from the rest of the people of Israel and make them ceremonially clean. Do this by sprinkling them with the water of purification, and have them shave their entire body and wash their clothing. Then they will be ceremonially clean. Have them bring a young bull and a grain offering of choice flour moistened with olive oil, along with a second young bull for a sin offering. Then assemble the whole community of Israel, and present the Levites at the entrance of the Tabernacle. When you present the Levites before the LORD, the people of Israel must lay their hands on them. Raising his hands, Aaron must then present the Levites to the LORD as a special offering from the people of Israel, thus dedicating them to the LORD's service.

"Next the Levites will lay their hands on the heads of the young bulls. Present one as a sin offering and the other as a burnt offering to the LORD, to purify the Levites and make them right with the LORD. Then have the Levites stand in front of Aaron and his sons, and raise your hands and present them as a special offering to the LORD. In this way, you will set the Levites apart from the rest of the people of Israel, and the Levites will belong to me. After this, they may go into the Tabernacle to do their work, because you have purified them and presented them as a special offering.

"Of all the people of Israel, the Levites are reserved for me. I have claimed them for myself in place of all the firstborn sons of the Israelites; I have taken the Levites as their substitutes. For all the firstborn males among the people of Israel are mine, both of people and of animals. I set them apart for myself on the day I struck down all the firstborn sons of the Egyptians. Yes, I have claimed the Levites in place of all the firstborn sons of Israel. And of all the Israelites, I have assigned the Levites to Aaron and his sons. They will serve in the Tabernacle on behalf of the Israelites and make sacrifices to purify the people so no plague will strike them when they approach the sanctuary."

So Moses, Aaron, and the whole community of Israel dedicated the Levites, carefully following all the LORD's instructions to Moses. The Levites purified themselves from sin and washed their clothes, and Aaron lifted them up and presented them to the LORD as a special offering. He then offered a sacrifice to purify them and make them right with the LORD. After that the Levites went into the Tabernacle to perform their duties, assisting Aaron and his sons. So they carried out all the commands that the LORD gave Moses concerning the Levites.

The LORD also instructed Moses, "This is the rule the Levites must follow: They must begin serving in the Tabernacle at the age of twenty-five, and they must retire at the age of fifty. After retirement they may assist their fellow Levites by serving as guards at the Tabernacle, but they may not officiate in the service. This is how you must assign duties to the Levites."

+

A year after Israel's departure from Egypt, the LORD spoke to Moses in the wilderness of Sinai. In the first month of that year he said, "Tell the Israelites to celebrate the Passover at the prescribed time, at twilight on the fourteenth day of the first month. Be sure to follow all my decrees and regulations concerning this celebration."

So Moses told the people to celebrate the Passover in the wilderness of Sinai as twilight fell on the fourteenth day of the month. And they celebrated the festival there, just as the LORD had commanded Moses. But some of the men had been ceremonially defiled by touching a dead body, so they could not celebrate the Passover that day. They came to Moses and Aaron that day and said, "We have become ceremonially unclean by touching a dead body. But why should we be prevented from presenting the LORD's offering at the proper time with the rest of the Israelites?"

Moses answered, "Wait here until I have received instructions for you from the LORD."

This was the LORD's reply to Moses. "Give the following instructions to the people of Israel: If any of the people now or in future generations are ceremonially unclean at Passover time because of touching a dead body, or if they are on a journey and cannot be present at the ceremony, they may still celebrate the LORD's Passover. They must offer the Passover sacrifice one month later, at twilight on the fourteenth day of the second month. They must eat the Passover lamb at that time with bitter salad greens and bread made without yeast. They must not leave any of the lamb until the next morning, and they must not break any of its bones. They must follow all the normal regulations concerning the Passover.

"But those who neglect to celebrate the Passover at the regular time, even though they are ceremonially clean and not away on a trip, will be cut off from the community of Israel. If they fail to present the LORD's offering at the proper time, they will suffer the consequences of their guilt. And if foreigners living among you want to celebrate the Passover to the LORD, they must follow these same decrees and regulations. The same laws apply both to native-born Israelites and to the foreigners living among you."

+

On the day the Tabernacle was set up, the cloud covered it. But from evening until morning the cloud over the Tabernacle looked like a pillar of fire. This was the regular pattern—at night the cloud that covered the Tabernacle had the appearance of fire. Whenever the cloud lifted from over the sacred tent, the people of Israel would break camp and follow it. And wherever the cloud settled, the people of Israel would set up camp. In this way, they traveled and camped at the LORD's command wherever he told them to go. Then they remained in their camp as long as the cloud stayed over the Tabernacle. If the cloud remained over the Tabernacle for a long time, the Israelites stayed and performed their duty to the LORD. Sometimes the cloud would stay over the Tabernacle for only a few days, so the people would stay for only a few days, as the LORD commanded. Then at the LORD's command they would break camp and move on. Sometimes the cloud stayed only overnight and lifted the next morning. But day or night, when the cloud lifted, the people broke camp and moved on. Whether the cloud stayed above the Tabernacle for two days, a month, or a year, the people of Israel stayed in camp and did not move on. But as soon as it lifted, they broke camp and moved on. So they camped or traveled at the LORD's command, and they did whatever the LORD told them through Moses.

✢ ✢ ✢

Now the LORD said to Moses, "Make two trumpets of hammered silver for calling the community to assemble and for signaling the breaking of camp. When both trumpets are blown, everyone must gather before you at the entrance of the Tabernacle. But if only one trumpet is blown, then only the leaders—the heads of the clans of Israel—must present themselves to you.

"When you sound the signal to move on, the tribes camped on the east side of the Tabernacle must break camp and move forward. When you sound the signal a second time, the tribes camped on the south will follow. You must sound short blasts as the signal for moving on. But when you call the people to an assembly, blow the trumpets with a different signal. Only the priests, Aaron's descendants, are allowed to blow the trumpets. This is a permanent law for you, to be observed from generation to generation.

"When you arrive in your own land and go to war against your enemies who attack you, sound the alarm with the trumpets. Then the LORD your God will remember you and rescue you from your enemies. Blow the trumpets in times of gladness, too, sounding them at your annual festivals and at the beginning of each month. And blow the trumpets over your burnt offerings and peace offerings. The trumpets will remind your God of his covenant with you. I am the LORD your God."

+ + +

In the second year after Israel's departure from Egypt—on the twentieth day of the second month—the cloud lifted from the Tabernacle of the Covenant. So the Israelites set out from the wilderness of Sinai and traveled on from place to place until the cloud stopped in the wilderness of Paran.

When the people set out for the first time, following the instructions the LORD had given through Moses, Judah's troops led the way. They marched behind their banner, and their leader was Nahshon son of Amminadab. They were joined by the troops of the tribe of Issachar, led by Nethanel son of Zuar, and the troops of the tribe of Zebulun, led by Eliab son of Helon.

Then the Tabernacle was taken down, and the Gershonite and Merarite divisions of the Levites were next in the line of march, carrying the Tabernacle with them. Reuben's troops went next, marching behind their banner. Their leader was Elizur son of Shedeur. They were joined by the troops of the tribe of Simeon, led by Shelumiel son of Zurishaddai, and the troops of the tribe of Gad, led by Eliasaph son of Deuel.

Next came the Kohathite division of the Levites, carrying the sacred objects from the Tabernacle. Before they arrived at the next camp, the Tabernacle would already be set up at its new location. Ephraim's troops went next, marching behind their banner. Their leader was Elishama son of Ammihud. They were joined by the troops of the tribe of Manasseh, led by Gamaliel son of Pedahzur, and the troops of the tribe of Benjamin, led by Abidan son of Gideoni.

Dan's troops went last, marching behind their banner and serving as the rear guard for all the tribal camps. Their leader was Ahiezer son of Ammishaddai. They were joined by the troops of the tribe of Asher, led by Pagiel son of Ocran, and the troops of the tribe of Naphtali, led by Ahira son of Enan.

This was the order in which the Israelites marched, division by division.

+

One day Moses said to his brother-in-law, Hobab son of Reuel the Midianite, "We are on our way to the place the LORD promised us, for he said, 'I will give it to you.' Come with us and we will treat you well, for the LORD has promised wonderful blessings for Israel!"

But Hobab replied, "No, I will not go. I must return to my own land and family."

"Please don't leave us," Moses pleaded. "You know the places in the wilderness where we should camp. Come, be our guide. If you do, we'll share with you all the blessings the LORD gives us."

They marched for three days after leaving the mountain of the LORD, with the Ark of the LORD's Covenant moving ahead of them to show them where to stop and rest. As they moved on each day, the cloud of the LORD hovered over them. And whenever the Ark set out, Moses would shout, "Arise, O LORD, and let your enemies be scattered! Let them flee before you!" And when the Ark was set down, he would say, "Return, O LORD, to the countless thousands of Israel!"

+

Soon the people began to complain about their hardship, and the LORD heard everything they said. Then the LORD's anger blazed against them, and he sent a fire to rage among them, and he destroyed some of the people in the outskirts of the camp. Then the people screamed to Moses for help, and when he prayed to the LORD, the fire stopped. After that, the area was known as Taberah (which means "the place of burning"), because fire from the LORD had burned among them there.

+

Then the foreign rabble who were traveling with the Israelites began to crave the good things of Egypt. And the people of Israel also began to complain. "Oh, for some meat!" they exclaimed. "We remember the fish we used to eat for free in Egypt. And we had all the cucumbers, melons, leeks, onions, and garlic we wanted. But now our appetites are gone. All we ever see is this manna!"

The manna looked like small coriander seeds, and it was pale yellow like gum resin. The people would go out and gather it from the ground. They made flour by grinding it with hand mills or pounding it in mortars. Then they boiled it in a pot and made it into flat cakes. These cakes tasted like pastries baked with olive oil. The manna came down on the camp with the dew during the night.

Moses heard all the families standing in the doorways of their tents whining, and the LORD became extremely angry. Moses was also very aggravated. And Moses said to the LORD, "Why are you treating me, your servant, so harshly? Have mercy on me! What did I do to deserve the burden of all these people? Did I give birth to them? Did I bring them into the world? Why did you tell me to carry them in my arms like a mother carries a nursing baby? How can I carry them to the land you swore to give their ancestors? Where am I supposed to get meat for all these people?

They keep whining to me, saying, 'Give us meat to eat!' I can't carry all these people by myself! The load is far too heavy! If this is how you intend to treat me, just go ahead and kill me. Do me a favor and spare me this misery!"

Then the LORD said to Moses, "Gather before me seventy men who are recognized as elders and leaders of Israel. Bring them to the Tabernacle to stand there with you. I will come down and talk to you there. I will take some of the Spirit that is upon you, and I will put the Spirit upon them also. They will bear the burden of the people along with you, so you will not have to carry it alone.

"And say to the people, 'Purify yourselves, for tomorrow you will have meat to eat. You were whining, and the LORD heard you when you cried, "Oh, for some meat! We were better off in Egypt!" Now the LORD will give you meat, and you will have to eat it. And it won't be for just a day or two, or for five or ten or even twenty. You will eat it for a whole month until you gag and are sick of it. For you have rejected the LORD, who is here among you, and you have whined to him, saying, "Why did we ever leave Egypt?"'"

But Moses responded to the LORD, "There are 600,000 foot soldiers here with me, and yet you say, 'I will give them meat for a whole month!' Even if we butchered all our flocks and herds, would that satisfy them? Even if we caught all the fish in the sea, would that be enough?"

Then the LORD said to Moses, "Has my arm lost its power? Now you will see whether or not my word comes true!"

So Moses went out and reported the LORD's words to the people. He gathered the seventy elders and stationed them around the Tabernacle. And the LORD came down in the cloud and spoke to Moses. Then he gave the seventy elders the same Spirit that was upon Moses. And when the Spirit rested upon them, they prophesied. But this never happened again.

Two men, Eldad and Medad, had stayed behind in the camp. They were listed among the elders, but they had not gone out to the Tabernacle. Yet the Spirit rested upon them as well, so they prophesied there in the camp. A young man ran and reported to Moses, "Eldad and Medad are prophesying in the camp!"

Joshua son of Nun, who had been Moses' assistant since his youth, protested, "Moses, my master, make them stop!"

But Moses replied, "Are you jealous for my sake? I wish that all the LORD's people were prophets and that the LORD would put his Spirit upon them all!" Then Moses returned to the camp with the elders of Israel.

Now the LORD sent a wind that brought quail from the sea and let them fall all around the camp. For miles in every direction there were quail flying about three feet above the ground. So the people went out and caught quail all that day and throughout the night and all the next day, too. No one gathered less than fifty bushels! They spread the quail all around the camp to dry. But while they were gorging themselves on the meat—while it was still in their mouths—the anger of the LORD blazed against the people, and he struck them with a severe plague. So that place was called Kibroth-hattaavah (which means "graves of gluttony") because there they buried the people who had craved meat from Egypt. From Kibroth-hattaavah the Israelites traveled to Hazeroth, where they stayed for some time.

+

While they were at Hazeroth, Miriam and Aaron criticized Moses because he had married a Cushite woman. They said, "Has the LORD spoken only through Moses? Hasn't he spoken through us, too?" But the LORD heard them. (Now Moses was very humble—more humble than any other person on earth.)

So immediately the LORD called to Moses, Aaron, and Miriam and said, "Go out to the Tabernacle, all three of you!" So the three of them went to the Tabernacle. Then the LORD descended in the pillar of cloud and stood at the entrance of the Tabernacle. "Aaron and Miriam!" he called, and they stepped forward. And the LORD said to them, "Now listen to what I say:

"If there were prophets among you,
    I, the LORD, would reveal myself in visions.
    I would speak to them in dreams.
But not with my servant Moses.
    Of all my house, he is the one I trust.
I speak to him face to face,
    clearly, and not in riddles!
    He sees the LORD as he is.
So why were you not afraid
    to criticize my servant Moses?"

The LORD was very angry with them, and he departed. As the cloud moved from above the Tabernacle, there stood Miriam, her skin as white as snow from leprosy. When Aaron saw what had happened to her, he cried out to Moses, "Oh, my master! Please don't punish us for this sin we have so foolishly committed. Don't let her be like a stillborn baby, already decayed at birth."

So Moses cried out to the LORD, "O God, I beg you, please heal her!"

But the LORD said to Moses, "If her father had done nothing more than spit in her face, wouldn't she be defiled for seven days? So keep her outside the camp for seven days, and after that she may be accepted back."

So Miriam was kept outside the camp for seven days, and the people waited until she was brought back before they traveled again. Then they left Hazeroth and camped in the wilderness of Paran.

+

The LORD now said to Moses, "Send out men to explore the land of Canaan, the land I am giving to the Israelites. Send one leader from each of the twelve ancestral tribes." So Moses did as the LORD commanded him. He sent out twelve men, all tribal leaders of Israel, from their camp in the wilderness of Paran. These were the tribes and the names of their leaders:

Tribe	*Leader*
Reuben	Shammua son of Zaccur
Simeon	Shaphat son of Hori
Judah	Caleb son of Jephunneh
Issachar	Igal son of Joseph
Ephraim	Hoshea son of Nun
Benjamin	Palti son of Raphu
Zebulun	Gaddiel son of Sodi
Manasseh son of Joseph	Gaddi son of Susi
Dan	Ammiel son of Gemalli
Asher	Sethur son of Michael
Naphtali	Nahbi son of Vophsi
Gad	Geuel son of Maki

These are the names of the men Moses sent out to explore the land. (Moses called Hoshea son of Nun by the name Joshua.)

Moses gave the men these instructions as he sent them out to explore the land: "Go north through the Negev into the hill country. See what the land is like, and find out whether the people living there are strong or weak, few or many. See what kind of land they live in. Is it good or bad? Do their towns have walls, or are they unprotected like open camps? Is the soil fertile or poor? Are there many trees? Do your best to bring back samples of the crops you see." (It happened to be the season for harvesting the first ripe grapes.)

So they went up and explored the land from the wilderness of Zin as far as Rehob, near Lebo-hamath. Going north, they passed through the Negev and arrived at Hebron, where Ahiman, Sheshai, and Talmai—all descendants of Anak—lived. (The ancient town of Hebron was founded seven years before the Egyptian city of Zoan.) When they came to the valley of Eshcol, they cut down a branch with a single cluster of grapes so large that it took two of them to carry it on a pole between them! They also brought back samples of the pomegranates and figs. That place was called the valley of Eshcol (which means "cluster"), because of the cluster of grapes the Israelite men cut there.

After exploring the land for forty days, the men returned to Moses, Aaron, and the whole community of Israel at Kadesh in the wilderness of Paran. They reported to the whole community what they had seen and showed them the fruit they had taken from the land. This was their report to Moses: "We entered the land you sent us to explore, and it is indeed a bountiful country—a land flowing with milk and honey. Here is the kind of fruit it produces. But the people living there are powerful, and their towns are large and fortified. We even saw giants there, the descendants of Anak! The Amalekites live in the Negev, and the Hittites, Jebusites, and Amorites live in the hill country. The Canaanites live along the coast of the Mediterranean Sea and along the Jordan Valley."

But Caleb tried to quiet the people as they stood before Moses. "Let's go at once to take the land," he said. "We can certainly conquer it!"

But the other men who had explored the land with him disagreed. "We can't go up against them! They are stronger than we are!" So they spread this bad report about the land among the Israelites: "The land we traveled through and explored will devour anyone who goes to live there. All the people we saw were huge. We even saw giants there, the descendants of Anak. Next to them we felt like grasshoppers, and that's what they thought, too!"

Then the whole community began weeping aloud, and they cried all night. Their voices rose in a great chorus of protest against Moses and Aaron. "If only we had died in Egypt, or even here in the wilderness!" they complained. "Why is the LORD taking us to this country only to have us die in battle? Our wives and our little ones will be carried off as plunder! Wouldn't it be better for us to return to Egypt?" Then they plotted among themselves, "Let's choose a new leader and go back to Egypt!"

Then Moses and Aaron fell face down on the ground before the whole community of Israel. Two of the men who had explored the land, Joshua son of Nun and Caleb son of Jephunneh, tore their clothing. They said to all the people of Israel, "The land we traveled through and explored is a wonderful land! And if the LORD is pleased with us, he will bring us safely into that land and give it to us. It is a rich land flowing with milk and honey. Do not rebel against the LORD, and don't be afraid of the people of the land. They are only helpless prey to us! They have no protection, but the LORD is with us! Don't be afraid of them!"

But the whole community began to talk about stoning Joshua and Caleb. Then the glorious presence of the LORD appeared to all the Israelites at the Tabernacle. And the Lord said to Moses, "How long will these people treat me with contempt? Will they never believe me, even after all the miraculous signs I have done among them? I will disown them and destroy them with a plague. Then I will make you into a nation greater and mightier than they are!"

But Moses objected. "What will the Egyptians think when they hear about it?" he asked the Lord. "They know full well the power you displayed in rescuing your people from Egypt. Now if you destroy them, the Egyptians will send a report to the inhabitants of this land, who have already heard that you live among your people. They know, Lord, that you have appeared to your people face to face and that your pillar of cloud hovers over them. They know that you go before them in the pillar of cloud by day and the pillar of fire by night. Now if you slaughter all these people with a single blow, the nations that have heard of your fame will say, 'The Lord was not able to bring them into the land he swore to give them, so he killed them in the wilderness.'

"Please, Lord, prove that your power is as great as you have claimed. For you said, 'The Lord is slow to anger and filled with unfailing love, forgiving every kind of sin and rebellion. But he does not excuse the guilty. He lays the sins of the parents upon their children; the entire family is affected—even children in the third and fourth generations.' In keeping with your magnificent, unfailing love, please pardon the sins of this people, just as you have forgiven them ever since they left Egypt."

Then the Lord said, "I will pardon them as you have requested. But as surely as I live, and as surely as the earth is filled with the Lord's glory, not one of these people will ever enter that land. They have all seen my glorious presence and the miraculous signs I performed both in Egypt and in the wilderness, but again and again they have tested me by refusing to listen to my voice. They will never even see the land I swore to give their ancestors. None of those who have treated me with contempt will ever see it. But my servant Caleb has a different attitude than the others have. He has remained loyal to me, so I will bring him into the land he explored. His descendants will possess their full share of that land. Now turn around, and don't go on toward the land where the Amalekites and Canaanites live. Tomorrow you must set out for the wilderness in the direction of the Red Sea."

Then the Lord said to Moses and Aaron, "How long must I put up with this wicked community and its complaints about me? Yes, I have heard the complaints the Israelites are making against me. Now tell them this: 'As surely as I live, declares the Lord, I will do to you the very things I heard you say. You will all drop dead in this wilderness! Because you complained against me, every one of you who is twenty years old or older and was included in the registration will die. You will not enter and occupy the land I swore to give you. The only exceptions will be Caleb son of Jephunneh and Joshua son of Nun.

"'You said your children would be carried off as plunder. Well, I will bring them safely into the land, and they will enjoy what you have despised. But as for you, you will drop dead in this wilderness. And your children will be like shepherds, wandering in the wilderness for forty years. In this way, they will pay for your faithlessness, until the last of you lies dead in the wilderness.

"'Because your men explored the land for forty days, you must wander in the wilderness for forty years—a year for each day, suffering the consequences of your sins. Then you will discover what it is like to have me for an enemy.' I, the LORD, have spoken! I will certainly do these things to every member of the community who has conspired against me. They will be destroyed here in this wilderness, and here they will die!"

The ten men Moses had sent to explore the land—the ones who incited rebellion against the LORD with their bad report—were struck dead with a plague before the LORD. Of the twelve who had explored the land, only Joshua and Caleb remained alive.

When Moses reported the LORD's words to all the Israelites, the people were filled with grief. Then they got up early the next morning and went to the top of the range of hills. "Let's go," they said. "We realize that we have sinned, but now we are ready to enter the land the LORD has promised us."

But Moses said, "Why are you now disobeying the LORD's orders to return to the wilderness? It won't work. Do not go up into the land now. You will only be crushed by your enemies because the LORD is not with you. When you face the Amalekites and Canaanites in battle, you will be slaughtered. The LORD will abandon you because you have abandoned the LORD."

But the people defiantly pushed ahead toward the hill country, even though neither Moses nor the Ark of the LORD's Covenant left the camp. Then the Amalekites and the Canaanites who lived in those hills came down and attacked them and chased them back as far as Hormah.

✦ ✦ ✦

Then the LORD told Moses, "Give the following instructions to the people of Israel.

"When you finally settle in the land I am giving you, you will offer special gifts as a pleasing aroma to the LORD. These gifts may take the form of a burnt offering, a sacrifice to fulfill a vow, a voluntary offering, or an offering at any of your annual festivals, and they may be taken from your herds of cattle or your flocks of sheep and goats. When you present these offerings, you must also give the LORD a grain offering of two quarts of choice flour mixed with one quart of olive oil. For each lamb offered as a burnt offering or a special sacrifice, you must also present one quart of wine as a liquid offering.

"If the sacrifice is a ram, give a grain offering of four quarts of choice flour mixed with a third of a gallon of olive oil, and give a third of a gallon of wine as a liquid offering. This will be a pleasing aroma to the LORD.

"When you present a young bull as a burnt offering or as a sacrifice to fulfill a vow or as a peace offering to the LORD, you must also give a grain offering of six quarts of choice flour mixed with two quarts of olive oil, and give two quarts of wine as a liquid offering. This will be a special gift, a pleasing aroma to the LORD.

"Each sacrifice of a bull, ram, lamb, or young goat should be prepared in this way. Follow these instructions with each offering you present. All of you native-born Israelites must follow these instructions when you offer a special gift as a pleasing aroma to the LORD. And if any foreigners visit you or live among you and want to present a special gift as a pleasing aroma to the LORD, they must follow these same procedures. Native-born Israelites and foreigners are equal before the LORD and are subject to the same decrees. This is a permanent law for you, to be observed from generation to generation. The same instructions and regulations will apply both to you and to the foreigners living among you."

Then the LORD said to Moses, "Give the following instructions to the people of Israel.

"When you arrive in the land where I am taking you, and you eat the crops that grow there, you must set some aside as a sacred offering to the LORD. Present a cake from the first of the flour you grind, and set it aside as a sacred offering, as you do with the first grain from the threshing floor. Throughout the generations to come, you are to present a sacred offering to the LORD each year from the first of your ground flour.

"But suppose you unintentionally fail to carry out all these commands that the LORD has given you through Moses. And suppose your descendants in the future fail to do everything the LORD has commanded through Moses. If the mistake was made unintentionally, and the community was unaware of it, the whole community must present a young bull for a burnt offering as a pleasing aroma to the LORD. It must be offered along with its prescribed grain offering and liquid offering and with one male goat for a sin offering. With it the priest will purify the whole community of Israel, making them right with the LORD, and they will be forgiven. For it was an unintentional sin, and they have corrected it with their offerings to the

LORD—the special gift and the sin offering. The whole community of Israel will be forgiven, including the foreigners living among you, for all the people were involved in the sin.

"If one individual commits an unintentional sin, the guilty person must bring a one-year-old female goat for a sin offering. The priest will sacrifice it to purify the guilty person before the LORD, and that person will be forgiven. These same instructions apply both to native-born Israelites and to the foreigners living among you.

"But those who brazenly violate the LORD's will, whether native-born Israelites or foreigners, have blasphemed the LORD, and they must be cut off from the community. Since they have treated the LORD's word with contempt and deliberately disobeyed his command, they must be completely cut off and suffer the punishment for their guilt."

+

One day while the people of Israel were in the wilderness, they discovered a man gathering wood on the Sabbath day. The people who found him doing this took him before Moses, Aaron, and the rest of the community. They held him in custody because they did not know what to do with him. Then the LORD said to Moses, "The man must be put to death! The whole community must stone him outside the camp." So the whole community took the man outside the camp and stoned him to death, just as the LORD had commanded Moses.

Then the LORD said to Moses, "Give the following instructions to the people of Israel: Throughout the generations to come you must make tassels for the hems of your clothing and attach them with a blue cord. When you see the tassels, you will remember and obey all the commands of the LORD instead of following your own desires and defiling yourselves, as you are prone to do. The tassels will help you remember that you must obey all my commands and be holy to your God. I am the LORD your God who brought you out of the land of Egypt that I might be your God. I am the LORD your God!"

+ + +

One day Korah son of Izhar, a descendant of Kohath son of Levi, conspired with Dathan and Abiram, the sons of Eliab, and On son of Peleth, from the tribe of Reuben. They incited a rebellion against Moses, along with 250 other leaders of the community, all prominent members of the assembly. They united against Moses and Aaron and said, "You have gone too far! The whole community of Israel has been set apart by the LORD, and he is with all of us. What right do you have to act as though you are greater than the rest of the LORD's people?"

When Moses heard what they were saying, he fell face down on the ground. Then he said to Korah and his followers, "Tomorrow morning the LORD will show us who belongs to him and who is holy. The LORD will allow only those whom he selects to enter his own presence. Korah, you and all your followers must prepare your incense burners. Light fires in them tomorrow, and burn incense before the LORD. Then we will see whom the LORD chooses as his holy one. You Levites are the ones who have gone too far!"

Then Moses spoke again to Korah: "Now listen, you Levites! Does it seem insignificant to you that the God of Israel has chosen you from among all the community of Israel to be near him so you can serve in the LORD's Tabernacle and stand before the people to minister to them? Korah, he has already given this special ministry to you and your fellow Levites. Are you now demanding the priesthood as well? The LORD is the one you and your followers are really revolting against! For who is Aaron that you are complaining about him?"

Then Moses summoned Dathan and Abiram, the sons of Eliab, but they replied, "We refuse to come before you! Isn't it enough that you brought us out of Egypt, a land flowing with milk and honey, to kill us here in this wilderness, and that you now treat us like your subjects? What's more, you haven't brought us into another land flowing with milk and honey. You haven't given us a new homeland with fields and vineyards. Are you trying to fool these men? We will not come."

Then Moses became very angry and said to the LORD, "Do not accept their grain offerings! I have not taken so much as a donkey from them, and I have never hurt a single one of them." And Moses said to Korah, "You and all your followers must come here tomorrow and present yourselves before the LORD. Aaron will also be here. You and each of your 250 followers must prepare an incense burner and put incense on it, so you can all present them before the LORD. Aaron will also bring his incense burner."

So each of these men prepared an incense burner, lit the fire, and placed incense on it. Then they all stood at the entrance of the Tabernacle with Moses and Aaron. Meanwhile, Korah had stirred up the entire community against Moses and Aaron, and they all gathered at the Tabernacle entrance. Then the glorious presence of the LORD appeared to the whole community, and the LORD said to Moses and Aaron, "Get away from all these people so that I may instantly destroy them!"

But Moses and Aaron fell face down on the ground. "O God," they pleaded, "you are the God who gives breath to all creatures. Must you be angry with all the people when only one man sins?"

And the Lord said to Moses, "Then tell all the people to get away from the tents of Korah, Dathan, and Abiram."

So Moses got up and rushed over to the tents of Dathan and Abiram, followed by the elders of Israel. "Quick!" he told the people. "Get away from the tents of these wicked men, and don't touch anything that belongs to them. If you do, you will be destroyed for their sins." So all the people stood back from the tents of Korah, Dathan, and Abiram. Then Dathan and Abiram came out and stood at the entrances of their tents, together with their wives and children and little ones.

And Moses said, "This is how you will know that the Lord has sent me to do all these things that I have done—for I have not done them on my own. If these men die a natural death, or if nothing unusual happens, then the Lord has not sent me. But if the Lord does something entirely new and the ground opens its mouth and swallows them and all their belongings, and they go down alive into the grave, then you will know that these men have shown contempt for the Lord."

He had hardly finished speaking the words when the ground suddenly split open beneath them. The earth opened its mouth and swallowed the men, along with their households and all their followers who were standing with them, and everything they owned. So they went down alive into the grave, along with all their belongings. The earth closed over them, and they all vanished from among the people of Israel. All the people around them fled when they heard their screams. "The earth will swallow us, too!" they cried. Then fire blazed forth from the Lord and burned up the 250 men who were offering incense.

And the Lord said to Moses, "Tell Eleazar son of Aaron the priest to pull all the incense burners from the fire, for they are holy. Also tell him to scatter the burning coals. Take the incense burners of these men who have sinned at the cost of their lives, and hammer the metal into a thin sheet to overlay the altar. Since these burners were used in the Lord's presence, they have become holy. Let them serve as a warning to the people of Israel."

So Eleazar the priest collected the 250 bronze incense burners that had been used by the men who died in the fire, and the bronze was hammered into a thin sheet to overlay the altar. This would warn the Israelites that no unauthorized person—no one who was not a descendant of Aaron—should ever enter the Lord's presence to burn incense. If anyone did, the same thing would happen to him as happened to Korah and his followers. So the Lord's instructions to Moses were carried out.

But the very next morning the whole community of Israel began muttering again against Moses and Aaron, saying, "You have killed the Lord's people!" As the community gathered to protest against Moses and Aaron, they turned toward the Tabernacle and saw that the cloud had covered it, and the glorious presence of the LORD appeared.

Moses and Aaron came and stood in front of the Tabernacle, and the LORD said to Moses, "Get away from all these people so that I can instantly destroy them!" But Moses and Aaron fell face down on the ground.

And Moses said to Aaron, "Quick, take an incense burner and place burning coals on it from the altar. Lay incense on it, and carry it out among the people to purify them and make them right with the LORD. The LORD's anger is blazing against them—the plague has already begun."

Aaron did as Moses told him and ran out among the people. The plague had already begun to strike down the people, but Aaron burned the incense and purified the people. He stood between the dead and the living, and the plague stopped. But 14,700 people died in that plague, in addition to those who had died in the affair involving Korah. Then because the plague had stopped, Aaron returned to Moses at the entrance of the Tabernacle.

Then the LORD said to Moses, "Tell the people of Israel to bring you twelve wooden staffs, one from each leader of Israel's ancestral tribes, and inscribe each leader's name on his staff. Inscribe Aaron's name on the staff of the tribe of Levi, for there must be one staff for the leader of each ancestral tribe. Place these staffs in the Tabernacle in front of the Ark containing the tablets of the Covenant, where I meet with you. Buds will sprout on the staff belonging to the man I choose. Then I will finally put an end to the people's murmuring and complaining against you."

So Moses gave the instructions to the people of Israel, and each of the twelve tribal leaders, including Aaron, brought Moses a staff. Moses placed the staffs in the LORD's presence in the Tabernacle of the Covenant. When he went into the Tabernacle of the Covenant the next day, he found that Aaron's staff, representing the tribe of Levi, had sprouted, budded, blossomed, and produced ripe almonds!

When Moses brought all the staffs out from the LORD's presence, he showed them to the people. Each man claimed his own staff. And the LORD said to Moses: "Place Aaron's staff permanently before the Ark of the Covenant to serve as a warning to rebels. This should put an end to their complaints against me and prevent any further deaths." So Moses did as the LORD commanded him.

Then the people of Israel said to Moses, "Look, we are doomed! We are dead! We are ruined! Everyone who even comes close to the Tabernacle of the LORD dies. Are we all doomed to die?"

+ + +

Then the LORD said to Aaron: "You, your sons, and your relatives from the tribe of Levi will be held responsible for any offenses related to the sanctuary. But you and your sons alone will be held responsible for violations connected with the priesthood.

"Bring your relatives of the tribe of Levi—your ancestral tribe—to assist you and your sons as you perform the sacred duties in front of the Tabernacle of the Covenant. But as the Levites go about all their assigned duties at the Tabernacle, they must be careful not to go near any of the sacred objects or the altar. If they do, both you and they will die. The Levites must join you in fulfilling their responsibilities for the care and maintenance of the Tabernacle, but no unauthorized person may assist you.

"You yourselves must perform the sacred duties inside the sanctuary and at the altar. If you follow these instructions, the LORD's anger will never again blaze against the people of Israel. I myself have chosen your fellow Levites from among the Israelites to be your special assistants. They are a gift to you, dedicated to the LORD for service in the Tabernacle. But you and your sons, the priests, must personally handle all the priestly rituals associated with the altar and with everything behind the inner curtain. I am giving you the priesthood as your special privilege of service. Any unauthorized person who comes too near the sanctuary will be put to death."

The LORD gave these further instructions to Aaron: "I myself have put you in charge of all the holy offerings that are brought to me by the people of Israel. I have given all these consecrated offerings to you and your sons as your permanent share. You are allotted the portion of the most holy offerings that is not burned on the fire. This portion of all the most holy offerings—including the grain offerings, sin offerings, and guilt offerings—will be most holy, and it belongs to you and your sons. You must eat it as a most holy offering. All the males may eat of it, and you must treat it as most holy.

"All the sacred offerings and special offerings presented to me when the Israelites lift them up before the altar also belong to you. I have given them to you and to your sons and daughters as your permanent share. Any member of your family who is ceremonially clean may eat of these offerings.

"I also give you the harvest gifts brought by the people as offerings to the LORD—the best of the olive oil, new wine, and grain. All the first crops of their land that the people present to the LORD belong to you. Any member of your family who is ceremonially clean may eat this food.

"Everything in Israel that is specially set apart for the LORD also belongs to you.

"The firstborn of every mother, whether human or animal, that is offered to the LORD will be yours. But you must always redeem your firstborn sons and the firstborn of ceremonially unclean animals. Redeem them when they are one month old. The redemption price is five pieces of silver (as measured by the weight of the sanctuary shekel, which equals twenty gerahs).

"However, you may not redeem the firstborn of cattle, sheep, or goats. They are holy and have been set apart for the LORD. Sprinkle their blood on the altar, and burn their fat as a special gift, a pleasing aroma to the LORD. The meat of these animals will be yours, just like the breast and right thigh that are presented by lifting them up as a special offering before the altar. Yes, I am giving you all these holy offerings that the people of Israel bring to the LORD. They are for you and your sons and daughters, to be eaten as your permanent share. This is an eternal and unbreakable covenant between the LORD and you, and it also applies to your descendants."

And the LORD said to Aaron, "You priests will receive no allotment of land or share of property among the people of Israel. I am your share and your allotment. As for the tribe of Levi, your relatives, I will compensate them for their service in the Tabernacle. Instead of an allotment of land, I will give them the tithes from the entire land of Israel.

"From now on, no Israelites except priests or Levites may approach the Tabernacle. If they come too near, they will be judged guilty and will die. Only the Levites may serve at the Tabernacle, and they will be held responsible for any offenses against it. This is a permanent law for you, to be observed from generation to generation. The Levites will receive no allotment of land among the Israelites, because I have given them the Israelites' tithes, which have been presented as sacred offerings to the LORD. This will be the Levites' share. That is why I said they would receive no allotment of land among the Israelites."

+

The LORD also told Moses, "Give these instructions to the Levites: When you receive from the people of Israel the tithes I have assigned as your allotment, give a tenth of the tithes you receive—a tithe of the tithe—to the LORD as a sacred offering. The LORD will consider this offering to be your harvest offering, as though it were the first grain from your own threshing floor or wine from your own winepress. You must present one-tenth of the tithe received from the Israelites as a sacred offering to the LORD. This is the LORD's sacred portion, and you must present it to Aaron the priest. Be sure to give to the LORD the best portions of the gifts given to you.

"Also, give these instructions to the Levites: When you present the best part as your offering, it will be considered as though it came from your own threshing floor or winepress. You Levites and your families may eat this food anywhere you wish, for it is your compensation for serving in the Tabernacle. You will not be considered guilty for accepting the Lord's tithes if you give the best portion to the priests. But be careful not to treat the holy gifts of the people of Israel as though they were common. If you do, you will die."

+

The Lord said to Moses and Aaron, "Here is another legal requirement commanded by the Lord: Tell the people of Israel to bring you a red heifer, a perfect animal that has no defects and has never been yoked to a plow. Give it to Eleazar the priest, and it will be taken outside the camp and slaughtered in his presence. Eleazar will take some of its blood on his finger and sprinkle it seven times toward the front of the Tabernacle. As Eleazar watches, the heifer must be burned—its hide, meat, blood, and dung. Eleazar the priest must then take a stick of cedar, a hyssop branch, and some scarlet yarn and throw them into the fire where the heifer is burning.

"Then the priest must wash his clothes and bathe himself in water. Afterward he may return to the camp, though he will remain ceremonially unclean until evening. The man who burns the animal must also wash his clothes and bathe himself in water, and he, too, will remain unclean until evening. Then someone who is ceremonially clean will gather up the ashes of the heifer and deposit them in a purified place outside the camp. They will be kept there for the community of Israel to use in the water for the purification ceremony. This ceremony is performed for the removal of sin. The man who gathers up the ashes of the heifer must also wash his clothes, and he will remain ceremonially unclean until evening. This is a permanent law for the people of Israel and any foreigners who live among them.

"All those who touch a dead human body will be ceremonially unclean for seven days. They must purify themselves on the third and seventh days with the water of purification; then they will be purified. But if they do not do this on the third and seventh days, they will continue to be unclean even after the seventh day. All those who touch a dead body and do not purify themselves in the proper way defile the Lord's Tabernacle, and they will be cut off from the community of Israel. Since the water of purification was not sprinkled on them, their defilement continues.

"This is the ritual law that applies when someone dies inside a tent: All those who enter that tent and those who were inside when the death occurred will be ceremonially unclean for seven days. Any open container in the tent that was not covered with a lid is also defiled. And if someone in an open field touches the corpse of someone who was killed with a sword or who died a natural death, or if someone touches a human bone or a grave, that person will be defiled for seven days.

"To remove the defilement, put some of the ashes from the burnt purification offering in a jar, and pour fresh water over them. Then someone who is ceremonially clean must take a hyssop branch and dip it into the water. That person must sprinkle the water on the tent, on all the furnishings in the tent, and on the people who were in the tent; also on the person who touched a human bone, or touched someone who was killed or who died naturally, or touched a grave. On the third and seventh days the person who is ceremonially clean must sprinkle the water on those who are defiled. Then on the seventh day the people being cleansed must wash their clothes and bathe themselves, and that evening they will be cleansed of their defilement.

"But those who become defiled and do not purify themselves will be cut off from the community, for they have defiled the sanctuary of the LORD. Since the water of purification has not been sprinkled on them, they remain defiled. This is a permanent law for the people. Those who sprinkle the water of purification must afterward wash their clothes, and anyone who then touches the water used for purification will remain defiled until evening. Anything and anyone that a defiled person touches will be ceremonially unclean until evening."

+ + +

In the first month of the year, the whole community of Israel arrived in the wilderness of Zin and camped at Kadesh. While they were there, Miriam died and was buried.

There was no water for the people to drink at that place, so they rebelled against Moses and Aaron. The people blamed Moses and said, "If only we had died in the LORD's presence with our brothers! Why have you brought the congregation of the LORD's people into this wilderness to die, along with all our livestock? Why did you make us leave Egypt and bring us here to this terrible place? This land has no grain, no figs, no grapes, no pomegranates, and no water to drink!"

Moses and Aaron turned away from the people and went to the entrance of the Tabernacle, where they fell face down on the ground. Then the glorious presence of the LORD appeared to them, and the LORD said to Moses, "You and Aaron must take the staff and assemble the entire community. As the people watch, speak to the rock over there, and it will pour out its water. You will provide enough water from the rock to satisfy the whole community and their livestock."

So Moses did as he was told. He took the staff from the place where it was kept before the LORD. Then he and Aaron summoned the people to come and gather at the rock. "Listen, you rebels!" he shouted. "Must we bring you water from this rock?" Then Moses raised his hand and struck the rock twice with the staff, and water gushed out. So the entire community and their livestock drank their fill.

But the LORD said to Moses and Aaron, "Because you did not trust me enough to demonstrate my holiness to the people of Israel, you will not lead them into the land I am giving them!" This place was known as the waters of Meribah (which means "arguing") because there the people of Israel argued with the LORD, and there he demonstrated his holiness among them.

✦

While Moses was at Kadesh, he sent ambassadors to the king of Edom with this message:

"This is what your relatives, the people of Israel, say: You know all the hardships we have been through. Our ancestors went down to Egypt, and we lived there a long time, and we and our ancestors were brutally mistreated by the Egyptians. But when we cried out to the LORD, he heard us and sent an angel who brought us out of Egypt. Now we are camped at Kadesh, a town on the border of your land. Please let us travel through your land. We will be careful not to go through your fields and vineyards. We won't even drink water from your wells. We will stay on the king's road and never leave it until we have passed through your territory."

But the king of Edom said, "Stay out of my land, or I will meet you with an army!"

The Israelites answered, "We will stay on the main road. If our livestock drink your water, we will pay for it. Just let us pass through your country. That's all we ask."

But the king of Edom replied, "Stay out! You may not pass through our land." With that he mobilized his army and marched out against them with an imposing force. Because Edom refused to allow Israel to pass through their country, Israel was forced to turn around.

✦

The whole community of Israel left Kadesh and arrived at Mount Hor. There, on the border of the land of Edom, the LORD said to Moses and Aaron, "The time has come for Aaron to join his ancestors in death. He will not enter the land I am giving the people of Israel, because the two of you rebelled against my instructions concerning the water at Meribah. Now take Aaron and his son Eleazar up Mount Hor. There you will remove Aaron's priestly garments and put them on Eleazar, his son. Aaron will die there and join his ancestors."

So Moses did as the LORD commanded. The three of them went up Mount Hor together as the whole community watched. At the summit, Moses removed the priestly garments from Aaron and put them on Eleazar, Aaron's son. Then Aaron died there on top of the mountain, and Moses and Eleazar went back down. When the people realized that Aaron had died, all Israel mourned for him thirty days.

+

The Canaanite king of Arad, who lived in the Negev, heard that the Israelites were approaching on the road through Atharim. So he attacked the Israelites and took some of them as prisoners. Then the people of Israel made this vow to the LORD: "If you will hand these people over to us, we will completely destroy all their towns." The LORD heard the Israelites' request and gave them victory over the Canaanites. The Israelites completely destroyed them and their towns, and the place has been called Hormah ever since.

+

Then the people of Israel set out from Mount Hor, taking the road to the Red Sea to go around the land of Edom. But the people grew impatient with the long journey, and they began to speak against God and Moses. "Why have you brought us out of Egypt to die here in the wilderness?" they complained. "There is nothing to eat here and nothing to drink. And we hate this horrible manna!"

So the LORD sent poisonous snakes among the people, and many were bitten and died. Then the people came to Moses and cried out, "We have sinned by speaking against the LORD and against you. Pray that the LORD will take away the snakes." So Moses prayed for the people.

Then the LORD told him, "Make a replica of a poisonous snake and attach it to a pole. All who are bitten will live if they simply look at it!" So Moses made a snake out of bronze and attached it to a pole. Then anyone who was bitten by a snake could look at the bronze snake and be healed!

✛

The Israelites traveled next to Oboth and camped there. Then they went on to Iye-abarim, in the wilderness on the eastern border of Moab. From there they traveled to the valley of Zered Brook and set up camp. Then they moved out and camped on the far side of the Arnon River, in the wilderness adjacent to the territory of the Amorites. The Arnon is the boundary line between the Moabites and the Amorites. For this reason *The Book of the Wars of the LORD* speaks of "the town of Waheb in the area of Suphah, and the ravines of the Arnon River, and the ravines that extend as far as the settlement of Ar on the border of Moab."

From there the Israelites traveled to Beer, which is the well where the LORD said to Moses, "Assemble the people, and I will give them water." There the Israelites sang this song:

"Spring up, O well!
    Yes, sing its praises!
Sing of this well,
    which princes dug,
which great leaders hollowed out
    with their scepters and staffs."

Then the Israelites left the wilderness and proceeded on through Mattanah, Nahaliel, and Bamoth. After that they went to the valley in Moab where Pisgah Peak overlooks the wasteland.

✛

The Israelites sent ambassadors to King Sihon of the Amorites with this message:

"Let us travel through your land. We will be careful not to go through your fields and vineyards. We won't even drink water from your wells. We will stay on the king's road until we have passed through your territory."

But King Sihon refused to let them cross his territory. Instead, he mobilized his entire army and attacked Israel in the wilderness, engaging them in battle at Jahaz. But the Israelites slaughtered them with their swords and occupied their land from the Arnon River to the Jabbok River. They went only as far as the Ammonite border because the boundary of the Ammonites was fortified.

So Israel captured all the towns of the Amorites and settled in them, including the city of Heshbon and its surrounding villages. Heshbon had been the capital of King Sihon of the Amorites. He had defeated a former Moabite king and seized all his land as far as the Arnon River. Therefore, the ancient poets wrote this about him:

"Come to Heshbon and let it be rebuilt!
　　Let the city of Sihon be restored.
A fire flamed forth from Heshbon,
　　a blaze from the city of Sihon.
It burned the city of Ar in Moab;
　　it destroyed the rulers of the Arnon heights.
What sorrow awaits you, O people of Moab!
　　You are finished, O worshipers of Chemosh!
Chemosh has left his sons as refugees,
　　his daughters as captives of Sihon, the Amorite king.
We have utterly destroyed them,
　　from Heshbon to Dibon.
We have completely wiped them out
　　as far away as Nophah and Medeba."

So the people of Israel occupied the territory of the Amorites. After Moses sent men to explore the Jazer area, they captured all the towns in the region and drove out the Amorites who lived there. Then they turned and marched up the road to Bashan, but King Og of Bashan and all his people attacked them at Edrei. The LORD said to Moses, "Do not be afraid of him, for I have handed him over to you, along with all his people and his land. Do the same to him as you did to King Sihon of the Amorites, who ruled in Heshbon." And Israel killed King Og, his sons, and all his subjects; not a single survivor remained. Then Israel occupied their land.

+

Then the people of Israel traveled to the plains of Moab and camped east of the Jordan River, across from Jericho. Balak son of Zippor, the Moabite king, had seen everything the Israelites did to the Amorites. And when the people of Moab saw how many Israelites there were, they were terrified. The king of Moab said to the elders of Midian, "This mob will devour everything in sight, like an ox devours grass in the field!"

So Balak, king of Moab, sent messengers to call Balaam son of Beor, who was living in his native land of Pethor near the Euphrates River. His message said:

"Look, a vast horde of people has arrived from Egypt. They cover the face of the earth and are threatening me. Please come and curse these people for me because they are too powerful for me. Then perhaps I will be able to conquer them and drive them from the land. I know that blessings fall on any people you bless, and curses fall on people you curse."

Balak's messengers, who were elders of Moab and Midian, set out with money to pay Balaam to place a curse upon Israel. They went to Balaam and delivered Balak's message to him. "Stay here overnight," Balaam said. "In the morning I will tell you whatever the LORD directs me to say." So the officials from Moab stayed there with Balaam.

That night God came to Balaam and asked him, "Who are these men visiting you?"

Balaam said to God, "Balak son of Zippor, king of Moab, has sent me this message: 'Look, a vast horde of people has arrived from Egypt, and they cover the face of the earth. Come and curse these people for me. Then perhaps I will be able to stand up to them and drive them from the land.'"

But God told Balaam, "Do not go with them. You are not to curse these people, for they have been blessed!"

The next morning Balaam got up and told Balak's officials, "Go on home! The LORD will not let me go with you."

So the Moabite officials returned to King Balak and reported, "Balaam refused to come with us." Then Balak tried again. This time he sent a larger number of even more distinguished officials than those he had sent the first time. They went to Balaam and delivered this message to him:

"This is what Balak son of Zippor says: Please don't let anything stop you from coming to help me. I will pay you very well and do whatever you tell me. Just come and curse these people for me!"

But Balaam responded to Balak's messengers, "Even if Balak were to give me his palace filled with silver and gold, I would be powerless to do anything against the will of the LORD my God. But stay here one more night, and I will see if the LORD has anything else to say to me."

That night God came to Balaam and told him, "Since these men have come for you, get up and go with them. But do only what I tell you to do."

So the next morning Balaam got up, saddled his donkey, and started off with the Moabite officials. But God was angry that Balaam was going, so he sent the angel of the LORD to stand in the road to block his way. As Balaam and two servants were riding along, Balaam's donkey saw the angel of the LORD standing in the road with a drawn sword in his hand. The donkey bolted off the road into a field, but Balaam beat it and turned it back onto the road. Then the angel of the LORD stood at a place where the road narrowed between two vineyard walls. When the donkey saw the angel of the LORD, it tried to squeeze by and crushed Balaam's foot against the wall. So Balaam beat the donkey again. Then the angel of the LORD moved farther down the road and stood in a place too narrow for the donkey to get by at all. This time when the donkey saw the angel, it lay down under Balaam. In a fit of rage Balaam beat the animal again with his staff.

Then the LORD gave the donkey the ability to speak. "What have I done to you that deserves your beating me three times?" it asked Balaam.

"You have made me look like a fool!" Balaam shouted. "If I had a sword with me, I would kill you!"

"But I am the same donkey you have ridden all your life," the donkey answered. "Have I ever done anything like this before?"

"No," Balaam admitted.

Then the LORD opened Balaam's eyes, and he saw the angel of the LORD standing in the roadway with a drawn sword in his hand. Balaam bowed his head and fell face down on the ground before him.

"Why did you beat your donkey those three times?" the angel of the LORD demanded. "Look, I have come to block your way because you are stubbornly resisting me. Three times the donkey saw me and shied away; otherwise, I would certainly have killed you by now and spared the donkey."

Then Balaam confessed to the angel of the LORD, "I have sinned. I didn't realize you were standing in the road to block my way. I will return home if you are against my going."

But the angel of the LORD told Balaam, "Go with these men, but say only what I tell you to say." So Balaam went on with Balak's officials.

When King Balak heard that Balaam was on the way, he went out to meet him at a Moabite town on the Arnon River at the farthest border of his land.

"Didn't I send you an urgent invitation? Why didn't you come right away?" Balak asked Balaam. "Didn't you believe me when I said I would reward you richly?"

Balaam replied, "Look, now I have come, but I have no power to say whatever I want. I will speak only the message that God puts in my mouth." Then Balaam accompanied Balak to Kiriath-huzoth, where the king sacrificed cattle and sheep. He sent portions of the meat to Balaam and the officials who were with him. The next morning Balak took Balaam up to Bamoth-baal. From there he could see some of the people of Israel spread out below him.

Then Balaam said to King Balak, "Build me seven altars here, and prepare seven young bulls and seven rams for me to sacrifice." Balak followed his instructions, and the two of them sacrificed a young bull and a ram on each altar.

Then Balaam said to Balak, "Stand here by your burnt offerings, and I will go to see if the LORD will respond to me. Then I will tell you whatever he reveals to me." So Balaam went alone to the top of a bare hill, and God met him there. Balaam said to him, "I have prepared seven altars and have sacrificed a young bull and a ram on each altar."

The LORD gave Balaam a message for King Balak. Then he said, "Go back to Balak and give him my message."

So Balaam returned and found the king standing beside his burnt offerings with all the officials of Moab. This was the message Balaam delivered:

> "Balak summoned me to come from Aram;
>> the king of Moab brought me from the eastern hills.
> 'Come,' he said, 'curse Jacob for me!
>> Come and announce Israel's doom.'
> But how can I curse those
>> whom God has not cursed?
> How can I condemn those
>> whom the LORD has not condemned?
> I see them from the cliff tops;
>> I watch them from the hills.
> I see a people who live by themselves,
>> set apart from other nations.
> Who can count Jacob's descendants, as numerous as dust?
>> Who can count even a fourth of Israel's people?
> Let me die like the righteous;
>> let my life end like theirs."

Then King Balak demanded of Balaam, "What have you done to me? I brought you to curse my enemies. Instead, you have blessed them!"

But Balaam replied, "I will speak only the message that the LORD puts in my mouth."

Then King Balak told him, "Come with me to another place. There you will see another part of the nation of Israel, but not all of them. Curse at least that many!" So Balak took Balaam to the plateau of Zophim on Pisgah Peak. He built seven altars there and offered a young bull and a ram on each altar.

Then Balaam said to the king, "Stand here by your burnt offerings while I go over there to meet the LORD."

And the LORD met Balaam and gave him a message. Then he said, "Go back to Balak and give him my message."

So Balaam returned and found the king standing beside his burnt offerings with all the officials of Moab. "What did the LORD say?" Balak asked eagerly.

This was the message Balaam delivered:

"Rise up, Balak, and listen!
  Hear me, son of Zippor.
God is not a man, so he does not lie.
  He is not human, so he does not change his mind.
Has he ever spoken and failed to act?
  Has he ever promised and not carried it through?
Listen, I received a command to bless;
  God has blessed, and I cannot reverse it!
No misfortune is in his plan for Jacob;
  no trouble is in store for Israel.
For the LORD their God is with them;
  he has been proclaimed their king.
God brought them out of Egypt;
  for them he is as strong as a wild ox.
No curse can touch Jacob;
  no magic has any power against Israel.
For now it will be said of Jacob,
  'What wonders God has done for Israel!'
These people rise up like a lioness,
  like a majestic lion rousing itself.
They refuse to rest
  until they have feasted on prey,
  drinking the blood of the slaughtered!"

Then Balak said to Balaam, "Fine, but if you won't curse them, at least don't bless them!"

But Balaam replied to Balak, "Didn't I tell you that I can do only what the LORD tells me?"

Then King Balak said to Balaam, "Come, I will take you to one more place. Perhaps it will please God to let you curse them from there."

So Balak took Balaam to the top of Mount Peor, overlooking the wasteland. Balaam again told Balak, "Build me seven altars, and prepare seven young bulls and seven rams for me to sacrifice." So Balak did as Balaam ordered and offered a young bull and a ram on each altar.

By now Balaam realized that the LORD was determined to bless Israel, so he did not resort to divination as before. Instead, he turned and looked out toward the wilderness, where he saw the people of Israel camped, tribe by tribe. Then the Spirit of God came upon him, and this is the message he delivered:

> "This is the message of Balaam son of Beor,
>   the message of the man whose eyes see clearly,
> the message of one who hears the words of God,
>   who sees a vision from the Almighty,
>   who bows down with eyes wide open:
> How beautiful are your tents, O Jacob;
>   how lovely are your homes, O Israel!
> They spread before me like palm groves,
>   like gardens by the riverside.
> They are like tall trees planted by the LORD,
>   like cedars beside the waters.
> Water will flow from their buckets;
>   their offspring have all they need.
> Their king will be greater than Agag;
>   their kingdom will be exalted.
> God brought them out of Egypt;
>   for them he is as strong as a wild ox.
> He devours all the nations that oppose him,
>   breaking their bones in pieces,
>   shooting them with arrows.
> Like a lion, Israel crouches and lies down;
>   like a lioness, who dares to arouse her?
> Blessed is everyone who blesses you, O Israel,
>   and cursed is everyone who curses you."

King Balak flew into a rage against Balaam. He angrily clapped his hands and shouted, "I called you to curse my enemies! Instead, you have blessed them three times. Now get out of here! Go back home! I promised to reward you richly, but the LORD has kept you from your reward."

Balaam told Balak, "Don't you remember what I told your messengers? I said, 'Even if Balak were to give me his palace filled with silver and gold, I would be powerless to do anything against the will of the LORD.' I told you that I could say only what the LORD says! Now I am returning to my own people. But first let me tell you what the Israelites will do to your people in the future."

This is the message Balaam delivered:

> "This is the message of Balaam son of Beor,
>   the message of the man whose eyes see clearly,

the message of one who hears the words of God,
   who has knowledge from the Most High,
who sees a vision from the Almighty,
   who bows down with eyes wide open:
I see him, but not here and now.
   I perceive him, but far in the distant future.
A star will rise from Jacob;
   a scepter will emerge from Israel.
It will crush the heads of Moab's people,
   cracking the skulls of the people of Sheth.
Edom will be taken over,
   and Seir, its enemy, will be conquered,
   while Israel marches on in triumph.
A ruler will rise in Jacob
   who will destroy the survivors of Ir."

Then Balaam looked over toward the people of Amalek and delivered this message:

"Amalek was the greatest of nations,
   but its destiny is destruction!"

Then he looked over toward the Kenites and delivered this message:

"Your home is secure;
   your nest is set in the rocks.
But the Kenites will be destroyed
   when Assyria takes you captive."

Balaam concluded his messages by saying:

"Alas, who can survive
   unless God has willed it?
Ships will come from the coasts of Cyprus;
   they will oppress Assyria and afflict Eber,
   but they, too, will be utterly destroyed."

Then Balaam left and returned home, and Balak also went on his way.

+

While the Israelites were camped at Acacia Grove, some of the men defiled themselves by having sexual relations with local Moabite women. These women invited them to attend sacrifices to their gods, so the Israelites feasted with them and worshiped the gods of Moab. In this way, Israel joined in the worship of Baal of Peor, causing the LORD's anger to blaze against his people.

The LORD issued the following command to Moses: "Seize all the ringleaders and execute them before the LORD in broad daylight, so his fierce anger will turn away from the people of Israel."

So Moses ordered Israel's judges, "Each of you must put to death the men under your authority who have joined in worshiping Baal of Peor."

Just then one of the Israelite men brought a Midianite woman into his tent, right before the eyes of Moses and all the people, as everyone was weeping at the entrance of the Tabernacle. When Phinehas son of Eleazar and grandson of Aaron the priest saw this, he jumped up and left the assembly. He took a spear and rushed after the man into his tent. Phinehas thrust the spear all the way through the man's body and into the woman's stomach. So the plague against the Israelites was stopped, but not before 24,000 people had died.

Then the LORD said to Moses, "Phinehas son of Eleazar and grandson of Aaron the priest has turned my anger away from the Israelites by being as zealous among them as I was. So I stopped destroying all Israel as I had intended to do in my zealous anger. Now tell him that I am making my special covenant of peace with him. In this covenant, I give him and his descendants a permanent right to the priesthood, for in his zeal for me, his God, he purified the people of Israel, making them right with me."

The Israelite man killed with the Midianite woman was named Zimri son of Salu, the leader of a family from the tribe of Simeon. The woman's name was Cozbi; she was the daughter of Zur, the leader of a Midianite clan.

Then the LORD said to Moses, "Attack the Midianites and destroy them, because they assaulted you with deceit and tricked you into worshiping Baal of Peor, and because of Cozbi, the daughter of a Midianite leader, who was killed at the time of the plague because of what happened at Peor."

+

After the plague had ended, the LORD said to Moses and to Eleazar son of Aaron the priest, "From the whole community of Israel, record the names of all the warriors by their families. List all the men twenty years old or older who are able to go to war."

So there on the plains of Moab beside the Jordan River, across from Jericho, Moses and Eleazar the priest issued these instructions to the leaders of Israel: "List all the men of Israel twenty years old and older, just as the LORD commanded Moses."

This is the record of all the descendants of Israel who came out of Egypt.

These were the clans descended from the sons of Reuben, Jacob's oldest son:

The Hanochite clan, named after their ancestor Hanoch.

The Palluite clan, named after their ancestor Pallu.

The Hezronite clan, named after their ancestor Hezron.

The Carmite clan, named after their ancestor Carmi.

These were the clans of Reuben. Their registered troops numbered 43,730.

Pallu was the ancestor of Eliab, and Eliab was the father of Nemuel, Dathan, and Abiram. This Dathan and Abiram are the same community leaders who conspired with Korah against Moses and Aaron, rebelling against the Lord. But the earth opened up its mouth and swallowed them with Korah, and fire devoured 250 of their followers. This served as a warning to the entire nation of Israel. However, the sons of Korah did not die that day.

These were the clans descended from the sons of Simeon:

The Jemuelite clan, named after their ancestor Jemuel.

The Jaminite clan, named after their ancestor Jamin.

The Jakinite clan, named after their ancestor Jakin.

The Zoharite clan, named after their ancestor Zohar.

The Shaulite clan, named after their ancestor Shaul.

These were the clans of Simeon. Their registered troops numbered 22,200.

These were the clans descended from the sons of Gad:

The Zephonite clan, named after their ancestor Zephon.

The Haggite clan, named after their ancestor Haggi.

The Shunite clan, named after their ancestor Shuni.

The Oznite clan, named after their ancestor Ozni.

The Erite clan, named after their ancestor Eri.

The Arodite clan, named after their ancestor Arodi.

The Arelite clan, named after their ancestor Areli.

These were the clans of Gad. Their registered troops numbered 40,500.

Judah had two sons, Er and Onan, who had died in the land of Canaan. These were the clans descended from Judah's surviving sons:

The Shelanite clan, named after their ancestor Shelah.

The Perezite clan, named after their ancestor Perez.

The Zerahite clan, named after their ancestor Zerah.

These were the subclans descended from the Perezites:

The Hezronites, named after their ancestor Hezron.

The Hamulites, named after their ancestor Hamul.

These were the clans of Judah. Their registered troops numbered 76,500.

These were the clans descended from the sons of Issachar:
  The Tolaite clan, named after their ancestor Tola.
  The Puite clan, named after their ancestor Puah.
  The Jashubite clan, named after their ancestor Jashub.
  The Shimronite clan, named after their ancestor Shimron.

These were the clans of Issachar. Their registered troops numbered 64,300.

These were the clans descended from the sons of Zebulun:
  The Seredite clan, named after their ancestor Sered.
  The Elonite clan, named after their ancestor Elon.
  The Jahleelite clan, named after their ancestor Jahleel.

These were the clans of Zebulun. Their registered troops numbered 60,500.

Two clans were descended from Joseph through Manasseh and Ephraim.

These were the clans descended from Manasseh:
  The Makirite clan, named after their ancestor Makir.
  The Gileadite clan, named after their ancestor Gilead, Makir's son.

These were the subclans descended from the Gileadites:
  The Iezerites, named after their ancestor Iezer.
  The Helekites, named after their ancestor Helek.
  The Asrielites, named after their ancestor Asriel.
  The Shechemites, named after their ancestor Shechem.
  The Shemidaites, named after their ancestor Shemida.
  The Hepherites, named after their ancestor Hepher.
  (One of Hepher's descendants, Zelophehad, had no sons, but his
     daughters' names were Mahlah, Noah, Hoglah, Milcah, and Tirzah.)

These were the clans of Manasseh. Their registered troops numbered 52,700.

These were the clans descended from the sons of Ephraim:
  The Shuthelahite clan, named after their ancestor Shuthelah.
  The Bekerite clan, named after their ancestor Beker.
  The Tahanite clan, named after their ancestor Tahan.

This was the subclan descended from the Shuthelahites:
  The Eranites, named after their ancestor Eran.

These were the clans of Ephraim. Their registered troops numbered 32,500.

These clans of Manasseh and Ephraim were all descendants of Joseph.

These were the clans descended from the sons of Benjamin:
    The Belaite clan, named after their ancestor Bela.
    The Ashbelite clan, named after their ancestor Ashbel.
    The Ahiramite clan, named after their ancestor Ahiram.
    The Shuphamite clan, named after their ancestor Shupham.
    The Huphamite clan, named after their ancestor Hupham.

These were the subclans descended from the Belaites:
    The Ardites, named after their ancestor Ard.
    The Naamites, named after their ancestor Naaman.

These were the clans of Benjamin. Their registered troops numbered 45,600.

These were the clans descended from the sons of Dan:
    The Shuhamite clan, named after their ancestor Shuham.

These were the Shuhamite clans of Dan. Their registered troops numbered 64,400.

These were the clans descended from the sons of Asher:
    The Imnite clan, named after their ancestor Imnah.
    The Ishvite clan, named after their ancestor Ishvi.
    The Beriite clan, named after their ancestor Beriah.

These were the subclans descended from the Beriites:
    The Heberites, named after their ancestor Heber.
    The Malkielites, named after their ancestor Malkiel.

Asher also had a daughter named Serah.

These were the clans of Asher. Their registered troops numbered 53,400.

These were the clans descended from the sons of Naphtali:
    The Jahzeelite clan, named after their ancestor Jahzeel.
    The Gunite clan, named after their ancestor Guni.
    The Jezerite clan, named after their ancestor Jezer.
    The Shillemite clan, named after their ancestor Shillem.

These were the clans of Naphtali. Their registered troops numbered 45,400.

In summary, the registered troops of all Israel numbered 601,730.

+

Then the LORD said to Moses, "Divide the land among the tribes, and distribute the grants of land in proportion to the tribes' populations, as indicated by the number of names on the list. Give the larger tribes more land and the smaller tribes less land, each group receiving a grant in proportion to the size of its population. But you must assign the land by lot, and give land to each ancestral tribe according to the number of names on the list. Each grant of land must be assigned by lot among the larger and smaller tribal groups."

This is the record of the Levites who were counted according to their clans:
The Gershonite clan, named after their ancestor Gershon.
The Kohathite clan, named after their ancestor Kohath.
The Merarite clan, named after their ancestor Merari.

The Libnites, the Hebronites, the Mahlites, the Mushites, and the Korahites were all subclans of the Levites.

Now Kohath was the ancestor of Amram, and Amram's wife was named Jochebed. She also was a descendant of Levi, born among the Levites in the land of Egypt. Amram and Jochebed became the parents of Aaron, Moses, and their sister, Miriam. To Aaron were born Nadab, Abihu, Eleazar, and Ithamar. But Nadab and Abihu died when they burned before the LORD the wrong kind of fire, different than he had commanded.

The men from the Levite clans who were one month old or older numbered 23,000. But the Levites were not included in the registration of the rest of the people of Israel because they were not given an allotment of land when it was divided among the Israelites.

So these are the results of the registration of the people of Israel as conducted by Moses and Eleazar the priest on the plains of Moab beside the Jordan River, across from Jericho. Not one person on this list had been among those listed in the previous registration taken by Moses and Aaron in the wilderness of Sinai. For the LORD had said of them, "They will all die in the wilderness." Not one of them survived except Caleb son of Jephunneh and Joshua son of Nun.

+

One day a petition was presented by the daughters of Zelophehad—Mahlah, Noah, Hoglah, Milcah, and Tirzah. Their father, Zelophehad, was a descendant of Hepher son of Gilead, son of Makir, son of Manasseh, son of Joseph. These women stood before Moses, Eleazar the priest, the tribal leaders, and the entire community at the entrance of the Tabernacle. "Our father died in the wilderness," they said. "He was not among Korah's followers, who rebelled against the LORD; he died because of his own sin. But he had no sons. Why should the name of our father disappear from his clan just because he had no sons? Give us property along with the rest of our relatives."

So Moses brought their case before the LORD. And the LORD replied to Moses, "The claim of the daughters of Zelophehad is legitimate. You must give them a grant of land along with their father's relatives. Assign them the property that would have been given to their father.

"And give the following instructions to the people of Israel: If a man dies and has no son, then give his inheritance to his daughters. And if he has no daughter either, transfer his inheritance to his brothers. If he has no brothers, give his inheritance to his father's brothers. But if his father has no brothers, give his inheritance to the nearest relative in his clan. This is a legal requirement for the people of Israel, just as the LORD commanded Moses."

+

One day the LORD said to Moses, "Climb one of the mountains east of the river, and look out over the land I have given the people of Israel. After you have seen it, you will die like your brother, Aaron, for you both rebelled against my instructions in the wilderness of Zin. When the people of Israel rebelled, you failed to demonstrate my holiness to them at the waters." (These are the waters of Meribah at Kadesh in the wilderness of Zin.)

Then Moses said to the LORD, "O LORD, you are the God who gives breath to all creatures. Please appoint a new man as leader for the community. Give them someone who will guide them wherever they go and will lead them into battle, so the community of the LORD will not be like sheep without a shepherd."

The LORD replied, "Take Joshua son of Nun, who has the Spirit in him, and lay your hands on him. Present him to Eleazar the priest before the whole community, and publicly commission him to lead the people. Transfer some of your authority to him so the whole community of Israel will obey him. When direction from the LORD is needed, Joshua will stand before Eleazar the priest, who will use the Urim—one of the sacred lots cast before the LORD—to determine his will. This is how Joshua and the rest of the community of Israel will determine everything they should do."

So Moses did as the LORD commanded. He presented Joshua to Eleazar the priest and the whole community. Moses laid his hands on him and commissioned him to lead the people, just as the LORD had commanded through Moses.

✦ ✦ ✦

The Lord said to Moses, "Give these instructions to the people of Israel: The offerings you present as special gifts are a pleasing aroma to me; they are my food. See to it that they are brought at the appointed times and offered according to my instructions.

"Say to the people: This is the special gift you must present to the Lord as your daily burnt offering. You must offer two one-year-old male lambs with no defects. Sacrifice one lamb in the morning and the other in the evening. With each lamb you must offer a grain offering of two quarts of choice flour mixed with one quart of pure oil of pressed olives. This is the regular burnt offering instituted at Mount Sinai as a special gift, a pleasing aroma to the Lord. Along with it you must present the proper liquid offering of one quart of alcoholic drink with each lamb, poured out in the Holy Place as an offering to the Lord. Offer the second lamb in the evening with the same grain offering and liquid offering. It, too, is a special gift, a pleasing aroma to the Lord.

"On the Sabbath day, sacrifice two one-year-old male lambs with no defects. They must be accompanied by a grain offering of four quarts of choice flour moistened with olive oil, and a liquid offering. This is the burnt offering to be presented each Sabbath day, in addition to the regular burnt offering and its accompanying liquid offering.

"On the first day of each month, present an extra burnt offering to the Lord of two young bulls, one ram, and seven one-year-old male lambs, all with no defects. These must be accompanied by grain offerings of choice flour moistened with olive oil—six quarts with each bull, four quarts with the ram, and two quarts with each lamb. This burnt offering will be a special gift, a pleasing aroma to the Lord. You must also present a liquid offering with each sacrifice: two quarts of wine for each bull, a third of a gallon for the ram, and one quart for each lamb. Present this monthly burnt offering on the first day of each month throughout the year.

"On the first day of each month, you must also offer one male goat for a sin offering to the Lord. This is in addition to the regular burnt offering and its accompanying liquid offering.

"On the fourteenth day of the first month, you must celebrate the Lord's Passover. On the following day—the fifteenth day of the month—a joyous, seven-day festival will begin, but no bread made with yeast may be eaten. The first day of the festival will be an official day for holy assembly, and no ordinary work may be done on that day. As a special gift you must present a burnt offering to the LORD—two young bulls, one ram, and seven one-year-old male lambs, all with no defects. These will be accompanied by grain offerings of choice flour moistened with olive oil—six quarts with each bull, four quarts with the ram, and two quarts with each of the seven lambs. You must also offer a male goat as a sin offering to purify yourselves and make yourselves right with the LORD. Present these offerings in addition to your regular morning burnt offering. On each of the seven days of the festival, this is how you must prepare the food offering that is presented as a special gift, a pleasing aroma to the LORD. These will be offered in addition to the regular burnt offerings and liquid offerings. The seventh day of the festival will be another official day for holy assembly, and no ordinary work may be done on that day.

"At the Festival of Harvest, when you present the first of your new grain to the LORD, you must call an official day for holy assembly, and you may do no ordinary work on that day. Present a special burnt offering on that day as a pleasing aroma to the LORD. It will consist of two young bulls, one ram, and seven one-year-old male lambs. These will be accompanied by grain offerings of choice flour moistened with olive oil—six quarts with each bull, four quarts with the ram, and two quarts with each of the seven lambs. Also, offer one male goat to purify yourselves and make yourselves right with the LORD. Prepare these special burnt offerings, along with their liquid offerings, in addition to the regular burnt offering and its accompanying grain offering. Be sure that all the animals you sacrifice have no defects.

"Celebrate the Festival of Trumpets each year on the first day of the appointed month in early autumn. You must call an official day for holy assembly, and you may do no ordinary work. On that day you must present a burnt offering as a pleasing aroma to the LORD. It will consist of one young bull, one ram, and seven one-year-old male lambs, all with no defects. These must be accompanied by grain offerings of choice flour moistened with olive oil—six quarts with the bull, four quarts with the ram, and two quarts with each of the seven lambs. In addition, you must sacrifice a male goat as a sin offering to purify yourselves and make yourselves right with the LORD. These special sacrifices are in addition to your regular monthly and daily burnt offerings, and they must be given with their prescribed grain offerings and liquid offerings. These offerings are given as a special gift to the LORD, a pleasing aroma to him.

"Ten days later, on the tenth day of the same month, you must call another holy assembly. On that day, the Day of Atonement, the people must go without food and must do no ordinary work. You must present a burnt offering as a pleasing aroma to the LORD. It will consist of one young bull, one ram, and seven one-year-old male lambs, all with no defects. These offerings must be accompanied by the prescribed grain offerings of choice flour moistened with olive oil—six quarts of choice flour with the bull, four quarts of choice flour with the ram, and two quarts of choice flour with each of the seven lambs. You must also sacrifice one male goat for a sin offering. This is in addition to the sin offering of atonement and the regular daily burnt offering with its grain offering, and their accompanying liquid offerings.

"Five days later, on the fifteenth day of the same month, you must call another holy assembly of all the people, and you may do no ordinary work on that day. It is the beginning of the Festival of Shelters, a seven-day festival to the LORD. On the first day of the festival, you must present a burnt offering as a special gift, a pleasing aroma to the LORD. It will consist of thirteen young bulls, two rams, and fourteen one-year-old male lambs, all with no defects. Each of these offerings must be accompanied by a grain offering of choice flour moistened with olive oil—six quarts for each of the thirteen bulls, four quarts for each of the two rams, and two quarts for each of the fourteen lambs. You must also sacrifice a male goat as a sin offering, in addition to the regular burnt offering with its accompanying grain offering and liquid offering.

"On the second day of this seven-day festival, sacrifice twelve young bulls, two rams, and fourteen one-year-old male lambs, all with no defects. Each of these offerings of bulls, rams, and lambs must be accompanied by its prescribed grain offering and liquid offering. You must also sacrifice a male goat as a sin offering, in addition to the regular burnt offering with its accompanying grain offering and liquid offering.

"On the third day of the festival, sacrifice eleven young bulls, two rams, and fourteen one-year-old male lambs, all with no defects. Each of these offerings of bulls, rams, and lambs must be accompanied by its prescribed grain offering and liquid offering. You must also sacrifice a male goat as a sin offering, in addition to the regular burnt offering with its accompanying grain offering and liquid offering.

"On the fourth day of the festival, sacrifice ten young bulls, two rams, and fourteen one-year-old male lambs, all with no defects. Each of these offerings of bulls, rams, and lambs must be accompanied by its prescribed grain offering and liquid offering. You must also sacrifice a male goat as a sin offering, in addition to the regular burnt offering with its accompanying grain offering and liquid offering.

"On the fifth day of the festival, sacrifice nine young bulls, two rams, and fourteen one-year-old male lambs, all with no defects. Each of these offerings of bulls, rams, and lambs must be accompanied by its prescribed grain offering and liquid offering. You must also sacrifice a male goat as a sin offering, in addition to the regular burnt offering with its accompanying grain offering and liquid offering.

"On the sixth day of the festival, sacrifice eight young bulls, two rams, and fourteen one-year-old male lambs, all with no defects. Each of these offerings of bulls, rams, and lambs must be accompanied by its prescribed grain offering and liquid offering. You must also sacrifice a male goat as a sin offering, in addition to the regular burnt offering with its accompanying grain offering and liquid offering.

"On the seventh day of the festival, sacrifice seven young bulls, two rams, and fourteen one-year-old male lambs, all with no defects. Each of these offerings of bulls, rams, and lambs must be accompanied by its prescribed grain offering and liquid offering. You must also sacrifice one male goat as a sin offering, in addition to the regular burnt offering with its accompanying grain offering and liquid offering.

"On the eighth day of the festival, proclaim another holy day. You must do no ordinary work on that day. You must present a burnt offering as a special gift, a pleasing aroma to the LORD. It will consist of one young bull, one ram, and seven one-year-old male lambs, all with no defects. Each of these offerings must be accompanied by its prescribed grain offering and liquid offering. You must also sacrifice one male goat as a sin offering, in addition to the regular burnt offering with its accompanying grain offering and liquid offering.

"You must present these offerings to the LORD at your annual festivals. These are in addition to the sacrifices and offerings you present in connection with vows, or as voluntary offerings, burnt offerings, grain offerings, liquid offerings, or peace offerings."

So Moses gave all of these instructions to the people of Israel as the LORD had commanded him.

+

Then Moses summoned the leaders of the tribes of Israel and told them, "This is what the LORD has commanded: A man who makes a vow to the LORD or makes a pledge under oath must never break it. He must do exactly what he said he would do.

"If a young woman makes a vow to the LORD or a pledge under oath while she is still living at her father's home, and her father hears of the vow or pledge and does not object to it, then all her vows and pledges will stand. But if her father refuses to let her fulfill the vow or pledge on the day he hears of it, then all her vows and pledges will become invalid. The LORD will forgive her because her father would not let her fulfill them.

"Now suppose a young woman makes a vow or binds herself with an impulsive pledge and later marries. If her husband learns of her vow or pledge and does not object on the day he hears of it, her vows and pledges will stand. But if her husband refuses to accept her vow or impulsive pledge on the day he hears of it, he nullifies her commitments, and the LORD will forgive her. If, however, a woman is a widow or is divorced, she must fulfill all her vows and pledges.

"But suppose a woman is married and living in her husband's home when she makes a vow or binds herself with a pledge. If her husband hears of it and does not object to it, her vow or pledge will stand. But if her husband refuses to accept it on the day he hears of it, her vow or pledge will be nullified, and the LORD will forgive her. So her husband may either confirm or nullify any vows or pledges she makes to deny herself. But if he does not object on the day he hears of it, then he is agreeing to all her vows and pledges. If he waits more than a day and then tries to nullify a vow or pledge, he will be punished for her guilt."

These are the regulations the LORD gave Moses concerning relationships between a man and his wife, and between a father and a young daughter who still lives at home.

+ + +

Then the LORD said to Moses, "On behalf of the people of Israel, take revenge on the Midianites for leading them into idolatry. After that, you will die and join your ancestors."

So Moses said to the people, "Choose some men, and arm them to fight the LORD's war of revenge against Midian. From each tribe of Israel, send 1,000 men into battle." So they chose 1,000 men from each tribe of Israel, a total of 12,000 men armed for battle. Then Moses sent them out, 1,000 men from each tribe, and Phinehas son of Eleazar the priest led them into battle. They carried along the holy objects of the sanctuary and the trumpets for sounding the charge. They attacked Midian as the LORD had commanded Moses, and they killed all the men. All five of the Midianite kings—Evi, Rekem, Zur, Hur, and Reba—died in the battle. They also killed Balaam son of Beor with the sword.

Then the Israelite army captured the Midianite women and children and seized their cattle and flocks and all their wealth as plunder. They burned all the towns and villages where the Midianites had lived. After they had gathered the plunder and captives, both people and animals, they brought them all to Moses and Eleazar the priest, and to the whole community of Israel, which was camped on the plains of Moab beside the Jordan River, across from Jericho. Moses, Eleazar the priest, and all the leaders of the community went to meet them outside the camp. But Moses was furious with all the generals and captains who had returned from the battle.

"Why have you let all the women live?" he demanded. "These are the very ones who followed Balaam's advice and caused the people of Israel to rebel against the LORD at Mount Peor. They are the ones who caused the plague to strike the LORD's people. So kill all the boys and all the women who have had intercourse with a man. Only the young girls who are virgins may live; you may keep them for yourselves. And all of you who have killed anyone or touched a dead body must stay outside the camp for seven days. You must purify yourselves and your captives on the third and seventh days. Purify all your clothing, too, and everything made of leather, goat hair, or wood."

Then Eleazar the priest said to the men who were in the battle, "The LORD has given Moses this legal requirement: Anything made of gold, silver, bronze, iron, tin, or lead—that is, all metals that do not burn—must be passed through fire in order to be made ceremonially pure. These metal objects must then be further purified with the water of purification. But everything that burns must be purified by the water alone. On the seventh day you must wash your clothes and be purified. Then you may return to the camp."

And the LORD said to Moses, "You and Eleazar the priest and the family leaders of each tribe are to make a list of all the plunder taken in the battle, including the people and animals. Then divide the plunder into two parts, and give half to the men who fought the battle and half to the rest of the people. From the army's portion, first give the LORD his share of the plunder—one of every 500 of the prisoners and of the cattle, donkeys, sheep, and goats. Give this share of the army's half to Eleazar the priest as an offering to the LORD. From the half that belongs to the people of Israel, take one of every fifty of the prisoners and of the cattle, donkeys, sheep, goats, and other animals. Give this share to the Levites, who are in charge of maintaining the LORD's Tabernacle." So Moses and Eleazar the priest did as the LORD commanded Moses.

The plunder remaining from everything the fighting men had taken totaled 675,000 sheep and goats, 72,000 cattle, 61,000 donkeys, and 32,000 virgin girls.

Half of the plunder was given to the fighting men. It totaled 337,500 sheep and goats, of which 675 were the LORD's share; 36,000 cattle, of which 72 were the LORD's share; 30,500 donkeys, of which 61 were the

Lord's share; and 16,000 virgin girls, of whom 32 were the Lord's share. Moses gave all the Lord's share to Eleazar the priest, just as the Lord had directed him.

Half of the plunder belonged to the people of Israel, and Moses separated it from the half belonging to the fighting men. It totaled 337,500 sheep and goats, 36,000 cattle, 30,500 donkeys, and 16,000 virgin girls. From the half-share given to the people, Moses took one of every fifty prisoners and animals and gave them to the Levites, who maintained the Lord's Tabernacle. All this was done as the Lord had commanded Moses.

Then all the generals and captains came to Moses and said, "We, your servants, have accounted for all the men who went out to battle under our command; not one of us is missing! So we are presenting the items of gold we captured as an offering to the Lord from our share of the plunder—armbands, bracelets, rings, earrings, and necklaces. This will purify our lives before the Lord and make us right with him."

So Moses and Eleazar the priest received the gold from all the military commanders—all kinds of jewelry and crafted objects. In all, the gold that the generals and captains presented as a gift to the Lord weighed about 420 pounds. All the fighting men had taken some of the plunder for themselves. So Moses and Eleazar the priest accepted the gifts from the generals and captains and brought the gold to the Tabernacle as a reminder to the Lord that the people of Israel belong to him.

✛

The tribes of Reuben and Gad owned vast numbers of livestock. So when they saw that the lands of Jazer and Gilead were ideally suited for their flocks and herds, they came to Moses, Eleazar the priest, and the other leaders of the community. They said, "Notice the towns of Ataroth, Dibon, Jazer, Nimrah, Heshbon, Elealeh, Sibmah, Nebo, and Beon. The Lord has conquered this whole area for the community of Israel, and it is ideally suited for all our livestock. If we have found favor with you, please let us have this land as our property instead of giving us land across the Jordan River."

"Do you intend to stay here while your brothers go across and do all the fighting?" Moses asked the men of Gad and Reuben. "Why do you want to discourage the rest of the people of Israel from going across to the land the Lord has given them? Your ancestors did the same thing when I sent them from Kadesh-barnea to explore the land. After they went up to the valley of Eshcol and explored the land, they discouraged the people of Israel from entering the land the Lord was giving them.

Then the LORD was very angry with them, and he vowed, 'Of all those I rescued from Egypt, no one who is twenty years old or older will ever see the land I swore to give to Abraham, Isaac, and Jacob, for they have not obeyed me wholeheartedly. The only exceptions are Caleb son of Jephunneh the Kenizzite and Joshua son of Nun, for they have wholeheartedly followed the LORD.'

"The LORD was angry with Israel and made them wander in the wilderness for forty years until the entire generation that sinned in the LORD's sight had died. But here you are, a brood of sinners, doing exactly the same thing! You are making the LORD even angrier with Israel. If you turn away from him like this and he abandons them again in the wilderness, you will be responsible for destroying this entire nation!"

But they approached Moses and said, "We simply want to build pens for our livestock and fortified towns for our wives and children. Then we will arm ourselves and lead our fellow Israelites into battle until we have brought them safely to their land. Meanwhile, our families will stay in the fortified towns we build here, so they will be safe from any attacks by the local people. We will not return to our homes until all the people of Israel have received their portions of land. But we do not claim any of the land on the other side of the Jordan. We would rather live here on the east side and accept this as our grant of land."

Then Moses said, "If you keep your word and arm yourselves for the LORD's battles, and if your troops cross the Jordan and keep fighting until the LORD has driven out his enemies, then you may return when the LORD has conquered the land. You will have fulfilled your duty to the LORD and to the rest of the people of Israel. And the land on the east side of the Jordan will be your property from the LORD. But if you fail to keep your word, then you will have sinned against the LORD, and you may be sure that your sin will find you out. Go ahead and build towns for your families and pens for your flocks, but do everything you have promised."

Then the men of Gad and Reuben replied, "We, your servants, will follow your instructions exactly. Our children, wives, flocks, and cattle will stay here in the towns of Gilead. But all who are able to bear arms will cross over to fight for the LORD, just as you have said."

So Moses gave orders to Eleazar the priest, Joshua son of Nun, and the leaders of the clans of Israel. He said, "The men of Gad and Reuben who are armed for battle must cross the Jordan with you to fight for the LORD. If they do, give them the land of Gilead as their property when the land is conquered. But if they refuse to arm themselves and cross over with you, then they must accept land with the rest of you in the land of Canaan."

The tribes of Gad and Reuben said again, "We are your servants, and we will do as the LORD has commanded! We will cross the Jordan into

Canaan fully armed to fight for the LORD, but our property will be here on this side of the Jordan."

So Moses assigned land to the tribes of Gad, Reuben, and half the tribe of Manasseh son of Joseph. He gave them the territory of King Sihon of the Amorites and the land of King Og of Bashan—the whole land with its cities and surrounding lands.

The descendants of Gad built the towns of Dibon, Ataroth, Aroer, Atroth-shophan, Jazer, Jogbehah, Beth-nimrah, and Beth-haran. These were all fortified towns with pens for their flocks.

The descendants of Reuben built the towns of Heshbon, Elealeh, Kiria-thaim, Nebo, Baal-meon, and Sibmah. They changed the names of some of the towns they conquered and rebuilt.

Then the descendants of Makir of the tribe of Manasseh went to Gilead and conquered it, and they drove out the Amorites living there. So Moses gave Gilead to the Makirites, descendants of Manasseh, and they settled there. The people of Jair, another clan of the tribe of Manasseh, captured many of the towns in Gilead and changed the name of that region to the Towns of Jair. Meanwhile, a man named Nobah captured the town of Ke-nath and its surrounding villages, and he renamed that area Nobah after himself.

+

This is the route the Israelites followed as they marched out of Egypt under the leadership of Moses and Aaron. At the LORD's direction, Moses kept a written record of their progress. These are the stages of their march, identi-fied by the different places where they stopped along the way.

They set out from the city of Rameses in early spring—on the fifteenth day of the first month—on the morning after the first Passover celebra-tion. The people of Israel left defiantly, in full view of all the Egyptians. Meanwhile, the Egyptians were burying all their firstborn sons, whom the LORD had killed the night before. The LORD had defeated the gods of Egypt that night with great acts of judgment!

After leaving Rameses, the Israelites set up camp at Succoth.
Then they left Succoth and camped at Etham on the edge of the
    wilderness.
They left Etham and turned back toward Pi-hahiroth, opposite Baal-
    zephon, and camped near Migdol.
They left Pi-hahiroth and crossed the Red Sea into the wilderness
    beyond. Then they traveled for three days into the Etham wilderness
    and camped at Marah.

They left Marah and camped at Elim, where there were twelve springs of water and seventy palm trees.

They left Elim and camped beside the Red Sea.

They left the Red Sea and camped in the wilderness of Sin.

They left the wilderness of Sin and camped at Dophkah.

They left Dophkah and camped at Alush.

They left Alush and camped at Rephidim, where there was no water for the people to drink.

They left Rephidim and camped in the wilderness of Sinai.

They left the wilderness of Sinai and camped at Kibroth-hattaavah.

They left Kibroth-hattaavah and camped at Hazeroth.

They left Hazeroth and camped at Rithmah.

They left Rithmah and camped at Rimmon-perez.

They left Rimmon-perez and camped at Libnah.

They left Libnah and camped at Rissah.

They left Rissah and camped at Kehelathah.

They left Kehelathah and camped at Mount Shepher.

They left Mount Shepher and camped at Haradah.

They left Haradah and camped at Makheloth.

They left Makheloth and camped at Tahath.

They left Tahath and camped at Terah.

They left Terah and camped at Mithcah.

They left Mithcah and camped at Hashmonah.

They left Hashmonah and camped at Moseroth.

They left Moseroth and camped at Bene-jaakan.

They left Bene-jaakan and camped at Hor-haggidgad.

They left Hor-haggidgad and camped at Jotbathah.

They left Jotbathah and camped at Abronah.

They left Abronah and camped at Ezion-geber.

They left Ezion-geber and camped at Kadesh in the wilderness of Zin.

They left Kadesh and camped at Mount Hor, at the border of Edom. While they were at the foot of Mount Hor, Aaron the priest was directed by the LORD to go up the mountain, and there he died. This happened in midsummer, on the first day of the fifth month of the fortieth year after Israel's departure from Egypt. Aaron was 123 years old when he died there on Mount Hor.

At that time the Canaanite king of Arad, who lived in the Negev in the land of Canaan, heard that the people of Israel were approaching his land.

Meanwhile, the Israelites left Mount Hor and camped at Zalmonah.

Then they left Zalmonah and camped at Punon.

They left Punon and camped at Oboth.

They left Oboth and camped at Iye-abarim on the border of Moab.

They left Iye-abarim and camped at Dibon-gad.

They left Dibon-gad and camped at Almon-diblathaim.

They left Almon-diblathaim and camped in the mountains east of the river, near Mount Nebo.

They left the mountains east of the river and camped on the plains of Moab beside the Jordan River, across from Jericho. Along the Jordan River they camped from Beth-jeshimoth as far as the meadows of Acacia on the plains of Moab.

✛ ✛ ✛

While they were camped near the Jordan River on the plains of Moab opposite Jericho, the LORD said to Moses, "Give the following instructions to the people of Israel: When you cross the Jordan River into the land of Canaan, you must drive out all the people living there. You must destroy all their carved and molten images and demolish all their pagan shrines. Take possession of the land and settle in it, because I have given it to you to occupy. You must distribute the land among the clans by sacred lot and in proportion to their size. A larger portion of land will be allotted to each of the larger clans, and a smaller portion will be allotted to each of the smaller clans. The decision of the sacred lot is final. In this way, the portions of land will be divided among your ancestral tribes. But if you fail to drive out the people who live in the land, those who remain will be like splinters in your eyes and thorns in your sides. They will harass you in the land where you live. And I will do to you what I had planned to do to them."

Then the LORD said to Moses, "Give these instructions to the Israelites: When you come into the land of Canaan, which I am giving you as your special possession, these will be the boundaries. The southern portion of your country will extend from the wilderness of Zin, along the edge of Edom. The southern boundary will begin on the east at the Dead Sea. It will then run south past Scorpion Pass in the direction of Zin. Its southernmost point will be Kadesh-barnea, from which it will go to Hazar-addar, and on to Azmon. From Azmon the boundary will turn toward the Brook of Egypt and end at the Mediterranean Sea.

"Your western boundary will be the coastline of the Mediterranean Sea.

"Your northern boundary will begin at the Mediterranean Sea and run east to Mount Hor, then to Lebo-hamath, and on through Zedad and Ziphron to Hazar-enan. This will be your northern boundary.

"The eastern boundary will start at Hazar-enan and run south to

Shepham, then down to Riblah on the east side of Ain. From there the boundary will run down along the eastern edge of the Sea of Galilee, and then along the Jordan River to the Dead Sea. These are the boundaries of your land."

Then Moses told the Israelites, "This territory is the homeland you are to divide among yourselves by sacred lot. The LORD has commanded that the land be divided among the nine and a half remaining tribes. The families of the tribes of Reuben, Gad, and half the tribe of Manasseh have already received their grants of land on the east side of the Jordan River, across from Jericho toward the sunrise."

And the LORD said to Moses, "Eleazar the priest and Joshua son of Nun are the men designated to divide the grants of land among the people. Enlist one leader from each tribe to help them with the task. These are the tribes and the names of the leaders:

Tribe	Leader
Judah	Caleb son of Jephunneh
Simeon	Shemuel son of Ammihud
Benjamin	Elidad son of Kislon
Dan	Bukki son of Jogli
Manasseh son of Joseph	Hanniel son of Ephod
Ephraim son of Joseph	Kemuel son of Shiphtan
Zebulun	Elizaphan son of Parnach
Issachar	Paltiel son of Azzan
Asher	Ahihud son of Shelomi
Naphtali	Pedahel son of Ammihud

These are the men the LORD has appointed to divide the grants of land in Canaan among the Israelites."

+

While Israel was camped beside the Jordan on the plains of Moab across from Jericho, the LORD said to Moses, "Command the people of Israel to give to the Levites from their property certain towns to live in, along with the surrounding pasturelands. These towns will be for the Levites to live in, and the surrounding lands will provide pasture for their cattle, flocks, and other livestock. The pastureland assigned to the Levites around these towns will extend 1,500 feet from the town walls in every direction. Measure off 3,000 feet outside the town walls in every direction—east, south, west, north—with the town at the center. This area will serve as the larger pastureland for the towns.

"Six of the towns you give the Levites will be cities of refuge, where a person who has accidentally killed someone can flee for safety. In addition, give them forty-two other towns. In all, forty-eight towns with the surrounding pastureland will be given to the Levites. These towns will come from the property of the people of Israel. The larger tribes will give more towns to the Levites, while the smaller tribes will give fewer. Each tribe will give property in proportion to the size of its land."

✝

The LORD said to Moses, "Give the following instructions to the people of Israel.

"When you cross the Jordan into the land of Canaan, designate cities of refuge to which people can flee if they have killed someone accidentally. These cities will be places of protection from a dead person's relatives who want to avenge the death. The slayer must not be put to death before being tried by the community. Designate six cities of refuge for yourselves, three on the east side of the Jordan River and three on the west in the land of Canaan. These cities are for the protection of Israelites, foreigners living among you, and traveling merchants. Anyone who accidentally kills someone may flee there for safety.

"But if someone strikes and kills another person with a piece of iron, it is murder, and the murderer must be executed. Or if someone with a stone in his hand strikes and kills another person, it is murder, and the murderer must be put to death. Or if someone strikes and kills another person with a wooden object, it is murder, and the murderer must be put to death. The victim's nearest relative is responsible for putting the murderer to death. When they meet, the avenger must put the murderer to death. So if someone hates another person and waits in ambush, then pushes him or throws something at him and he dies, it is murder. Or if someone hates another person and hits him with a fist and he dies, it is murder. In such cases, the avenger must put the murderer to death when they meet.

"But suppose someone pushes another person without having shown previous hostility, or throws something that unintentionally hits another person, or accidentally drops a huge stone on someone, though they were not enemies, and the person dies. If this should happen, the community must follow these regulations in making a judgment between the slayer and the avenger, the victim's nearest relative: The community must protect the slayer from the avenger and must escort the slayer back to live in the city of refuge to which he fled. There he must remain until the death of the high priest, who was anointed with the sacred oil.

"But if the slayer ever leaves the limits of the city of refuge, and the avenger finds him outside the city and kills him, it will not be considered murder. The slayer should have stayed inside the city of refuge until the death of the high priest. But after the death of the high priest, the slayer may return to his own property. These are legal requirements for you to observe from generation to generation, wherever you may live.

"All murderers must be put to death, but only if evidence is presented by more than one witness. No one may be put to death on the testimony of only one witness. Also, you must never accept a ransom payment for the life of someone judged guilty of murder and subject to execution; murderers must always be put to death. And never accept a ransom payment from someone who has fled to a city of refuge, allowing a slayer to return to his property before the death of the high priest. This will ensure that the land where you live will not be polluted, for murder pollutes the land. And no sacrifice except the execution of the murderer can purify the land from murder. You must not defile the land where you live, for I live there myself. I am the LORD, who lives among the people of Israel."

+ + +

Then the heads of the clans of Gilead—descendants of Makir, son of Manasseh, son of Joseph—came to Moses and the family leaders of Israel with a petition. They said, "Sir, the LORD instructed you to divide the land by sacred lot among the people of Israel. You were told by the LORD to give the grant of land owned by our brother Zelophehad to his daughters. But if they marry men from another tribe, their grants of land will go with them to the tribe into which they marry. In this way, the total area of our tribal land will be reduced. Then when the Year of Jubilee comes, their portion of land will be added to that of the new tribe, causing it to be lost forever to our ancestral tribe."

So Moses gave the Israelites this command from the LORD: "The claim of the men of the tribe of Joseph is legitimate. This is what the LORD commands concerning the daughters of Zelophehad: Let them marry anyone they like, as long as it is within their own ancestral tribe. None of the territorial land may pass from tribe to tribe, for all the land given to each tribe must remain within the tribe to which it was first allotted. The daughters throughout the tribes of Israel who are in line to inherit property must marry within their tribe, so that all the Israelites will keep their ancestral property. No grant of land may pass from one tribe to another; each tribe of Israel must keep its allotted portion of land."

The daughters of Zelophehad did as the LORD commanded Moses. Mahlah, Tirzah, Hoglah, Milcah, and Noah all married cousins on their father's side. They married into the clans of Manasseh son of Joseph. Thus, their inheritance of land remained within their ancestral tribe.

These are the commands and regulations that the LORD gave to the people of Israel through Moses while they were camped on the plains of Moab beside the Jordan River, across from Jericho.

IMMERSED IN DEUTERONOMY

THE ANCIENT NATION OF ISRAEL is finally poised to enter the land God promised to their ancestor Abraham. The books of Exodus, Leviticus, and Numbers have told the story of Israel's journey from Egypt to the edge of Canaan. God has freed his people from their slavery in Egypt and promised them a homeland of their own. The terms of God's covenant with them have been delivered in parts from Mount Sinai, from the Tabernacle, and along the route to Canaan. Now, just before he dies, Moses conveys the terms of the covenant again, all at once.

Moses uses a literary form well suited to his purpose, adapting the kind of treaty that a high king would use in making an agreement with other kings who are subject to him. The covenant was made using this culturally familiar and accepted treaty form. It would govern the relationship between the LORD and the Israelites, his "kingdom of priests" and "holy nation." It is also worth noting that the Ten Commandments are actually a miniature version of this kind of treaty.

The nation has been wandering in the wilderness for forty years, during which time the disobedient generation has died out. Moses knows that the new generation needs to hear and understand their covenant with God and embrace it for themselves. The book of Deuteronomy is the final message delivered by Moses to this next generation of God's covenant people.

The book of Deuteronomy has six distinct parts that reflect the elements in a treaty between a high king and those subject to him.

Credentials of the High King's representative (p. 273)
What God has done for Israel (pp. 273-279)
The expectation of exclusive allegiance to God (pp. 279-281)
Israel's duties under God (pp. 281-310)
Blessings or curses (pp. 310-315)
Israel's oath and witnesses (pp. 315-327)

The treaty begins by listing the High King's name and titles. In Deuteronomy, the credentials of Moses are given because he is acting as God's representative.

Next comes a description of what the High King has done for his subjects. Deuteronomy emphasizes what the LORD has done for Israel, concentrating on God's provision and protection during the nation's wilderness journey.

The next part of the treaty makes a demand for exclusive allegiance. Moses explains how the Israelites are to live out their exclusive allegiance by welcoming each new generation into the covenant. Also, they are to protect their relationship with God in their new land by completely shunning the worship of foreign gods.

Deuteronomy next describes the High King's other expectations. An extensive body of law regarding offerings and festivals, community leaders, safeguards of justice, warfare, sexual relations, and much more shows that loyalty to God is to be expressed in every aspect of life.

This is followed by a list of blessings for keeping the treaty and a list of curses for breaking it. As we will see in the story that follows Deuteronomy, the consequences flowing from the treaty will determine Israel's future.

Finally, the treaty is witnessed and copies are safeguarded. The "entire body of instruction" in Deuteronomy is written in a book and given for safekeeping to "the priests who carried the Ark of the LORD's Covenant." And as Moses names the treaty's witnesses he also pulls together its main themes: "Today I have given you the choice between life and death, between blessings and curses. Now I call on heaven and earth to witness the choice you make. Oh, that you would choose life, so that you and your descendants might live!"

DEUTERONOMY

✣

These are the words that Moses spoke to all the people of Israel while they were in the wilderness east of the Jordan River. They were camped in the Jordan Valley near Suph, between Paran on one side and Tophel, Laban, Hazeroth, and Di-zahab on the other.

Normally it takes only eleven days to travel from Mount Sinai to Kadesh-barnea, going by way of Mount Seir. But forty years after the Israelites left Egypt, on the first day of the eleventh month, Moses addressed the people of Israel, telling them everything the LORD had commanded him to say. This took place after he had defeated King Sihon of the Amorites, who ruled in Heshbon, and at Edrei had defeated King Og of Bashan, who ruled in Ashtaroth.

✣ ✣ ✣

While the Israelites were in the land of Moab east of the Jordan River, Moses carefully explained the LORD's instructions as follows.

"When we were at Mount Sinai, the LORD our God said to us, 'You have stayed at this mountain long enough. It is time to break camp and move on. Go to the hill country of the Amorites and to all the neighboring regions—the Jordan Valley, the hill country, the western foothills, the Negev, and the coastal plain. Go to the land of the Canaanites and to Lebanon, and all the way to the great Euphrates River. Look, I am giving all this land to you! Go in and occupy it, for it is the land the LORD swore to give to your ancestors Abraham, Isaac, and Jacob, and to all their descendants.'"

Moses continued, "At that time I told you, 'You are too great a burden for me to carry all by myself. The LORD your God has increased your population, making you as numerous as the stars! And may the LORD, the God of your ancestors, multiply you a thousand times more and bless you as he promised! But you are such a heavy load to carry! How can I deal with all your problems and bickering? Choose some well-respected men from each tribe who are known for their wisdom and understanding, and I will appoint them as your leaders.'

"Then you responded, 'Your plan is a good one.' So I took the wise and respected men you had selected from your tribes and appointed them to serve as judges and officials over you. Some were responsible for a thousand people, some for a hundred, some for fifty, and some for ten.

"At that time I instructed the judges, 'You must hear the cases of your fellow Israelites and the foreigners living among you. Be perfectly fair in your decisions and impartial in your judgments. Hear the cases of those who are poor as well as those who are rich. Don't be afraid of anyone's anger, for the decision you make is God's decision. Bring me any cases that are too difficult for you, and I will handle them.'

"At that time I gave you instructions about everything you were to do.

"Then, just as the LORD our God commanded us, we left Mount Sinai and traveled through the great and terrifying wilderness, as you yourselves remember, and headed toward the hill country of the Amorites. When we arrived at Kadesh-barnea, I said to you, 'You have now reached the hill country of the Amorites that the LORD our God is giving us. Look! He has placed the land in front of you. Go and occupy it as the LORD, the God of your ancestors, has promised you. Don't be afraid! Don't be discouraged!'

"But you all came to me and said, 'First, let's send out scouts to explore the land for us. They will advise us on the best route to take and which towns we should enter.'

"This seemed like a good idea to me, so I chose twelve scouts, one from each of your tribes. They headed for the hill country and came to the valley of Eshcol and explored it. They picked some of its fruit and brought it back to us. And they reported, 'The land the LORD our God has given us is indeed a good land.'

"But you rebelled against the command of the LORD your God and refused to go in. You complained in your tents and said, 'The LORD must hate us. That's why he has brought us here from Egypt—to hand us over to the Amorites to be slaughtered. Where can we go? Our brothers have demoralized us with their report. They tell us, "The people of the land are taller and more powerful than we are, and their towns are large, with walls rising high into the sky! We even saw giants there—the descendants of Anak!"'

"But I said to you, 'Don't be shocked or afraid of them! The LORD your God is going ahead of you. He will fight for you, just as you saw him do in Egypt. And you saw how the LORD your God cared for you all along the way as you traveled through the wilderness, just as a father cares for his child. Now he has brought you to this place.'

"But even after all he did, you refused to trust the LORD your God, who goes before you looking for the best places to camp, guiding you with a pillar of fire by night and a pillar of cloud by day.

"When the Lord heard your complaining, he became very angry. So he solemnly swore, 'Not one of you from this wicked generation will live to see the good land I swore to give your ancestors, except Caleb son of Jephunneh. He will see this land because he has followed the Lord completely. I will give to him and his descendants some of the very land he explored during his scouting mission.'

"And the Lord was also angry with me because of you. He said to me, 'Moses, not even you will enter the Promised Land! Instead, your assistant, Joshua son of Nun, will lead the people into the land. Encourage him, for he will lead Israel as they take possession of it. I will give the land to your little ones—your innocent children. You were afraid they would be captured, but they will be the ones who occupy it. As for you, turn around now and go on back through the wilderness toward the Red Sea.'

"Then you confessed, 'We have sinned against the Lord! We will go into the land and fight for it, as the Lord our God has commanded us.' So your men strapped on their weapons, thinking it would be easy to attack the hill country.

"But the Lord told me to tell you, 'Do not attack, for I am not with you. If you go ahead on your own, you will be crushed by your enemies.'

"This is what I told you, but you would not listen. Instead, you again rebelled against the Lord's command and arrogantly went into the hill country to fight. But the Amorites who lived there came out against you like a swarm of bees. They chased and battered you all the way from Seir to Hormah. Then you returned and wept before the Lord, but he refused to listen. So you stayed there at Kadesh for a long time.

"Then we turned around and headed back across the wilderness toward the Red Sea, just as the Lord had instructed me, and we wandered around in the region of Mount Seir for a long time.

"Then at last the Lord said to me, 'You have been wandering around in this hill country long enough; turn to the north. Give these orders to the people: "You will pass through the country belonging to your relatives the Edomites, the descendants of Esau, who live in Seir. The Edomites will feel threatened, so be careful. Do not bother them, for I have given them all the hill country around Mount Seir as their property, and I will not give you even one square foot of their land. If you need food to eat or water to drink, pay them for it. For the Lord your God has blessed you in everything you have done. He has watched your every step through this great wilderness. During these forty years, the Lord your God has been with you, and you have lacked nothing."'

"So we bypassed the territory of our relatives, the descendants of Esau, who live in Seir. We avoided the road through the Arabah Valley that comes up from Elath and Ezion-geber.

"Then as we turned north along the desert route through Moab, the LORD warned us, 'Do not bother the Moabites, the descendants of Lot, or start a war with them. I have given them Ar as their property, and I will not give you any of their land.'"

(A race of giants called the Emites had once lived in the area of Ar. They were as strong and numerous and tall as the Anakites, another race of giants. Both the Emites and the Anakites are also known as the Rephaites, though the Moabites call them Emites. In earlier times the Horites had lived in Seir, but they were driven out and displaced by the descendants of Esau, just as Israel drove out the people of Canaan when the LORD gave Israel their land.)

Moses continued, "Then the LORD said to us, 'Get moving. Cross the Zered Brook.' So we crossed the brook.

"Thirty-eight years passed from the time we first left Kadesh-barnea until we finally crossed the Zered Brook! By then, all the men old enough to fight in battle had died in the wilderness, as the LORD had vowed would happen. The LORD struck them down until they had all been eliminated from the community.

"When all the men of fighting age had died, the LORD said to me, 'Today you will cross the border of Moab at Ar and enter the land of the Ammonites, the descendants of Lot. But do not bother them or start a war with them. I have given the land of Ammon to them as their property, and I will not give you any of their land.'"

(That area was once considered the land of the Rephaites, who had lived there, though the Ammonites call them Zamzummites. They were also as strong and numerous and tall as the Anakites. But the LORD destroyed them so the Ammonites could occupy their land. He had done the same for the descendants of Esau who lived in Seir, for he destroyed the Horites so they could settle there in their place. The descendants of Esau live there to this day. A similar thing happened when the Caphtorites from Crete invaded and destroyed the Avvites, who had lived in villages in the area of Gaza.)

Moses continued, "Then the LORD said, 'Now get moving! Cross the Arnon Gorge. Look, I will hand over to you Sihon the Amorite, king of Heshbon, and I will give you his land. Attack him and begin to occupy the land. Beginning today I will make people throughout the earth terrified because of you. When they hear reports about you, they will tremble with dread and fear.'"

Moses continued, "From the wilderness of Kedemoth I sent ambassadors to King Sihon of Heshbon with this proposal of peace:

'Let us travel through your land. We will stay on the main road and won't turn off into the fields on either side. Sell us food to eat and water to drink, and we will pay for it. All we want is permission to pass through your land. The descendants of Esau who live in Seir allowed us to go through their country, and so did the Moabites, who live in Ar. Let us pass through until we cross the Jordan into the land the LORD our God is giving us.'

"But King Sihon of Heshbon refused to allow us to pass through, because the LORD your God made Sihon stubborn and defiant so he could help you defeat him, as he has now done.

"Then the LORD said to me, 'Look, I have begun to hand King Sihon and his land over to you. Begin now to conquer and occupy his land.'

"Then King Sihon declared war on us and mobilized his forces at Jahaz. But the LORD our God handed him over to us, and we crushed him, his sons, and all his people. We conquered all his towns and completely destroyed everyone—men, women, and children. Not a single person was spared. We took all the livestock as plunder for ourselves, along with anything of value from the towns we ransacked.

"The LORD our God also helped us conquer Aroer on the edge of the Arnon Gorge, and the town in the gorge, and the whole area as far as Gilead. No town had walls too strong for us. However, we avoided the land of the Ammonites all along the Jabbok River and the towns in the hill country—all the places the LORD our God had commanded us to leave alone.

"Next we turned and headed for the land of Bashan, where King Og and his entire army attacked us at Edrei. But the LORD told me, 'Do not be afraid of him, for I have given you victory over Og and his entire army, and I will give you all his land. Treat him just as you treated King Sihon of the Amorites, who ruled in Heshbon.'

"So the LORD our God handed King Og and all his people over to us, and we killed them all. Not a single person survived. We conquered all sixty of his towns—the entire Argob region in his kingdom of Bashan. Not a single town escaped our conquest. These towns were all fortified with high walls and barred gates. We also took many unwalled villages at the same time. We completely destroyed the kingdom of Bashan, just as we had destroyed King Sihon of Heshbon. We destroyed all the people in every town we conquered—men, women, and children alike. But we kept all the livestock for ourselves and took plunder from all the towns.

"So we took the land of the two Amorite kings east of the Jordan River—all the way from the Arnon Gorge to Mount Hermon. (Mount Hermon is called Sirion by the Sidonians, and the Amorites call it Senir.) We had now conquered all the cities on the plateau and all Gilead and Bashan, as far as the towns of Salecah and Edrei, which were part of Og's kingdom in Bashan. (King Og of Bashan was the last survivor of the giant Rephaites. His bed was made of iron and was more than thirteen feet long and six feet wide. It can still be seen in the Ammonite city of Rabbah.)

"When we took possession of this land, I gave to the tribes of Reuben and Gad the territory beyond Aroer along the Arnon Gorge, plus half of the hill country of Gilead with its towns. Then I gave the rest of Gilead and all of Bashan—Og's former kingdom—to the half-tribe of Manasseh. (This entire Argob region of Bashan used to be known as the land of the Rephaites. Jair, a leader from the tribe of Manasseh, conquered the whole Argob region in Bashan, all the way to the border of the Geshurites and Maacathites. Jair renamed this region after himself, calling it the Towns of Jair, as it is still known today.) I gave Gilead to the clan of Makir. But I also gave part of Gilead to the tribes of Reuben and Gad. The area I gave them extended from the middle of the Arnon Gorge in the south to the Jabbok River on the Ammonite frontier. They also received the Jordan Valley, all the way from the Sea of Galilee down to the Dead Sea, with the Jordan River serving as the western boundary. To the east were the slopes of Pisgah.

"At that time I gave this command to the tribes that would live east of the Jordan: 'Although the LORD your God has given you this land as your property, all your fighting men must cross the Jordan ahead of your Israelite relatives, armed and ready to assist them. Your wives, children, and numerous livestock, however, may stay behind in the towns I have given you. When the LORD has given security to the rest of the Israelites, as he has to you, and when they occupy the land the LORD your God is giving them across the Jordan River, then you may all return here to the land I have given you.'

"At that time I gave Joshua this charge: 'You have seen for yourself everything the LORD your God has done to these two kings. He will do the same to all the kingdoms on the west side of the Jordan. Do not be afraid of the nations there, for the LORD your God will fight for you.'

"At that time I pleaded with the LORD and said, 'O Sovereign LORD, you have only begun to show your greatness and the strength of your hand to me, your servant. Is there any god in heaven or on earth who can perform such great and mighty deeds as you do? Please let me cross the Jordan to see the wonderful land on the other side, the beautiful hill country and the Lebanon mountains.'

"But the LORD was angry with me because of you, and he would not listen to me. 'That's enough!' he declared. 'Speak of it no more. But go up to Pisgah Peak, and look over the land in every direction. Take a good look, but you may not cross the Jordan River. Instead, commission Joshua and encourage and strengthen him, for he will lead the people across the Jordan. He will give them all the land you now see before you as their possession.' So we stayed in the valley near Beth-peor.

✛ ✛ ✛

"And now, Israel, listen carefully to these decrees and regulations that I am about to teach you. Obey them so that you may live, so you may enter and occupy the land that the LORD, the God of your ancestors, is giving you. Do not add to or subtract from these commands I am giving you. Just obey the commands of the LORD your God that I am giving you.

"You saw for yourself what the LORD did to you at Baal-peor. There the LORD your God destroyed everyone who had worshiped Baal, the god of Peor. But all of you who were faithful to the LORD your God are still alive today—every one of you.

"Look, I now teach you these decrees and regulations just as the LORD my God commanded me, so that you may obey them in the land you are about to enter and occupy. Obey them completely, and you will display your wisdom and intelligence among the surrounding nations. When they hear all these decrees, they will exclaim, 'How wise and prudent are the people of this great nation!' For what great nation has a god as near to them as the LORD our God is near to us whenever we call on him? And what great nation has decrees and regulations as righteous and fair as this body of instructions that I am giving you today?

"But watch out! Be careful never to forget what you yourself have seen. Do not let these memories escape from your mind as long as you live! And be sure to pass them on to your children and grandchildren. Never forget the day when you stood before the LORD your God at Mount Sinai, where he told me, 'Summon the people before me, and I will personally instruct them. Then they will learn to fear me as long as they live, and they will teach their children to fear me also.'

"You came near and stood at the foot of the mountain, while flames from the mountain shot into the sky. The mountain was shrouded in black clouds and deep darkness. And the LORD spoke to you from the heart of the fire. You heard the sound of his words but didn't see his form; there was only a voice. He proclaimed his covenant—the Ten Commandments—which he commanded you to keep, and which he wrote on two stone tablets. It was at that time that the LORD commanded me to teach you his decrees and regulations so you would obey them in the land you are about to enter and occupy.

"But be very careful! You did not see the LORD's form on the day he spoke to you from the heart of the fire at Mount Sinai. So do not corrupt yourselves by making an idol in any form—whether of a man or a woman, an animal on the ground, a bird in the sky, a small animal that scurries along the ground, or a fish in the deepest sea. And when you look up into the sky and see the sun, moon, and stars—all the forces of heaven—don't be seduced into worshiping them. The LORD your God gave them to all the peoples of the earth. Remember that the LORD rescued you from the iron-smelting furnace of Egypt in order to make you his very own people and his special possession, which is what you are today.

"But the LORD was angry with me because of you. He vowed that I would not cross the Jordan River into the good land the LORD your God is giving you as your special possession. You will cross the Jordan to occupy the land, but I will not. Instead, I will die here on the east side of the river. So be careful not to break the covenant the LORD your God has made with you. Do not make idols of any shape or form, for the LORD your God has forbidden this. The LORD your God is a devouring fire; he is a jealous God.

"In the future, when you have children and grandchildren and have lived in the land a long time, do not corrupt yourselves by making idols of any kind. This is evil in the sight of the LORD your God and will arouse his anger.

"Today I call on heaven and earth as witnesses against you. If you break my covenant, you will quickly disappear from the land you are crossing the Jordan to occupy. You will live there only a short time; then you will be utterly destroyed. For the LORD will scatter you among the nations, where only a few of you will survive. There, in a foreign land, you will worship idols made from wood and stone—gods that neither see nor hear nor eat nor smell. But from there you will search again for the LORD your God. And if you search for him with all your heart and soul, you will find him.

"In the distant future, when you are suffering all these things, you will finally return to the LORD your God and listen to what he tells you. For the LORD your God is a merciful God; he will not abandon you or destroy you or forget the solemn covenant he made with your ancestors.

"Now search all of history, from the time God created people on the earth until now, and search from one end of the heavens to the other. Has anything as great as this ever been seen or heard before? Has any nation ever heard the voice of God speaking from fire—as you did—and survived? Has any other god dared to take a nation for himself out of another nation by means of trials, miraculous signs, wonders, war, a strong hand, a powerful arm, and terrifying acts? Yet that is what the LORD your God did for you in Egypt, right before your eyes.

"He showed you these things so you would know that the LORD is God and there is no other. He let you hear his voice from heaven so he could instruct you. He let you see his great fire here on earth so he could speak to you from it. Because he loved your ancestors, he chose to bless their descendants, and he personally brought you out of Egypt with a great display of power. He drove out nations far greater than you, so he could bring you in and give you their land as your special possession, as it is today.

"So remember this and keep it firmly in mind: The LORD is God both in heaven and on earth, and there is no other. If you obey all the decrees and commands I am giving you today, all will be well with you and your children. I am giving you these instructions so you will enjoy a long life in the land the LORD your God is giving you for all time."

Then Moses set apart three cities of refuge east of the Jordan River. Anyone who killed another person unintentionally, without previous hostility, could flee there to live in safety. These were the cities: Bezer on the wilderness plateau for the tribe of Reuben; Ramoth in Gilead for the tribe of Gad; Golan in Bashan for the tribe of Manasseh.

+ + +

This is the body of instruction that Moses presented to the Israelites. These are the laws, decrees, and regulations that Moses gave to the people of Israel when they left Egypt, and as they camped in the valley near Beth-peor east of the Jordan River. (This land was formerly occupied by the Amorites under King Sihon, who ruled from Heshbon. But Moses and the Israelites destroyed him and his people when they came up from Egypt. Israel took possession of his land and that of King Og of Bashan—the two Amorite kings east of the Jordan. So Israel conquered the entire area from Aroer at the edge of the Arnon Gorge all the way to Mount Sirion, also called Mount Hermon. And they conquered the eastern bank of the Jordan River as far south as the Dead Sea, below the slopes of Pisgah.)

Moses called all the people of Israel together and said, "Listen carefully, Israel. Hear the decrees and regulations I am giving you today, so you may learn them and obey them!

"The LORD our God made a covenant with us at Mount Sinai. The LORD did not make this covenant with our ancestors, but with all of us who are alive today. At the mountain the LORD spoke to you face to face from the heart of the fire. I stood as an intermediary between you and the LORD, for you were afraid of the fire and did not want to approach the mountain. He spoke to me, and I passed his words on to you. This is what he said:

"I am the LORD your God, who rescued you from the land of Egypt, the place of your slavery.

"You must not have any other god but me.

"You must not make for yourself an idol of any kind, or an image of anything in the heavens or on the earth or in the sea. You must not bow down to them or worship them, for I, the LORD your God, am a jealous God who will not tolerate your affection for any other gods. I lay the sins of the parents upon their children; the entire family is affected—even children in the third and fourth generations of those who reject me. But I lavish unfailing love for a thousand generations on those who love me and obey my commands.

"You must not misuse the name of the LORD your God. The LORD will not let you go unpunished if you misuse his name.

"Observe the Sabbath day by keeping it holy, as the LORD your God has commanded you. You have six days each week for your ordinary work, but the seventh day is a Sabbath day of rest dedicated to the LORD your God. On that day no one in your household may do any work. This includes you, your sons and daughters, your male and female servants, your oxen and donkeys and other livestock, and any foreigners living among you. All your male and female servants must rest as you do. Remember that you were once slaves in Egypt, but the LORD your God brought you out with his strong hand and powerful arm. That is why the LORD your God has commanded you to rest on the Sabbath day.

"Honor your father and mother, as the LORD your God commanded you. Then you will live a long, full life in the land the LORD your God is giving you.

"You must not murder.

"You must not commit adultery.

"You must not steal.

"You must not testify falsely against your neighbor.

"You must not covet your neighbor's wife. You must not covet your neighbor's house or land, male or female servant, ox or donkey, or anything else that belongs to your neighbor.

"The LORD spoke these words to all of you assembled there at the foot of the mountain. He spoke with a loud voice from the heart of the fire, surrounded by clouds and deep darkness. This was all he said at that time, and he wrote his words on two stone tablets and gave them to me.

"But when you heard the voice from the heart of the darkness, while the mountain was blazing with fire, all your tribal leaders and elders came to me. They said, 'Look, the LORD our God has shown us his glory and greatness, and we have heard his voice from the heart of the fire. Today we have seen that God can speak to us humans, and yet we live! But now, why should we risk death again? If the LORD our God speaks to us again, we will certainly die and be consumed by this awesome fire. Can any living thing hear the voice of the living God from the heart of the fire as we did and yet survive? Go yourself and listen to what the LORD our God says. Then come and tell us everything he tells you, and we will listen and obey.'

"The LORD heard the request you made to me. And he said, 'I have heard what the people said to you, and they are right. Oh, that they would always have hearts like this, that they might fear me and obey all my commands! If they did, they and their descendants would prosper forever. Go and tell them, "Return to your tents." But you stand here with me so I can give you all my commands, decrees, and regulations. You must teach them to the people so they can obey them in the land I am giving them as their possession.'"

So Moses told the people, "You must be careful to obey all the commands of the LORD your God, following his instructions in every detail. Stay on the path that the LORD your God has commanded you to follow. Then you will live long and prosperous lives in the land you are about to enter and occupy.

"These are the commands, decrees, and regulations that the LORD your God commanded me to teach you. You must obey them in the land you are about to enter and occupy, and you and your children and grandchildren must fear the LORD your God as long as you live. If you obey all his decrees and commands, you will enjoy a long life. Listen closely, Israel, and be careful to obey. Then all will go well with you, and you will have many children in the land flowing with milk and honey, just as the LORD, the God of your ancestors, promised you.

"Listen, O Israel! The LORD is our God, the LORD alone. And you must love the LORD your God with all your heart, all your soul, and all your strength. And you must commit yourselves wholeheartedly to these commands that I am giving you today. Repeat them again and again to your children. Talk about them when you are at home and when you are on the road, when you are going to bed and when you are getting up. Tie them to your hands and wear them on your forehead as reminders. Write them on the doorposts of your house and on your gates.

"The LORD your God will soon bring you into the land he swore to give you when he made a vow to your ancestors Abraham, Isaac, and Jacob. It is a land with large, prosperous cities that you did not build. The houses will be richly stocked with goods you did not produce. You will draw water from cisterns you did not dig, and you will eat from vineyards and olive trees you did not plant. When you have eaten your fill in this land, be careful not to forget the LORD, who rescued you from slavery in the land of Egypt. You must fear the LORD your God and serve him. When you take an oath, you must use only his name.

"You must not worship any of the gods of neighboring nations, for the LORD your God, who lives among you, is a jealous God. His anger will flare up against you, and he will wipe you from the face of the earth. You must not test the LORD your God as you did when you complained at Massah. You must diligently obey the commands of the LORD your God—all the laws and decrees he has given you. Do what is right and good in the LORD's sight, so all will go well with you. Then you will enter and occupy the good land that the LORD swore to give your ancestors. You will drive out all the enemies living in the land, just as the LORD said you would.

"In the future your children will ask you, 'What is the meaning of these laws, decrees, and regulations that the LORD our God has commanded us to obey?'

"Then you must tell them, 'We were Pharaoh's slaves in Egypt, but the LORD brought us out of Egypt with his strong hand. The LORD did miraculous signs and wonders before our eyes, dealing terrifying blows against Egypt and Pharaoh and all his people. He brought us out of Egypt so he could give us this land he had sworn to give our ancestors. And the LORD our God commanded us to obey all these decrees and to fear him so he can continue to bless us and preserve our lives, as he has done to this day. For we will be counted as righteous when we obey all the commands the LORD our God has given us.'

"When the LORD your God brings you into the land you are about to enter and occupy, he will clear away many nations ahead of you: the Hittites, Girgashites, Amorites, Canaanites, Perizzites, Hivites, and Jebusites. These seven nations are greater and more numerous than you. When the LORD your God hands these nations over to you and you conquer them, you must completely destroy them. Make no treaties with them and show them no mercy. You must not intermarry with them. Do not let your daughters and sons marry their sons and daughters, for they will lead your children away from me to worship other gods. Then the anger of the LORD will burn against you, and he will quickly destroy you. This is what you must do. You must break down their pagan altars and shatter their sacred pillars. Cut down their Asherah poles and burn their idols. For you are a holy people, who belong to the LORD your God. Of all the people on earth, the LORD your God has chosen you to be his own special treasure.

"The LORD did not set his heart on you and choose you because you were more numerous than other nations, for you were the smallest of all nations! Rather, it was simply that the LORD loves you, and he was keeping the oath he had sworn to your ancestors. That is why the LORD rescued you with such a strong hand from your slavery and from the oppressive hand of Pharaoh, king of Egypt. Understand, therefore, that the LORD your God is indeed God. He is the faithful God who keeps his covenant for a thousand generations and lavishes his unfailing love on those who love him and obey his commands. But he does not hesitate to punish and destroy those who reject him. Therefore, you must obey all these commands, decrees, and regulations I am giving you today.

"If you listen to these regulations and faithfully obey them, the LORD your God will keep his covenant of unfailing love with you, as he promised with an oath to your ancestors. He will love you and bless you, and he will give you many children. He will give fertility to your land and your animals. When you arrive in the land he swore to give your ancestors, you will have large harvests of grain, new wine, and olive oil, and great herds of cattle, sheep, and goats. You will be blessed above all the nations of the earth. None of your men or women will be childless, and all your livestock will bear young. And the LORD will protect you from all sickness. He will not let you suffer from the terrible diseases you knew in Egypt, but he will inflict them on all your enemies!

"You must destroy all the nations the LORD your God hands over to you. Show them no mercy, and do not worship their gods, or they will trap you. Perhaps you will think to yourselves, 'How can we ever conquer these nations that are so much more powerful than we are?' But don't be afraid of them! Just remember what the LORD your God did to Pharaoh and to all the land of Egypt. Remember the great terrors the LORD your God sent against them. You saw it all with your own eyes! And remember the miraculous signs and wonders, and the strong hand and powerful arm with which he brought you out of Egypt. The LORD your God will use this same power against all the people you fear. And then the LORD your God will send terror to drive out the few survivors still hiding from you!

"No, do not be afraid of those nations, for the LORD your God is among you, and he is a great and awesome God. The LORD your God will drive those nations out ahead of you little by little. You will not clear them away all at once, otherwise the wild animals would multiply too quickly for you. But the LORD your God will hand them over to you. He will throw them into complete confusion until they are destroyed. He will put their kings in your power, and you will erase their names from the face of the earth. No one will be able to stand against you, and you will destroy them all.

"You must burn their idols in fire, and you must not covet the silver or gold that covers them. You must not take it or it will become a trap to you, for it is detestable to the LORD your God. Do not bring any detestable objects into your home, for then you will be destroyed, just like them. You must utterly detest such things, for they are set apart for destruction.

"Be careful to obey all the commands I am giving you today. Then you will live and multiply, and you will enter and occupy the land the LORD swore to give your ancestors. Remember how the LORD your God led you through the wilderness for these forty years, humbling you and testing you to prove your character, and to find out whether or not you would obey his commands. Yes, he humbled you by letting you go hungry and then feeding you with manna, a food previously unknown to you and your ancestors. He did it to teach you that people do not live by bread alone; rather, we live by every word that comes from the mouth of the LORD. For all these forty years your clothes didn't wear out, and your feet didn't blister or swell. Think about it: Just as a parent disciplines a child, the LORD your God disciplines you for your own good.

"So obey the commands of the LORD your God by walking in his ways and fearing him. For the LORD your God is bringing you into a good land of flowing streams and pools of water, with fountains and springs that gush out in the valleys and hills. It is a land of wheat and barley; of grapevines, fig trees, and pomegranates; of olive oil and honey. It is a land where food is plentiful and nothing is lacking. It is a land where iron is as common as stone, and copper is abundant in the hills. When you have eaten your fill, be sure to praise the LORD your God for the good land he has given you.

"But that is the time to be careful! Beware that in your plenty you do not forget the LORD your God and disobey his commands, regulations, and decrees that I am giving you today. For when you have become full and prosperous and have built fine homes to live in, and when your flocks and herds have become very large and your silver and gold have multiplied along with everything else, be careful! Do not become proud at that time and forget the LORD your God, who rescued you from slavery in the land of Egypt. Do not forget that he led you through the great and terrifying wilderness with its poisonous snakes and scorpions, where it was so hot and dry. He gave you water from the rock! He fed you with manna in the wilderness, a food unknown to your ancestors. He did this to humble you and test you for your own good. He did all this so you would never say to yourself, 'I have achieved this wealth with my own strength and energy.' Remember the LORD your God. He is the one who gives you power to be successful, in order to fulfill the covenant he confirmed to your ancestors with an oath.

"But I assure you of this: If you ever forget the LORD your God and follow other gods, worshiping and bowing down to them, you will certainly be destroyed. Just as the LORD has destroyed other nations in your path, you also will be destroyed if you refuse to obey the LORD your God.

"Listen, O Israel! Today you are about to cross the Jordan River to take over the land belonging to nations much greater and more powerful than you. They live in cities with walls that reach to the sky! The people are strong and tall—descendants of the famous Anakite giants. You've heard the saying, 'Who can stand up to the Anakites?' But recognize today that the LORD your God is the one who will cross over ahead of you like a devouring fire to destroy them. He will subdue them so that you will quickly conquer them and drive them out, just as the LORD has promised.

"After the LORD your God has done this for you, don't say in your hearts, 'The LORD has given us this land because we are such good people!' No, it is because of the wickedness of the other nations that he is pushing them out of your way. It is not because you are so good or have such integrity that you are about to occupy their land. The LORD your God will drive these nations out ahead of you only because of their wickedness, and to fulfill the oath he swore to your ancestors Abraham, Isaac, and Jacob. You must recognize that the LORD your God is not giving you this good land because you are good, for you are not—you are a stubborn people.

"Remember and never forget how angry you made the LORD your God out in the wilderness. From the day you left Egypt until now, you have been constantly rebelling against him. Even at Mount Sinai you made the LORD so angry he was ready to destroy you. This happened when I was on the mountain receiving the tablets of stone inscribed with the words of the covenant that the LORD had made with you. I was there for forty days and forty nights, and all that time I ate no food and drank no water. The LORD gave me the two tablets on which God had written with his own finger all the words he had spoken to you from the heart of the fire when you were assembled at the mountain.

"At the end of the forty days and nights, the LORD handed me the two stone tablets inscribed with the words of the covenant. Then the LORD said to me, 'Get up! Go down immediately, for the people you brought out of Egypt have corrupted themselves. How quickly they have turned away from the way I commanded them to live! They have melted gold and made an idol for themselves!'

"The LORD also said to me, 'I have seen how stubborn and rebellious these people are. Leave me alone so I may destroy them and erase their name from under heaven. Then I will make a mighty nation of your descendants, a nation larger and more powerful than they are.'

"So while the mountain was blazing with fire I turned and came down, holding in my hands the two stone tablets inscribed with the terms of the covenant. There below me I could see that you had sinned against the LORD your God. You had melted gold and made a calf idol for yourselves. How quickly you had turned away from the path the LORD had commanded you to follow! So I took the stone tablets and threw them to the ground, smashing them before your eyes.

"Then, as before, I threw myself down before the LORD for forty days and nights. I ate no bread and drank no water because of the great sin you had committed by doing what the LORD hated, provoking him to anger. I feared that the furious anger of the LORD, which turned him against you, would drive him to destroy you. But again he listened to me. The LORD was so angry with Aaron that he wanted to destroy him, too. But I prayed for Aaron, and the LORD spared him. I took your sin—the calf you had made—and I melted it down in the fire and ground it into fine dust. Then I threw the dust into the stream that flows down the mountain.

"You also made the LORD angry at Taberah, Massah, and Kibroth-hattaavah. And at Kadesh-barnea the LORD sent you out with this command: 'Go up and take over the land I have given you.' But you rebelled against the command of the LORD your God and refused to put your trust in him or obey him. Yes, you have been rebelling against the LORD as long as I have known you.

"That is why I threw myself down before the LORD for forty days and nights—for the LORD said he would destroy you. I prayed to the LORD and said, 'O Sovereign LORD, do not destroy them. They are your own people. They are your special possession, whom you redeemed from Egypt by your mighty power and your strong hand. Please overlook the stubbornness and the awful sin of these people, and remember instead your servants Abraham, Isaac, and Jacob. If you destroy these people, the Egyptians will say, "The Israelites died because the LORD wasn't able to bring them to the land he had promised to give them." Or they might say, "He destroyed them because he hated them; he deliberately took them into the wilderness to slaughter them." But they are your people and your special possession, whom you brought out of Egypt by your great strength and powerful arm.'

"At that time the LORD said to me, 'Chisel out two stone tablets like the first ones. Also make a wooden Ark—a sacred chest to store them in. Come up to me on the mountain, and I will write on the tablets the same words that were on the ones you smashed. Then place the tablets in the Ark.'

"So I made an Ark of acacia wood and cut two stone tablets like the first two. Then I went up the mountain with the tablets in my hand. Once again the LORD wrote the Ten Commandments on the tablets and gave them to me. They were the same words the LORD had spoken to you from the heart of the fire on the day you were assembled at the foot of the mountain. Then I turned and came down the mountain and placed the tablets in the Ark of the Covenant, which I had made, just as the LORD commanded me. And the tablets are still there in the Ark."

(The people of Israel set out from the wells of the people of Jaakan and traveled to Moserah, where Aaron died and was buried. His son Eleazar ministered as high priest in his place. Then they journeyed to Gudgodah, and from there to Jotbathah, a land with many brooks and streams. At that time the LORD set apart the tribe of Levi to carry the Ark of the LORD's Covenant, and to stand before the LORD as his ministers, and to pronounce blessings in his name. These are their duties to this day. That is why the Levites have no share of property or possession of land among the other Israelite tribes. The LORD himself is their special possession, as the LORD your God told them.)

"As for me, I stayed on the mountain in the LORD's presence for forty days and nights, as I had done the first time. And once again the LORD listened to my pleas and agreed not to destroy you. Then the LORD said to me, 'Get up and resume the journey, and lead the people to the land I swore to give to their ancestors, so they may take possession of it.'

"And now, Israel, what does the LORD your God require of you? He requires only that you fear the LORD your God, and live in a way that pleases him, and love him and serve him with all your heart and soul. And you must always obey the LORD's commands and decrees that I am giving you today for your own good.

"Look, the highest heavens and the earth and everything in it all belong to the LORD your God. Yet the LORD chose your ancestors as the objects of his love. And he chose you, their descendants, above all other nations, as is evident today. Therefore, change your hearts and stop being stubborn.

"For the LORD your God is the God of gods and Lord of lords. He is the great God, the mighty and awesome God, who shows no partiality and cannot be bribed. He ensures that orphans and widows receive justice. He shows love to the foreigners living among you and gives them food and clothing. So you, too, must show love to foreigners, for you yourselves were once foreigners in the land of Egypt. You must fear the LORD your God and worship him and cling to him. Your oaths must be in his name alone. He alone is your God, the only one who is worthy of your praise, the one who has done these mighty miracles that you have seen with your own eyes. When your ancestors went down into Egypt, there were only seventy of them. But now the LORD your God has made you as numerous as the stars in the sky!

"You must love the LORD your God and always obey his requirements, decrees, regulations, and commands. Keep in mind that I am not talking now to your children, who have never experienced the discipline of the LORD your God or seen his greatness and his strong hand and powerful arm. They didn't see the miraculous signs and wonders he performed in Egypt against Pharaoh and all his land. They didn't see what the LORD did to the armies of Egypt and to their horses and chariots—how he drowned them in the Red Sea as they were chasing you. He destroyed them, and they have not recovered to this very day!

"Your children didn't see how the LORD cared for you in the wilderness until you arrived here. They didn't see what he did to Dathan and Abiram (the sons of Eliab, a descendant of Reuben) when the earth opened its mouth in the Israelite camp and swallowed them, along with their households and tents and every living thing that belonged to them. But you have seen the LORD perform all these mighty deeds with your own eyes!

"Therefore, be careful to obey every command I am giving you today, so you may have strength to go in and take over the land you are about to enter. If you obey, you will enjoy a long life in the land the LORD swore to give to your ancestors and to you, their descendants—a land flowing with milk and honey! For the land you are about to enter and take over is not like the land of Egypt from which you came, where you planted your seed and made irrigation ditches with your foot as in a vegetable garden. Rather, the land you will soon take over is a land of hills and valleys with plenty of rain—a land that the LORD your God cares for. He watches over it through each season of the year!

"If you carefully obey the commands I am giving you today, and if you love the LORD your God and serve him with all your heart and soul, then he will send the rains in their proper seasons—the early and late rains—so you can bring in your harvests of grain, new wine, and olive oil. He will give you lush pastureland for your livestock, and you yourselves will have all you want to eat.

"But be careful. Don't let your heart be deceived so that you turn away from the LORD and serve and worship other gods. If you do, the LORD's anger will burn against you. He will shut up the sky and hold back the rain, and the ground will fail to produce its harvests. Then you will quickly die in that good land the LORD is giving you.

"So commit yourselves wholeheartedly to these words of mine. Tie them to your hands and wear them on your forehead as reminders. Teach them to your children. Talk about them when you are at home and when you are on the road, when you are going to bed and when you are getting up. Write them on the doorposts of your house and on your gates, so that as long as the sky remains above the earth, you and your children may flourish in the land the LORD swore to give your ancestors.

"Be careful to obey all these commands I am giving you. Show love to the LORD your God by walking in his ways and holding tightly to him. Then the LORD will drive out all the nations ahead of you, though they are much greater and stronger than you, and you will take over their land. Wherever you set foot, that land will be yours. Your frontiers will stretch from the wilderness in the south to Lebanon in the north, and from the Euphrates River in the east to the Mediterranean Sea in the west. No one will be able to stand against you, for the LORD your God will cause the people to fear and dread you, as he promised, wherever you go in the whole land.

"Look, today I am giving you the choice between a blessing and a curse! You will be blessed if you obey the commands of the LORD your God that I am giving you today. But you will be cursed if you reject the commands of the LORD your God and turn away from him and worship gods you have not known before.

"When the LORD your God brings you into the land and helps you take possession of it, you must pronounce the blessing at Mount Gerizim and the curse at Mount Ebal. (These two mountains are west of the Jordan River in the land of the Canaanites who live in the Jordan Valley, near the town of Gilgal, not far from the oaks of Moreh.) For you are about to cross the Jordan River to take over the land the LORD your God is giving you. When you take that land and are living in it, you must be careful to obey all the decrees and regulations I am giving you today.

✛

"These are the decrees and regulations you must be careful to obey when you live in the land that the LORD, the God of your ancestors, is giving you. You must obey them as long as you live.

"When you drive out the nations that live there, you must destroy all the places where they worship their gods—high on the mountains, up on the hills, and under every green tree. Break down their altars and smash their sacred pillars. Burn their Asherah poles and cut down their carved idols. Completely erase the names of their gods!

"Do not worship the LORD your God in the way these pagan peoples worship their gods. Rather, you must seek the LORD your God at the place of worship he himself will choose from among all the tribes—the place where his name will be honored. There you will bring your burnt offerings, your sacrifices, your tithes, your sacred offerings, your offerings to fulfill a vow, your voluntary offerings, and your offerings of the firstborn animals of your herds and flocks. There you and your families will feast in the presence of the LORD your God, and you will rejoice in all you have accomplished because the LORD your God has blessed you.

"Your pattern of worship will change. Today all of you are doing as you please, because you have not yet arrived at the place of rest, the land the LORD your God is giving you as your special possession. But you will soon cross the Jordan River and live in the land the LORD your God is giving you. When he gives you rest from all your enemies and you're living safely in the land, you must bring everything I command you—your burnt offerings, your sacrifices, your tithes, your sacred offerings, and your offerings to fulfill a vow—to the designated place of worship, the place the LORD your God chooses for his name to be honored.

"You must celebrate there in the presence of the LORD your God with your sons and daughters and all your servants. And remember to include the Levites who live in your towns, for they will receive no allotment of land among you. Be careful not to sacrifice your burnt offerings just anywhere you like. You may do so only at the place the LORD will choose within one of your tribal territories. There you must offer your burnt offerings and do everything I command you.

"But you may butcher your animals and eat their meat in any town whenever you want. You may freely eat the animals with which the LORD your God blesses you. All of you, whether ceremonially clean or unclean, may eat that meat, just as you now eat gazelle and deer. But you must not consume the blood. You must pour it out on the ground like water.

"But you may not eat your offerings in your hometown—neither the tithe of your grain and new wine and olive oil, nor the firstborn of your flocks and herds, nor any offering to fulfill a vow, nor your voluntary offerings, nor your sacred offerings. You must eat these in the presence of the LORD your God at the place he will choose. Eat them there with your children, your servants, and the Levites who live in your towns, celebrating in the presence of the LORD your God in all you do. And be very careful never to neglect the Levites as long as you live in your land.

"When the LORD your God expands your territory as he has promised, and you have the urge to eat meat, you may freely eat meat whenever you want. It might happen that the designated place of worship—the place the LORD your God chooses for his name to be honored—is a long way from your home. If so, you may butcher any of the cattle, sheep, or goats the LORD has given you, and you may freely eat the meat in your hometown, as I have commanded you. Anyone, whether ceremonially clean or unclean, may eat that meat, just as you do now with gazelle and deer.

But never consume the blood, for the blood is the life, and you must not consume the lifeblood with the meat. Instead, pour out the blood on the ground like water. Do not consume the blood, so that all may go well with you and your children after you, because you will be doing what pleases the Lord.

"Take your sacred gifts and your offerings given to fulfill a vow to the place the Lord chooses. You must offer the meat and blood of your burnt offerings on the altar of the Lord your God. The blood of your other sacrifices must be poured out on the altar of the Lord your God, but you may eat the meat. Be careful to obey all my commands, so that all will go well with you and your children after you, because you will be doing what is good and pleasing to the Lord your God.

"When the Lord your God goes ahead of you and destroys the nations and you drive them out and live in their land, do not fall into the trap of following their customs and worshiping their gods. Do not inquire about their gods, saying, 'How do these nations worship their gods? I want to follow their example.' You must not worship the Lord your God the way the other nations worship their gods, for they perform for their gods every detestable act that the Lord hates. They even burn their sons and daughters as sacrifices to their gods.

"So be careful to obey all the commands I give you. You must not add anything to them or subtract anything from them.

"Suppose there are prophets among you or those who dream dreams about the future, and they promise you signs or miracles, and the predicted signs or miracles occur. If they then say, 'Come, let us worship other gods'—gods you have not known before—do not listen to them. The Lord your God is testing you to see if you truly love him with all your heart and soul. Serve only the Lord your God and fear him alone. Obey his commands, listen to his voice, and cling to him. The false prophets or visionaries who try to lead you astray must be put to death, for they encourage rebellion against the Lord your God, who redeemed you from slavery and brought you out of the land of Egypt. Since they try to lead you astray from the way the Lord your God commanded you to live, you must put them to death. In this way you will purge the evil from among you.

"Suppose someone secretly entices you—even your brother, your son or daughter, your beloved wife, or your closest friend—and says, 'Let us go worship other gods'—gods that neither you nor your ancestors have known. They might suggest that you worship the gods of peoples who live nearby or who come from the ends of the earth. But do not give in or listen. Have no pity, and do not spare or protect them. You must put them to death! Strike the first blow yourself, and then all the people must join in. Stone the guilty ones to death because they have tried to draw you away from the LORD your God, who rescued you from the land of Egypt, the place of slavery. Then all Israel will hear about it and be afraid, and no one will act so wickedly again.

"When you begin living in the towns the LORD your God is giving you, you may hear that scoundrels among you are leading their fellow citizens astray by saying, 'Let us go worship other gods'—gods you have not known before. In such cases, you must examine the facts carefully. If you find that the report is true and such a detestable act has been committed among you, you must attack that town and completely destroy all its inhabitants, as well as all the livestock. Then you must pile all the plunder in the middle of the open square and burn it. Burn the entire town as a burnt offering to the LORD your God. That town must remain a ruin forever; it may never be rebuilt. Keep none of the plunder that has been set apart for destruction. Then the LORD will turn from his fierce anger and be merciful to you. He will have compassion on you and make you a large nation, just as he swore to your ancestors.

"The LORD your God will be merciful only if you listen to his voice and keep all his commands that I am giving you today, doing what pleases him.

"Since you are the people of the LORD your God, never cut yourselves or shave the hair above your foreheads in mourning for the dead. You have been set apart as holy to the LORD your God, and he has chosen you from all the nations of the earth to be his own special treasure.

"You must not eat any detestable animals that are ceremonially unclean. These are the animals you may eat: the ox, the sheep, the goat, the deer, the gazelle, the roe deer, the wild goat, the addax, the antelope, and the mountain sheep.

"You may eat any animal that has completely split hooves and chews the cud, but if the animal doesn't have both, it may not be eaten. So you may not eat the camel, the hare, or the hyrax. They chew the cud but do not have split hooves, so they are ceremonially unclean for you. And you may not eat the pig. It has split hooves but does not chew the cud, so it is ceremonially unclean for you. You may not eat the meat of these animals or even touch their carcasses.

"Of all the marine animals, you may eat whatever has both fins and scales. You may not, however, eat marine animals that do not have both fins and scales. They are ceremonially unclean for you.

"You may eat any bird that is ceremonially clean. These are the birds you may not eat: the griffon vulture, the bearded vulture, the black vulture, the kite, the falcon, buzzards of all kinds, ravens of all kinds, the eagle owl, the short-eared owl, the seagull, hawks of all kinds, the little owl, the great owl, the barn owl, the desert owl, the Egyptian vulture, the cormorant, the stork, herons of all kinds, the hoopoe, and the bat.

"All winged insects that walk along the ground are ceremonially unclean for you and may not be eaten. But you may eat any winged bird or insect that is ceremonially clean.

"You must not eat anything that has died a natural death. You may give it to a foreigner living in your town, or you may sell it to a stranger. But do not eat it yourselves, for you are set apart as holy to the LORD your God.

"You must not cook a young goat in its mother's milk.

+

"You must set aside a tithe of your crops—one-tenth of all the crops you harvest each year. Bring this tithe to the designated place of worship—the place the LORD your God chooses for his name to be honored—and eat it there in his presence. This applies to your tithes of grain, new wine, olive oil, and the firstborn males of your flocks and herds. Doing this will teach you always to fear the LORD your God.

"Now when the LORD your God blesses you with a good harvest, the place of worship he chooses for his name to be honored might be too far for you to bring the tithe. If so, you may sell the tithe portion of your crops and herds, put the money in a pouch, and go to the place the LORD your God has chosen. When you arrive, you may use the money to buy any kind of food you want—cattle, sheep, goats, wine, or other alcoholic drink. Then feast there in the presence of the LORD your God and celebrate with your household. And do not neglect the Levites in your town, for they will receive no allotment of land among you.

"At the end of every third year, bring the entire tithe of that year's harvest and store it in the nearest town. Give it to the Levites, who will receive no allotment of land among you, as well as to the foreigners living among you, the orphans, and the widows in your towns, so they can eat and be satisfied. Then the LORD your God will bless you in all your work.

"At the end of every seventh year you must cancel the debts of everyone who owes you money. This is how it must be done. Everyone must cancel the loans they have made to their fellow Israelites. They must not demand payment from their neighbors or relatives, for the LORD's time of release has arrived. This release from debt, however, applies only to your fellow Israelites—not to the foreigners living among you.

"There should be no poor among you, for the LORD your God will greatly bless you in the land he is giving you as a special possession. You will receive this blessing if you are careful to obey all the commands of the LORD your God that I am giving you today. The LORD your God will bless you as he has promised. You will lend money to many nations but will never need to borrow. You will rule many nations, but they will not rule over you.

"But if there are any poor Israelites in your towns when you arrive in the land the LORD your God is giving you, do not be hard-hearted or tight-fisted toward them. Instead, be generous and lend them whatever they need. Do not be mean-spirited and refuse someone a loan because the year for canceling debts is close at hand. If you refuse to make the loan and the needy person cries out to the LORD, you will be considered guilty of sin. Give generously to the poor, not grudgingly, for the LORD your God will bless you in everything you do. There will always be some in the land who are poor. That is why I am commanding you to share freely with the poor and with other Israelites in need.

"If a fellow Hebrew sells himself or herself to be your servant and serves you for six years, in the seventh year you must set that servant free.

"When you release a male servant, do not send him away empty-handed. Give him a generous farewell gift from your flock, your threshing floor, and your winepress. Share with him some of the bounty with which the LORD your God has blessed you. Remember that you were once slaves in the land of Egypt and the LORD your God redeemed you! That is why I am giving you this command.

"But suppose your servant says, 'I will not leave you,' because he loves you and your family, and he has done well with you. In that case, take an awl and push it through his earlobe into the door. After that, he will be your servant for life. And do the same for your female servants.

"You must not consider it a hardship when you release your servants. Remember that for six years they have given you services worth double the wages of hired workers, and the LORD your God will bless you in all you do.

"You must set aside for the LORD your God all the firstborn males from your flocks and herds. Do not use the firstborn of your herds to work your fields, and do not shear the firstborn of your flocks. Instead, you and your family must eat these animals in the presence of the LORD your God each year at the place he chooses. But if this firstborn animal has any defect, such as lameness or blindness, or if anything else is wrong with it, you must not sacrifice it to the LORD your God. Instead, use it for food for your family in your hometown. Anyone, whether ceremonially clean or unclean, may eat it, just as anyone may eat a gazelle or deer. But you must not consume the blood. You must pour it out on the ground like water.

"In honor of the LORD your God, celebrate the Passover each year in the early spring, in the month of Abib, for that was the month in which the LORD your God brought you out of Egypt by night. Your Passover sacrifice may be from either the flock or the herd, and it must be sacrificed to the LORD your God at the designated place of worship—the place he chooses for his name to be honored. Eat it with bread made without yeast. For seven days the bread you eat must be made without yeast, as when you escaped from Egypt in such a hurry. Eat this bread—the bread of suffering—so that as long as you live you will remember the day you departed from Egypt. Let no yeast be found in any house throughout your land for those seven days. And when you sacrifice the Passover lamb on the evening of the first day, do not let any of the meat remain until the next morning.

"You may not sacrifice the Passover in just any of the towns that the LORD your God is giving you. You must offer it only at the designated place of worship—the place the LORD your God chooses for his name to be honored. Sacrifice it there in the evening as the sun goes down on the anniversary of your exodus from Egypt. Roast the lamb and eat it in the place the LORD your God chooses. Then you may go back to your tents the next morning. For the next six days you may not eat any bread made with yeast. On the seventh day proclaim another holy day in honor of the LORD your God, and no work may be done on that day.

"Count off seven weeks from when you first begin to cut the grain at the time of harvest. Then celebrate the Festival of Harvest to honor the LORD your God. Bring him a voluntary offering in proportion to the blessings you have received from him. This is a time to celebrate before the LORD your God at the designated place of worship he will choose for his name to be honored. Celebrate with your sons and daughters, your male and female servants, the Levites from your towns, and the foreigners, orphans, and widows who live among you. Remember that you were once slaves in Egypt, so be careful to obey all these decrees.

"You must observe the Festival of Shelters for seven days at the end of the harvest season, after the grain has been threshed and the grapes have been pressed. This festival will be a happy time of celebrating with your sons and daughters, your male and female servants, and the Levites, foreigners, orphans, and widows from your towns. For seven days you must celebrate this festival to honor the LORD your God at the place he chooses, for it is he who blesses you with bountiful harvests and gives you success in all your work. This festival will be a time of great joy for all.

"Each year every man in Israel must celebrate these three festivals: the Festival of Unleavened Bread, the Festival of Harvest, and the Festival of Shelters. On each of these occasions, all men must appear before the LORD your God at the place he chooses, but they must not appear before the

LORD without a gift for him. All must give as they are able, according to
the blessings given to them by the LORD your God.

+

"Appoint judges and officials for yourselves from each of your tribes in all
the towns the LORD your God is giving you. They must judge the people
fairly. You must never twist justice or show partiality. Never accept a bribe,
for bribes blind the eyes of the wise and corrupt the decisions of the godly.
Let true justice prevail, so you may live and occupy the land that the LORD
your God is giving you.

"You must never set up a wooden Asherah pole beside the altar you build
for the LORD your God. And never set up sacred pillars for worship, for
the LORD your God hates them.

  "Never sacrifice sick or defective cattle, sheep, or goats to the LORD your
God, for he detests such gifts.

  "When you begin living in the towns the LORD your God is giving you,
a man or woman among you might do evil in the sight of the LORD your
God and violate the covenant. For instance, they might serve other gods
or worship the sun, the moon, or any of the stars—the forces of heaven—
which I have strictly forbidden. When you hear about it, investigate the
matter thoroughly. If it is true that this detestable thing has been done in
Israel, then the man or woman who has committed such an evil act must be
taken to the gates of the town and stoned to death. But never put a person
to death on the testimony of only one witness. There must always be two
or three witnesses. The witnesses must throw the first stones, and then all
the people may join in. In this way, you will purge the evil from among you.

"Suppose a case arises in a local court that is too hard for you to decide—
for instance, whether someone is guilty of murder or only of manslaughter,
or a difficult lawsuit, or a case involving different kinds of assault. Take
such legal cases to the place the LORD your God will choose, and present
them to the Levitical priests or the judge on duty at that time. They will
hear the case and declare the verdict. You must carry out the verdict they
announce and the sentence they prescribe at the place the LORD chooses.
You must do exactly what they say. After they have interpreted the law and
declared their verdict, the sentence they impose must be fully executed; do
not modify it in any way. Anyone arrogant enough to reject the verdict of
the judge or of the priest who represents the LORD your God must die. In
this way you will purge the evil from Israel. Then everyone else will hear
about it and be afraid to act so arrogantly.

"You are about to enter the land the LORD your God is giving you. When you take it over and settle there, you may think, 'We should select a king to rule over us like the other nations around us.' If this happens, be sure to select as king the man the LORD your God chooses. You must appoint a fellow Israelite; he may not be a foreigner.

"The king must not build up a large stable of horses for himself or send his people to Egypt to buy horses, for the LORD has told you, 'You must never return to Egypt.' The king must not take many wives for himself, because they will turn his heart away from the LORD. And he must not accumulate large amounts of wealth in silver and gold for himself.

"When he sits on the throne as king, he must copy for himself this body of instruction on a scroll in the presence of the Levitical priests. He must always keep that copy with him and read it daily as long as he lives. That way he will learn to fear the LORD his God by obeying all the terms of these instructions and decrees. This regular reading will prevent him from becoming proud and acting as if he is above his fellow citizens. It will also prevent him from turning away from these commands in the smallest way. And it will ensure that he and his descendants will reign for many generations in Israel.

"Remember that the Levitical priests—that is, the whole of the tribe of Levi—will receive no allotment of land among the other tribes in Israel. Instead, the priests and Levites will eat from the special gifts given to the LORD, for that is their share. They will have no land of their own among the Israelites. The LORD himself is their special possession, just as he promised them.

"These are the parts the priests may claim as their share from the cattle, sheep, and goats that the people bring as offerings: the shoulder, the cheeks, and the stomach. You must also give to the priests the first share of the grain, the new wine, the olive oil, and the wool at shearing time. For the LORD your God chose the tribe of Levi out of all your tribes to minister in the LORD's name forever.

"Suppose a Levite chooses to move from his town in Israel, wherever he is living, to the place the LORD chooses for worship. He may minister there in the name of the LORD his God, just like all his fellow Levites who are serving the LORD there. He may eat his share of the sacrifices and offerings, even if he also receives support from his family.

"When you enter the land the LORD your God is giving you, be very careful not to imitate the detestable customs of the nations living there. For example, never sacrifice your son or daughter as a burnt offering. And do not let your people practice fortune-telling, or use sorcery, or interpret omens, or engage in witchcraft, or cast spells, or function as mediums or psychics, or call forth the spirits of the dead. Anyone who does these things is detestable to the LORD. It is because the other nations have done these detestable things that the LORD your God will drive them out ahead of you. But you must be blameless before the LORD your God. The nations you are about to displace consult sorcerers and fortune-tellers, but the LORD your God forbids you to do such things."

Moses continued, "The LORD your God will raise up for you a prophet like me from among your fellow Israelites. You must listen to him. For this is what you yourselves requested of the LORD your God when you were assembled at Mount Sinai. You said, 'Don't let us hear the voice of the LORD our God anymore or see this blazing fire, for we will die.'

"Then the LORD said to me, 'What they have said is right. I will raise up a prophet like you from among their fellow Israelites. I will put my words in his mouth, and he will tell the people everything I command him. I will personally deal with anyone who will not listen to the messages the prophet proclaims on my behalf. But any prophet who falsely claims to speak in my name or who speaks in the name of another god must die.'

"But you may wonder, 'How will we know whether or not a prophecy is from the LORD?' If the prophet speaks in the LORD's name but his prediction does not happen or come true, you will know that the LORD did not give that message. That prophet has spoken without my authority and need not be feared.

+

"When the LORD your God destroys the nations whose land he is giving you, you will take over their land and settle in their towns and homes. Then you must set apart three cities of refuge in the land the LORD your God is giving you. Survey the territory, and divide the land the LORD your God is giving you into three districts, with one of these cities in each district. Then anyone who has killed someone can flee to one of the cities of refuge for safety.

"If someone kills another person unintentionally, without previous hostility, the slayer may flee to any of these cities to live in safety. For example, suppose someone goes into the forest with a neighbor to cut wood. And suppose one of them swings an ax to chop down a tree, and the ax head flies off the handle, killing the other person. In such cases, the slayer may flee to one of the cities of refuge to live in safety.

"If the distance to the nearest city of refuge is too far, an enraged avenger might be able to chase down and kill the person who caused the death. Then the slayer would die unfairly, since he had never shown hostility toward the person who died. That is why I am commanding you to set aside three cities of refuge.

"And if the LORD your God enlarges your territory, as he swore to your ancestors, and gives you all the land he promised them, you must designate three additional cities of refuge. (He will give you this land if you are careful to obey all the commands I have given you—if you always love the LORD your God and walk in his ways.) That way you will prevent the death of innocent people in the land the LORD your God is giving you as your special possession. You will not be held responsible for the death of innocent people.

"But suppose someone is hostile toward a neighbor and deliberately ambushes and murders him and then flees to one of the cities of refuge. In that case, the elders of the murderer's hometown must send agents to the city of refuge to bring him back and hand him over to the dead person's avenger to be put to death. Do not feel sorry for that murderer! Purge from Israel the guilt of murdering innocent people; then all will go well with you.

"When you arrive in the land the LORD your God is giving you as your special possession, you must never steal anyone's land by moving the boundary markers your ancestors set up to mark their property.

"You must not convict anyone of a crime on the testimony of only one witness. The facts of the case must be established by the testimony of two or three witnesses.

"If a malicious witness comes forward and accuses someone of a crime, then both the accuser and accused must appear before the LORD by coming to the priests and judges in office at that time. The judges must investigate the case thoroughly. If the accuser has brought false charges against his fellow Israelite, you must impose on the accuser the sentence he intended for the other person. In this way, you will purge such evil from among you. Then the rest of the people will hear about it and be afraid to do such an evil thing. You must show no pity for the guilty! Your rule should be life for life, eye for eye, tooth for tooth, hand for hand, foot for foot.

+

"When you go out to fight your enemies and you face horses and chariots and an army greater than your own, do not be afraid. The LORD your God, who brought you out of the land of Egypt, is with you! When you prepare for battle, the priest must come forward to speak to the troops. He will say to them, 'Listen to me, all you men of Israel! Do not be afraid as you go out to fight your enemies today! Do not lose heart or panic or tremble before them. For the LORD your God is going with you! He will fight for you against your enemies, and he will give you victory!'

"Then the officers of the army must address the troops and say, 'Has anyone here just built a new house but not yet dedicated it? If so, you may go home! You might be killed in the battle, and someone else would dedicate your house. Has anyone here just planted a vineyard but not yet eaten any of its fruit? If so, you may go home! You might die in battle, and someone else would eat the first fruit. Has anyone here just become engaged to a woman but not yet married her? Well, you may go home and get married! You might die in the battle, and someone else would marry her.'

"Then the officers will also say, 'Is anyone here afraid or worried? If you are, you may go home before you frighten anyone else.' When the officers have finished speaking to their troops, they will appoint the unit commanders.

"As you approach a town to attack it, you must first offer its people terms for peace. If they accept your terms and open the gates to you, then all the people inside will serve you in forced labor. But if they refuse to make peace and prepare to fight, you must attack the town. When the LORD your God hands the town over to you, use your swords to kill every man in the town. But you may keep for yourselves all the women, children, livestock, and other plunder. You may enjoy the plunder from your enemies that the LORD your God has given you.

"But these instructions apply only to distant towns, not to the towns of the nations in the land you will enter. In those towns that the LORD your God is giving you as a special possession, destroy every living thing. You must completely destroy the Hittites, Amorites, Canaanites, Perizzites, Hivites, and Jebusites, just as the LORD your God has commanded you. This will prevent the people of the land from teaching you to imitate their detestable customs in the worship of their gods, which would cause you to sin deeply against the LORD your God.

"When you are attacking a town and the war drags on, you must not cut down the trees with your axes. You may eat the fruit, but do not cut down the trees. Are the trees your enemies, that you should attack them? You may only cut down trees that you know are not valuable for food. Use them to make the equipment you need to attack the enemy town until it falls.

+

"When you are in the land the LORD your God is giving you, someone may be found murdered in a field, and you don't know who committed the murder. In such a case, your elders and judges must measure the distance from the site of the crime to the nearby towns. When the nearest town has been determined, that town's elders must select from the herd a heifer that has never been trained or yoked to a plow. They must lead it down to a valley that has not been plowed or planted and that has a stream running through it. There in the valley they must break the heifer's neck. Then the Levitical priests must step forward, for the LORD your God has chosen them to minister before him and to pronounce blessings in the LORD's name. They are to decide all legal and criminal cases.

"The elders of the town must wash their hands over the heifer whose neck was broken. Then they must say, 'Our hands did not shed this person's blood, nor did we see it happen. O LORD, forgive your people Israel whom you have redeemed. Do not charge your people with the guilt of murdering an innocent person.' Then they will be absolved of the guilt of this person's blood. By following these instructions, you will do what is right in the LORD's sight and will cleanse the guilt of murder from your community.

"Suppose you go out to war against your enemies and the LORD your God hands them over to you, and you take some of them as captives. And suppose you see among the captives a beautiful woman, and you are attracted to her and want to marry her. If this happens, you may take her to your home, where she must shave her head, cut her nails, and change the clothes she was wearing when she was captured. She will stay in your home, but let her mourn for her father and mother for a full month. Then you may marry her, and you will be her husband and she will be your wife. But if you marry her and she does not please you, you must let her go free. You may not sell her or treat her as a slave, for you have humiliated her.

"Suppose a man has two wives, but he loves one and not the other, and both have given him sons. And suppose the firstborn son is the son of the wife he does not love. When the man divides his inheritance, he may not give the larger inheritance to his younger son, the son of the wife he loves, as if he were the firstborn son. He must recognize the rights of his oldest son, the son of the wife he does not love, by giving him a double portion. He is the first son of his father's virility, and the rights of the firstborn belong to him.

"Suppose a man has a stubborn and rebellious son who will not obey his father or mother, even though they discipline him. In such a case, the father and mother must take the son to the elders as they hold court at the town gate. The parents must say to the elders, 'This son of ours is stubborn and rebellious and refuses to obey. He is a glutton and a drunkard.' Then all the men of his town must stone him to death. In this way, you will purge this evil from among you, and all Israel will hear about it and be afraid.

"If someone has committed a crime worthy of death and is executed and hung on a tree, the body must not remain hanging from the tree overnight. You must bury the body that same day, for anyone who is hung is cursed in the sight of God. In this way, you will prevent the defilement of the land the LORD your God is giving you as your special possession.

"If you see your neighbor's ox or sheep or goat wandering away, don't ignore your responsibility. Take it back to its owner. If its owner does not live nearby or you don't know who the owner is, take it to your place and keep it until the owner comes looking for it. Then you must return it. Do the same if you find your neighbor's donkey, clothing, or anything else your neighbor loses. Don't ignore your responsibility.

"If you see that your neighbor's donkey or ox has collapsed on the road, do not look the other way. Go and help your neighbor get it back on its feet!

"A woman must not put on men's clothing, and a man must not wear women's clothing. Anyone who does this is detestable in the sight of the LORD your God.

"If you happen to find a bird's nest in a tree or on the ground, and there are young ones or eggs in it with the mother sitting in the nest, do not take the mother with the young. You may take the young, but let the mother go, so that you may prosper and enjoy a long life.

"When you build a new house, you must build a railing around the edge of its flat roof. That way you will not be considered guilty of murder if someone falls from the roof.

"You must not plant any other crop between the rows of your vineyard. If you do, you are forbidden to use either the grapes from the vineyard or the other crop.

"You must not plow with an ox and a donkey harnessed together.

"You must not wear clothing made of wool and linen woven together.

"You must put four tassels on the hem of the cloak with which you cover yourself—on the front, back, and sides.

"Suppose a man marries a woman, but after sleeping with her, he turns against her and publicly accuses her of shameful conduct, saying, 'When I married this woman, I discovered she was not a virgin.' Then the woman's father and mother must bring the proof of her virginity to the elders as they hold court at the town gate. Her father must say to them, 'I gave my daughter to this man to be his wife, and now he has turned against her.

He has accused her of shameful conduct, saying, "I discovered that your daughter was not a virgin." But here is the proof of my daughter's virginity.' Then they must spread her bed sheet before the elders. The elders must then take the man and punish him. They must also fine him 100 pieces of silver, which he must pay to the woman's father because he publicly accused a virgin of Israel of shameful conduct. The woman will then remain the man's wife, and he may never divorce her.

"But suppose the man's accusations are true, and he can show that she was not a virgin. The woman must be taken to the door of her father's home, and there the men of the town must stone her to death, for she has committed a disgraceful crime in Israel by being promiscuous while living in her parents' home. In this way, you will purge this evil from among you.

"If a man is discovered committing adultery, both he and the woman must die. In this way, you will purge Israel of such evil.

"Suppose a man meets a young woman, a virgin who is engaged to be married, and he has sexual intercourse with her. If this happens within a town, you must take both of them to the gates of that town and stone them to death. The woman is guilty because she did not scream for help. The man must die because he violated another man's wife. In this way, you will purge this evil from among you.

"But if the man meets the engaged woman out in the country, and he rapes her, then only the man must die. Do nothing to the young woman; she has committed no crime worthy of death. She is as innocent as a murder victim. Since the man raped her out in the country, it must be assumed that she screamed, but there was no one to rescue her.

"Suppose a man has intercourse with a young woman who is a virgin but is not engaged to be married. If they are discovered, he must pay her father fifty pieces of silver. Then he must marry the young woman because he violated her, and he may never divorce her as long as he lives.

"A man must not marry his father's former wife, for this would violate his father.

"If a man's testicles are crushed or his penis is cut off, he may not be admitted to the assembly of the LORD.

"If a person is illegitimate by birth, neither he nor his descendants for ten generations may be admitted to the assembly of the LORD.

"No Ammonite or Moabite or any of their descendants for ten generations may be admitted to the assembly of the LORD. These nations did not welcome you with food and water when you came out of Egypt. Instead, they hired Balaam son of Beor from Pethor in distant Aram-naharaim to curse you. But the LORD your God refused to listen to Balaam. He turned the intended curse into a blessing because the LORD your God loves you. As long as you live, you must never promote the welfare and prosperity of the Ammonites or Moabites.

"Do not detest the Edomites or the Egyptians, because the Edomites are your relatives and you lived as foreigners among the Egyptians. The third generation of Edomites and Egyptians may enter the assembly of the LORD.

"When you go to war against your enemies, be sure to stay away from anything that is impure.

"Any man who becomes ceremonially defiled because of a nocturnal emission must leave the camp and stay away all day. Toward evening he must bathe himself, and at sunset he may return to the camp.

"You must have a designated area outside the camp where you can go to relieve yourself. Each of you must have a spade as part of your equipment. Whenever you relieve yourself, dig a hole with the spade and cover the excrement. The camp must be holy, for the LORD your God moves around in your camp to protect you and to defeat your enemies. He must not see any shameful thing among you, or he will turn away from you.

"If slaves should escape from their masters and take refuge with you, you must not hand them over to their masters. Let them live among you in any town they choose, and do not oppress them.

"No Israelite, whether man or woman, may become a temple prostitute. When you are bringing an offering to fulfill a vow, you must not bring to the house of the LORD your God any offering from the earnings of a prostitute, whether a man or a woman, for both are detestable to the LORD your God.

"Do not charge interest on the loans you make to a fellow Israelite, whether you loan money, or food, or anything else. You may charge interest to foreigners, but you may not charge interest to Israelites, so that the LORD your God may bless you in everything you do in the land you are about to enter and occupy.

"When you make a vow to the LORD your God, be prompt in fulfilling whatever you promised him. For the LORD your God demands that you promptly fulfill all your vows, or you will be guilty of sin. However, it is not a sin to refrain from making a vow. But once you have voluntarily made a vow, be careful to fulfill your promise to the LORD your God.

"When you enter your neighbor's vineyard, you may eat your fill of grapes, but you must not carry any away in a basket. And when you enter your neighbor's field of grain, you may pluck the heads of grain with your hand, but you must not harvest it with a sickle.

"Suppose a man marries a woman but she does not please him. Having discovered something wrong with her, he writes a document of divorce, hands it to her, and sends her away from his house. When she leaves his house, she is free to marry another man. But if the second husband also turns against her, writes a document of divorce, hands it to her, and sends her away, or if he dies, the first husband may not marry her again, for she has been defiled. That would be detestable to the LORD. You must not bring guilt upon the land the LORD your God is giving you as a special possession.

"A newly married man must not be drafted into the army or be given any other official responsibilities. He must be free to spend one year at home, bringing happiness to the wife he has married.

"It is wrong to take a set of millstones, or even just the upper millstone, as security for a loan, for the owner uses it to make a living.

"If anyone kidnaps a fellow Israelite and treats him as a slave or sells him, the kidnapper must die. In this way, you will purge the evil from among you.

"In all cases involving serious skin diseases, be careful to follow the instructions of the Levitical priests; obey all the commands I have given them. Remember what the LORD your God did to Miriam as you were coming from Egypt.

"If you lend anything to your neighbor, do not enter his house to pick up the item he is giving as security. You must wait outside while he goes in and brings it out to you. If your neighbor is poor and gives you his cloak as security for a loan, do not keep the cloak overnight. Return the cloak to its owner by sunset so he can stay warm through the night and bless you, and the LORD your God will count you as righteous.

"Never take advantage of poor and destitute laborers, whether they are fellow Israelites or foreigners living in your towns. You must pay them their wages each day before sunset because they are poor and are counting on it. If you don't, they might cry out to the LORD against you, and it would be counted against you as sin.

"Parents must not be put to death for the sins of their children, nor children for the sins of their parents. Those deserving to die must be put to death for their own crimes.

"True justice must be given to foreigners living among you and to orphans, and you must never accept a widow's garment as security for her debt. Always remember that you were slaves in Egypt and that the LORD your God redeemed you from your slavery. That is why I have given you this command.

"When you are harvesting your crops and forget to bring in a bundle of grain from your field, don't go back to get it. Leave it for the foreigners, orphans, and widows. Then the LORD your God will bless you in all you do. When you beat the olives from your olive trees, don't go over the boughs twice. Leave the remaining olives for the foreigners, orphans, and widows. When you gather the grapes in your vineyard, don't glean the vines after they are picked. Leave the remaining grapes for the foreigners, orphans, and widows. Remember that you were slaves in the land of Egypt. That is why I am giving you this command.

"Suppose two people take a dispute to court, and the judges declare that one is right and the other is wrong. If the person in the wrong is sentenced to be flogged, the judge must command him to lie down and be beaten in his presence with the number of lashes appropriate to the crime. But never give more than forty lashes; more than forty lashes would publicly humiliate your neighbor.

"You must not muzzle an ox to keep it from eating as it treads out the grain.

"If two brothers are living together on the same property and one of them dies without a son, his widow may not be married to anyone from outside the family. Instead, her husband's brother should marry her and have intercourse with her to fulfill the duties of a brother-in-law. The first son she bears to him will be considered the son of the dead brother, so that his name will not be forgotten in Israel.

"But if the man refuses to marry his brother's widow, she must go to the town gate and say to the elders assembled there, 'My husband's brother refuses to preserve his brother's name in Israel—he refuses to fulfill the duties of a brother-in-law by marrying me.' The elders of the town will then summon him and talk with him. If he still refuses and says, 'I don't want to marry her,' the widow must walk over to him in the presence of the elders, pull his sandal from his foot, and spit in his face. Then she must declare, 'This is what happens to a man who refuses to provide his brother with children.' Ever afterward in Israel his family will be referred to as 'the family of the man whose sandal was pulled off'!

"If two Israelite men get into a fight and the wife of one tries to rescue her husband by grabbing the testicles of the other man, you must cut off her hand. Show her no pity.

"You must use accurate scales when you weigh out merchandise, and you must use full and honest measures. Yes, always use honest weights and measures, so that you may enjoy a long life in the land the LORD your God is giving you. All who cheat with dishonest weights and measures are detestable to the LORD your God.

"Never forget what the Amalekites did to you as you came from Egypt. They attacked you when you were exhausted and weary, and they struck down those who were straggling behind. They had no fear of God. Therefore, when the LORD your God has given you rest from all your enemies in the land he is giving you as a special possession, you must destroy the Amalekites and erase their memory from under heaven. Never forget this!

"When you enter the land the Lord your God is giving you as a special possession and you have conquered it and settled there, put some of the first produce from each crop you harvest into a basket and bring it to the designated place of worship—the place the Lord your God chooses for his name to be honored. Go to the priest in charge at that time and say to him, 'With this gift I acknowledge to the Lord your God that I have entered the land he swore to our ancestors he would give us.' The priest will then take the basket from your hand and set it before the altar of the Lord your God.

"You must then say in the presence of the Lord your God, 'My ancestor Jacob was a wandering Aramean who went to live as a foreigner in Egypt. His family arrived few in number, but in Egypt they became a large and mighty nation. When the Egyptians oppressed and humiliated us by making us their slaves, we cried out to the Lord, the God of our ancestors. He heard our cries and saw our hardship, toil, and oppression. So the Lord brought us out of Egypt with a strong hand and powerful arm, with overwhelming terror, and with miraculous signs and wonders. He brought us to this place and gave us this land flowing with milk and honey! And now, O Lord, I have brought you the first portion of the harvest you have given me from the ground.' Then place the produce before the Lord your God, and bow to the ground in worship before him. Afterward you may go and celebrate because of all the good things the Lord your God has given to you and your household. Remember to include the Levites and the foreigners living among you in the celebration.

"Every third year you must offer a special tithe of your crops. In this year of the special tithe you must give your tithes to the Levites, foreigners, orphans, and widows, so that they will have enough to eat in your towns. Then you must declare in the presence of the Lord your God, 'I have taken the sacred gift from my house and have given it to the Levites, foreigners, orphans, and widows, just as you commanded me. I have not violated or forgotten any of your commands. I have not eaten any of it while in mourning; I have not handled it while I was ceremonially unclean; and I have not offered any of it to the dead. I have obeyed the Lord my God and have done everything you commanded me. Now look down from your holy dwelling place in heaven and bless your people Israel and the land you swore to our ancestors to give us—a land flowing with milk and honey.'

"Today the LORD your God has commanded you to obey all these decrees and regulations. So be careful to obey them wholeheartedly. You have declared today that the LORD is your God. And you have promised to walk in his ways, and to obey his decrees, commands, and regulations, and to do everything he tells you. The LORD has declared today that you are his people, his own special treasure, just as he promised, and that you must obey all his commands. And if you do, he will set you high above all the other nations he has made. Then you will receive praise, honor, and renown. You will be a nation that is holy to the LORD your God, just as he promised."

+ + +

Then Moses and the leaders of Israel gave this charge to the people: "Obey all these commands that I am giving you today. When you cross the Jordan River and enter the land the LORD your God is giving you, set up some large stones and coat them with plaster. Write this whole body of instruction on them when you cross the river to enter the land the LORD your God is giving you—a land flowing with milk and honey, just as the LORD, the God of your ancestors, promised you. When you cross the Jordan, set up these stones at Mount Ebal and coat them with plaster, as I am commanding you today.

"Then build an altar there to the LORD your God, using natural, uncut stones. You must not shape the stones with an iron tool. Build the altar of uncut stones, and use it to offer burnt offerings to the LORD your God. Also sacrifice peace offerings on it, and celebrate by feasting there before the LORD your God. You must clearly write all these instructions on the stones coated with plaster."

Then Moses and the Levitical priests addressed all Israel as follows: "O Israel, be quiet and listen! Today you have become the people of the LORD your God. So you must obey the LORD your God by keeping all these commands and decrees that I am giving you today."

That same day Moses also gave this charge to the people: "When you cross the Jordan River, the tribes of Simeon, Levi, Judah, Issachar, Joseph, and Benjamin must stand on Mount Gerizim to proclaim a blessing over the people. And the tribes of Reuben, Gad, Asher, Zebulun, Dan, and Naphtali must stand on Mount Ebal to proclaim a curse.

"Then the Levites will shout to all the people of Israel:

'Cursed is anyone who carves or casts an idol and secretly sets it up.
    These idols, the work of craftsmen, are detestable to the LORD.'
        And all the people will reply, 'Amen.'

'Cursed is anyone who dishonors father or mother.'
  And all the people will reply, 'Amen.'

'Cursed is anyone who steals property from a neighbor by moving a
  boundary marker.'
  And all the people will reply, 'Amen.'

'Cursed is anyone who leads a blind person astray on the road.'
  And all the people will reply, 'Amen.'

'Cursed is anyone who denies justice to foreigners, orphans, or widows.'
  And all the people will reply, 'Amen.'

'Cursed is anyone who has sexual intercourse with one of his father's
  wives, for he has violated his father.'
  And all the people will reply, 'Amen.'

'Cursed is anyone who has sexual intercourse with an animal.'
  And all the people will reply, 'Amen.'

'Cursed is anyone who has sexual intercourse with his sister, whether she
  is the daughter of his father or his mother.'
  And all the people will reply, 'Amen.'

'Cursed is anyone who has sexual intercourse with his mother-in-law.'
  And all the people will reply, 'Amen.'

'Cursed is anyone who attacks a neighbor in secret.'
  And all the people will reply, 'Amen.'

'Cursed is anyone who accepts payment to kill an innocent person.'
  And all the people will reply, 'Amen.'

'Cursed is anyone who does not affirm and obey the terms of these
  instructions.'
  And all the people will reply, 'Amen.'

"If you fully obey the LORD your God and carefully keep all his commands
that I am giving you today, the LORD your God will set you high above all
the nations of the world. You will experience all these blessings if you obey
the LORD your God:

  Your towns and your fields
    will be blessed.
  Your children and your crops
    will be blessed.
  The offspring of your herds and flocks
    will be blessed.

Your fruit baskets and breadboards
  will be blessed.
Wherever you go and whatever you do,
  you will be blessed.

"The Lord will conquer your enemies when they attack you. They will attack you from one direction, but they will scatter from you in seven!

"The Lord will guarantee a blessing on everything you do and will fill your storehouses with grain. The Lord your God will bless you in the land he is giving you.

"If you obey the commands of the Lord your God and walk in his ways, the Lord will establish you as his holy people as he swore he would do. Then all the nations of the world will see that you are a people claimed by the Lord, and they will stand in awe of you.

"The Lord will give you prosperity in the land he swore to your ancestors to give you, blessing you with many children, numerous livestock, and abundant crops. The Lord will send rain at the proper time from his rich treasury in the heavens and will bless all the work you do. You will lend to many nations, but you will never need to borrow from them. If you listen to these commands of the Lord your God that I am giving you today, and if you carefully obey them, the Lord will make you the head and not the tail, and you will always be on top and never at the bottom. You must not turn away from any of the commands I am giving you today, nor follow after other gods and worship them.

"But if you refuse to listen to the Lord your God and do not obey all the commands and decrees I am giving you today, all these curses will come and overwhelm you:

Your towns and your fields
  will be cursed.
Your fruit baskets and breadboards
  will be cursed.
Your children and your crops
  will be cursed.
The offspring of your herds and flocks
  will be cursed.
Wherever you go and whatever you do,
  you will be cursed.

"The Lord himself will send on you curses, confusion, and frustration in everything you do, until at last you are completely destroyed for doing evil and abandoning me. The Lord will afflict you with diseases until none of you are left in the land you are about to enter and occupy. The

LORD will strike you with wasting diseases, fever, and inflammation, with scorching heat and drought, and with blight and mildew. These disasters will pursue you until you die. The skies above will be as unyielding as bronze, and the earth beneath will be as hard as iron. The LORD will change the rain that falls on your land into powder, and dust will pour down from the sky until you are destroyed.

"The LORD will cause you to be defeated by your enemies. You will attack your enemies from one direction, but you will scatter from them in seven! You will be an object of horror to all the kingdoms of the earth. Your corpses will be food for all the scavenging birds and wild animals, and no one will be there to chase them away.

"The LORD will afflict you with the boils of Egypt and with tumors, scurvy, and the itch, from which you cannot be cured. The LORD will strike you with madness, blindness, and panic. You will grope around in broad daylight like a blind person groping in the darkness, but you will not find your way. You will be oppressed and robbed continually, and no one will come to save you.

"You will be engaged to a woman, but another man will sleep with her. You will build a house, but someone else will live in it. You will plant a vineyard, but you will never enjoy its fruit. Your ox will be butchered before your eyes, but you will not eat a single bite of the meat. Your donkey will be taken from you, never to be returned. Your sheep and goats will be given to your enemies, and no one will be there to help you. You will watch as your sons and daughters are taken away as slaves. Your heart will break for them, but you won't be able to help them. A foreign nation you have never heard about will eat the crops you worked so hard to grow. You will suffer under constant oppression and harsh treatment. You will go mad because of all the tragedy you see around you. The LORD will cover your knees and legs with incurable boils. In fact, you will be covered from head to foot.

"The LORD will exile you and your king to a nation unknown to you and your ancestors. There in exile you will worship gods of wood and stone! You will become an object of horror, ridicule, and mockery among all the nations to which the LORD sends you.

"You will plant much but harvest little, for locusts will eat your crops. You will plant vineyards and care for them, but you will not drink the wine or eat the grapes, for worms will destroy the vines. You will grow olive trees throughout your land, but you will never use the olive oil, for the fruit will drop before it ripens. You will have sons and daughters, but you will lose them, for they will be led away into captivity. Swarms of insects will destroy your trees and crops.

"The foreigners living among you will become stronger and stronger, while you become weaker and weaker. They will lend money to you, but you will not lend to them. They will be the head, and you will be the tail!

"If you refuse to listen to the LORD your God and to obey the commands and decrees he has given you, all these curses will pursue and overtake you until you are destroyed. These horrors will serve as a sign and warning among you and your descendants forever. If you do not serve the LORD your God with joy and enthusiasm for the abundant benefits you have received, you will serve your enemies whom the LORD will send against you. You will be left hungry, thirsty, naked, and lacking in everything. The LORD will put an iron yoke on your neck, oppressing you harshly until he has destroyed you.

"The LORD will bring a distant nation against you from the end of the earth, and it will swoop down on you like a vulture. It is a nation whose language you do not understand, a fierce and heartless nation that shows no respect for the old and no pity for the young. Its armies will devour your livestock and crops, and you will be destroyed. They will leave you no grain, new wine, olive oil, calves, or lambs, and you will starve to death. They will attack your cities until all the fortified walls in your land—the walls you trusted to protect you—are knocked down. They will attack all the towns in the land the LORD your God has given you.

"The siege and terrible distress of the enemy's attack will be so severe that you will eat the flesh of your own sons and daughters, whom the LORD your God has given you. The most tenderhearted man among you will have no compassion for his own brother, his beloved wife, and his surviving children. He will refuse to share with them the flesh he is devouring—the flesh of one of his own children—because he has nothing else to eat during the siege and terrible distress that your enemy will inflict on all your towns. The most tender and delicate woman among you—so delicate she would not so much as touch the ground with her foot—will be selfish toward the husband she loves and toward her own son or daughter. She will hide from them the afterbirth and the new baby she has borne, so that she herself can secretly eat them. She will have nothing else to eat during the siege and terrible distress that your enemy will inflict on all your towns.

"If you refuse to obey all the words of instruction that are written in this book, and if you do not fear the glorious and awesome name of the LORD your God, then the LORD will overwhelm you and your children with indescribable plagues. These plagues will be intense and without relief, making you miserable and unbearably sick. He will afflict you with all the diseases of Egypt that you feared so much, and you will have no relief. The LORD will afflict you with every sickness and plague there is, even those not mentioned in this Book of Instruction, until you are destroyed.

Though you become as numerous as the stars in the sky, few of you will be left because you would not listen to the LORD your God.

"Just as the LORD has found great pleasure in causing you to prosper and multiply, the LORD will find pleasure in destroying you. You will be torn from the land you are about to enter and occupy. For the LORD will scatter you among all the nations from one end of the earth to the other. There you will worship foreign gods that neither you nor your ancestors have known, gods made of wood and stone! There among those nations you will find no peace or place to rest. And the LORD will cause your heart to tremble, your eyesight to fail, and your soul to despair. Your life will constantly hang in the balance. You will live night and day in fear, unsure if you will survive. In the morning you will say, 'If only it were night!' And in the evening you will say, 'If only it were morning!' For you will be terrified by the awful horrors you see around you. Then the LORD will send you back to Egypt in ships, to a destination I promised you would never see again. There you will offer to sell yourselves to your enemies as slaves, but no one will buy you."

+ + +

These are the terms of the covenant the LORD commanded Moses to make with the Israelites while they were in the land of Moab, in addition to the covenant he had made with them at Mount Sinai.

Moses summoned all the Israelites and said to them, "You have seen with your own eyes everything the LORD did in the land of Egypt to Pharaoh and to all his servants and to his whole country—all the great tests of strength, the miraculous signs, and the amazing wonders. But to this day the LORD has not given you minds that understand, nor eyes that see, nor ears that hear! For forty years I led you through the wilderness, yet your clothes and sandals did not wear out. You ate no bread and drank no wine or other alcoholic drink, but he provided for you so you would know that he is the LORD your God.

"When we came here, King Sihon of Heshbon and King Og of Bashan came out to fight against us, but we defeated them. We took their land and gave it to the tribes of Reuben and Gad and to the half-tribe of Manasseh as their grant of land.

"Therefore, obey the terms of this covenant so that you will prosper in everything you do. All of you—tribal leaders, elders, officers, all the men of Israel—are standing today in the presence of the LORD your God. Your little ones and your wives are with you, as well as the foreigners living among you who chop your wood and carry your water. You are standing here today to enter into the covenant of the LORD your God. The LORD is making this covenant, including the curses. By entering into the covenant today, he will establish you as his people and confirm that he is your God, just as he promised you and as he swore to your ancestors Abraham, Isaac, and Jacob.

"But you are not the only ones with whom I am making this covenant with its curses. I am making this covenant both with you who stand here today in the presence of the LORD our God, and also with the future generations who are not standing here today.

"You remember how we lived in the land of Egypt and how we traveled through the lands of enemy nations as we left. You have seen their detestable practices and their idols made of wood, stone, silver, and gold. I am making this covenant with you so that no one among you—no man, woman, clan, or tribe—will turn away from the LORD our God to worship these gods of other nations, and so that no root among you bears bitter and poisonous fruit.

"Those who hear the warnings of this curse should not congratulate themselves, thinking, 'I am safe, even though I am following the desires of my own stubborn heart.' This would lead to utter ruin! The LORD will never pardon such people. Instead his anger and jealousy will burn against them. All the curses written in this book will come down on them, and the LORD will erase their names from under heaven. The LORD will separate them from all the tribes of Israel, to pour out on them all the curses of the covenant recorded in this Book of Instruction.

"Then the generations to come, both your own descendants and the foreigners who come from distant lands, will see the devastation of the land and the diseases the LORD inflicts on it. They will exclaim, 'The whole land is devastated by sulfur and salt. It is a wasteland with nothing planted and nothing growing, not even a blade of grass. It is like the cities of Sodom and Gomorrah, Admah and Zeboiim, which the LORD destroyed in his intense anger.'

"And all the surrounding nations will ask, 'Why has the LORD done this to this land? Why was he so angry?'

"And the answer will be, 'This happened because the people of the land abandoned the covenant that the LORD, the God of their ancestors, made with them when he brought them out of the land of Egypt. Instead, they turned away to serve and worship gods they had not known before, gods that were not from the LORD. That is why the LORD's anger has burned against this land, bringing down on it every curse recorded in this book. In great anger and fury the LORD uprooted his people from their land and banished them to another land, where they still live today!'

"The LORD our God has secrets known to no one. We are not accountable for them, but we and our children are accountable forever for all that he has revealed to us, so that we may obey all the terms of these instructions.

"In the future, when you experience all these blessings and curses I have listed for you, and when you are living among the nations to which the LORD your God has exiled you, take to heart all these instructions. If at that time you and your children return to the LORD your God, and if you obey with all your heart and all your soul all the commands I have given you today, then the LORD your God will restore your fortunes. He will have mercy on you and gather you back from all the nations where he has scattered you. Even though you are banished to the ends of the earth, the LORD your God will gather you from there and bring you back again. The LORD your God will return you to the land that belonged to your ancestors, and you will possess that land again. Then he will make you even more prosperous and numerous than your ancestors!

"The LORD your God will change your heart and the hearts of all your descendants, so that you will love him with all your heart and soul and so you may live! The LORD your God will inflict all these curses on your enemies and on those who hate and persecute you. Then you will again obey the LORD and keep all his commands that I am giving you today.

"The LORD your God will then make you successful in everything you do. He will give you many children and numerous livestock, and he will cause your fields to produce abundant harvests, for the LORD will again delight in being good to you as he was to your ancestors. The LORD your God will delight in you if you obey his voice and keep the commands and decrees written in this Book of Instruction, and if you turn to the LORD your God with all your heart and soul.

"This command I am giving you today is not too difficult for you, and it is not beyond your reach. It is not kept in heaven, so distant that you must ask, 'Who will go up to heaven and bring it down so we can hear it and obey?' It is not kept beyond the sea, so far away that you must ask, 'Who will cross the sea to bring it to us so we can hear it and obey?' No, the message is very close at hand; it is on your lips and in your heart so that you can obey it.

"Now listen! Today I am giving you a choice between life and death, between prosperity and disaster. For I command you this day to love the LORD your God and to keep his commands, decrees, and regulations by walking in his ways. If you do this, you will live and multiply, and the LORD your God will bless you and the land you are about to enter and occupy.

"But if your heart turns away and you refuse to listen, and if you are drawn away to serve and worship other gods, then I warn you now that you will certainly be destroyed. You will not live a long, good life in the land you are crossing the Jordan to occupy.

"Today I have given you the choice between life and death, between blessings and curses. Now I call on heaven and earth to witness the choice you make. Oh, that you would choose life, so that you and your descendants might live! You can make this choice by loving the LORD your God, obeying him, and committing yourself firmly to him. This is the key to your life. And if you love and obey the LORD, you will live long in the land the LORD swore to give your ancestors Abraham, Isaac, and Jacob."

When Moses had finished giving these instructions to all the people of Israel, he said, "I am now 120 years old, and I am no longer able to lead you. The LORD has told me, 'You will not cross the Jordan River.' But the LORD your God himself will cross over ahead of you. He will destroy the nations living there, and you will take possession of their land. Joshua will lead you across the river, just as the LORD promised.

"The LORD will destroy the nations living in the land, just as he destroyed Sihon and Og, the kings of the Amorites. The LORD will hand over to you the people who live there, and you must deal with them as I have commanded you. So be strong and courageous! Do not be afraid and do not panic before them. For the LORD your God will personally go ahead of you. He will neither fail you nor abandon you."

Then Moses called for Joshua, and as all Israel watched, he said to him, "Be strong and courageous! For you will lead these people into the land that the LORD swore to their ancestors he would give them. You are the one who will divide it among them as their grants of land. Do not be afraid or discouraged, for the LORD will personally go ahead of you. He will be with you; he will neither fail you nor abandon you."

So Moses wrote this entire body of instruction in a book and gave it to the priests, who carried the Ark of the LORD's Covenant, and to the elders of Israel. Then Moses gave them this command: "At the end of every seventh year, the Year of Release, during the Festival of Shelters, you must read this Book of Instruction to all the people of Israel when they assemble before the LORD your God at the place he chooses. Call them all together—men, women, children, and the foreigners living in your towns—so they may hear this Book of Instruction and learn to fear the LORD your God and carefully obey all the terms of these instructions. Do this so that your children who have not known these instructions will hear them and will learn to fear the LORD your God. Do this as long as you live in the land you are crossing the Jordan to occupy."

+

Then the LORD said to Moses, "The time has come for you to die. Call Joshua and present yourselves at the Tabernacle, so that I may commission him there." So Moses and Joshua went and presented themselves at the Tabernacle. And the LORD appeared to them in a pillar of cloud that stood at the entrance to the sacred tent.

The LORD said to Moses, "You are about to die and join your ancestors. After you are gone, these people will begin to worship foreign gods, the gods of the land where they are going. They will abandon me and break my covenant that I have made with them. Then my anger will blaze forth against them. I will abandon them, hiding my face from them, and they will be devoured. Terrible trouble will come down on them, and on that day they will say, 'These disasters have come down on us because God is no longer among us!' At that time I will hide my face from them on account of all the evil they commit by worshiping other gods.

"So write down the words of this song, and teach it to the people of Israel. Help them learn it, so it may serve as a witness for me against them. For I will bring them into the land I swore to give their ancestors—a land flowing with milk and honey. There they will become prosperous, eat all the food they want, and become fat. But they will begin to worship other gods; they will despise me and break my covenant. And when great disasters come down on them, this song will stand as evidence against them, for it will never be forgotten by their descendants. I know the intentions of these people, even now before they have entered the land I swore to give them."

So that very day Moses wrote down the words of the song and taught it to the Israelites.

Then the LORD commissioned Joshua son of Nun with these words: "Be strong and courageous, for you must bring the people of Israel into the land I swore to give them. I will be with you."

When Moses had finished writing this entire body of instruction in a book, he gave this command to the Levites who carried the Ark of the LORD's Covenant: "Take this Book of Instruction and place it beside the Ark of the Covenant of the LORD your God, so it may remain there as a witness against the people of Israel. For I know how rebellious and stubborn you are. Even now, while I am still alive and am here with you, you have rebelled against the LORD. How much more rebellious will you be after my death!

"Now summon all the elders and officials of your tribes, so that I can speak to them directly and call heaven and earth to witness against them. I know that after my death you will become utterly corrupt and will turn from the way I have commanded you to follow. In the days to come, disaster will come down on you, for you will do what is evil in the LORD's sight, making him very angry with your actions."

So Moses recited this entire song publicly to the assembly of Israel:

"Listen, O heavens, and I will speak!
    Hear, O earth, the words that I say!
Let my teaching fall on you like rain;
    let my speech settle like dew.
Let my words fall like rain on tender grass,
    like gentle showers on young plants.
I will proclaim the name of the LORD;
    how glorious is our God!
He is the Rock; his deeds are perfect.
    Everything he does is just and fair.
He is a faithful God who does no wrong;
    how just and upright he is!

"But they have acted corruptly toward him;
    when they act so perversely,
are they really his children?
    They are a deceitful and twisted generation.
Is this the way you repay the LORD,
    you foolish and senseless people?
Isn't he your Father who created you?
    Has he not made you and established you?
Remember the days of long ago;
    think about the generations past.
Ask your father, and he will inform you.
    Inquire of your elders, and they will tell you.
When the Most High assigned lands to the nations,
    when he divided up the human race,
he established the boundaries of the peoples
    according to the number in his heavenly court.

"For the people of Israel belong to the LORD;
    Jacob is his special possession.
He found them in a desert land,
    in an empty, howling wasteland.
He surrounded them and watched over them;
    he guarded them as he would guard his own eyes.
Like an eagle that rouses her chicks
    and hovers over her young,
so he spread his wings to take them up
    and carried them safely on his pinions.
The LORD alone guided them;
    they followed no foreign gods.

He let them ride over the highlands
    and feast on the crops of the fields.
He nourished them with honey from the rock
    and olive oil from the stony ground.
He fed them yogurt from the herd
    and milk from the flock,
      together with the fat of lambs.
He gave them choice rams from Bashan, and goats,
    together with the choicest wheat.
You drank the finest wine,
    made from the juice of grapes.

"But Israel soon became fat and unruly;
    the people grew heavy, plump, and stuffed!
Then they abandoned the God who had made them;
    they made light of the Rock of their salvation.
They stirred up his jealousy by worshiping foreign gods;
    they provoked his fury with detestable deeds.
They offered sacrifices to demons, which are not God,
    to gods they had not known before,
to new gods only recently arrived,
    to gods their ancestors had never feared.
You neglected the Rock who had fathered you;
    you forgot the God who had given you birth.

"The LORD saw this and drew back,
    provoked to anger by his own sons and daughters.
He said, 'I will abandon them;
    then see what becomes of them.
For they are a twisted generation,
    children without integrity.
They have roused my jealousy by worshiping things that
      are not God;
    they have provoked my anger with their useless idols.
Now I will rouse their jealousy through people who are not
      even a people;
    I will provoke their anger through the foolish Gentiles.
For my anger blazes forth like fire
    and burns to the depths of the grave.
It devours the earth and all its crops
    and ignites the foundations of the mountains.
I will heap disasters upon them
    and shoot them down with my arrows.

I will weaken them with famine,
   burning fever, and deadly disease.
I will send the fangs of wild beasts
   and poisonous snakes that glide in the dust.
Outside, the sword will bring death,
   and inside, terror will strike
both young men and young women,
   both infants and the aged.
I would have annihilated them,
   wiping out even the memory of them.
But I feared the taunt of Israel's enemy,
   who might misunderstand and say,
"Our own power has triumphed!
   The LORD had nothing to do with this!"'

"But Israel is a senseless nation;
   the people are foolish, without understanding.
Oh, that they were wise and could understand this!
   Oh, that they might know their fate!
How could one person chase a thousand of them,
   and two people put ten thousand to flight,
unless their Rock had sold them,
   unless the LORD had given them up?
But the rock of our enemies is not like our Rock,
   as even they recognize.
Their vine grows from the vine of Sodom,
   from the vineyards of Gomorrah.
Their grapes are poison,
   and their clusters are bitter.
Their wine is the venom of serpents,
   the deadly poison of cobras.

"The LORD says, 'Am I not storing up these things,
   sealing them away in my treasury?
I will take revenge; I will pay them back.
   In due time their feet will slip.
Their day of disaster will arrive,
   and their destiny will overtake them.'

"Indeed, the LORD will give justice to his people,
   and he will change his mind about his servants,
when he sees their strength is gone
   and no one is left, slave or free.

Then he will ask, 'Where are their gods,
   the rocks they fled to for refuge?
Where now are those gods,
   who ate the fat of their sacrifices
   and drank the wine of their offerings?
Let those gods arise and help you!
   Let them provide you with shelter!
Look now; I myself am he!
   There is no other god but me!
I am the one who kills and gives life;
   I am the one who wounds and heals;
   no one can be rescued from my powerful hand!
Now I raise my hand to heaven
   and declare, "As surely as I live,
when I sharpen my flashing sword
   and begin to carry out justice,
I will take revenge on my enemies
   and repay those who reject me.
I will make my arrows drunk with blood,
   and my sword will devour flesh—
the blood of the slaughtered and the captives,
   and the heads of the enemy leaders."'

"Rejoice with him, you heavens,
   and let all of God's angels worship him.
Rejoice with his people, you Gentiles,
   and let all the angels be strengthened in him.
For he will avenge the blood of his children;
   he will take revenge against his enemies.
He will repay those who hate him
   and cleanse his people's land."

So Moses came with Joshua son of Nun and recited all the words of this song to the people.

When Moses had finished reciting all these words to the people of Israel, he added: "Take to heart all the words of warning I have given you today. Pass them on as a command to your children so they will obey every word of these instructions. These instructions are not empty words—they are your life! By obeying them you will enjoy a long life in the land you will occupy when you cross the Jordan River."

+ + +

That same day the LORD said to Moses, "Go to Moab, to the mountains east of the river, and climb Mount Nebo, which is across from Jericho. Look out across the land of Canaan, the land I am giving to the people of Israel as their own special possession. Then you will die there on the mountain. You will join your ancestors, just as Aaron, your brother, died on Mount Hor and joined his ancestors. For both of you betrayed me with the Israelites at the waters of Meribah at Kadesh in the wilderness of Zin. You failed to demonstrate my holiness to the people of Israel there. So you will see the land from a distance, but you may not enter the land I am giving to the people of Israel."

This is the blessing that Moses, the man of God, gave to the people of Israel before his death:

> "The LORD came from Mount Sinai
>   and dawned upon us from Mount Seir;
> he shone forth from Mount Paran
>   and came from Meribah-kadesh
>   with flaming fire at his right hand.
> Indeed, he loves his people;
>   all his holy ones are in his hands.
> They follow in his steps
>   and accept his teaching.
> Moses gave us the LORD's instruction,
>   the special possession of the people of Israel.
> The LORD became king in Israel—
>   when the leaders of the people assembled,
>   when the tribes of Israel gathered as one."

Moses said this about the tribe of Reuben:

> "Let the tribe of Reuben live and not die out,
>   though they are few in number."

Moses said this about the tribe of Judah:

> "O LORD, hear the cry of Judah
>   and bring them together as a people.
> Give them strength to defend their cause;
>   help them against their enemies!"

Moses said this about the tribe of Levi:

"O Lord, you have given your Thummim and Urim—the sacred
    lots—
  to your faithful servants the Levites.
You put them to the test at Massah
  and struggled with them at the waters of Meribah.
The Levites obeyed your word
  and guarded your covenant.
They were more loyal to you
  than to their own parents.
They ignored their relatives
  and did not acknowledge their own children.
They teach your regulations to Jacob;
  they give your instructions to Israel.
They present incense before you
  and offer whole burnt offerings on the altar.
Bless the ministry of the Levites, O Lord,
  and accept all the work of their hands.
Hit their enemies where it hurts the most;
  strike down their foes so they never rise again."

Moses said this about the tribe of Benjamin:

"The people of Benjamin are loved by the Lord
  and live in safety beside him.
He surrounds them continuously
  and preserves them from every harm."

Moses said this about the tribes of Joseph:

"May their land be blessed by the Lord
  with the precious gift of dew from the heavens
  and water from beneath the earth;
with the rich fruit that grows in the sun,
  and the rich harvest produced each month;
with the finest crops of the ancient mountains,
  and the abundance from the everlasting hills;
with the best gifts of the earth and its bounty,
  and the favor of the one who appeared in the burning bush.
May these blessings rest on Joseph's head,
  crowning the brow of the prince among his brothers.
Joseph has the majesty of a young bull;
  he has the horns of a wild ox.
He will gore distant nations,
  even to the ends of the earth.

This is my blessing for the multitudes of Ephraim
 and the thousands of Manasseh."

Moses said this about the tribes of Zebulun and Issachar:

"May the people of Zebulun prosper in their travels.
 May the people of Issachar prosper at home in their tents.
They summon the people to the mountain
 to offer proper sacrifices there.
They benefit from the riches of the sea
 and the hidden treasures in the sand."

Moses said this about the tribe of Gad:

"Blessed is the one who enlarges Gad's territory!
 Gad is poised there like a lion
 to tear off an arm or a head.
The people of Gad took the best land for themselves;
 a leader's share was assigned to them.
When the leaders of the people were assembled,
 they carried out the LORD's justice
 and obeyed his regulations for Israel."

Moses said this about the tribe of Dan:

"Dan is a lion's cub,
 leaping out from Bashan."

Moses said this about the tribe of Naphtali:

"O Naphtali, you are rich in favor
 and full of the LORD's blessings;
 may you possess the west and the south."

Moses said this about the tribe of Asher:

"May Asher be blessed above other sons;
 may he be esteemed by his brothers;
 may he bathe his feet in olive oil.
May the bolts of your gates be of iron and bronze;
 may you be secure all your days."

"There is no one like the God of Israel.
 He rides across the heavens to help you,
 across the skies in majestic splendor.
The eternal God is your refuge,
 and his everlasting arms are under you.

He drives out the enemy before you;
    he cries out, 'Destroy them!'
So Israel will live in safety,
    prosperous Jacob in security,
in a land of grain and new wine,
    while the heavens drop down dew.
How blessed you are, O Israel!
    Who else is like you, a people saved by the LORD?
He is your protecting shield
    and your triumphant sword!
Your enemies will cringe before you,
    and you will stomp on their backs!"

Then Moses went up to Mount Nebo from the plains of Moab and climbed Pisgah Peak, which is across from Jericho. And the LORD showed him the whole land, from Gilead as far as Dan; all the land of Naphtali; the land of Ephraim and Manasseh; all the land of Judah, extending to the Mediterranean Sea; the Negev; the Jordan Valley with Jericho—the city of palms—as far as Zoar. Then the LORD said to Moses, "This is the land I promised on oath to Abraham, Isaac, and Jacob when I said, 'I will give it to your descendants.' I have now allowed you to see it with your own eyes, but you will not enter the land."

So Moses, the servant of the LORD, died there in the land of Moab, just as the LORD had said. The LORD buried him in a valley near Beth-peor in Moab, but to this day no one knows the exact place. Moses was 120 years old when he died, yet his eyesight was clear, and he was as strong as ever. The people of Israel mourned for Moses on the plains of Moab for thirty days, until the customary period of mourning was over.

Now Joshua son of Nun was full of the spirit of wisdom, for Moses had laid his hands on him. So the people of Israel obeyed him, doing just as the LORD had commanded Moses.

There has never been another prophet in Israel like Moses, whom the LORD knew face to face. The LORD sent him to perform all the miraculous signs and wonders in the land of Egypt against Pharaoh, and all his servants, and his entire land. With mighty power, Moses performed terrifying acts in the sight of all Israel.

THE STORIES AND THE STORY
How the Bible Works

The Bible is a gift. The Creator of all things has entered into our human story, and he has spoken. Working through all the authors of the Bible's various writings, God brings wisdom into our lives and light to our path. But his biggest intention for the Bible is to invite us into its Story. What God wants from us, more than anything else, is to make the Bible's great drama of restoration and new life the story of our lives too.

The appropriate way to receive a gift like this is to come to know the Bible deeply, to lose ourselves in it precisely so that we can find ourselves in it. In other words, the best thing we can do with the Bible is to immerse ourselves in it.

The first step on this journey of immersion is to become intimately familiar with the Bible's individual books—the songs and stories, the visions and letters. These books reflect different kinds of writing, and each book with its various parts must first be read and understood on its own terms. Your *Immerse Bible* is designed to help you easily see what kind of writing is found in each book. This will foster a better reading experience that leads to reading more and to reading in context.

But there is an even bigger goal than understanding the individual books. At its heart, the Bible is God's grand narrative of the world and his intentions for it. By reading whole books and then reading them as a collection of writings, we discover how the Bible presents God's big story—*the* Story. The true destination of Bible reading is for us to inhabit the Story. All the smaller parts of the Bible—Gospels and histories, proverbs and prophecies—take their rightful places in revealing the saving drama of God.

As we begin our journey deep into the heart of the Bible, we come across many stories. The plots and subplots of these stories fit together to tell the Bible's big Story. All the characters, communities, and covenants play a part in bringing the overall Story to its fitting conclusion. That is, they are related to each other and work together to reveal God's bigger purposes for the world.

But how are they related?

The following overview of the main stories that make up the Story will help you understand the overall flow of the Bible. It will reveal how the major stories in the Bible are really subplots of the big Story. As each new subplot is introduced, we will see how it serves the bigger narrative, particularly the story that immediately precedes it.

The Bible is a connected, multi-layered story, and Jesus the Messiah is directly at the center of it all. Sent by the Father and empowered by the Spirit, he is the One who ultimately brings resolution to all the stories. He is the thread—the beginning and the end—that ties the Scriptures together. Jesus the Messiah makes the Story's good ending possible, enabling the completion of God's one, big, saving purpose for all things.

1. The Story of God and His World

In the beginning God made everything and said it was all very good. It is evident from the rich variety of interconnected living things in his created order that God delights in flourishing life. This thriving, teeming world brings God glory and reveals his power.

When we read the Bible in its ancient Near Eastern context, something else also becomes clear. The opening song of creation shows us that God intends for the entire cosmos to be his temple, the place where he makes his home. When the Bible says God "rested" on the seventh day, it doesn't simply mean he stopped working. In the ancient world, a deity "rested" in order to take up residence within a temple. So the new world God made becomes his creation-temple, and he rules over it, bringing peace and life.

This is the Bible's first account, and it forms the frame for everything else that happens. God's creation is the stage for all the acts of the Story going forward. And the role of others in the drama will determine whether or not the Creator's plan for flourishing life will be realized.

2. The Story of Humanity

Humans come into the creation story in a special way. They are portrayed as being formed from the earth itself, establishing their permanent connection with the rest of the creation. Yet they are set apart from the beginning with a unique calling: stewardship. Out of all the creatures, only humans are made in the image of God himself and are to bring God's intentions for his creation to fruition. Their job is to rule over all things, helping life to flourish. Humanity is God's plan for managing his world. As priests in the temple of God's creation, humans—more than any other creature—will determine the success or failure of God's purposes for the world.

However, there are also other forces at work. Evil powers exist and are in a position to influence humans, drawing them away from God and interfering with his aims. God's people are lured into self-assertion and rebellion. This disrupts not only their relationship with God but also the way they function in the world. Because of humanity's bond with the rest of creation and their special vocation within it, great tragedy comes into the world. As their own humanity is twisted out of shape, guilt, pain, violence, and death begin to wreak havoc throughout God's good creation. Human beings are made for worship, created to bring glory to the Creator. But when humans direct their worship elsewhere, the damage reverberates throughout the world.

You'd think this would be enough to make God reject humans completely. But instead, God makes a promise to Adam and Eve that he will continue to work in and through human beings. In fact, it will be an offspring of the woman who will defeat the powers of evil. God will overcome the moral chaos of the world, and he will do it in partnership with humanity. In the Bible's Story, the fate of humanity and the rest of creation are irrevocably bound together.

But the question then becomes: How will God do this?

3. The Story of Abraham and His Family

The book of Genesis reveals a surprising answer: God is going to mend the world and bring his blessing to all the families on earth through one man and his descendants. God calls Abram (his name is later changed to Abraham) to leave his home and go to a new land and a new future. God narrows his focus to one family for a time as the means for bringing restoration to all the world's families.

From this point on, the big stories of humanity and of creation will hinge on what happens in the smaller story of Abraham's descendants. God intends for this family to be an agent for the renewal of the world. This plan begins with God's making promises to Abraham—to bless him, to make his family into a great nation, and to bring blessing to all nations. Over time, God makes a series of these promises, or covenantal agreements, with Abraham's family. Each new covenant moves the story forward and makes God's ultimate intentions more clear.

Early in the narrative, Abraham's descendants go down to Egypt and are eventually enslaved there. But God comes down to set them free and bring them into their own land, an event known as the Exodus. This great act of liberation becomes the template, or pattern, for all the acts of deliverance that God will bring in the future. (The nation that comes from Abraham's descendants becomes known as Israel, named after Abraham's grandson.)

As part of the Exodus, God gives his Law to the people through the great leader Moses, and this Law becomes an important part of his covenantal agreement with Israel. In revealing his mandates to Israel, God expects Israel to become a light to the nations. God wants his people to show the rest of the world what it looks like to live well under God's rule.

Another critical event in the Exodus occurs when God's personal presence comes down and inhabits the Tabernacle (a great tent set up at the center of Israel's camp). This Tabernacle becomes God's house in the midst of his people and is filled with symbols of the earth and sky. It is thus a miniature picture of the cosmos, revealing God's desire to cleanse and renew the whole creation and to make his home with us here once again.

God is present with his people in their new land, keeping the promises he made through Moses. But Israel struggles to honor its covenantal obligations. Throughout the story of Israel, the nation turns away from God again and again. This breakdown threatens the covenant itself. God is committed to working through his people. So if they fail, then his restoration project cannot move forward.

But this story is full of God's surprises. Along the way, God establishes a further covenant with Israel's king David. God assures David of a dynasty of kings on which the promises and hopes of Israel will be concentrated. The destiny of Israel as the beginning of God's new humanity is now focused here.

However, the people of Israel persist in rejecting God's covenant—worshiping idols, inflicting injustice on the poor, and looking out only for themselves. In anger and frustration, God finally intervenes. He exiles his people from their own land and withdraws his presence from them. Others now rule over Abraham's family, and Israel's role in the divine drama seems to have disappeared. A key biblical truth is revealed here: There can be no renewal, for Israel or the wider world, until evil and wrongdoing are dealt with. Judgment is part of setting things right.

The failure of Israel is critical for the overall Story. Israel was called to be the means by which God saves the world, but now the rescue party itself needs rescuing. Everything God intended for his people—indeed, for the entire creation—now seems in doubt.

God sees everything that has gone wrong. But wrongdoing, violence, and death will not get the last word—not in God's Story. He has another promise. Through his prophets, God brings a vision of a new future, one aligned with his founding purpose. He will establish a new covenant, one that completes and surpasses all the covenants that came before. God himself will return to his people and restore them. They will be the light they were always meant to be. So the people wait—praying, worshiping, longing—for one more promise to come true.

4. The Story of Messiah Jesus
By the first century AD, Israel had been suffering under foreign rule for centuries. Now subjugated by the Roman Empire, God's people are divided

about what to do. Zealous factions advocate violent rebellion. Many teachers and other religious leaders are urging people to get more serious about following Israel's distinctive way of life under God's law. And those running the Temple in Jerusalem survive by making compromises with their Roman overlords.

Israel's ancient prophet Isaiah had foretold a time when a messenger would come to Jerusalem proclaiming the good news that God is returning at last, that his people are being saved. But Rome had its own version of the good news, and it wasn't about Israel's God. The empire's gospel was about the great blessings brought by their own powerful leader, Caesar Augustus. He is, they said, "a savior for us and those who come after us, to make war to cease, to create order everywhere. The birthday of the god Augustus was the beginning for the world of the good tidings that have come to men through him" (from the Priene Calendar Inscription in Asia Minor, ca. 9 BC).

Into this world a child is born in Israel. He is a descendant of King David, but he comes from a humble family. An angel speaks to his mother, Mary, before he is born. He tells her that this child will be the long-promised and long-awaited Messiah, Israel's King, the One who will fulfill their history. Remarkably, Scripture's account of the ministry of Jesus echoes particulars of Israel's history.

Before Israel's Exodus, Pharaoh killed many Israelite babies, but Israel's deliverer, Moses, escaped; King Herod also kills many Israelite babies in trying to kill Jesus, but Jesus also escapes. The family of Israel went to Egypt to survive a deadly famine; the family of Jesus also survives by going to Egypt. Israel passed through the Jordan River to enter the Promised Land; Jesus is baptized in the Jordan River before beginning his ministry in Israel. Israel spent forty years in the wilderness, where they struggled with temptation; Jesus spends forty days fasting in the wilderness and is tempted by the devil. And as Israel had twelve sons who fathered twelve tribes, Jesus chooses twelve men to be his closest followers. In all of this, Jesus is reliving aspects of the ancient narrative of Israel, but now with a different outcome. Jesus is refreshing Israel's story and renewing Israel itself—through himself.

In his opening message to the people of Israel, Jesus calls them to be the light they were always meant to be, announcing the Good News that something unprecedented is happening in Israel's story. He demonstrates in powerful words and miraculous deeds what it looks like when God comes as King—teaching, correcting, and healing. Jesus is widely recognized as a rabbi and a mighty prophet in Israel, but the current religious leaders see him as a dangerous new problem. Jesus critiques their leadership, thus threatening their positions of power.

This tension between Jesus and the Jewish religious leaders rises until Jesus travels to Jerusalem for a final confrontation. His twelve disciples now recognize him as the Son of David, the Messiah, but they still don't understand his mission. They assume Jesus is going to fight his enemies and claim the throne. But Jesus talks about fighting a different kind of battle. He says his struggle is against the powers of darkness and the spiritual ruler of this world.

Then during Israel's annual celebration of the Exodus, Jesus shares a final Passover meal with his disciples. He tells them that his death will inaugurate the new covenant promised by the prophets. He is arrested by the religious leaders and handed over to the Romans for execution. He is nailed to a cross, with a mocking sign posted above his head that reads "The King of the Jews." It certainly looks as though Jesus has lost, that he is no king after all. But three days later, Jesus is raised from the dead and appears to his disciples.

It turns out that Jesus willingly went to his death as a sacrifice for the sins of his people. Through his sacrifice, he wins a surprising victory over the spiritual powers of darkness. He takes on sin and death directly—ironically, through death—emptying them of their power over humanity, and he rises from the dead to confirm his triumph. This unexpected story of Israel's Messiah reveals God's long-term plan. All the earlier covenants were leading to this one. The life and ministry of Jesus brings all the narrative threads in the Scriptures together into a single, coherent Story.

5. All the Stories in One

So we see that the story of Jesus does not simply stand alone. The Bible presents his narrative as intimately tied to all the plots and subplots that came before him. Jesus, crucified and raised, is God's answer to Israel's previous failure, humanity's wrongdoing and death, and the curse on all creation.

Jesus fulfills Israel's story and successfully plays the role of rescuer given to Abraham's family. He is Abraham's faithful descendant and David's powerful son, the Messiah. He is the light the nations have been longing for. People from every tribe, nation, and community can now join Abraham's family through belief in Jesus the Messiah. As the true Israelite, Jesus is also a new Adam, a fresh start for the human race. He has defeated our archenemies sin and death, restoring our relationship with God and ushering us into the life that is truly life. The new covenant in Jesus introduces a new world.

Jesus opens the doorway to the true worship of God, and we recover our God-given vocation to be his image-bearers through our stewardship of the world. As the new Adam, Jesus brings flourishing life back into the world. He embodies the new creation in his resurrection, blazing a path of future renewal for everything in heaven and on earth.

Jesus also launches a new community of God's people—the church—creating the renewed humanity that God envisioned from the beginning. This community is the focus of God's work on the way to a completely restored and healed creation. The book of Acts and the letters of the New Testament record how the earliest churches continued the ministry of God's coming reign that Jesus had begun. The context of this ministry changes over time and in location, but the ministry itself remains the same for God's new family: to embody and proclaim the Good News of God's victory through the Messiah.

In the end, the discovery of the narrative unity we find in the Scriptures is not merely for the purpose of information. The Bible is an invitation. It calls us to join the Story and take up our own role in God's ongoing redemptive drama. We read the Bible deeply and well in order to learn the true story of our lives within God's bigger Story of the world. We read the Bible to grasp the cosmic scope and meaning of Jesus' victory. And we read the Bible to know what it means to follow Jesus ourselves. The path of the cross—selfless love and sacrifice—is the path for us, too. But that path also ends in our own resurrection when the Messiah returns.

> Yet what we suffer now is nothing compared to the glory he will reveal to us later. For all creation is waiting eagerly for that future day when God will reveal who his children really are. Against its will, all creation was subjected to God's curse. But with eager hope, the creation looks forward to the day when it will join God's children in glorious freedom from death and decay. For we know that all creation has been groaning as in the pains of childbirth right up to the present time. And we believers also groan, even though we have the Holy Spirit within us as a foretaste of future glory, for we long for our bodies to be released from sin and suffering. We, too, wait with eager hope for the day when God will give us our full rights as his adopted children, including the new bodies he has promised us. We were given this hope when we were saved.
>
> From Paul's letter to the Romans

The final theme of the biblical chronicle is life, the same theme that began the Story. Through the power of the Spirit and the action of the Son, the Father's intention will be realized in a new heaven and a new earth.

Introducing

IMMERSE
The Reading Bible

Many people feel discouraged in their Bible reading. The size and scope (not to mention the tiny fonts and the thin pages) intimidate new and seasoned readers alike, keeping them from diving into and immersing themselves in the word of God. The Bible itself is not the problem; how the Bible has been presented to readers for generations is.

Our Bibles currently look like reference books—a resource to put on the shelf and consult only when needed. So we read it like a reference book: infrequently and in small pieces. But the Bible is a collection of good writings that invite us to good reading—and it's God's word! There is an urgent need today for Christians to know the word of God, and the best way to do so is by reading the Bible. However, we need to understand the Bible on its own terms. We need to become deeply acquainted with whole books by reading them at length. And we can learn how to read the Bible well by altering a few of our current Bible reading habits.

First, we need to think about the Bible as a collection of writings written in various literary forms known as *genres*. Each literary form, or genre, used in the Bible—such as a poem, story, or letter—was chosen because, along with the words, it works to communicate truths about God to real people. (See "The Literary Forms of the Bible," p. 341, for a further explanation of some of these genres.) A complete book can be composed in a single genre, or the author may use several genres to tell one story. And even when books of the Bible are made up of several different compositions, as in the book of Psalms, those components are drawn together in such a way as to give each book an overall unity as a distinct work in itself.

Second, recognizing that the Bible is made up of whole books that tell a complete story, we should seek to understand the Bible's teaching and live out its story. To help readers better understand and read the Bible as whole books, we've removed any additives from the Bible text. Those additions, while inserted with good intentions, have accumulated over the centuries, changing how people view the Bible and, therefore, what they think they're supposed to do with it.

Chapters and verses aren't the original units of the Bible. The latest books of the Bible were written in the first century AD; however, chapter divisions were added in the thirteenth century, and the verse divisions we use today appeared in the middle of the sixteenth century. So for the majority of its history, the Bible had no chapters or verses. They were introduced so that reference works like commentaries and concordances could be created. But if we rely on these later additions to guide our reading of the Bible, we often miss the original, natural structure. This also puts us at risk of missing the message and meaning of the Bible. For this reason, we have removed the chapter and verse markers from the text. (We do, however, include a verse range at the top of each page, allowing for easy reference.)

This edition also removes the section headings that are found in most Bibles. These are also not original but the work of modern publishers. These headings create the impression that the Bible is made up of short, encyclopedic sections. So, like chapters and verses, they can encourage us to treat the Bible as a kind of reference work rather than a collection of good writings that invite good reading. Many headings may also spoil the suspense that the inspired storytellers sought to create and use to such good effect. (For example, a heading that often appears in the book of Acts announces in advance "Peter's Miraculous Escape from Prison.")

So, in place of section headings, *Immerse: The Reading Bible* uses line spacing and graphic markers to simply and elegantly reflect the natural structures of the Bible's books. For example, in the letter known as 1 Corinthians, Paul addresses twelve issues in the life of the community in Corinth. In this edition, double line breaks and a single cross mark off the teaching Paul offers for each issue. Single line breaks separate different phases of the longer arguments Paul makes to support his teaching. And triple line breaks with three crosses set off the opening and closing of the letter from the main body. By contrast, the section headings in a typical Bible divide 1 Corinthians into nearly thirty parts. These divisions give no indication of which parts speak together to the same issue or where the letter's main body begins and ends.

Modern Bibles also include hundreds of footnotes and often include cross-references throughout the text. While these features provide information that can be helpful in certain settings, there's a danger that they, too, can encourage us to treat the Bible as a reference work. Constantly going back and forth between the text and the notes doesn't really qualify as being immersed in reading the Bible.

Third, the order in which the books appear is another important factor in reading the Bible well and at length. For the majority of the Bible's history, its books were not arranged in any fixed order. Instead, they were placed in a great variety of orders, depending on the needs and goals of each presentation. In some cases, books from the same time period were put together. In other cases, similar kinds of writing were set side by side. And often the Bible's books were organized according to the way the community used them in worship.

The order of books that we know today didn't become fixed until near the time of the invention of the printing press in the fifteenth century. This ordering has many drawbacks. For example, it presents Paul's letters in order of length (longest to shortest) rather than in the order in which he wrote them. Also, in this order, the books of the prophets are divided into groups by size, and the smaller books are then organized based on phrases they share. This arrangement puts them out of historical order and sends the reader swinging back and forth between centuries. And there are many other similar concerns in what we know as the traditional order.

This edition returns to the church's longstanding tradition of arranging the Bible's books to best meet the goals of a given presentation. To help readers delve deeper into the Story of the Bible, it places Paul's letters in their likely historical order. The books of the prophets are arranged in similar fashion. Furthermore, the collection of prophetic books is placed immediately after the story of Israel because the prophets were God's messengers to the people during the unfolding of that story. The remaining books of the First Testament, known traditionally as the "Writings," are placed after the prophets and arranged by type of writing. The introductions to the various groups of books in this Bible will explain more about how they are arranged and why.

Finally, some complete books of the Bible were broken into parts over time. The books of Samuel and Kings originally made up one long book, but they were separated into four parts so they would fit conveniently on ancient papyrus scrolls. The books of Chronicles, Ezra, and Nehemiah are similarly the divided parts of an originally unified composition. In this edition, both of these two longer works are put back together as Samuel–Kings and Chronicles–Ezra–Nehemiah. Luke and Acts were written as a unified story of the life of Jesus and the birth of the community of his followers. These two volumes had been separated so that Luke could be placed with the other Gospels. But since the two parts were meant to be read together, they have been reunited here as Luke–Acts.

All of this is presented in a clean, single-column format, allowing each of the Bible's basic units to be read like the books they are. The lines of Hebrew poetry can easily be seen, and stories, proverbs, letters, and other genres can readily be identified. In short, *Immerse: The Reading Bible* takes full advantage of good visual design to provide a more authentic encounter with God's sacred words.

It is our prayer that the combined effect of these changes to the visual layout of the Bible will enhance your reading experience. We believe these changes serve the Scriptures well and will allow you to receive these books on their own terms. The goal, after all, is to let the Bible be the book that God inspired so it can do its powerful work in our lives.

THE LITERARY FORMS OF THE BIBLE

Just as God's word uses existing human language, the inspired authors also employ existing human literary forms that enable words to be arranged in meaningful ways. These different types of writing are called *genres*.

Today most of us are probably more familiar with the concept of genre from watching movies. By watching the opening scene, we can identify whether it's a Western, a science fiction thriller, a romantic comedy, or a documentary. Once we know what kind of film it is, we know what expectations we should have about what can or can't happen, how things are likely to develop, and how we should interpret what is being shown. These expectations, created by previous films and respected by filmmakers, are like an agreement with the audience about how its message will be communicated and should be interpreted.

Likewise, the Bible's authors and editors, through God's inspiration, used and respected the genres of their day. We may be able to recognize some of them as similar to genres we know today, but others may be less familiar.

Since understanding genres is critical to reading the Bible well, we will describe the key types below. The compositions that reflect these genres make up either whole Bible books or smaller sections of larger books, so some Bible books are written partly in one genre and partly in another. (Many of the genres introduced here will be further explained in the introductions to books or sections of the Bible.) As indicated below, the specific genres employed in the Bible can be divided into two general categories of writing: prose and poetry.

PROSE GENRES

- *Stories.* Narrative—or stories—weave together events in a way that shows they have a larger meaning. Typically, a story situates the reader in a place and time and then introduces a conflict. This conflict intensifies until it reaches a climax, which is followed by a resolution.

  Narrative is the most common genre used in the Bible, emphasizing that God primarily makes himself known through his words and actions in specific historical events. The Bible doesn't teach about God merely in the abstract; its historical narratives are intentionally shaped to highlight key points about God and how he relates to people and the world.

The Bible features two special types of stories-within-stories. Sometimes a person will tell a story to illustrate a point about the larger narrative that person is in. These stories are called *parables* and were a favorite teaching tool of Jesus. They usually describe real-life situations but sometimes can be fanciful, like Jotham's parable in the book of Judges, which uses talking trees as the characters. People in a story may also relate *dreams* and *visions* that they've had. In this case they're not making up a story but reporting one they've seen. This subset of narrative speaks in pictures and uses symbols to represent realities.

- *Apocalypse.* Meaning "unveiling," apocalypse is an ancient genre structured as a narrative but composed entirely of *visions* employing vivid symbols which a heavenly visitor reveals to a person. These visions disclose the secrets of the spiritual world and, often, the future. The book of Revelation is a complete apocalypse, while the book of Daniel is split between narrative and apocalypse. Elements of apocalypse also appear in Isaiah, Ezekiel, and Zechariah.

- *Letters.* About one-third of the Bible's books are letters that were originally written by one person to another person or to a group. Letters in the Bible, following the form of ancient letters, have three parts: the opening, the main body, and the closing. In the opening, writers typically give their name, say who they're writing to, and offer a word of thanksgiving or prayer. The main body deals with the business of the letter. In the closing, the writer extends greetings, shares prayer requests, and offers a prayer for God to bless the recipients. Letters in the Bible are typically used by leaders to present their authoritative teaching to a community when they aren't physically present.

- *Laws.* Also known as commands, these are instructions for what to do in specific situations in order to live as God intends. Less frequently, laws are statements of general principles to follow. Many biblical laws have been gathered into large collections, but sometimes they are placed within narratives as part of the resolution after a conflict. God's instructions are most often presented in the Bible as part of his covenantal agreements with his people, contributing to his larger saving purposes.

- *Sermons.* These are public addresses to groups that have gathered for worship or for the celebration of a special occasion. They typically explain the meaning of earlier parts of the Bible's story for people living in a later part of that story. Most sermons in the Bible are found within narratives, but the book of Hebrews comprises four sermons that were collected and then sent out in the same letter.

The book of Deuteronomy is a series of sermons by Moses to the people of Israel as they were about to enter the Promised Land. Parts of it take the form of a *treaty* that high kings would make with the kings who served them. The Ten Commandments are a miniature version of that kind of treaty.

- **Prayers.** These are addressed to God and are usually offered in a public setting in the Bible, though sometimes they are private. They can include praise, thanksgiving, confession, and requests.

- **Lists.** Many kinds of lists are found in the Bible. One of the most common types, *genealogy*, is a record of a person's ancestors or descendants. The Bible also includes lists of things like offerings, building materials, assigned territories, stops along journeys, court officials, population counts, and so on. Lists in the Bible are not merely informative but usually make a theological point or provide verification of someone's connection to God's people.

POETRY GENRES

Hebrew poetry is based not on the repetition of sound (rhyme) but on the repetition of meaning. Its essential unit, the couplet, features a form of parallelism. One line states something, and the next line repeats, contrasts, or elaborates on the first line, intensifying its meaning. This feature is sometimes expanded to a triplet (three-line unit) for greater emphasis.

Poetry frequently uses metaphors and other figurative language to communicate messages with greater strength and emotion.

- **Proverbs.** These are short sayings, typically two lines in length (though sometimes longer), that teach practical lessons for life in God's world. Proverbs are not necessarily promises about how things will work out; mainly they are descriptions of wise ways to live.

- **Songs.** Poetry set to music. In the Bible, songs are used primarily for celebration or for mourning (in which case they are called *laments*). They are often found within narratives, but some books of the Bible are whole collections of songs.

  Psalms are songs used by people gathered for worship. These songs are most often addressed to God as prayers set to music.

- **Oracles.** These are messages from God delivered by prophets. In the Bible, oracles are most often recorded in poetry; originally, they may have been sung. Some oracles are in prose, but even those often use symbolic language similar to dreams and visions. Most biblical oracles are found within larger collections from the same prophet; however, the book of Obadiah consists of a single oracle.

- *Poetic dialogue.* Utilized in a number of ancient writings, poetic dialogue is a conversation in which each participant speaks in a form of poetry. In the Bible, this genre is found only in the book of Job.

Reading the Bible well starts with recognizing and then honoring each book's genre. Following this practice will help prevent mistakes in interpretation and allow us to discover the meaning that the Bible's creators originally intended.

NLT: A NOTE TO READERS

The *Holy Bible,* New Living Translation, was first published in 1996. It quickly became one of the most popular Bible translations in the English-speaking world. While the NLT's influence was rapidly growing, the Bible Translation Committee determined that an additional investment in scholarly review and text refinement could make it even better. So shortly after its initial publication, the committee began an eight-year process with the purpose of increasing the level of the NLT's precision without sacrificing its easy-to-understand quality. This second-generation text was completed in 2004, with minor changes subsequently introduced in 2007, 2013, and 2015.

The goal of any Bible translation is to convey the meaning and content of the ancient Hebrew, Aramaic, and Greek texts as accurately as possible to contemporary readers. The challenge for our translators was to create a text that would communicate as clearly and powerfully to today's readers as the original texts did to readers and listeners in the ancient biblical world. The resulting translation is easy to read and understand, while also accurately communicating the meaning and content of the original biblical texts. The NLT is a general-purpose text especially good for study, devotional reading, and reading aloud in worship services.

We believe that the New Living Translation—which combines the latest biblical scholarship with a clear, dynamic writing style—will communicate God's word powerfully to all who read it. We publish it with the prayer that God will use it to speak his timeless truth to the church and the world in a fresh, new way.

The Publishers

A full introduction to the NLT can be found at:
http://newlivingtranslation.com/05discoverthenlt/nltintro.asp

A complete list of the translators can be found at:
http://newlivingtranslation.com/05discoverthenlt/meetthescholars.asp

WORLD OF THE PATRIARCHS

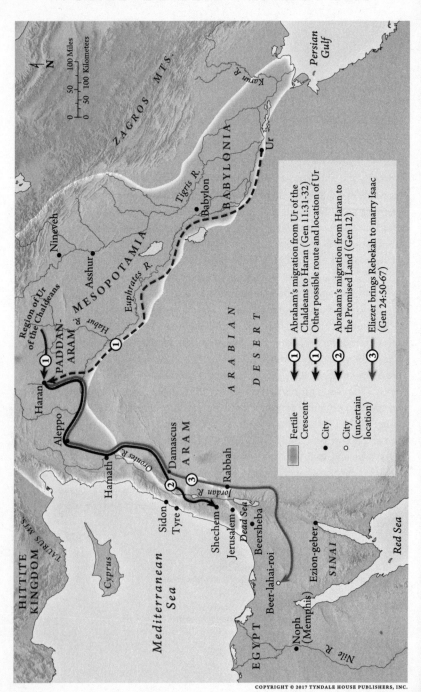

EXODUS FROM EGYPT

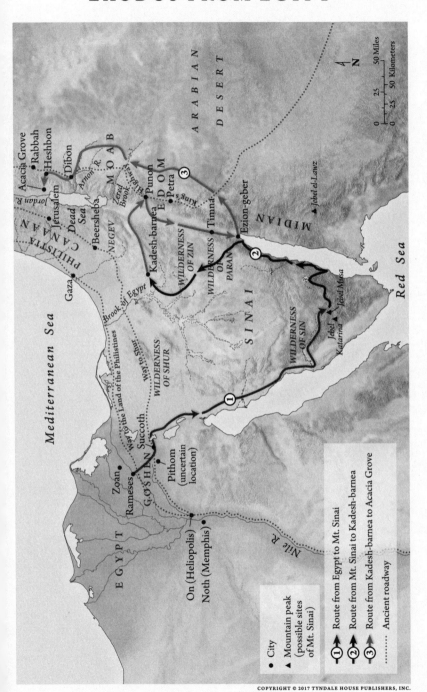

THE IMMERSE BIBLE SERIES

IMMERSE: THE READING BIBLE comes in six volumes and presents each Bible book without the distractions of chapter and verse numbers, subject headers, or footnotes. It's designed for reading—especially for reading with others. By committing to just two eight-week sessions per year (spring and fall), you can read through the entire Bible in three years. And online video and audio support tools make it easy to read together in groups. Step into this three-year Immerse Bible reading cycle with your friends; then do it again—and again—for a lifetime of life-giving, life-changing Bible engagement!

Immerse: Beginnings includes the first five books of the Bible, known as the *Torah* (meaning "instruction"). These books describe the origins of God's creation, the human rebellion, and the family of Israel—the people God chose to be a light to all peoples. We follow the covenant community from its earliest ancestors to the time it is about to enter the Promised Land.

Immerse: Kingdoms tells the story of Israel from the time of its conquest of Canaan (Joshua) through its struggle to settle the land (Judges, Ruth) and the establishment of Israel's kingdom, which ends in a forced exile (Samuel–Kings). The nation of Israel, commissioned to be God's light to the nations, falls to division and then foreign conquest for rejecting God's rule.

Immerse: Prophets presents the First Testament prophets in groupings that generally represent four historical periods: before the fall of Israel's northern kingdom (Amos, Hosea, Micah, Isaiah), before the fall of the southern kingdom (Zephaniah, Nahum, Habakkuk), around the time of Jerusalem's destruction (Jeremiah, Obadiah, Ezekiel), and after the return from exile (Haggai, Zechariah, Malachi, Joel, Jonah).

Immerse: Poets presents the poetical books of the First Testament in two groupings, dividing the books between songs (Psalms, Lamentations, Song of Songs) and wisdom writings (Proverbs, Ecclesiastes, Job). These writings all reflect the daily, down-to-earth faith of God's people as they live out their covenant relationship with him in worship and wise living.

Immerse: Chronicles contains the remaining First Testament books: Chronicles–Ezra–Nehemiah, Esther, and Daniel. These works were all written after the Jewish people fell under the control of foreign empires and were scattered among the nations. They remind God's chastened people of their identity and calling to faithfully represent God to the nations and that there is still hope for the struggling dynasty of David.

Immerse: Messiah provides a unique guided journey through the entire New Testament. Each major section is anchored by one of the Gospels, highlighting the richness of Scripture's fourfold witness to Jesus the Messiah. This creates a fresh reading of the New Testament centered on Christ.